ALSO BY JACK F. MATLOCK, JR.

AUTOPSY ON AN EMPIRE:
The American Ambassador's Account
of the Collapse of the Soviet Union

REAGAN

AND

GORBACHEV

REAGAN

AND

GORBACHEV

HOW THE COLD
WAR ENDED

Jack F. Matlock, Jr.

RANDOM HOUSE

NEW YORK

Library of Congress Cataloging-in-Publication Data
Matlock, Jack F.
Reagan and Gorbachev / by Jack F. Matlock, Jr.
p.   cm.
Includes bibliographical references (p.) and index.
ISBN 0-679-46323-2
1. Reagan, Ronald. 2. Gorbachev, Mikhail Sergeevich, 1931– 3. Summit meetings—
Switzerland—Geneva. 4. Summit meetings—Iceland—Reykjavík. 5. United States—
Foreign relations—Soviet Union. 6. Soviet Union—Foreign relations—United States.
7. United States—Foreign relations—1981–1989. I. Title.
E183.8.S65M3724 2004
327.73047—dc22   2003069368

Printed in the United States of America on acid-free paper
Random House website address: www.atrandom.com
2 4 6 8 9 7 5 3 1
First Edition

Book design by Victoria Wong

To

Rebecca Burrum Matlock,

who helped make the good things happen

FOREWORD

*Some of the NSC staff are too hard line
and don't think any approach should be made to the Soviets.
I think I'm hard line and will never appease.
But I do want to try to let them see there is a better world
if they'll show* by deed *that they want to get along with the free world.*
—RONALD REAGAN, diary entry of April 6, 1983[1]

I WAS CHANGING for dinner in my dressing room in the ornate, imitation-French-chateau residence of the American ambassador in Prague when the telephone rang. Prague was not one of our most active diplomatic posts in 1983 and telephone calls at awkward times were not common. In fact, during my eighteen months in Prague, nobody had dared ring me when I was dressing.

Nevertheless, the call pleased me. I had often wondered why my predecessor had installed a telephone in the dressing room. Now I could testify to the wisdom of providing for contingencies, however unlikely.

When I picked up the receiver, I heard the excited voice of the Czech international operator, whose anxiety was all but palpable: "Pane Velvyslanče (Mr. Ambassador), excuse me for ringing you at home, but the White House is calling from Washington." Twenty-five years of communism had not sufficed to extinguish totally the traditional Czech sense of propriety: one does *not* disturb an ambassador just before the dinner hour for any but the supreme interests of state.

"Děkuji, pěkně rozumím (Thanks, I understand perfectly)," I muttered, amused at her agitation. First, I was not about to be upset over a call when I was dressing, since it was—up to then—a unique experience. Rather like General Halftrack in the comic strip Camp Swampy, at times I wondered if Washington knew we were there. Second, her assumption that the call was important, just because it emanated from the White House, was touching in its naïveté. I well knew that *important* business from the White House or

State Department was not conducted on open telephone lines. Therefore, the call was most likely to alert me to the travel of a congressman or to cadge an invitation to an embassy dinner for some White House staffer's friend who would be traveling in the area.

It was my turn to register surprise when the White House operator, having established that I was in fact Ambassador Matlock, informed me that Judge Clark was calling. I felt a surge of distinctly mixed emotion: it was flattering to be remembered by the president's assistant for national security, and it was always pleasant to talk to Bill Clark, whom I had known since he came to Washington as deputy secretary of state.

Nevertheless, I suddenly recalled a conversation with Clark in Washington the year before: he had asked if I was interested in the position of Soviet specialist on the National Security Council staff when Richard Pipes returned to Harvard. I told him that I would prefer to stay in Prague, since I had been there only a year. There were certainly plenty of people available in Washington who could handle the Soviet "portfolio," which, in any case, was not a very active one in the fall of 1982. I returned to Prague believing that this question was behind me and I could look forward to another couple of years looking after American interests in Czechoslovakia.

My suspicion about the subject of the call proved accurate. The question I thought had been resolved was still open.

"Jack, I know we are on an open line and can't discuss details, but you will recall our conversation last November. I just wanted you to know that we are reorganizing, and we'd like you to take over a bigger job. It will include all of Europe, your specialty, and Canada to boot. Could you come to Washington next week and talk about it? George Shultz thinks you are the right person, and we have some special projects in mind we'd like to discuss."

I answered that I would be delighted to come to Washington and talk it over, but made it clear that I was not eager to leave Czechoslovakia and reenter the bruising arena of Washington politics.

No sooner had I laid the telephone receiver on its cradle and started for Rebecca's dressing room (as I said, it is a palatial residence), to let her know that an abrupt change in our lives might be in the offing, than the ringing resumed. (How prescient my predecessor now seemed!) This time it was Mark Palmer in the State Department.

"Jack," he began, "I wanted you to know that you'll be getting a call soon from Judge Clark, and . . ."

"I already have," I interrupted.

"Oh, in that case, all I have to say is I hope you didn't say no this time.

The secretary really wants you to take this job and he's going to be mighty annoyed if you keep turning it down. Will we see you next week?"

"Yes, you'll see me next week. But I'm just not sure about the job. My place is in the field. I like to work in embassies, and like to deal with other countries. That's why I joined the foreign service. I detest the Washington bureaucracy, and I am sure the feeling is reciprocated. I don't think I'm the person you need there now. Besides, I haven't even spoken to Rebecca about it yet."

"All right, just don't say no until we have a chance to talk. And, by the way, don't think Shultz is going to put you up for another embassy if you disappoint him now."

"I get the picture, but I'm not convinced. See you next week."

JUDGE CLARK IS an early riser, so it was no surprise when I was invited for a working breakfast at seven the day after I arrived in Washington. We met at the White House mess. Not in the larger room to which every deputy assistant to the president and even most special assistants to the president (the next rung down on the White House bureaucratic ladder) have access, but in the small one reserved for what is known in the West Wing as "senior staff"—the chief of staff and the full-fledged assistants to the president.

There were four of us at the table. Robert McFarlane, Clark's deputy, whom even casual acquaintances called "Bud," and Admiral John Poindexter, then in the number three position of executive secretary, joined the judge and me. At first we talked about Prague, Soviet leader Yuri Andropov's health, and the staff reorganization at the NSC. Geographic and functional specialties would be grouped as they were at the State Department, meaning that there would be a section to cover Europe and Canada, which would include the USSR. "Vancouver to Vladivostok—the long way round" was the apt description of the portfolio offered.

At seven-thirty Judge Clark left for a meeting with the president and asked McFarlane and Poindexter to brief me on the special project he had mentioned when he telephoned.

"When the president came to office," McFarlane began (I paraphrase from memory), "he felt that we were too weak to negotiate effectively with the Soviets. Therefore, his first priority was to restore our strength. There is still a lot to do, but the president is satisfied that he has restored enough momentum to our defense programs to deal with the Soviets effectively. In fact, he feels it is time to pursue negotiations aggressively.

"A lot of people don't understand the president's goal. They interpret what he says as belligerence, when it is merely realism. We'll get nowhere if we encourage illusions about the nature of the Soviet system.

"Anyway, for better or for worse, the president has decided it's time to negotiate. But we have a problem. Here on the NSC staff we have nobody with experience dealing with the Soviets. Theoreticians, yes. But now it is no longer theory. We need street smarts. We know you have dealt with the Soviets a lot, and you are not soft. What we want you to do is put together a realistic program for negotiation and help us carry it out. But don't think just about the Soviet Union: bear in mind that we have to keep the allies with us, and also convince Congress and the American public."

Before I left the West Wing, I was discussing dates with John Poindexter. I agreed to come on the staff immediately, provided my family could stay in Prague for the summer. I called Rebecca to let her know that the offer was one I could not refuse.

We were reluctant to leave Prague at that time. U.S. relations were strained with the Czechoslovak government the Soviet leaders had installed following their invasion in 1968 to end Alexander Dubček's "Prague Spring." We traveled about the country often and developed as many acquaintances as we could outside official circles. Most Czechs and Slovaks were eager for contact with Americans but feared harassment or worse from their security police, prone to suspect political disloyalty on the part of those with Western contacts. To protect our acquaintances we concentrated on our interest in the country and its culture, and reminded them of the American role in creating an independent Czechoslovakia and liberating part of the country from the Nazis in World War II. Czechs and Slovaks did not need to be told why communism was bad for them. They knew that very well. They needed assurance that they had not been forgotten by the United States.

Rebecca took the lead in developing ties with artists, musicians, and writers. When we met with officials, she would often put in a word in favor of a local issue such as historic preservation. We were told later by Czech friends that her appeals on behalf of the Tugenhat House in Brno, one of Mies van der Rohe's early creations that had fallen into disrepair, was a factor in the local government's decision to restore it.

Although we were happy in Prague and felt that we were making progress in convincing Czechs and Slovaks that the United States had an interest in their fate, Rebecca agreed to the transfer without hesitation. Washington had been home for us throughout our foreign service career. We had many friends there and our children, then grown or in college, were not far away. Though I did not relish having to deal with the government bureaucracy, we both knew that if the president wanted help to prepare negotiations with the Soviet leaders, Washington was where we should be.

Until fall, I would spend two or three weeks each month in Washington and a week or two in Prague. From the fall of 1983 to the end of 1986, when I was asked by President Reagan to go to Moscow as American ambassador to the Soviet Union, I worked full-time on the NSC staff as senior director for European and Soviet affairs.

MORE THAN A decade has now passed since the policies worked out in Washington in the mid-eighties were applied, negotiated, and brought to fruition. The Cold War ended, fulfilling their ultimate goal. But then, before the public could grasp the implications of this great shift, Communist rule disintegrated in the Soviet Union, which itself then fragmented and disappeared from political maps of the globe—two developments that were not among Reagan's goals. The world was suddenly transformed in ways we are still trying to understand.

It would seem politicians, journalists, and scholars have fallen over themselves in a rush to explain what happened. But with a few notable exceptions, most interpretations offered so far do not square with the events as I remember them. Some observers, like the journalist Peter Schweizer, attribute all three seismic events to Reagan's military buildup and economic pressure on the Soviet Union.[2] But it really was not so simple. The Soviet Union could have weathered that pressure for a decade or more so long as the Communist Party remained in firm control of the country and did not try to match the U.S. defense effort. The Soviet economic decline would have continued, but the political problems that ensued could have been contained for a long time had there not been an attempt to change the system.

Others have argued that Reagan's policies had nothing to do with the end of the Cold War. They argue that it was solely Mikhail Gorbachev's courage and genius that brought peace, which could have occurred earlier if only Reagan had been more pliable. This view has as little to commend it as do excessive claims for Reagan's policies. Without the military and economic pressure from the United States it is most unlikely that Gorbachev could have persuaded his generals to acquiesce to the arms cuts the Soviet Union itself desperately needed, and without which internal reform would have been unthinkable.

Furthermore, the policies the Reagan administration followed to end the Cold War were in place before Mikhail Gorbachev became general secretary of the Communist Party of the Soviet Union in March 1985. He and Reagan skirmished over them for two years, but from 1987 they engaged each other in negotiations dealing with the entire range of issues that had accumulated. Equally important, these negotiations fitted the framework that had been worked out in Washington in 1983 and announced as official U.S. policy in 1984: a four-part agenda that comprised protection for human rights, opening the Soviet Union, reducing weaponry, and disengaging from armed conflicts in third countries.

Gorbachev, too, has his critics, particularly in Russia. Anatoly Dobrynin, the longtime Soviet ambassador in the United States, has joined some other Soviet officials active during the Cold War in accusing Gorbachev of making unnecessary and one-sided concessions to the United States. In fact, however, Gorbachev's "concessions" were neither unnecessary (since he could not have reached agreements without them) nor one-sided, except as measured on the distorted scale of Soviet geopolitical thinking. Every one of the agreements he concluded was in the Soviet interest—assuming the Soviet Union was prepared to live in peace with its neighbors and not try to impose an alien political system on them.

There are also those who see Reagan as one who changed course between his first and second terms of office, suddenly seeing the error of his earlier ways (or—depending on the point of view—deviating from the true path) and making deals instead of using his bully pulpit to lambaste the evil empire.[3] But in Reagan's mind his policy was consistent throughout. He wanted to reduce the threat of war, to convince the Soviet leaders that cooperation could serve the Soviet peoples better than confrontation, and to encourage openness and democracy in the Soviet Union. He was convinced that a free people with a say in their government's policies would be no threat to their neighbors or to the United States. Unlike many of his advisers, he believed that, if given the chance, he could convince the Soviet leaders that these goals were in the Soviet Union's interest—provided, and only provided, they came to understand that military competition with the United States was a losing strategy.

By the time Ronald Reagan left office in January 1989 the Cold War had ended in principle, with both the United States and Soviet Union avowing the same goals. The countries of Eastern Europe were still to be liberated and Germany to be unified, but the principles Gorbachev announced at the United Nations in December 1988 implied that the Soviet Union no longer intended to use force to ensure its domination of the area. At the time, many may have questioned whether Gorbachev really meant what he said; the events in the fall of 1989, when the countries of Central and Eastern Europe asserted their independence and the Berlin Wall was dismantled without a shot fired in anger, proved conclusively that he did.

In January 1989 the agreements that united Europe and wound up the East-West military confrontation were still to come. They were negotiated with skill by the first Bush administration. Nevertheless, from the time Gorbachev renounced the class struggle as the basis of Soviet foreign policy, the Cold War lost its rationale. The confrontation that had begun with the Bolshevik victory in Russia in 1917 and 1918 and had become, since 1946, an armed rivalry that threatened literally to end the possibility of human life on this earth was suddenly over.

Many readers will take issue with some of these statements. But if we take a close look at what really happened in the crucial years of the 1980s, I believe we will find a preponderance of fact in support of my conclusions. During those years I was privileged to observe U.S.-Soviet relations from the American embassy in Moscow in 1981 when I was chargé d'affaires, from our embassy in Prague from November 1981 until the spring of 1983, from Washington as a member of the National Security Council staff until the end of 1986, and again from Moscow from early 1987, when I was sent as ambassador by President Reagan.

In my account, I have availed myself, of course, of much more than my own memory and the notes I made at the time. I have reread most of the key documents and the messages and reports that have been declassified. I have discussed the events with both American and Soviet colleagues of those years and consulted the many memoirs that have been published in both countries. I have interviewed, sometimes repeatedly, most of the key figures on both sides. I am particularly indebted to former president Gorbachev for his responsiveness and the access he and his colleagues granted me to the archives he retains of his period in office. Their cooperation has enabled me to tell Moscow's side of the story with a confidence nearly as solid as that I feel for the events I witnessed on the American side.

CONTENTS

REAGAN

AND

GORBACHEV

I

1981–82

REAGAN'S CHALLENGE

And I have to believe that our greatest goal must be peace.
—RONALD REAGAN, June 16, 1981[1]

*I've always recognized that ultimately there's got to be a settlement, a
solution.*
—RONALD REAGAN, December 23, 1981[2]

*[A] Soviet leadership devoted to improving its people's lives, rather than
expanding its armed conquests, will find a sympathetic partner in the West.*
—RONALD REAGAN, May 9, 1982[3]

READERS MAY SUSPECT that the dates of the quotations set forth
above are mistaken. After all, doesn't everyone know that President
Reagan spent his first term bashing the Soviet Union and showed an interest
in serious negotiations only in his second term? Such is the myth that has developed of late.

The dates are correct. All of the remarks quoted were made during the
first eighteen months of Reagan's first administration. And they were not ex-
ceptional. These thoughts were present or clearly implied in virtually everything Reagan and his first secretary of state, Alexander Haig, said about
relations with the Soviet Union from the outset of their terms in office.

Of course, these were not the only thoughts they expressed. Other statements, particularly when taken out of context, gave rise to the distorted impression that came to prevail in American and foreign opinion. Let us look
carefully at what President Reagan said and how he said it.

During his first press conference as president, on January 29, 1981, Reagan stated that he was in favor of negotiating to achieve "an actual reduction

in the numbers of nuclear weapons" on a basis that would be verifiable. He also declared that during any negotiation one had to take into account "other things that are going on," and for that reason he believed in "linkage."

A journalist asked what he thought of "the long-range intentions of the Soviet Union" and whether "the Kremlin is bent on world domination that might lead to a continuation of the cold war" or whether "under other circumstances détente is possible." Addressing this convoluted question, Reagan replied that "so far détente has been a one-way street that the Soviet Union has used to pursue its own aims," and that as far as Soviet intentions are concerned, their leaders have consistently said that "their goal must be the promotion of world revolution and a one-world Socialist or Communist state."

Then he went on to add: "Now, as long as they do that and as long as they, at the same time, have openly and publicly declared that the only morality they recognize is what will further their cause, meaning they reserve unto themselves the right to commit any crime, to lie, to cheat, in order to attain that, and that is moral, not immoral, and we operate on a different set of standards, I think when you do business with them, even at a détente, you keep that in mind."[4]

Press and television reporters repeated his words about lying and cheating as if they were the heart of his approach.* Only an extraordinarily attentive reader would have grasped that Reagan referred to lying and cheating not as a personal moral defect of the Soviet leaders but as a feature of the philosophy they held. When asked about the remark subsequently, he denied that he was "castigating" the Soviet leaders "for lack of character," and explained, "It's just that they don't think like we do."[5]

In fact, Reagan cited in his first press conference several themes that remained in the bedrock of his policy toward the Soviet Union throughout his eight years in office: arms reduction to equal levels, as deep as the Soviet Union would accept; verification of agreements; linkage of arms control negotiations with Soviet behavior, in particular Soviet use of arms outside its borders; and reciprocity, inasmuch as the Soviet Union had taken advantage of the relaxed atmosphere of the 1970s ("détente") to its own advantage. Additional themes and many details were added to his "Soviet agenda" over the next three years, but Reagan never altered his commitment to the goals he enunciated on January 29, 1981.

---

* For example, the *New York Times* headlined its report on the news conference "President Reagan Assails Soviet Leaders for Reserving Right to 'Commit Any Crime, to Lie and Cheat.' "

A Different Policy

PRESIDENT REAGAN WAS convinced that the strategy the United States had followed previously in dealing with the Soviet Union had not been effective. He expressed that judgment repeatedly during his campaigns for the presidency. Once he took office he was determined to do things differently.

The approach he described in his first press conference represented significant departures from President Jimmy Carter's. In proposing an actual reduction in nuclear weapons, he was implicitly critical of the SALT II treaty that Carter had signed and the "Vladivostok agreement" concluded by President Gerald Ford, both of which would have placed limits on numbers of weapons without requiring a substantial reduction of existing arsenals. The condition that any agreement be verifiable was also intended to contrast Reagan's approach with Carter's, since Reagan and his supporters considered the verification provisions of SALT II inadequate.

Reagan's endorsement of linkage was also the opposite of Carter's policy, which had explicitly delinked arms control negotiations from other issues. Political reality had relinked the two, however, with the result that the Soviet invasion of Afghanistan was the final blow that prevented Senate ratification of SALT II.*

Reagan's goal was to shift the U.S. strategy from reacting to challenges and limiting damage to a concerted effort to change Soviet behavior. His approach constituted a direct challenge to the Soviet leadership since it explicitly denied fundamental tenets of Communist ideology and required a Soviet about-face on many issues under negotiation. It was a challenge to think differently about Soviet security, the place of the Soviet Union in the world, and the nature of Soviet society. It altered both the substance of negotiations and the way the dialogue was conducted, but it did not require the Soviet Union to compromise its own security. Soviet claims to the contrary, it never threatened military action against the Soviet Union itself.

---

* When the SALT II treaty was before the U.S. Senate for ratification in 1979, I was a strong and vocal supporter of it. My support was not solely because, as a foreign service officer on active duty, I was obligated to support the president's policy. I also judged that SALT II was the best that could be achieved at that time and that it could act as a brake on the arms race and open the door to significant reductions in the future. The Soviet invasion of Afghanistan in December 1979 changed my mind. It proved to me that the Soviet leaders were more interested in using force for geopolitical gain than in reducing arms, which ultimately would have made any arms limitation agreement a source of contention rather than a step toward ending the arms race. Furthermore, the reaction of the Senate and the American public demonstrated that separating the arms reduction process from other issues was not politically tenable in the United States.

During his first two years in office, Reagan explained his policies to the public piecemeal and not always with coherence, but there was an inner consistency: to deter further aggressive behavior by the Soviet Union, to make sure the Soviet leaders could never have the illusion that they could win a war with the United States, and, having ensured against that, to prepare the United States for successful negotiations. He had no secret strategy, but described every element of his policy to the public.

Hindsight allows us to group Reagan's early policies toward the Soviet Union in a few major tendencies, interrelated but distinct: telling the truth about the Soviet Union, restoring U.S. and allied strength, deterring aggression, and establishing reciprocity.

Setting the Record Straight

REAGAN WAS CONVINCED that U.S. presidents had normally refrained from frank criticism of the Soviet Union when they tried to cooperate with it. During World War II he had seen how Hollywood, with encouragement from Washington, had created a picture of a benign "Uncle Joe" Stalin, a personally modest man dedicated to bringing about democracy and social justice to his backward country. In the interest of making Americans feel good about their Soviet ally, moviemakers of the day flagrantly distorted history, as in the film version of Joseph Davies's *Mission to Moscow,* which portrays the innocent victims of Stalin's purge trials as traitors, justly accused of treason.

Wouldn't it have been better, Reagan asked, if Franklin Roosevelt had been more candid about the nature of the alliance with the Soviet Union? It really had nothing to do with whether the Soviet Union was a democracy or not, but whether cooperation was essential to defeat Hitler. It was, and it could be justified on that basis, without arousing extravagant expectations about the prospects for close postwar collaboration.

Later, other presidents had seemed to ignore the nature of the Soviet system whenever there was an effort to expand cooperation and control the arms race. Too often, he felt, this practice resulted in one-sided agreements that the Soviets exploited to their advantage. Even when balanced agreements were reached, the public was led to expect too much from them, and this could lead to overreaction if expectations were not met. Take the Soviet invasion of Afghanistan: didn't Carter's zeal to get the SALT II agreement ratified cause him to ignore the signs that the Soviets were preparing to enforce the Brezhnev Doctrine in Afghanistan? Carter said the Soviet invasion surprised him, but why, if he understood the Soviet system, should he have been surprised?

Far better, in Reagan's view, to level with the American people and tell it like it really was. Only that would encourage realistic public expectations and the understanding that we were dealing with a power based on an ideology that permitted—indeed required—ethical standards quite different from those we professed and usually observed.

Nevertheless, he did not lead with his criticism of the Soviet Union, nor did he dwell on it in his prepared speeches early in his administration. Usually his comments were elicited by questions that he answered in the following spirit: "Yes, this is how they are and we need to keep that in mind when we deal with them. We don't wish ill of them, but they've got to stop pushing other people around. It's in their own interest to stop that, and if they do we can even cooperate."

President Reagan did not himself offer a comprehensive statement regarding his policy toward the Soviet Union for more than a year. However, Secretary of State Alexander Haig spelled out U.S. policy in considerable detail, repeatedly emphasizing that it was not necessary for the Soviet Union to change internally "for East and West to manage their affairs in more constructive ways."[6] He stressed that the U.S. goal was "to demonstrate to the Soviet Union that aggressive and violent behavior will threaten Moscow's own interests." He added, "Only the U.S. has the power to persuade the Soviet leaders that improved relations with us serve Soviet as well as American interests."[7]

Both Reagan and Haig talked of the Soviet Union as a failed system facing increasing difficulties, but they felt that increasing Soviet reliance on military power abroad was both a danger to the peace and a source of weakness at home. Thus, in their view, if the United States could demonstrate to the Soviet leaders that they could not save their faltering system with military victories abroad and could not win an arms race with us, they would have no choice but to seek accommodation with the West in order to deal with their mounting problems at home. Haig put it most clearly in an address to the U.S. Chamber of Commerce in April 1982 when he remarked, "We must place our policy in the context of important changes that are taking place in the world and in the Soviet empire that may make Moscow more amenable to the virtues of restraint. The Soviet attempt to change the balance of power has produced a backlash of increasing international resistance. . . . As a consequence, the Soviet leaders may find it increasingly difficult to sustain the status quo at home while exporting a failed ideology abroad."[8]

Reagan was nearly a year and a half into his presidency when he delivered his first speech dealing in a comprehensive way with U.S.-Soviet relations. Pulling together thoughts that he had expressed piecemeal before, and repeating in his own words the ideas Haig had put forth, he announced: "I'm optimistic that we can build a more constructive relationship with the Soviet Union. . . . The Soviet empire is faltering because it is rigid; . . . in the end, this course will undermine the foundations of the Soviet system."9

Part of setting the record straight was to document and call attention to Soviet violations of previous agreements. Therefore, the White House ordered the U.S. intelligence community to study the record of Soviet compliance with agreements it had entered into with the United States or the international community. That study established what specialists already knew: The Soviet Union was continuing to violate several obligations it had undertaken. While some were relatively minor and technical, a few were important and blatant.

For example, most Soviet underground nuclear testing had resulted in venting more radioactive debris into the atmosphere than permitted by the Limited Test Ban Treaty, concluded in 1963 by President John Kennedy and General Secretary Nikita Khrushchev. U.S. protests had been met by denial rather than corrective action. An outbreak of anthrax near Sverdlovsk in 1979 seemed caused by a leak from a biological warfare facility—banned by a 1972 treaty—but the Soviet government claimed implausibly that it was caused by consumption of infected meat. Overhead pictures revealed that the Soviet Union was constructing a giant phased-array radar station not far from Krasnoyarsk in Siberia. Their intent was obvious: to cover a gap in their early-warning radar system. The 1972 ABM Treaty with the United States specified that such stations could be built only near a country's borders and have an outward orientation. The station near Krasnoyarsk was thousands of miles inland and was oriented to cover much of northern Siberia. Nevertheless, the Soviets claimed that it was only for "deep space tracking" and therefore not relevant to obligations under the ABM Treaty.

These were specific actions that unquestionably violated legal obligations freely undertaken by the Soviet Union. Not all agreements, however, had been legally binding treaties. A number of declarations of intent or principle had been issued over the years, documents such as the Universal Declaration of Human Rights, the U.S.-Soviet Declaration of Principles of 1972, and, in 1975, the Helsinki Final Act. These were political rather than legal commitments, and Soviet leaders generally ignored them unless they contained provisions that could be used against the West. In the case of the Helsinki accord, which obligated the signatories to respect and enforce an extensive list of human rights, there had not been the slightest effort to bring Soviet practices in harmony with the principles established. Soviet officials often refused even to discuss violations of these principles, on grounds that they were purely matters of internal jurisdiction.

The general conclusion drawn by President Reagan and his secretaries of state was not that treaties with the Soviet Union were worthless. They recognized that the Soviet Union had complied with many of the provisions of the legally binding treaties. Soviet leaders had fulfilled treaty obligations whenever they considered it more in their interest to comply than to violate. However, the violations demonstrated the importance of negotiating a treaty with great care and ensuring that the United States could determine what was going on. Experience with past treaties suggested that it was unwise to sweep violations under the rug in the hope that the Soviet authorities would quietly correct the situation and do better next time. So long as their tendency was to deny that the violation had occurred, this would not work.

As for the agreements involving political obligations, the conclusion was different. While it was important to keep calling attention to violations in the hope that eventually this might have some effect, such commitments up to then had proven hollow. There was no need to negotiate any more of this type until there was a better record of compliance with those already signed.

EVIDENCE WAS ACCUMULATING that the Soviet Union was involved in the support of terrorist groups to a greater extent than had been thought. Philosophically, Communist leaders had always condemned terrorism, but by this they meant random acts of violence by groups they did not control, with a political purpose they did not approve. They had always considered violence for the sake of "revolution" not only acceptable but necessary. They had indulged in political assassinations outside their borders and supported, at least indirectly, Marxist groups that used terrorist tactics as part of their revolutionary technique. Nevertheless, they publicly condemned some of the more notorious international terrorists of the day.

During the 1970s things began to happen that challenged a complacent attitude regarding Soviet ties to international terrorism. Soviet hand-held surface-to-air missiles were intercepted in transit by the Italian police in the mid-1970s. They had been shipped to Italy in a Libyan diplomatic pouch and intended for terrorists to use against civilian aircraft. Where did the Libyans get them if not from the Soviets? A Turkish citizen with ties to the

Bulgarian secret police (itself under the control of the KGB) had attempted to assassinate the pope after passing through Sofia on his way to Vatican City. Other incidents seemed to indicate Soviet involvement.

Shortly after taking office, Reagan ordered a study of Soviet ties to international terrorist groups. It was completed in May and bore a Top Secret classification. It was so nuanced that its "key judgments" covered three pages. It found "conclusive evidence that the USSR directly or indirectly supports a large number of national insurgencies and some separatist-irredentist groups. Many of these entities, of both types, carry out terrorist activities as part of their larger programs of revolutionary violence."[10]

The Soviet Union also provided support to "certain allied and friendly governments and entities—notably Libya, certain Palestinian groups, East European states, South Yemen, and Cuba—which in turn" supported terrorist activities.

One example the report cited of direct Soviet involvement in terrorism was the supply of arms to revolutionary groups in El Salvador. It gave a specific description of the way the supply was organized:

> Moscow has provided funding assistance and has coordinated the weapons supply from its allies, including East European countries, Vietnam and Ethiopia. The Soviets have facilitated the quest for arms of El Salvador's Unified Revolutionary Directorate (DRU), an umbrella organization comprising five guerrilla/terrorist groups. The Soviets have urged Palestinian groups to provide training and other support to the Salvadoran revolutionaries, and have coordinated the support infrastructure abroad with assistance such as the provision of safe houses and travel arrangements for Salvadoran rebel leaders.[11]

Was the CIA mistaken, or driven to misinterpret evidence to make a political point? Hardly. Here is what Dmitri Volkogonov, a Soviet military historian who studied secret KGB and Communist Party archives after the Soviet Union's collapse, said on the issue: "It is no secret that the Soviet secret service maintained covert links with terrorist organizations, some of which received arms from the USSR. Many terrorists received ideological and special training in the Soviet Union, and some were given asylum." As for arms to El Salvador in particular, Volkogonov found in Andropov's secret archive a Politburo decision to supply arms to rebels in El Salvador.[12]

Secretary Haig made both the general issue of Soviet support for terrorism and the specific case of El Salvador central elements in his description of Soviet behavior that would have to be restrained if there was to be improvement in U.S.-Soviet relations.

Basically, his and Reagan's view was that until there was a clear understanding of the nature of the Soviet system and of the way it operated, it was impossible to devise a strategy to deal with it. Setting the record straight was only the start of the task, however.

Accumulating Chips

REAGAN WAS CONVINCED that U.S. defenses had been allowed to deteriorate during the 1970s, and that this condition had left the United States vulnerable. In his view, an imbalance could encourage the Soviet leaders to believe that they could use their superior military strength to blackmail the U.S. and split its alliances. He also felt that U.S. weakness left him without much to trade when it came to negotiations on arms reduction. He was well aware that the Soviet Union normally insisted on equal reductions; if he began to negotiate when the Soviets had superior forces, he doubted that they could be induced to reduce them to a common level.

For both reasons, Reagan sought a substantial increase in U.S. defense spending—even more than Carter had proposed in his last budget request. He also announced that he wished to restore some programs canceled by Carter, such as the "enhanced radiation" weapon (neutron bomb) and the B-1 bomber. At first Congress was supportive, particularly since Carter had also sought sharply increased defense funding at the close of his administration, but by the end of 1981 it was clear that one program the Reagan administration considered vital for balancing Soviet forces and providing potential trade-offs was in trouble. This was the new U.S. heavy intercontinental ballistic missile (ICBM), designated the MX. Congress did not oppose the idea of a new heavy missile in principle—the USSR had been building them in large numbers—but rather feared public opposition to their deployment. Nobody wanted them in his backyard, and moving them on railways or interstate highways was not acceptable either. If they were in fixed locations, they would be vulnerable to a surprise attack; if they were mobile, an accident could have disastrous consequences for people in the vicinity.

Did we really need more nuclear-armed missiles when both the U.S. and USSR had enough to wipe out life on earth several times over? By the logic of deterrence, we did. After all, the pertinent consideration was not how much the weapons could destroy if they were used, but rather how to ensure that they would never be used. We faced an adversary with a large stock of land-based heavy ICBMs, each with ten nuclear warheads that could be aimed with great accuracy. The United States, in all its nuclear forces, had nothing comparable. Our land-based missiles were smaller in size and carried fewer warheads; missiles launched from submarines were not accurate enough for precise targeting of Soviet missile silos; aircraft carrying gravity bombs or cruise missiles might not penetrate Soviet air defenses. They were all designed for retaliation, not preemptive attack.

In short, the United States was not capable of carrying out a first-strike strategy, an attempt to deal a crushing blow to the other side and avoid a devastating counterstrike. In theory, at least, the Soviet Union did have a first-strike capability with its heavy missiles. It could have wiped out the bulk of the U.S. land-based ICBMs in a surprise attack and then confronted the U.S. president with a choice of submitting to some demand or committing mutual suicide by launching a retaliatory attack on the Soviet Union, which would still have enough weapons left to devastate population centers in the U.S. Not a pretty prospect.

This was theory, of course, and many argued that it was only that. There was no evidence that the Soviet leaders had adopted a first-strike strategy. Nevertheless, sound security policy cannot rest on factors as vague, indeterminate, and subject to change as presumed intentions. If a possibility exists, it must be taken seriously. While there was no evidence of Soviet intent to unleash a nuclear war, the United States was aware that both Soviet military doctrine and senior Soviet military leaders held that the USSR could prevail if a nuclear war broke out.*

There were only two potential solutions to the first-strike dilemma. The simplest would have been for both sides to reduce the number of weapons that could be used for this purpose below the quantity required to deliver a disarming first strike. The second would be to build a defense to protect missile sites and cities. However, the first required Soviet agreement, and Soviet negotiators had steadfastly refused to make deep cuts in the missiles the United States considered most threatening. After all, the U.S. had nothing comparable to trade. The second required an enormous and expensive effort, without guarantee that it would be successful, and, even if it were, it would require modification or abandonment of the 1972 Treaty on Anti-Ballistic Missile Systems (ABM).

As Congress objected to the MX—for sound political and environmental

---

* Critics of Reagan's policy frequently denied that this was the case—as if they could know. However, Dmitri Yazov, USSR minister of defense from 1987 to 1991, said to me and to other foreign visitors that he had believed the Soviet Union could prevail in a nuclear war before the disaster at the Chernobyl nuclear power station in 1986 convinced him otherwise. He realized then that even a conventional war could wreak nuclear devastation and that a nation could be destroyed by fallout from nuclear power plants attacked by conventional weapons.

reasons—the Reagan administration was forced to consider other means of dealing with the Soviet superiority in heavy ICBMs.

WHEN REAGAN SPOKE of negotiating from strength, he did not mean merely military strength. He was also convinced that the 1970s had left the United States with a weakened economy (high inflation and unemployment) and a lack of political will (the "post-Vietnam syndrome," Carter's talk of national "malaise"). In Reagan's mind, efforts to forge a renewed sense of national purpose and to stimulate the economy by cutting taxes were not only important in themselves, but also components of his strategy to improve his negotiating posture vis-à-vis the Soviet leaders.

Sanctions could also be used as bargaining chips, and they were a favorite tool of many officials in the Reagan administration. Reagan's attitude toward them was ambiguous, however. Though he could be persuaded at times to apply or threaten economic sanctions, he preferred to avoid them. In the case of the Soviet Union, he inherited sanctions on about everything that could be sanctioned, and he felt that some were ill advised since they damaged U.S. more than Soviet interests. Nevertheless, there were strong arguments against lifting them without any Soviet concession. These conflicting considerations produced a fluctuating policy toward sanctions during Reagan's first term.

Just a few months after taking office he lifted the ban President Carter had imposed on grain sales to the Soviet Union above the eight million tons a year guaranteed by treaty. The grain "embargo"* had been imposed following the Soviet invasion of Afghanistan. Secretary of State Haig opposed lifting the ban since the Soviet Union was continuing the war and refusing even to discuss leaving. However, Reagan had promised during his campaign to lift the embargo and did so to carry out his promise.

In contrast to his action regarding grain sales, Reagan approved efforts to persuade our European allies to refuse construction of a large pipeline to supply natural gas from western Siberia to Central Europe. The rationale was that the Soviet economy should not be strengthened by profits from the gas, and that Western Europe should not make itself dependent on the Soviet Union for its energy.

Despite strong efforts by Reagan and Haig to achieve allied solidarity, the

---

* It was not technically an embargo since sales of eight million tons a year were permitted. Under the U.S.-USSR long-term agreement, the Soviet government had a right to buy up to that amount without the approval of the U.S. government. Sales above that amount required approval, which gave Carter the right to stop them.

Europeans refused to block the pipeline. It was constructed in due course even though Washington imposed a unilateral embargo on oil and gas equipment. After December 1981, when General Wojciech Jaruzelski, the Polish leader, declared martial law in his country under Soviet pressure, further attempts were made to persuade the Europeans to restrict credits and investment in the Soviet Union. These efforts, like those to block the pipeline, turned out to be futile. The Europeans were simply not willing to agree to economic sanctions aside from restrictions on the export of items that would directly enhance the Soviet military potential.

The U.S. government soon relaxed its pressure on its allies. Alliance solidarity was due for a severe test in 1983 when the time would come, absent a prior agreement with the Soviet Union, to deploy American intermediate-range nuclear missiles in Europe. Differences over trade with the Soviet Union could not be allowed to divide the alliance.

Deterring Aggression

THE SOVIET INVASION of Afghanistan in December 1979 had caused the final demise of détente. The American inability to prevent the invasion had contributed to Carter's electoral defeat. It was important to the Reagan administration not only to keep pressure on the Soviet Union to leave Afghanistan, but also to prevent further Soviet attempts to intervene with military force outside its borders.

Soon after he took office, Secretary Haig demanded that the Soviet Union cease supplying arms to rebels in El Salvador, and made an issue of Soviet support for terrorism in general. Even graver concern developed regarding Poland. As the free trade union Solidarity gained momentum and turned into a mass movement demanding the end of Communist rule, Moscow's reaction was ominous. Throughout late spring and summer its sharp criticism of the Polish leaders and military exercises along the Polish border were distressingly reminiscent of the Soviet reaction to Alexander Dubček's "socialism with a human face" in Czechoslovakia before it was crushed by Soviet tanks in August 1968.

I was in charge of the American embassy in Moscow in 1981 as Soviet pressures on Poland mounted. Reporting on Soviet intentions was our top priority. The embassy sent several messages every day, relaying every scrap of information that came its way bearing on the Soviet attitude toward Poland. From time to time I would analyze the developing situation. I reported that the Soviet leaders were deeply disturbed by the rise of Solidarity and were seriously considering intervention, but that they would not do so lightly. They had learned in Afghanistan that interventions were not necessarily quick and successful, and they could not be certain that the Poles would not resist. They had also learned that the Western reaction to intervention could be costly, particularly in political terms, and probably understood that reaction to a Soviet invasion of Poland would harm them far more than the intervention in Afghanistan had. Therefore, they would attempt to pressure the Polish government to contain Solidarity for them.[13]

That is, in fact, what happened when General Jaruzelski declared martial law. Bad as this was, a Soviet invasion would have been much worse, and the U.S. reaction was largely rhetorical.* When the Europeans refused to restrict investments and credits, there was little left that the United States could do to penalize the Soviet Union, even though all understood that Jaruzelski had acted under Soviet pressure.

As for Afghanistan, U.S. attention focused on ways to support the opposition that had developed locally to the Soviet invasion and the Afghan regime the Soviets had installed. Most of the things the Carter administration had done had been either spectacular "one-shot" gestures, such as boycotting the 1980 Olympic Games in Moscow, or actions that harmed U.S. interests more than they hurt the Soviet Union, such as closing the Soviet consulate general in New York (and leaving there a UN mission with more than seven hundred people) and the American consulate general in Kiev (and leaving there nobody to take care of American interests or follow political developments in Ukraine).

Except for the grain "embargo," Reagan felt unable to end other ineffective boycotts immediately, lest he send a signal that the Soviet intervention in Afghanistan did not matter. Instead, a strategy developed to provide concrete assistance to the mujahedin in Afghanistan and, as it became effective, to phase out self-defeating sanctions.

Establishing Reciprocity

REAGAN ONLY OCCASIONALLY mentioned reciprocity in his early comments on policy toward the Soviet Union, but the principle was embedded in his approach. It was Secretary of State Alexander Haig who spelled out what the administration had in mind. On substance, it obviously meant that the

---

* The U.S. Information Agency prepared a film, *Let Poland Be Poland!*, condemning the suppression of Solidarity, which it showed throughout the world, particularly in Europe.

United States expected any agreements to contain a balance of benefits. It also meant that the U.S. expected a reciprocity of behavior. As Haig put it: "We want the competition of democracy and communism to be conducted in peaceful and political terms, but we will provide other means if the Soviet Union insists upon violent methods of struggle. There must be a single standard."[14]

The reason the Reagan administration placed such stress on reciprocity was its conviction that the Soviet Union had sought and obtained one-sided advantages during the 1970s. In 1972, Richard Nixon and Leonid Brezhnev had signed a Declaration of Principles in which, among other commitments, both pledged not to seek "unilateral advantage." Nevertheless, from 1977 the USSR began to deploy large numbers of nuclear-tipped missiles (SS-20s) capable of reaching all NATO capitals in Europe with unprecedented accuracy. NATO had no comparable weapons, so the previous balance in Europe became a Soviet advantage.

Furthermore, even before these deployments, Soviet arms and military advisers began to turn up in hot spots in Africa and troubled areas of Central America. In some local wars, such as those between Somalia and Ethiopia and the civil war in Angola, Cuban troops, armed and financed by the Soviet Union, participated actively in the fighting. Soviet arms bolstered Arab countries opposed to peace with Israel, such as Syria and Iraq. Terrorists were routinely using Soviet arms, not only in the Middle East but elsewhere. These questionable activities were followed in December 1979 by an outright invasion of Afghanistan by Soviet forces. There was no way these activities could be reconciled with the commitment in 1972 to refrain from seeking unilateral advantage.

The Reagan-Haig concept of reciprocity went beyond Soviet military activity. The Soviet propaganda machine had operated on a Cold War basis even at the height of détente when Western governments muted their criticism of the Soviet Union. Soviet citizens were reminded periodically that a relaxation (détente) "in the sphere of interstate relations" did not mean that "the ideological struggle" was over. It was a struggle involving much more than mere propaganda—putting out tendentious and misleading information. Denying the Soviet people information from abroad was a critical feature of the ideological struggle. Western radio stations were jammed, domestic dissent suppressed, and foreigners excluded from the Soviet mass media unless they were known to be sympathetic to the Soviet Union.

Moscow also conducted a clandestine campaign to spread fabrications ("disinformation" was the term usually applied) in ostensibly independent publications. These operations were normally conducted by KGB agents in the field, who planted deliberate falsehoods in newspapers that were covertly financed by the Soviet Union or fed them to corrupt journalists with appropriate bribes.* The entire operation was mounted and controlled by a special section of the Central Committee Secretariat in Moscow.

The Reagan administration never attempted to establish reciprocity by exchanging falsehoods with the Soviet Union, but stepped up efforts to expose Soviet lies. Reagan was convinced that deliberate disinformation and the isolation of the Soviet public were major impediments to better relations. His attitude echoed the comment Adlai Stevenson made in one of his election campaigns: "If you don't stop telling lies about me, I'll start telling the truth about you."

Reciprocity also applied to the manner in which relations were conducted. Beginning in the first Nixon administration, senior American officials had developed a habit of using Soviet ambassador Anatoly Dobrynin for their most sensitive communications, bypassing the American ambassador in Moscow and, until Dr. Henry Kissinger was named secretary of state, the State Department as well. The Carter administration made more use of its ambassador in Moscow, but still entrusted Dobrynin with some of its most sensitive communications. To avoid attracting public attention to his special relationship, he was accorded privileges not offered any other ambassador in Washington, even those of our closest allies: a direct telephone line to the secretary of state and the use of a private entrance into the State Department.

The practice of using Dobrynin exclusively for the most important communications with the Soviet leadership made about as much sense as it would to hire an opponent's lawyer to represent both parties in a litigation. The reason Dobrynin was used as a "special channel" obviously had nothing to do with enhancing American diplomacy; the objective was simply to withhold information from others in the American government. Kissinger's initial bureaucratic strategy was to exclude Secretary of State William Rogers from arms control negotiations with the Soviet Union; even after he became secretary of state himself, he continued his secretive practices, apparently to control not only access to the information but the very record of

---

* Once, when I was assigned to the American embassy in Accra, Ghana, in the 1960s, I was witness to a revealing encounter. While I was chatting at a reception with several Soviet embassy officers in Russian, a Ghanaian journalist approached the group and, not realizing that I was American, said to the Soviet press attaché, "I haven't gotten my case of whiskey this month." The Soviet diplomat grabbed his arm and rushed him out of my hearing, but not before I recognized the journalist. His by-line often appeared on the most vicious anti-American diatribes in the local press.

negotiation as well. He usually dealt with Dobrynin in private, and when he spoke to Soviet officials in Moscow who did not speak English, he used the Soviet interpreter. Thus, he personally could control what was put into—and left out of—the record available to other Americans.

Carter administration officials began using American interpreters, but still used Dobrynin on matters considered particularly sensitive. The reasons, again, stemmed from bureaucratic rivalry. There were times when State Department officials did not want Zbigniew Brzezinski, Carter's assistant for national security, to be aware of what they had told Dobrynin. If they had put it in a telegram to the American ambassador in Moscow, a copy would have gone to the White House and Brzezinski would have known what was said and possibly protested to President Carter. Brzezinski also dealt directly with Dobrynin without informing the State Department or the U.S. embassy in Moscow.

There was nothing inherently wrong with U.S. officials dealing with Dobrynin, or even with making special arrangements to shield their contacts from public attention. It was unwise, however, to grant privileges and access to the Soviet ambassador without requiring that the American ambassador in Moscow be given comparable treatment. As it was, the American ambassador was not given appointments in most ministries except for those dealing with foreign affairs and foreign trade, and was never allowed to talk to officials in the Communist Party Secretariat, who acted as personal advisers to the general secretary. He was never accorded private access to the Soviet foreign ministry or to the Kremlin. Thus, while Dobrynin was welcomed everywhere he wished to go in Washington, American representatives were restricted to very limited contacts in Moscow.

From the beginning, the Reagan administration acted to correct the imbalance. It continued, of course, to do business with the Soviet embassy in Washington, but required the Soviet ambassador to enter the State Department through the diplomatic entrance other ambassadors used. Important messages for the Soviet government were sent to the American embassy in Moscow for delivery and discussion; if the Soviet embassy in Washington wished further clarification, its diplomats were received at the bureaucratic level equivalent to that at which discussions had occurred in Moscow. Though the national security adviser continued to have occasional contacts with Dobrynin (usually with a State Department officer present), he made it clear that routine contacts between the Soviet embassy and the White House staff would depend on the willingness of Soviet authorities to allow American diplomats to meet with members of the Central Committee staff.

All of this may smack of silly bureaucratic game playing, but it was not that. The former arrangements had severely handicapped the U.S. government in any effort to communicate with the Soviet leadership. In the first place, it made private U.S. messages hostage to the Soviet ambassador's goodwill and competence, and however high one might rate the latter, it was not prudent to depend on the former. Furthermore, the practice allowed Soviet foreign minister Gromyko to play his own bureaucratic games in Moscow. Dobrynin's messages went to the Ministry of Foreign Affairs, which would put its spin on them before reporting them to the general secretary and his staff. Sometimes the ministry failed to pass them to the general secretary altogether.

Some of the tussles between the U.S. and USSR early in the Reagan administration involved these issues of reciprocity. American journalists often reported them in distorted fashion, suggesting that the Reagan administration had deliberately set out to insult the Soviet Union and its representatives.

Thus, when Dobrynin was invited to his first meeting with Haig, his office was informed that he should enter through the normal diplomatic entrance rather than through the basement entrance he had used previously. Shortly before the appointment, an official on the Soviet desk in the State Department called Dobrynin's protocol assistant to remind him where Dobrynin should come. Nevertheless, Dobrynin's driver tried to take him into the basement entrance and was turned back by State Department security guards. Reporters who were waiting at the diplomatic entrance observed what happened, and their stories gave rise to a flurry of media comment that blamed the Reagan administration for planning an incident to embarrass Dobrynin. Walter Cronkite spent several minutes of a rare on-camera interview with President Reagan questioning what he termed "childish" treatment of the Soviet ambassador.[15]

I was personally involved in another of the early skirmishes over reciprocity. When the Soviet media distorted Reagan's intent to the point of charging that he was planning a war against the Soviet Union, the State Department made a formal request that I be allowed to appear on Soviet television to discuss American policy and answer questions about it. I was the senior officer at the American embassy in Moscow at the time. Since I speak Russian, I would have been able to appear without an interpreter. The request was still pending when Dr. Georgy Arbatov, the director of the USA-Canada Institute in Moscow, was traveling in the United States and giving interviews to newspapers and television stations. He was invited to appear on a major U.S. network a few days after his visa here was to expire, and he requested an extension to do the interview. This presented an opportunity to invoke the principle of reciprocity. The Soviet government was informed that Arbatov's visa would be extended if the senior American diplomat in Moscow was allowed to discuss U.S. policy on Soviet television. The request was not granted, so the State Department refused to extend Arbatov's stay in the United States.

Later, on July 4, 1981, I was offered five minutes of prime time on Soviet television to deliver a message to the Soviet people on our national day. It was a normal Soviet practice to offer foreign ambassadors such an opportunity once a year, but U.S. ambassador Thomas Watson had been refused the year before because his planned address contained a reference to Soviet intervention in Afghanistan. I thought I could get the point across without triggering a Pavlovian reaction, so I talked about American values and how our nation was pleased that "not a single American soldier is engaged in combat anywhere in the world." Since the Soviet media were accusing the United States of "warmongering," it was important to call attention to this fact. After all, my Soviet listeners knew who was fighting in Afghanistan, and they weren't happy about it.

My experience with this brief address was revealing in several respects. Since the available time was short, I prepared carefully, with help from Helen Semler, who had grown up in a Russian-speaking émigré family and whose husband, Peter, was an embassy counselor. I wanted to describe the American government in Abraham Lincoln's phrase "of the people, by the people, for the people," but found that it was difficult to get the idea across in simple phrases. We could translate the words literally, of course, but their meaning would have been unclear to Soviet listeners, whose government pretended to be all those things, but was in fact quite different. We had to explain each phrase if our listeners were to understand. This brought home to me how difficult it was going to be to bridge the cultural and semantic gap that history and Communist ideology had created between our peoples. We had to be very careful to make sure that the words I used would be understood as intended.

The second thing that struck me was how the Soviet newscasters did their best to help me make an effective presentation. The address was prerecorded, so I could repeat my delivery until I got it right. Svetlana Starodumskaya, one of the prominent anchors of the day, coached me on phrasing, tempo, and pauses, which greatly improved the final version. In part, Svetlana and the others who helped did so out of professional pride, not wanting a dull presentation to mar their newscast. But I had the impression it was more than that. They really wanted to hear, and for their listeners to hear, an American point of view.

The impact of this brief presentation surpassed all expectations. For years, Soviet citizens would quote back to me things I said on television that day. It was so unusual for them to hear a foreign representative challenge Soviet propaganda stereotypes—even with cautious indirection—that people noticed and remembered. Opening the Soviet media had to be a prime U.S. objective if relations were to improve, and the degree to which it was opened would be an important test of the regime's commitment to reform. For this reason, access to the Soviet media continued to be an issue between the United States and the Soviet Union for several years.

There was less hesitation on the Soviet part to accept our efforts to make the official dialogue reciprocal. Soviet officials in Moscow seemed pleased that American diplomats were doing more business directly with them than they had before.

Reaching Out: Private Communication

JUST TWO MONTHS into his presidency, Reagan was critically wounded by a would-be assassin's bullet. He underwent an emergency operation at George Washington University Hospital in Washington and spent several weeks there before returning to the White House and work. While in the hospital he resolved to communicate his desire for better relations to Brezhnev. When he returned to the White House, he drafted a personal letter, but Secretary Haig objected that it would convey the wrong signal to Brezhnev, particularly as it coincided with his decision to lift the grain "embargo." After all, the Soviets were not winding down the war in Afghanistan, which had precipitated the embargo in the first place.

At Haig's direction, the State Department drafted a replacement letter designed to stress that an end to the grain embargo did not mean that the United States considered the Soviet intervention in Afghanistan acceptable. Reagan insisted on sending his personal appeal too, and both letters were finally delivered at the same time.[16] Reagan's personal letter was a genuine attempt to reach out, but by then it was beyond Brezhnev's capacity to respond positively. His reply did not go beyond a stiff, staff-drafted rejection of everything Reagan had written. As Soviet ambassador Anatoly Dobrynin wrote subsequently, "Brezhnev's letter . . . was cast in the standard polemical form stressing their differences, without any attempt to emphasize the necessity of developing their personal relations. The tone could not possibly have built a personal bridge."[17]

Throughout the spring and summer of 1981, American officials conducted detailed discussions with Soviet officials both in Moscow and in Washington. Haig saw Dobrynin from time to time for lengthy discussions, and I was frequently instructed to explain U.S. policy in Moscow to Gromyko's principal deputy, Georgy Korniyenko. Most of these meetings focused on complaints about Soviet actions or evidence of Soviet treaty violations, but their intent was constructive. We felt we had to impress upon the Soviet government that its continued support of violence outside its borders was not consistent with improved relations, and that the United States would take account of Soviet use of armed force and its record in complying with treaty obligations as it developed its policy on arms control. Alexander Haig puts it this way in his memoirs:

> If the Reagan Administration came into office with the determination to resist Soviet adventurism, it arrived also with the idea of reopening a realistic dialogue with Moscow. We wanted to identify questions on which the U.S. and the Soviets could accommodate their interests in ways that advanced peace and social justice. But before that could happen, the Soviets must believe that it was better to accommodate to the United States and the West than to go on marauding against their interests and security.[18]

Both Reagan and Haig wanted to conduct their contacts with the Soviet leaders in confidence. Only when he was accused repeatedly of not communicating with the Soviet leaders did Reagan speak of his handwritten letter to Brezhnev. Conversations between American and Soviet diplomats rarely stayed off the public record for long, however. Leaks abounded, just as they had during previous American administrations. Some officials wanted to demonstrate how tough Reagan was; some wanted to prove to journalist friends that they were in the know; others wanted to advance, or more often defeat, some particular idea. Most of the time leaks were symptoms of jockeying for position within the new administration. They made confidential communication most difficult and suggested to the suspicious Soviets that much of what the administration said was meant only for public consumption.

For these reasons, Haig was quickly persuaded that we needed a better way to communicate confidentially. In the past, this had been done through Ambassador Dobrynin, but for the reasons already mentioned, that particular "special channel" was not acceptable. We needed one that would ensure access to the Soviet decision makers without the distorting lens of a Soviet intermediary.

An approach was made to me in Moscow in the summer that seemed to be a request for a confidential dialogue. A Soviet acquaintance invited my wife and me to dinner "in order to meet someone you should know." This was a typical way to bring embassy personnel in contact with a KGB officer—frequently for purposes of blackmail or recruitment. But that was clearly not the intent in this case because I was invited to come with my wife. With State Department approval, Rebecca and I accepted the invitation.

The guest to whom I was introduced, Vasili Sytnikov, held a position with the State Committee on Publishing, but we did not talk about books or magazines. He made a long pitch over dinner about the lack of communication between our governments and about our need to establish an unofficial and purely private dialogue if we were to make any progress. He also mentioned that he had taken "back-channel" messages to Ambassador Llewelyn Thompson during negotiations on the status of Berlin. Though Sytnikov did most of the talking at dinner, Vadim Zagladin, a deputy chief of the Central Committee International Department, and his wife were also guests. He generally endorsed Sytnikov's comments about the need for better communication, and I naturally took this as a signal that Sytnikov was acting with the approval of senior members of the Central Committee staff.

When Rebecca and I left the dinner, Sytnikov asked for a ride. He got out of the car in front of our embassy, in plain view of the KGB guards, and spoke in a loud voice that they could overhear, repeating his basic points about needing a private channel of communication. These actions were obviously intended to demonstrate to me that he was acting on higher authority. Otherwise, he would have avoided riding in my car with a Soviet driver (who would report him to the KGB), or having any contact in sight of the Soviet embassy guards.

The next day I checked embassy records regarding Sytnikov. They confirmed that he was a presumed KGB officer who had been involved in some back-channel messages to Ambassador Thompson. When I reported the approach to Secretary Haig with the recommendation to offer a discussion of Afghanistan, I was immediately authorized to do so. I invited Sytnikov to a reception at my apartment and, when the other guests had left, took him to the library to deliver a message. It was that the United States was prepared to hold a confidential discussion, entirely off the record, with him or whomever his authorities might designate, regarding the conditions under which the Soviet Union could withdraw its military forces from Afghanistan.

In return for a Soviet decision to withdraw its armed forces, the United States would discuss ways to ensure the security of the Soviet Union's southern border and also make a commitment not to use the territory of Afghanistan against the Soviet Union. The United States had no desire, I pointed out, to encourage an Afghanistan hostile to the Soviet Union. It would be pleased to see an independent Afghanistan with close and friendly relations with the Soviet Union, like Finland's for example. What we found unacceptable was the creation of a Soviet satellite by military force.

Visibly nervous, Sytnikov carefully wrote down the points in the message, and then remarked that he would report the matter and let me know. He wasn't sure his people wanted to talk about Afghanistan; they had the SALT treaty in mind.

I told him that we were not ruling out future discussions on arms reduction, but that our position had not yet been developed to the point that talking about it would be useful. The Soviet authorities should recognize that it was their invasion of Afghanistan, more than anything else, that had prevented ratification of the SALT II treaty. If the Soviet Union could find a way to leave Afghanistan, it would be a boost to negotiations in other areas, including arms control. He seemed reassured and promised a reply.

It never came. Sytnikov did not respond to future invitations from me and did not come to any of the functions he would normally have attended by virtue of his cover job (such as the opening of a book fair). We could only conclude that whoever authorized the initial contact had decided against a private discussion of Afghanistan at that point. The Soviet leaders still expected to win.

Reagan Replaces His Quarterback

IN JUNE 1982, President Reagan tapped George Shultz to replace Alexander Haig as secretary of state. Shultz was to become, despite determined resistance from other members of Reagan's team, the president's principal lieutenant in both formulating policy toward the Soviet Union and implementing it.

Whether General Haig could have done the same, we cannot say, but we can be certain that if he had remained in office, he would have done it differently. He was less sanguine than Reagan and Shultz that the Soviet Union could change, and therefore posed more limited goals for U.S. policy than they eventually did. If the Soviet leaders had been willing to curb Soviet military support for third world insurgencies, had refrained from threatening to intervene in Poland, and had agreed to reduce military arsenals to a verifiable parity, he very likely would have settled for something resembling a cease-fire in place. This would have reduced pressure for internal reform in the Soviet Union and left the ideological basis for the Cold War in effect, though muted. The world would have seemed safer to Western publics, but the East-West divide would have remained. The Cold War would perhaps have been dormant for a time, but would not have ended as a result.

Haig was replaced, however, not because of the policies he espoused but because he had offended key members of Reagan's administration. Some of his cabinet colleagues and members of the senior White House staff resented his attempts to be the president's "vicar." If Haig had remained in office, his confrontational approach would probably have prevented the effective coordination of any truly innovative policy.

Nevertheless, Alexander Haig's imprint on Reagan administration policy was significant and, in fact, facilitated the progress subsequently made. His stress on reciprocity remained basic to Reagan's policy throughout both terms, and Haig's insistence on using American representatives to deliver important messages to the Soviet government established a more effective pattern of communication that well served both Reagan and Shultz—and, after them, George H.W. Bush and his secretary of state. His concept of linkage, as we shall see, not only survived him, but remained an essential element of U.S. foreign policy for at least a decade.

Secretary of State Shultz combined qualities that made him one of the most effective statesmen of the twentieth century. A man of deep experience in the three worlds of government, business, and academia, he was able to probe the details of a subject without losing sight of the larger picture. As a manager, he inspired teamwork, bringing the key players in his and other relevant departments into his counsel and keeping them informed of his decisions. A good listener, he sought differing points of view before every important decision and, when possible, took time to reflect before making up his mind. A master negotiator, he understood the importance and the limitations of personal chemistry in a negotiation.

His weaknesses were few and of lesser importance: His disputes with some of his colleagues sometimes colored his attitude toward their departments and conditioned him to allow debilitating turf fights by his staff. There also were times—fortunately rare—that he would opt out of important decisions in a sulk rather than carry his views directly and vigorously to the president—something his rivals never hesitated to do.

George Shultz's qualities complemented some of Ronald Reagan's weak points. Shultz mastered details that bored Reagan, exhibited greater stamina in negotiations, and had a keener sense of the value of consistency in overall policy. In contrast, Reagan was more effective on a public platform. While Shultz's carefully crafted speeches were persuasive to diplomats and foreign governments, they had little resonance with the broader American public that seemed to thrill at Reagan's every phrase.

II

1981–82

MOSCOW'S TRUCULENCE

*As we in the Soviet Union saw it, Reagan was embarked on a path of breaking
the military and strategic parity between the two nations. With
characteristically reactive behavior, the Soviet leadership . . . viewed Reagan
with great indignation and suspicion.*
— ANATOLY DOBRYNIN, 1995[1]

IN THE FALL of 1980, Soviet leaders expected Jimmy Carter to defeat
Ronald Reagan. They had been severely disappointed with Carter, considering him unpredictable and unreliable. He had come to office with stri-
dent denunciations of Soviet human rights abuses, yet entered into no
negotiations on the issue and even ended those that had begun during the
Ford administration. He had abruptly altered the U.S. negotiating position
on strategic arms. When an agreement, known as SALT II, was finally
reached, its ratification was poorly managed. After the Soviet invasion of
Afghanistan, all hope of ratification disappeared and Carter had withdrawn
the treaty from Senate consideration. Soviet officials suspected that Carter
had deliberately maneuvered to prevent ratification. They had received little
complaint about their buildup in Afghanistan before their invasion. In their
eyes, Carter was using an issue of no real importance to the United States in
order to scuttle the arms control agreement he had concluded with them.

Even with all these complaints, however, Soviet leaders considered Carter
the lesser evil. They believed Reagan came out of the extreme right wing

of the Republican Party and was committed to militant anti-communism. Furthermore, he seemed to them irresponsible and capable of dangerous things. This was, after all, what their ambassador in Washington, Anatoly Dobrynin, was reporting, and he was in close touch with Washington insiders eager to share their doubts about the former actor from California who consistently challenged the Washington establishment to which they belonged. It was also what some of the country's most prominent newspapers and television commentators were suggesting.

It was not that the Soviet leaders had any problem with Republicans as such. Since Franklin Roosevelt's death, they had come to prefer dealing with Republicans. They thought Republicans were more businesslike than Democrats, less given to ideological tantrums, and suspected that Republicans had the *real* power in the United States, even if they occasionally allowed a Democrat to occupy the White House as a form of window dressing. Wall Street, as every good Marxist knew, was the locus of real power in the United States, and Wall Street was notoriously Republican. That was why Republicans could deliver on their promises and Democrats were prone to renege. Thus, in the Soviet view, Eisenhower was easier to deal with than Truman; Nixon and Ford seemed to them more "realistic" than Kennedy and Johnson. Many Soviet officials considered Watergate an anti-Soviet conspiracy: in their eyes, the charges against Nixon were so insubstantial that they could have been only a cover for the real reason to force him from office—his attempt to do business with the Soviet Union.

Thus, the Soviet leaders would have been inclined to cheer if a Nixon II had defeated Carter in 1980. But they believed that Reagan was different, a fanatical extremist. Oblivious to the message of American public opinion polls on the eve of the election, they expected Carter to win and were shocked by Reagan's triumph. As the shock wore off, they expected the worst, and this expectation, buoyed by partisan gossip within the Washington Beltway and the alarmist attitude of many Western journalists, led them to exaggerate Reagan's hostility and to ignore his attempts to establish a frank dialogue and to reduce tensions. Soviet ambassador Dobrynin subsequently explained that what upset the Soviet leaders most was Reagan's "apparent determination to regain military superiority" and his "ideological offensive," which could "foment trouble inside the country and among Soviet allies."[2]

Furthermore—more important to the Soviet leaders than the rhetoric—Reagan showed absolutely no interest in resuming negotiations on arms control on the basis the Soviets demanded: primarily to preserve existing Soviet advantages. The Soviet leaders genuinely wanted to avoid an unrestrained arms race, which they already understood they were unlikely to win if the United States summoned the will to race. But they doubted that the American public was willing to sustain a prolonged effort.* They also understood that their influence in the world and hold on their own people rested preeminently and primarily on their military power.

Soviet Leaders: The Brezhnev Generation

DURING REAGAN'S FIRST term Soviet foreign policy was firmly in the hands of Foreign Minister Andrei Gromyko, a man less dour personally than the "Mr. Nyet" image that stuck with the Western public. On policy issues, however, he was as rigid as his public image suggested. He took particular care not to cross the most conservative of his Politburo colleagues. He invariably supported hardline Defense Minister Dmitri Ustinov, who died just after Reagan was reelected in 1984.

The ideological world in which Gromyko, Ustinov, and Viktor Chebrikov (the KGB chairman) lived can be illustrated by their attitude toward Nikita Khrushchev's denunciation of Stalin. They expressed it clearly during a Politburo discussion in 1984 of a proposal to restore Georgy Malenkov and Lazar Kaganovich to Communist Party membership. (Formerly members of Stalin's Politburo, they had been expelled during Khrushchev's tenure.) Here are some telling excerpts from the minutes of the meeting:

USTINOV: . . . I will say frankly, that if not for Khrushchev, then the decision to expel these people from the party would not have been taken. And in general those scandalous disgraces which Khrushchev committed in relation to Stalin would never have occurred. . . . No one enemy brought us so much harm as Khrushchev did in his policy towards the past of our party and our state, and towards Stalin. . . .

CHEBRIKOV: Besides that, a whole list of individuals were illegally rehabili-

---

* The remarks of a Soviet official in the spring of 1981, when I argued that it was in the Soviet interest to leave Afghanistan and offer major cuts in nuclear weapons, illustrate this attitude. "You are wrong," he said. "We will stay in Afghanistan as long as necessary. We remember that it took over a decade to subdue the resistance in Central Asia, but we had the political stamina to stay the course. We'll do the same in Afghanistan. And we will always be able to turn out more missiles than you. The reason is that our people are willing to sacrifice for these things, and yours are not. Our people don't require a dozen colors of toilet paper in six different scents to be happy. Americans do now; for that reason you will never be able to sustain public support for military expenditures so long as you are not directly attacked."

tated. As a matter of fact they were rightly punished. Take, for example, Solzhenitsyn. . . .

USTINOV: I will stand by my evaluation of Khrushchev's activity, as they say, until I die. He did us a lot of damage. Think about what he did to our history, to Stalin.

GROMYKO: He rendered an irreversible blow to the positive image of the Soviet Union in the eyes of the outside world.

USTINOV: It's not a secret that the westerners never loved us. But Khrushchev gave them such arguments, such material, that we have been discredited for many years.[3]

What, precisely, was the damage Khrushchev's "scandalous disgraces" inflicted on the Communist Party, Soviet state, and Stalin personally? He told the truth about Stalin's mass murders—only part of the truth to be sure, but nevertheless the truth.

EVEN BEFORE REAGAN was inaugurated, Soviet information media attacked him as an anti-Soviet ideologue who might risk war. Verbal attacks were repeated in a rising drumbeat after his first press conference when he mentioned lying and cheating. Brezhnev mentioned the possibility of a meeting with Reagan in his address to the Communist Party Congress in February, but this was hardly a serious proposal. The Reagan administration treated it courteously, welcoming a dialogue, but noting that any Reagan-Brezhnev meeting should be well prepared.

No doubt if Reagan had proposed an early meeting the Soviets would have found reasons to delay it, probably by setting conditions that Reagan was unwilling to meet, such as resubmitting the SALT II treaty to the Senate and recommending its ratification. Brezhnev was no longer capable of discussing even trivial issues coherently. His colleagues would have avoided a face-to-face meeting with the American president at almost any cost.

I was able to observe Brezhnev at ceremonial functions in the spring and summer of 1981 when I was in charge of the American embassy in Moscow. He was not only incapable of speaking without a script, but often had trouble reading even simple texts. Moscow intellectuals would joke about their leader's condition. One prominent writer regaled us over dinner with Brezhnev imitations. One of them went as follows:

Brezhnev goes to the airport to greet Margaret Thatcher. When she comes out of the plane, he goes forward, looks at the paper in his hand, and reads, "Welcome, Indira Gandhi!"

Gromyko, standing beside him, whispers, "Not Indira Gandhi, Margaret Thatcher."

Brezhnev looks at the paper again and repeats, "Welcome, Indira Gandhi."

"Margaret Thatcher, Margaret Thatcher," Gromyko prompts, voice rising.

Brezhnev turns to him and, waving his script, says, "I know she is Margaret Thatcher, but it says here Indira Gandhi."

This was only a slight exaggeration. When Brezhnev was seeing off a visiting chief of state at the VIP airport terminal west of Moscow, he and Gromyko walked past a group of journalists there covering the event. One called out in Russian, "How did the meeting go?" The voice was loud and clear but Brezhnev did not understand. The journalist repeated the question, even louder. Brezhnev turned to Gromyko, walking beside him, and asked, "Chto on skazal?" (What'd he say?). Gromyko replied, "Skazhi khorosho" (Just say fine). Brezhnev thereupon turned to the journalists and, face beaming with the satisfaction of a person who has just solved an intricate puzzle, said, "Khorosho. Khorosho" (Fine. Fine).

An inner group of senior Politburo members actually made policy: former KGB chief Yuri Andropov, who was acting as de facto "second secretary," Foreign Minister Andrei Gromyko, and Defense Minister Dmitri Ustinov. With rare exceptions, Brezhnev simply accepted what his colleagues prepared for him.

There is at least one documented occasion in 1981, however, when Brezhnev declined to rubber-stamp a proposal made by his colleagues. On August 28, five Politburo members including Gromyko, Andropov, and Ustinov proposed extensive mobilization of Soviet forces along the Polish border in order to intervene in Poland "in the event of a further worsening of the situation." Brezhnev read the memorandum and muttered, "Let's wait a bit."[4]

This incident makes clear that a Soviet invasion of Poland was a serious possibility in the summer and fall of 1981. The concern Reagan and Haig expressed was not misplaced, nor were the reports from the U.S. embassy in Moscow that the public charges against the Polish leaders could be used to justify military intervention.

In fact, the Soviet invasion did not occur. It was made unnecessary, in Soviet eyes, by General Wojciech Jaruzelski's decision in December 1981 to use Polish forces to suppress Solidarity.

Defense Minister Dmitri Ustinov stated Soviet policy clearly and forcefully in a major address toward the end of Reagan's first year as president.*

---

* His language may require some explanation for those not versed in Orwellian Soviet speak, so I have provided in parentheses translations of the major points.

Speaking officially on behalf of the Politburo, he accused the United States of "undermining the military-strategic balance" and seeking military superiority (by countering Soviet missiles deployed in Europe after a "balance" was declared), of attempting to stop "forces of national and social liberation" (opposing Soviet proxy wars), and of seeking to "besiege" the socialist countries (by insisting that Soviet troops leave Afghanistan and not intervene in Poland). Responding to U.S. charges of Soviet support for terrorists, he accused the United States and NATO of employing "the methods of international terrorism" (arming resistance forces opposed to Soviet-backed violence). The U.S., he added, had called into question "all that had been jointly achieved" (by insisting that détente be a two-way street), but pledged that the Soviet Union would strengthen its defenses to meet the "uncontrolled military threat" of imperialists (it would hang on to military superiority, come what may).

Then, what was intended as a clincher: the Soviet Union, he asserted, "has never embarked and will never embark on the road of aggression." (The Finns, of course, started the Winter War, the Baltic countries chose to enter the Soviet Union, Communist governments ruled Eastern Europe because they were elected, and Soviet troops were in Afghanistan only to help a neighbor fight off bandits.)[5]

This, of course, was public rhetoric designed for the anniversary of the Bolshevik Revolution, a celebratory occasion normally marked by braggadocio and self-congratulation. It was also more than that. Defense Minister Ustinov—and the entire Politburo that had approved the speech—really meant it. Soviet leaders were oblivious to the irony my interpretations highlight. Whatever the Politburo had declared to be the truth was the truth. Anyone who questioned it was an enemy. Every one of Ustinov's themes was a staple of Soviet diplomacy throughout Reagan's first term.

Public Anxieties

THE EXCHANGE OF polemics between Moscow and Washington and the publicized increases in the U.S. defense budget had an impact on public opinion everywhere. Even though it was the Soviet Union that was supporting a hot war in Afghanistan and the Soviet Union that had built up its armed forces steadily in the late 1970s when the United States was reducing its forces, many people ignored those facts and blamed the United States for what they saw as a "renewed Cold War" and a new spiral in the arms race.

U.S. Allies: Partners and Problems

THE REAGAN ADMINISTRATION was united in its conviction that it was vitally important to maintain and strengthen U.S. alliances abroad, particularly with NATO countries and Japan. Although their opinions were divided on many other points, this was one on which Haig (and subsequently Shultz) could agree with Secretary of Defense Caspar Weinberger, and both with the president's assistant for national security, whoever he was at the moment. Everyone recognized that if the Soviet Union managed to drive wedges between the United States and its allies, it would be much more difficult to induce the Soviet leaders to adopt policies of restraint. If Soviet blackmail worked, it would be continued—and then nothing would fall into place.

Given agreement on this point, it is remarkable how maladroit the administration was, during its first two years, in managing its alliances. In trying to bring additional pressure to bear on Moscow by economic sanctions, it instead brought pressure on the NATO alliance. Most proposals for sanctions, even after martial law was declared in Poland, had to be dropped when the allies persisted in their opposition.

Resistance to American efforts to block construction of a pipeline to supply Soviet gas to Europe emerged in July 1981 when Reagan met other members of the Group of Seven in Ottawa. French president François Mitterrand made clear that he would not agree to an "economic blockade" of the Soviet Union, and complained that Reagan was willing to sell grain to the Soviet Union while pressing the Europeans not to buy Soviet gas. Reagan responded that it was one thing to make the Soviets dependent on the West and quite another to make one's country dependent on them. Mitterrand was not prepared to agree.[6]

German chancellor Helmut Schmidt was even more vehement than Mitterrand in his opposition to sanctions, and to any public pressure on the Soviet Union in regard to Poland and other countries in Eastern Europe. Poland, he argued, was firmly in the Soviet orbit, and that could not be changed without risking war. To alleviate the crisis caused by Jaruzelski's declaration of martial law, Schmidt advised using carrots (offers of massive economic aid to Poland in return for freedom for Solidarity) instead of sticks (sanctions against Poland or the Soviet Union).[7]

Gradually, the Reagan administration eased its pressure on the allies to apply broad economic sanctions on the Soviet Union, contenting itself with unilateral sanctions that applied only to American firms. This did little to penalize the Soviet Union, which simply switched its procurement of items such as equipment for oil and gas production to other countries. The sanctions made hardliners in the administration feel good, however, and allowed them to brag that the United States was bringing pressure to bear on the Soviet Union.

U.S. relations with its allies improved after 1982 as a result of several factors. George Shultz, who became secretary of state in July, was more understanding of allied concerns than Haig had been. He used less confrontational tactics in dealing with them. This helped, particularly after Helmut Kohl replaced Helmut Schmidt as German chancellor in October 1982. Schmidt had never concealed his contempt for the intellectual deficiencies he perceived in most of his interlocutors. His attitude created a personal animus that exacerbated even minor differences in viewpoint. Kohl was a German politician much more in tune with Reagan, not only philosophically, but in his personal manner. He became a true partner, and this was to pay dividends, both to the alliance and—eventually—to Germany's future.

Reagan's most stalwart partner abroad, however, was British prime minister Margaret Thatcher. Their philosophies on the role of government, the economy, and the approach to Cold War issues were nearly identical, even though Thatcher did not share Reagan's dream of eliminating nuclear weapons or his enthusiasm for missile defense. Unlike some of her colleagues on the European continent, she seemed to understand Reagan's qualities as a leader.[8] She became, in her words, "his principal cheerleader in NATO."

Her influence on Reagan surpassed that of any other foreign leader. In fact, it exceeded that of most of his own cabinet members. One of her early contributions was her advice to avoid public talk of "the rising tide of neutralism" in Europe—a favorite theme of some of Reagan's speechwriters. Thatcher agreed that there was such a tide and that it was deeply troubling, but understood that talking about it would only make it worse.[9]

Reagan took her advice to heart and generally avoided public arguments with the leaders of allied countries. Unfortunately, he did not enforce this restraint on all members of his administration. Careless comments, particularly from Weinberger's Department of Defense, repeatedly caused disputes to flare up in Europe and required fire brigades from the State Department and White House to rush around the NATO capitals dousing flames before they spread.

U.S. Public

RONALD REAGAN WAS remarkably popular with the American public, particularly after his gallant response to the attempt on his life in March 1981. Nevertheless, apprehension about his foreign policy, already high when he took office, grew as arms control negotiations were delayed and it appeared that the arms race had taken on new life with his defense budgets. Though few disagreed with his harsh words about the Soviet system, many felt that it was unwise to voice them, and suspected that they revealed a willingness to risk war.

Public opinion is influenced as much by symbols as by facts, and meetings between U.S. and Soviet leaders had come to symbolize the commitment of both the United States and the Soviet Union to avoid war and work out their differences by negotiation. Of course, summit meetings can be helpful under the right circumstances. Face-to-face contact between national leaders is sometimes necessary to find solutions to negotiating deadlocks. When a meeting has been agreed, both usually press their respective bureaucracies to reach as much agreement as they can. If the principals like one another (not a given, by any means!), personal chemistry can act as a catalyst to future problem solving. Communication, direct or indirect, is always essential if problems are not to get out of hand.

All these things are true, but even so, the virtues of U.S.-Soviet summitry had been oversold to the public. By starting the tradition of making U.S.-Soviet summit meetings largely a show of signing agreements, most of which were negotiated before the meeting, Nixon and Brezhnev had unwittingly made summitry in times of tension more difficult than it should have been. The public had been conditioned to think that the principal objective of summit meetings was to sign agreements. It was an easy step from this idea to a conviction that agreements were impossible without summit meetings, and—by extension—if there were no agreements, it was because the U.S. and Soviet leaders were not meeting each other.

These misperceptions had begun to act as a barrier rather than a stimulus to such meetings. Neither the American president nor the Soviet general secretary wanted to go into a meeting that would be considered a failure. Neither wanted to be under pressure to conclude agreements just to make their meeting look successful. Public expectations, therefore, required both to insist that a "positive outcome" be assured before a meeting could be agreed upon.

The U.S. and Soviet leaders were no longer free to do what they really needed to do (and what allies did all the time), which was to get together, get to know each other, and try to clear the air regarding policy differences. The most useful summit meetings would not waste time signing agreements at all, but would concentrate on disagreements and ways to reduce them.

Misled more by the media than by the administration, the American public did not see it that way. The prospects, or lack thereof, of a meeting between President Reagan and the Soviet leader became staples of media attention on the false assumption that such meetings provided a barometer of the state of the U.S.-Soviet relationship. This attitude would have made an early summit meeting between Reagan and Brezhnev impossible even if Brezhnev's health had permitted one.

Gradually, as the infirmity of successive Soviet leaders became obvious, the question of summitry became less important in American politics. When Walter Mondale tried to use the issue in his 1984 campaign for the presidency, Reagan could simply shrug and remark, "Well, they keep dying on me."

Whereas the summit issue faded from 1982 on, public worries about the arms race grew. A campaign in favor of a nuclear freeze began. A freeze would have barred implementation of NATO's 1979 "dual-track" decision: to deploy American intermediate-range nuclear missiles in Europe unless the Soviet Union agreed to eliminate or reduce the number of its SS-20s, a powerful new missile that threatened the capitals of all NATO countries on the European continent. Concern about the electoral impact of Reagan's foreign policy grew in the White House, particularly when it seemed to be a factor in the 1982 congressional elections. Democrats came out with a majority of seats in the House of Representatives and narrowed the Republican lead in the Senate.

The peace movement in the United States and in Europe grew most rapidly in 1983 and 1984. Even though it directed its fire at several of Reagan's key policies, he never treated members of the movement as enemies. He refused to do so not only because of his personal decency and sense of political effect, but also—and even more fundamentally—because he agreed that nuclear weapons were an intolerable threat to mankind and should eventually be abolished. He disagreed not with the goals of the peace movement, but with the steps it demanded to reach them.

For this reason, he never overreacted to criticism the way Richard Nixon had done during the Vietnam War. He compiled no enemies lists and made no effort to get back at critics. Confident that he was on the right track, Reagan was content to explain why he thought his methods would preserve peace and result in fewer weapons while other strategies would run a greater risk and force the arms race into new directions.

"Nations don't fear each other because they are armed," he used to say. "They arm because they fear each other."

Simplistic? Yes. Not always true? Also, yes. Even so, it was not a bad maxim for someone determined to get at the root of distrust and bring about a reduction of weaponry, with or without formal agreements.

Soviet Public

SOVIET MEDIA WERE unanimous in their characterization of President Reagan. He was an aggressive imperialist actively seeking military superiority so that he could unleash a war against the Soviet Union and destroy it. Any treatment of what he said used carefully selected quotations, usually out of context, to substantiate the hostile interpretation. Soviet media said even less than the American media about his expressions of desire to cooperate. They hardly ever mentioned what his specific criticisms of Soviet policy were. They did their best to make it seem that his criticisms were leveled at the Soviet people and Soviet society rather than the political leadership and its ideology.

It is hard to say what impact this had on the thinking of average Soviet citizens. There were no opinion polls conducted on a scientific basis that were released to the public. Those of us who visited the Soviet Union during this period and talked to people got the impression that most Soviet citizens considered Reagan an attractive figure and a natural leader. The most common reaction was something like: "You Americans are lucky, as usual. You have a president who knows how to be a leader. Not like the doddering old fools we have to put up with!"

Most Soviet citizens had learned to distrust their own propaganda. Many even took Soviet official statements as representing the opposite of the truth. This undermined the effectiveness of Soviet leaders' hostile propaganda. On the negative side, however, Soviet citizens had no real understanding of why Reagan had said the things he did, or what he really wanted. The Soviet system had been more effective denying its people information than actively misleading them.

Not until Gorbachev introduced his policies of perestroika, and from 1987 began to open the Soviet Union to outside influences, was it possible for the United States or other foreign countries to communicate directly with the Soviet people. There were, of course, radio broadcasts from the Voice of America, Radio Liberty, the BBC, and other Western stations, but most were jammed in urban areas. It took great effort and no little risk for Soviet citizens to receive these broadcasts until jamming ended in 1987.

It was often said that the Soviet leaders did not care about public opinion, but that was wrong. They did, but they were confident they could manipulate their public, partly by tailoring information, partly by inventing it, and partly by denying it. Brezhnev's generation of Soviet leaders understood very well the threat the truth about the system and its past could pose to their rule. That is why they maintained an Iron Curtain, not only against the outside world, but also against the facts of their own history.

This is why the Reagan administration devoted so much energy to breaking through the Iron Curtain and getting its message across to the people there. It is also why Brezhnev, Andropov, and Chernenko were determined to prevent that from happening.

Formal Negotiations Finally Start

CONVINCED THAT THE Soviet leaders were not yet ready to accept meaningful cuts in weaponry and divided in its own councils as to what sort of agreement it needed, the United States was slow to resume negotiations with the Soviet Union on strategic arms. However, negotiations on intermediate-range missiles in Europe could not be postponed without serious damage to the NATO alliance. Accordingly, the U.S. informed its allies in May 1981 that it would begin negotiations with the Soviet Union on the issue, and negotiations started in Geneva that November. Negotiations on strategic arms, however, were not resumed until June 1982.

Intermediate-Range Nuclear Forces (INF)

IN 1977 the Soviet Union began replacing missiles with single nuclear warheads deployed against NATO targets with a new mobile nuclear missile with three independently targeted warheads. NATO called it the SS-20.* It also had greater range and much greater accuracy. It could strike the capitals of European NATO countries in four or five minutes.

The SS-20s changed the nuclear balance in Europe, particularly as it became clear that the older Soviet missiles were being replaced, not warhead for warhead, but with a substantially larger number of the more capable weapon. European NATO countries took alarm and pressed the United States to help them deal with what they saw as a new Soviet threat. The result was a decision made by NATO in December 1979 (more than a year before Reagan took office) to deploy a new generation of U.S. missiles in

---

* The Soviet designation was RSD-10, but Soviet security agencies carried secrecy to the point that they classified the names of their nuclear weapons and other advanced weaponry. NATO, therefore, applied its own name to Soviet weapons as they were developed, even though it normally was aware of the secret Soviet designation. Since Soviet negotiators were prohibited from using their own name in public, they accepted the NATO designation for the purpose of negotiation and public discussion.

Europe unless an agreement could be reached with the Soviet Union to reduce the threat posed by the SS-20s. This decision, envisioning deployment
only if negotiations failed, was called the "dual-track" decision since preparations to deploy proceeded simultaneously with negotiations to make deployment unnecessary.[10]

Plans therefore went forward to develop and manufacture two new U.S.
weapons: a ballistic missile called the Pershing II (P2 for short) and a
ground-launched cruise missile (GLCM) called the Tomahawk. A maximum of 572—108 Pershing IIs and 464 GLCMs—were to be deployed in
the fall of 1983 unless a successfully negotiated agreement made them unnecessary.

Two features of NATO's plans deserve emphasis. First, the deployments
NATO projected did not match the Soviet SS-20s missile for missile or warhead for warhead. The numbers were smaller and the destructive power
much less. Second, the mix of Pershing IIs and GLCMs, with a predominance of the latter, was designed to make clear that NATO was not attempting to acquire a first-strike capability. The Pershing IIs could not reach
Moscow (although Soviet leaders feared they could) or most Soviet ICBM
sites. Even if all those planned had been deployed, the NATO forces would
only partially balance the SS-20s. U.S. officials believed that no reasonable
person who understood the facts could conclude that they threatened to
ratchet up the arms race. Soviet claims that the NATO aim was to acquire
military superiority struck American officials as disingenuous—evidence
that the Soviet Union was determined to maintain superiority in Europe in
both conventional and nuclear weapons.

In the Soviet view, the prospect of Pershing IIs deployed in Germany was
directly threatening. Soviet specialists believed that their range was greater
than the United States claimed—that it was closer to 2,500 kilometers rather
than the 1,600 kilometers the U.S. (accurately) claimed. Had this mistaken
belief been true, the Pershing II, given its short flight time, would pose a direct threat to the Soviet leadership in Moscow. In Soviet eyes, though not in
reality, it was a potentially decapitating weapon.[11]

The United States worried mainly about the political effect the SS-20s
might have on the NATO alliance. Potentially, the SS-20s could "decouple"
European nuclear security from the American nuclear umbrella. How could
Europeans count on an American president retaliating for a nuclear attack
on European allies if it exposed American cities to a Soviet nuclear attack?
With U.S. missiles in Europe, a U.S. president could retaliate without using
America's strategic arsenal. Until 1987, Soviet leaders seemed incapable of

understanding the reason NATO governments considered the SS-20s a threat that had to be removed or countered.

A perceived vulnerability can have a political effect even if war never breaks out. Both sides were determined to prevent war, but if Europeans became convinced that Soviet weaponry held them hostage, they might begin to weaken their ties to NATO and make separate deals in the hope of protecting themselves. This was mainly what both Europeans and Americans worried about as they sought a solution to the dilemma posed by the Soviet SS-20s.

The initial American proposal was simple: if the Soviet Union removed the SS-20s, the United States would not deploy Pershing IIs and GLCMs in Europe. This would create a balance of weapons in this category of zero on both sides, whence the term "zero/zero proposal," or sometimes "zero option."

In contrast, Soviet leaders looked at the INF negotiations as an opportunity to equate the SS-20s with British and French nuclear weapons and U.S. "forward-based systems"—nuclear-armed short-range aircraft.[12] The U.S. perception of the problem differed totally from the Soviet position; not only were British and French nuclear forces not intermediate-range forces, they were not committed to defend other NATO countries, but only to deter an attack on the United Kingdom or France. Furthermore, both the British and French governments strongly opposed the inclusion of their weapons in any U.S.-Soviet agreement. U.S. forward-based systems were also of a different type from the SS-20s, were much less destructive and accurate, and had missions that did not involve the Soviet Union at all. Thus, they were not primarily Cold War weapons, nor did they have the sort of first-strike capacity of the SS-20 against European targets.

Those who designed the zero/zero proposal knew very well that the Soviet leaders at that time were unlikely to accept it. The Soviet leaders had claimed against all logic that the SS-20s did not alter the balance of forces and that any attempt to redress the imbalance they had created would be considered an attempt to gain superiority. Furthermore, traditionally they had not been willing to reduce the number of weapons unless the other side had something to trade.

For President Reagan, the question was not whether the Soviets would accept the proposal, but whether it would solve the decoupling dilemma, reduce weaponry, and be fair. It met all these criteria, and he endorsed it. He did not consider his proposal a take-it-or-leave-it proposition, as both he and Secretary Haig made clear in public statements. Haig told the Senate Foreign Relations Committee in November that the United States sought "a verifiable agreement that would achieve significant reductions on both sides, leading to equal ceilings at the lowest possible levels—levels which ideally could be zero." When questioned on this point, Reagan remarked that, going into a negotiation, one always asks for more than he may be prepared to accept.

A Walk That Went Nowhere

IN JULY 1982, Paul Nitze, the chief American negotiator in the INF talks, tried to see if U.S. and Soviet differences could be bridged. Six months of negotiation had brought the parties no closer to agreement. The prospect of step-by-step concessions was exceedingly dim. Both sides were entrenched in positions each defined as matters of principle not subject to negotiation. Each feared that any concrete concession would simply be accepted by the other side and not reciprocated with one of comparable value.

The Soviet negotiator, Yuli Kvitsinsky, had told Nitze that officials in Moscow would review their policy during the summer and thereafter the Soviet position would be difficult to change. Nitze decided that he should make a serious effort to find out whether an acceptable compromise was possible before that happened. He invited Kvitsinsky to a Saturday outing where they could talk out of the earshot of colleagues and microphones.[13]

During their stroll, Nitze presented Kvitsinsky with an intricate set of ideas, making plain that he had not cleared them in Washington and therefore could not guarantee that the United States would buy them. (Nitze had revealed his ideas only to Eugene Rostow, the head of ACDA, the U.S. Arms Control and Disarmament Agency.) Nevertheless, if the ideas seemed acceptable to Soviet decision makers, Nitze would try to persuade his government to approve them. Nitze also warned that his ideas were offered as a package of mutual concessions; all had to be acceptable or none could be offered. As he put it, "nothing is agreed, or even proposed, until everything has been agreed."[14]

Nitze's central idea was to permit seventy-five medium-range nuclear missile systems in Europe on each side. For the Soviet Union they would be SS-20s; for NATO they would all be ground-launched cruise missiles. The United States would thus forgo deploying the Pershing II and balance the SS-20 with less threatening GLCMs. The idea implied concessions on both sides and represented a reasonable compromise in theory. However, an agreement on this basis would have been most difficult to verify without measures more intrusive than the Soviets had thus far been willing to permit.

Kvitsinsky expressed doubt that several elements in the proposal would be acceptable to Moscow, but he took detailed notes and promised to notify Nitze of Moscow's reaction. He asked Nitze not to discuss the ideas with the president or other U.S. officials until he had sent notification of Moscow's serious interest.

Nitze says that he made no such promise. Kvitsinsky says that Nitze nodded, a gesture he interpreted as agreement. Probably both are right in their own minds: Nitze, in his conviction that he avoided a promise not to inform the president of the conversation until he got a positive signal from Kvitsinsky; Kvitsinsky, in his belief that Nitze had signaled assent. In fact, Nitze informed President Reagan and a small group of close advisers, including both Shultz and Weinberger, as soon as he returned to Washington. If he had not done so, he would have destroyed his credibility with his own government.

Nitze's impression was that Reagan had a generally positive reaction. If the Soviet leadership had shown a serious interest, Reagan probably would have authorized negotiations designed to achieve that result, at least as an interim measure. For weeks, however, there was no word from Kvitsinsky, and in time various objections to the arrangement Nitze discussed emerged in Washington.

Most objections centered on tactics rather than substance. Few denied that Nitze's suggestions might be acceptable as the end product of a negotiating process, but many objected to showing the U.S. hand prematurely. They seemed to think that if Soviet negotiators could be induced to make the proposal, the United States could accept it, but if the U.S. made the proposal first, the Soviets would pick out those elements they favored and refuse the compensating concessions.

Kvitsinsky has published a detailed account of his efforts to interest the Soviet leadership in Nitze's ideas.[15] There is no reason to doubt that he shared Nitze's interest in finding a negotiated solution. However, his efforts were in vain. In Moscow, both the foreign and defense ministries dismissed Nitze's ideas as a trick. They refused even to authorize a negative signal to Nitze, despite Kvitsinsky's argument that silence or rejection could be used by the Americans to prove that the Soviet Union was inflexible and unwilling to negotiate.

Despite the foreign ministry's lack of support, Kvitsinsky nevertheless described Nitze's ideas to Vadim Zagladin in the International Department of the Central Committee Secretariat, who arranged for Kvitsinsky to brief Yuri Andropov. (This was when Leonid Brezhnev was no longer totally compos mentis and Andropov was acting as "second secretary" of the Communist Party.) Andropov seemed to agree that there should be at least a pretense of negotiating and ordered a review of the Soviet position. Nevertheless, key officials were reluctant to work during the vacation season (it was August), and the Soviet military refused either to remove some of the SS-20s they had deployed or to accept any new U.S. missiles in Europe. This left Kvitsinsky with no prospect of a Soviet position the United States might accept.

Kvitsinsky returned to Geneva at the end of September with the message that Moscow was "wholly negative" to Nitze's ideas and that any INF agreement would have to include several features that the United States had always considered out of the question, such as compensation for British and French nuclear systems, no limits on Soviet INF deployments outside Europe, and equal reductions in nuclear-capable medium-range aircraft, whether land- or sea-based. Nitze's ideas had met none of these requirements, but had suggested U.S. concessions to justify Soviet abandonment of them.[16]

When reports of the "walk-in-the-woods" episode leaked to the press, several inconsistent versions developed. Some said it was a reasonable U.S. proposal that the Soviets rejected and thereby proved that they had no interest in an agreement. Others claimed that the United States had "turned down" the idea even before there was a Soviet reply, so there was no reason for the Soviets to take it seriously. Still others described it as a proposal rejected by both sides.

There are elements of truth in all these interpretations, but they miss the real point. There never was a proposal for the respective governments to accept or reject, but rather a set of ideas that could have been used by both sides as goals in the negotiation. Judging from Kvitsinsky's account, as well as the testimony of other Soviet officials involved, there was little prospect that the Soviet leadership in 1982 or 1983 would have accepted anything like the walk-in-the-woods formula. However, the Soviets could have gained powerful leverage over NATO's ability to deploy if they had agreed to negotiate on that basis. If they had, the Reagan administration would probably have been forced, despite the reservations many of its officials held, to adopt the positions Nitze had outlined. Otherwise, opposition to the U.S. deployments, already dangerously high, would have grown in Europe. The terms Nitze suggested would probably have proven acceptable, though marginally, to the U.S. and the other NATO governments, provided adequate verification measures could have been negotiated. Verification, however, would have proven a most difficult issue, and the negotiations could easily have stalled. In that case, NATO would probably have found it politically impossible to proceed with the deployments planned for the fall of 1983.

Nitze continued for more than a year to seek a solution that would make U.S. deployments unnecessary, but his subsequent ideas, like those he advanced during the walk in the woods, usually evoked charges of bad faith and a public debate over who proposed what, rather than any real progress toward an agreement. As Kvitsinsky concluded in September 1982, the Soviet government had no real interest in an agreement. It put all its energy into blocking U.S. deployments through support of the peace movement in Western Europe, and calculated—inaccurately—that serious negotiations would undermine their allies in the European anti-nuclear movements. In reality, the United States and its NATO allies had more to fear from inconclusive negotiations than did the Soviet Union.

There is a double irony in the initial Soviet position on the INF question. By failing to recognize that Reagan's zero/zero proposal was in the Soviet strategic interest, Soviet leaders missed an early opportunity to prevent the deployment of U.S. nuclear missiles in Europe that could reach the Soviet Union (their prime objective in that negotiation) and to slow the arms race without making concessions in other areas (their more fundamental objective). Also, by refusing the opportunity to negotiate on the terms Nitze suggested during the walk in the woods, the Soviets undermined their own strategy of encouraging European publics to prevent U.S. deployments. Until Gorbachev changed the policy of his predecessors, the Soviet position was both strategically blind and tactically self-defeating.

The failure of informal talks between the Soviet and American INF negotiators revealed inherent problems both sides faced in dealing with each other. Both countries were publicly committed to positions the other had rejected. If there was to be an agreement, a way had to be found to define it so that both sides could credibly claim that they had not backed down under pressure and that their interests were served. So long as negotiations were conducted in public there would be a tendency to read every change of position as a win or loss, stimulating groups with a stake in some particular feature to hold an agreement hostage to their particular interest. To avoid this danger, negotiators needed the freedom to explore ideas before they were officially adopted, without the fear that these ideas would become the focus of public debate preceding the overall context of an agreement.

The informal talks between Nitze and Kvitsinsky highlighted that it was practically impossible to break through stalemated positions using only the official negotiators. Both sides assumed that any "informal suggestion" by representatives of the other was officially inspired and probably a trick. After all, if such proposals were accepted, the originating side could disavow them and ask for more. If they were rejected, it could claim that it had shown its flexibility, but the other side refused to negotiate.

In the case of the INF negotiations in 1982 and 1983, no amount of creativity on the part of the negotiators could result in an agreement so long as the Soviet leaders thought they could block U.S. deployments by political action in Western Europe. If there had been the possibility of an agreement, it would have required precisely the sort of initiative Nitze had taken. This was recognized in the Reagan White House and, beginning in 1983, stimulated renewed efforts to establish some sort of private channel to the Soviet leadership.

Negotiations on Strategic Arms

NEGOTIATIONS ON STRATEGIC arms opened in Geneva at the end of June 1982, just after Alexander Haig resigned as secretary of state. The U.S. position had developed during his tenure, however, and was not changed significantly by his successor, George Shultz.

Reagan's critics made much the same charge regarding the U.S. position in the Strategic Arms Reduction Talks (START)* as they had of the zero/zero proposal in INF: it was not negotiable with the Soviet Union, they said, because it would require a radical change in the structure of Soviet strategic forces. They were right about the latter: the proposal did reduce the most threatening Soviet systems, the heavy ICBMs, and encourage a shift to sea-based systems, specifically ballistic missiles launched from submarines (SLBMs).

The United States was technologically ahead in developing sea-based missiles, but this does not mean that its proposal was entirely self-serving. The Soviet heavy ICBMs were so numerous and accurate that they could have wiped out the U.S. ICBMs in a surprise attack. They were, therefore, preeminently first-strike weapons. Submarine-launched missiles were not so accurate and could not be confidently aimed at reinforced missile silos. Relatively invulnerable to a first strike themselves, they were primarily useful in a retaliatory strike. Furthermore, the Soviets had up to then demonstrated a capability of closing every technological gap the Americans had opened. In the period envisioned for reducing the number of strategic weapons, the Soviets could have changed their mix of forces to place a greater

* START instead of SALT—Strategic Arms Limitation Talks—for the Soviets accepted Reagan's proposal to aim for reductions rather than limitations.

proportion of weapons at sea. The result would have created greater stability and thus benefited both sides. However, it would have required major expenditures on new weapons just when the Soviet leaders were looking for ways to trim defense outlays.

The U.S. proposal in START, like that in INF, was a statement of what the Reagan administration considered the optimum outcome. Negotiations were expected, and if they were serious, compromises would have been made. There is no question, however, that Reagan and his advisers were determined to deal with the threat they saw in the Soviet heavy ICBMs. They still hoped that Congress would approve the MX and thus provide a counter to the Soviet systems and something to trade for them. If the Soviets refused substantial reductions in their land-based ICBMs (50 percent was the goal), the administration preferred to live without an agreement.

The Soviet delegation at Geneva flatly rejected the U.S. proposal and insisted on a treaty that did little more than SALT II to meet U.S. concerns. Negotiations stalled from their first day and, when congressional opposition to the MX delayed its production, President Reagan began to think about building defenses to protect the United States from a potential first strike.

Rhetoric and Reality, or Truth and Its Consequences

ONE QUESTION CRITICS of Reagan's rhetoric rarely asked was whether his statements were true or not. There were occasions when he might justly be deemed to have exaggerated. When he said that the Soviet Union was "the focus of evil in the modern world," he should have said "a focus of evil" so as not to imply that it was the only one. Some of the "quotations" he cited from Lenin were not authentic in the sense that they could be documented with evidence then available,* but most captured the essence of actual Soviet behavior. While Lenin may not have said anything as vivid as "promises are like pie crusts, made to be broken," he and his successors acted as if they believed it. We were dealing with a system that deserved to be called an "evil empire." Soviet leaders did indeed lie and cheat, even if they did not always proclaim their adherence to "world revolution" as openly as Reagan thought.

One blatant web of lies was being flogged by Soviet propaganda on Polit-

* Many of Lenin's authentic writings were suppressed by Soviet censorship. Some of the suppressed material has since been published and may authenticate some of Reagan's quotations that could not be documented when he used them.

buro orders precisely when Reagan made his comment about lying and cheating. It misrepresented what occurred when Soviet forces invaded Afghanistan in December 1979. Soviet military forces invaded the country the day after a contingent of KGB troops had attacked the presidential palace in Kabul, killing Prime Minister Amin, his family, and all others who happened to be in the building at the time. This action was outright treachery, since the KGB troops were ostensibly in Kabul to protect the Afghan president. The Soviets then installed their candidate, Babrak Karmal, to head the regime in Kabul that had earlier declared itself "socialist."

Dmitri Volkogonov, who studied Politburo records of the operation, describes the instructions issued by the Party Central Committee as follows:

> [Soviet media] were told to say that the Afghan leadership "repeatedly, at least fourteen times, asked us to send Soviet troops." Karmal, they must say, had returned to the country illegally in the second half of October 1979, soon after the murder of Taraki by Amin. . . . "On the night of 27/28 December 1979," the official version must say, "the underground, that is members of the PDPA, came out, as a result of which the Amin regime was overthrown." . . .[17]

Volkogonov then comments that "[t]here was not a single word of truth in this 'interpretation,' but the propaganda and international information departments of the Central Committee were past masters at fooling the Soviet public, and most people swallowed it."[18] The cover story fooled not only the Soviet public. It was accepted at face value by many in the West. Elements of it persist in responsible Western journalism and scholarship. For example, if we check the entry for the "Afghan Civil War of 1979" in the respected *Facts on File Encyclopedia of the 20th Century* published in 1991, we find the following account:

> In 1978 Khalq militants assassinated Afghanistan's first president; a Khalq leader became president but was ousted by his prime minister (September 1979), who himself was overthrown (December 27, 1979) by another leftist, Babrak Karmal, who had Soviet backing. When Karmal's attempt to impose Russianization met with armed resistance, he asked for Soviet aid to crush the opposition.[19]

Cover story swallowed, hook, line, and sinker! Unfortunately, this is only one of thousands of Soviet fabrications, on matters large and small, now embedded in respectable scholarship. It will take generations to weed out the lies, and many will never be expunged since there will always be people who preserve them to "prove" pet theories or gain notoriety.*

So it was true that the Soviet leaders lied and cheated, but did they do this because they believed in world revolution, as Reagan thought? In fact, they didn't use the words "world revolution" very much anymore, but we should think a bit about what they actually meant by their "international duty." The straightforward meaning was that they believed they had a right to intervene in any "revolution" if they thought it would benefit them. (Of course, only revolutionaries friendly to the Soviet Union were true Marxists. Others were by Soviet definition counterrevolutionaries, to be opposed by any feasible means.) Despite his lack of sophistication and ignorance of many details and nuances, Ronald Reagan had a knack for cutting right to the core of an issue and expressing it in a way ordinary people could understand.

OF COURSE THE Soviet leaders did not like Reagan's condemnation of their system, and they responded with personal invective that he never reciprocated. It was not pleasant for them to have their lies challenged. As Soviet ambassador Dobrynin puts it in his memoirs: "The Soviet leadership was at times extremely thin-skinned, forgetting that they also engaged in the same kind of propaganda against the United States from time to time. He [Reagan] was giving them a dose of their own medicine."[20]

Thin skins provide only a partial explanation for the extreme sensitivity in Moscow to Reagan's comments. Soviet leaders were determined to conceal from the Soviet public nasty facts about the Communist system. Try as they might to suppress the thought, the Soviet leaders knew that they were vulnerable to Reagan's charges: many families had lost members to Stalin's purges and labor camps; body bags were beginning to come back from Afghanistan; those in power continually lied to them; the Communist system was not delivering what it had promised. To many Soviet citizens, at last a foreign leader had appeared who was not afraid to tell the truth. What worried most Soviet citizens was not Reagan's condemnation of communism, but the fear, assiduously promoted by their Communist bosses, that his words might be a prelude to an American nuclear attack on the Soviet Union.

---

* One of the most outrageous lies originated by KGB disinformation linked the CIA to the assassination of President John F. Kennedy. Like others, it was fed first to an Italian newspaper, *Paese Sera,* and then cited by Soviet media in order to spread the story. It was this fabrication that was used by New Orleans district attorney Jim Garrison to open an investigation, and by Oliver Stone for his film *JFK.* See Max Holland, "The Lie That Linked CIA to the Kennedy Assassination," *Studies in Intelligence* 11 (Fall/Winter 2001–2002): 5–17.

Andropov Replaces Brezhnev

BREZHNEV DIED IN November 1982 and was replaced by Yuri Andropov, the former KGB chairman who had increased his power as Brezhnev's health declined and persons close to Brezhnev were charged with corruption. President Reagan sent Vice President Bush to attend Brezhnev's funeral and made the unusual gesture of going to the Soviet embassy in Washington to sign the condolence book. It was a signal that he was ready to improve communication with the new Soviet leader.

In Moscow and abroad, KGB propagandists worked hard to convince the world that Andropov would bring a new dynamism to Soviet policy. They spread tales of Andropov's "Western" ways, including a fondness for Scotch whiskey and jazz, and praised him as a good manager, a man of foresight, and one who knew that the Soviet Union needed to change.

Officials in Washington were not persuaded. There was no reason to think that Andropov was "liberal" in any respect. He had been Soviet ambassador to Hungary in 1956, and thus was reputed to have designed and directed the Soviet intervention that ended the Hungarian revolution with Soviet troops, murdering Hungarian leader Imre Nagy in the process.

Andropov was aware that the Soviet Union faced problems in its economy. He ordered two of the younger members of the Central Committee Secretariat, Mikhail Gorbachev and Nikolai Ryzhkov, to work quietly on a program of cautious reforms. Illness overtook Andropov before any were implemented, but they amounted to no more than tinkering with a dysfunctional mechanism. When Gorbachev later put them into practice in 1985 and 1986, they failed to stem the Soviet economy's downward spiral.

In foreign affairs, Andropov brought no change to the Soviet posture. On key issues he was in agreement with his contemporaries Andrei Gromyko and Dmitri Ustinov. Even Gorbachev, his protégé, wrote later that he was a man with the limitations of his generation of Communist leaders, incapable of transcending the ideological imperatives on which Communist rule was based.[21]

Relations in December 1982

MOST OBSERVERS ASSESSED U.S.-Soviet relations at the end of 1982 as probably worse, and certainly no better, than they were when Reagan became president. It was true that Soviet propaganda was more shrill in its attacks on the American president than it had been in most of the 1970s and that the American president was sharper in his criticism of the Soviet system than many of his predecessors, except for Jimmy Carter in the final year of his presidency. Nevertheless, there was no evidence then, and none has emerged subsequently, to suggest that the United States and the Soviet Union were at any time in the 1980s close to war with each other.

Nuclear threats, such as those posed by the Soviet leadership in 1956 when the British and French seized the Suez Canal, or by Nikita Khrushchev in 1962 when he placed nuclear weapons on Cuba, or by the United States in ordering a Defcon 3 alert during the 1973 war in the Middle East, were notably absent. While the Soviet leaders accused Reagan of planning to attack the Soviet Union, there was not a shred of evidence to substantiate this fear. Reagan himself said repeatedly that he did not believe the Soviet leaders wanted war. If he had been planning one, surely he would have accused the Soviets of doing the same. Furthermore, he consistently proposed deep cuts in those weapons that might be used to start one.

Reagan's political opponents never convincingly explained how war could come about as a result of his policies. They blamed him rather than Soviet intransigence for what they considered lack of "progress" in U.S.-Soviet relations. They viewed his reorientation of U.S. policy as provocative rather than constructive, and charged that Reagan was attempting to avoid genuine negotiation.

On most of these points they were wrong, as subsequent events demonstrated, but the critics were correct in concluding that Reagan was not eager to take up serious negotiation with the Soviet Union the moment he took the oath of office. Neither were the Soviet leaders prepared for real negotiation with the United States, despite their claims to the contrary. Even so, war between the two superpowers was a more remote possibility than it had been during most of the Cold War up to then.

IN 1981 AND 1982, Ronald Reagan challenged the Soviet leaders to think differently about their security and their interests. They refused to listen and were mentally unprepared to understand what he meant even if they had paid attention. At that time, the Soviet Union did not have a leader capable of coming to terms with the outside world, or even of grasping that this was what, above all, his country needed.

Andropov's coming to power was not the generational change in the Soviet leadership that people everywhere were waiting for. Nevertheless, Andropov seemed more competent than Brezhnev was toward his end, and one could speculate that Andropov had a more objective view of the Soviet Union's malaise than Brezhnev, with his self-satisfied "life-has-never-been-better" romanticism. In any event, the United States had no choice but to deal with Andropov, even though he, and others of his generation, could be presumed to be nothing more than transitional figures.

Reagan's will bolstered by growing defense budgets, he began to think more seriously about what he could do with a new-style Soviet leadership, should one eventually emerge—and, also, how he might help it understand where real Soviet interests lay. That's why he went to the Soviet embassy in Washington to sign the condolence book for Brezhnev, and why he began to insist on a more positive and comprehensive negotiating plan for the United States.

III

1983

SUMMIT HOPES DASHED

If anyone had any illusions about the possibility of an evolution for the better in the policy of the present American administration, recent events have dispelled them once and for all.
— Yuri Andropov, September 28, 1983[1]

Two years into the Reagan presidency, the U.S. government finally formulated for internal use a statement of its policy toward the Soviet Union. The directive had been delayed by internal disputes, personnel shifts, and the absence of any sense of urgency. It had been obvious that the Soviet leaders were not willing to negotiate seriously on terms acceptable to the United States. Nevertheless, with Brezhnev's death and Yuri Andropov's succession as general secretary, the president, supported by Secretary of State George Shultz and most of his White House advisers, thought that new efforts should be made to communicate with the Soviet leaders. Therefore Reagan insisted that the bureaucracy stop spinning its wheels and produce an authoritative statement that he could sign.

The result was National Security Decision Directive Number 75 (NSDD-75) entitled "U.S. Relations with the USSR," issued on January 17, 1983. Classified "Secret—Sensitive," it was binding on all U.S. government agencies dealing in foreign affairs. Though a secret policy statement, it was consistent with what Reagan and his secretaries of state had been saying in

public. It focused on Soviet behavior outside the USSR and the domestic political structures that fostered aggression. In only one respect was it more explicit than public statements: it set a goal to reduce the power of the Soviet
"ruling elite" by encouraging a pluralistic society. It contained no suggestion of a desire to destroy the Soviet Union, to establish U.S. military superiority, or to force the Soviet Union to jeopardize its own security. In fact, it
aimed for agreements that not only enhanced U.S. interests and were reciprocal, but also served a "mutual interest." This clearly implied two important
things: (1) that there *were* common interests to be found between the United
States and the Soviet Union, and (2) that the Soviet Union could not be
forced to sign an agreement that was not in its interest.[2]

Summary of NSDD-75
U.S. Relations with the USSR

U.S. policy toward the Soviet Union will consist of three elements: external
resistance to Soviet imperialism; internal pressure on the USSR to weaken the
sources of Soviet imperialism; and negotiations to eliminate, on the basis of
strict reciprocity, outstanding disagreements. Specifically, U.S. tasks are:

1. To contain and over time reverse Soviet expansionism by competing effectively on a sustained basis with the Soviet Union in all international
   arenas—particularly in the overall military balance and in geographical
   regions of priority concern to the United States. This will remain the primary focus of U.S. policy toward the USSR.
2. To promote, within the narrow limits available to us, the process of change
   in the Soviet Union toward a more pluralistic political and economic system in which the power of the privileged ruling elite is gradually reduced.
   The U.S. recognizes that Soviet aggressiveness has deep roots in the internal system, and that relations with the USSR should therefore take into account whether or not they help to strengthen this system and its capacity to
   engage in aggression.
3. To engage the Soviet Union in negotiations to attempt to reach agreements
   which protect and enhance U.S. interests and which are consistent with the
   principle of strict reciprocity and mutual interest. This is important when
   the Soviet Union is in the midst of a process of political succession.

In order to implement this threefold strategy, the U.S. must convey clearly to
Moscow that unacceptable behavior will incur costs that would outweigh any

gains. At the same time, the U.S. must make clear to the Soviets that genuine restraint in their behavior would create the possibility of an East-West relationship that might bring important benefits for the Soviet Union. It is particularly important that this message be conveyed clearly during the succession period, since this may be a particularly opportune time for external forces to affect the policies of Brezhnev's successors.

The Dialogue Quickens

GIVEN THE DEGREE of mutual recrimination that had marked U.S.-Soviet relations during the preceding three years, it was unlikely that U.S. goals could be reached without new and prolonged attempts to engage the Soviet leaders. They obviously had not yet grasped that what Reagan was requesting was consistent with the long-term interests of the Soviet Union. Secretary of State Shultz brooded over the lack of real communication and viewed William Clark and his National Security Council staff as responsible for preventing President Reagan from following his natural proclivities.[3] When Shultz and his wife were invited to a private dinner with the Reagans on February 12, 1983 (a heavy snowstorm in Washington had prevented the Reagans' normal weekend trip to Camp David), he discussed the situation with the president and persuaded him to meet with Soviet ambassador Anatoly Dobrynin.

Three days later, Shultz invited Dobrynin to the State Department, then, without advance warning, took him to the White House residence for a secret meeting with Reagan.[4] During a two-hour discussion Reagan reviewed the principal issues in dispute with the Soviet Union and made one specific request: that the Soviet authorities allow the seven Pentecostal Christians who had taken refuge in the American embassy in Moscow to leave the Soviet Union.[5] He assured Dobrynin that if the Vashchenko and Chmykhalov families were allowed to emigrate he would not embarrass the Soviet government "by undue publicity, by claims of credit for ourselves, or by 'crowing.' "[6] It was not his first request on behalf of these families, but by making it directly and emphatically himself, he gave it special force.

The process turned out to be extraordinarily complicated, but within a few months both families, along with close relatives who had remained in Siberia, were allowed to depart the Soviet Union. Reagan kept his word not to "crow" and considered the Soviet action a conciliatory gesture that justified a more active engagement.

We must go more deeply into the U.S. experience with the Vashchenkos and Chmykhalovs to understand why it was a testing point in Reagan's mind.

The Pentecostalists and Reagan's View of Human Rights

RONALD REAGAN WAS intensely interested in the fate of individuals in trouble. He wanted to do everything in his power to help them. His harsh judgment of the Soviet leaders was based, more than any other single factor, not on the ideology he talked about so much, but on his perception of the way they treated their own people.

When I first met him in November 1981, I had just come from several months in Moscow in charge of our embassy and was on my way to Prague as U.S. ambassador. My family and I were invited to join the president in the Oval Office for a photograph. I expected him to ask me some questions about the Soviet position on arms control, or perhaps Afghanistan, or maybe whether I thought the USSR might invade Poland. He chose to inquire about none of those hot issues. Instead, he asked whether we were making the Pentecostalists who had taken refuge in our embassy as comfortable as possible. When I assured him that we were doing the best we could with very limited facilities, he prolonged the meeting beyond schedule to inquire further.

"Why don't the Soviets let them go?" he asked, genuinely perplexed as to what might motivate a government to keep its people captive. I tried to explain why the Soviet leaders had refused to acknowledge that their citizens had a right to leave the country. In part they had the attitude of landlords with slaves or serfs: that people who choose to settle elsewhere were, in effect, property stolen by the country to which they fled. Even more important, however, was their inchoate but powerful understanding that the Soviet system could not withstand the free movement of its people. It was a system based on falsehoods; unfettered contact with the outside world would expose the lies and undermine the entire structure. Upon occasion, Communist leaders would make deals regarding individuals or families, but would insist on retaining control of foreign travel. The concept that people had rights that no government could properly infringe had never penetrated their thinking. They considered the public clamor in the United States and Western Europe over human rights a form of political warfare, designed only to embarrass and bring pressure to bear on the Soviet Union.

Reagan was fascinated by Soviet psychology and would have prolonged the discussion (we had already taken more than double the time officially allotted) if Richard Allen, his assistant for national security, had not reminded him that others were waiting and he was falling behind schedule.

The president's questions and comments impressed me. It was obvious that he felt a deep commitment to help people whose rights had been denied, and he genuinely wanted to understand the mentality of the Soviet leaders. When I had assured him about the treatment of the people who had taken refuge in our embassy, he could have dismissed the matter with a shrug, saying something like "I guess the Commies are acting true to form; they have to keep their people prisoner so the word won't get out how bad conditions are there." Or maybe even "Gee, that shows why those Soviets can't be trusted to do anything decently!"

Instead, he had wanted to penetrate an alien mode of thought. His questions were not those of a man determined to crush an adversary at all costs, but of one mentally preparing himself to deal with that adversary. They were also the questions of a man who recognized that there was a lot he didn't know but was eager to learn. When I came to work in the White House a year and a half after this conversation, the insights I derived from that brief exchange served me well.

As regards the Vashchenko and Chmykhalov families, I had been part of their saga from the start, for I had been in charge of the American embassy in Moscow in June 1978 when they pushed past the Soviet guards to enter the embassy's consular section. The guards seized seventeen-year-old Ivan Vashchenko and beat him severely, but seven—Peter and Augustina Vashchenko and three of their daughters, along with Maria Chmykhalova and her teenage son Timofei—got through. They all wanted to go to the United States, but the Soviet government would not issue the exit visas required to leave the country.

Although we explained that U.S. visas would be useless without Soviet exit permission, and that the Soviet government would not give them this permission while they were in the American embassy, the Vashchenkos and Chmykhalovs refused to leave the embassy. I decided, without explicit authority from the State Department, not to force them out when the consular section closed for the day. Our apartment was just above the embassy's consular waiting room, and my wife, Rebecca, brought food to them. For several weeks they lived in the waiting room. When it became apparent that they could not be persuaded to leave the embassy voluntarily, we let them use space in the basement—spartan, but in some respects better than their normal accommodations in Siberia.

I met with both families frequently and developed a deep respect for their commitment to their faith and their willingness to risk everything in order to worship in freedom. Peter Vashchenko, the leader of the group, had been to the embassy before. Just after New Year's Day in 1963, when I was a junior political officer in the embassy, he had been among a group of Siberian families who swept past the Soviet guards at the embassy (with some assistance from me, since I happened to be entering the building at the same time) and requested asylum. There had been thirty-two in the group—far more than could be accommodated in our overcrowded compound. After a few hours, we had persuaded them to leave the embassy, with assurance from the Soviet Ministry of Foreign Affairs that they would not be punished for entering the embassy.[7]

We learned some years later to our surprise that the Soviet authorities had kept their word. They did not punish the Pentecostalists for going to the U.S. embassy in Moscow and actually left them alone for a while. But when the authorities started drafting the young men (they were pacifists) and sending their children to boarding schools where they were taught atheism, the Vashchenko and Chmykhalov families decided that their conscience required them to go to a country where they could practice their religion unhindered. They were immovable in their determination to stay in the embassy until they had permission to leave the country.

The Vashchenko and Chmykhalov families quickly found a place in the embassy community. Though cramped in small apartments themselves, embassy families were supportive. Our guests helped out in the snack bar and assisted the Catholic chaplain. (Protestant services were held outside the embassy compound, where they would not venture.) The younger members of the families started learning English and typing. This went on for five years.

PERMISSION FOR THE Vashchenko and Chmykhalov families to leave the Soviet Union did not follow automatically or smoothly—or necessarily as the result of the approach to Dobrynin. In fact, Dobrynin was never permitted to give explicit assurances that they would be allowed to leave. The reply to Reagan's request was that the Pentecostalists would have to leave the embassy and return to their residence in Siberia, after which "the question of their leaving the USSR will be considered." Without more assurance than this, they would never have agreed to leave the embassy.

Max Kampelman, the U.S. ambassador to the Conference on Security and Cooperation in Europe (CSCE) in Madrid, managed to obtain more direct assurances from Sergei Kondrashev, a Soviet diplomat assigned to the conference. Though he had diplomatic cover, Kondrashev was known to be a senior officer in the KGB. Presumably, he could communicate with the general secretary by KGB channels, bypassing the foreign ministry. Kampelman had initiated an unofficial (that is, off the formal record) dialogue with him in an attempt to obtain the release of Anatoly Shcharansky and several other dissidents and Jewish refuseniks. Several weeks after Reagan's approach to Dobrynin, Kampelman called Kondrashev's attention to the Pentecostalists and explained that we requested the departure not only of the seven persons who had taken refuge in the embassy, but also of their family members who had remained in Siberia.

After checking with Moscow, Kondrashev told Kampelman that all would be released provided they went first to Israel and not to the United States directly. He also warned that matters discussed with him should not be mentioned to any other Soviet official.[8] With Kondrashev's assurances, and help from Dr. Olin Robison, president of Middlebury College and a prominent Baptist who had befriended the Vashchenko and Chmykhalov families, American officials managed to persuade them to leave the embassy, go home to Siberia, and apply to emigrate to Israel.

The Kampelman-Kondrashev dialogue contributed to ending the plight of the Pentecostalists and nearly succeeded in arranging Shcharansky's release,* but unfortunately it ended before more people could be helped. The reason is instructive. An American diplomat ignored Kondrashev's warning not to involve other Soviet officials and mentioned to a Soviet diplomat something Kondrashev had said. The Kondrashev-Kampelman "channel" thus came to the attention of the Soviet ambassador in Madrid, who informed Gromyko. When he learned that the channel was no longer private, Gromyko ordered it shut down.

The problem was not, as most Americans would suspect, that Kampelman's unofficial contacts were conducted without Gromyko's knowledge. Gromyko almost certainly knew of them, and even approved them. But the condition that they not be mentioned to other Soviet officials was important. Once these discussions entered foreign ministry channels, they became official. Gromyko would then be an implicit party to any agreement reached. If they stayed out of official channels, any settlements reached would be off the record. Gromyko was not necessarily opposed to solving such problems so long as the Soviet government did not have to acknowledge dealing with a foreign power on matters it claimed were purely domestic.

---

* Kondrashev told Kampelman that Shcharansky would be allowed to leave if he made a written request to be released from prison. Shcharansky refused to do so and remained in a Soviet prison for several additional months. After his subsequent emigration to Israel, he called himself Natan Sharansky.

Senior American officials, including most secretaries of state, seemed incapable of grasping the bureaucratic thinking that lay behind Groymko's attitude. They were to stumble over it repeatedly in attempting, out of courtesy, to notify Gromyko of informal contacts.

Reagan's Strategic Defense Initiative (SDI)

WHILE NEGOTIATIONS WERE still under way in Madrid concerning human rights issues and Secretary Shultz was preparing to activate the U.S.-Soviet dialogue, President Reagan made a speech that injected a new element into the U.S. negotiating posture: an element that persisted as both stimulus and stumbling block well beyond his administration. On March 23, 1983, he delivered an address to the American people that stressed the alarming Soviet arms buildup that had occurred during the 1970s. He ended the speech by announcing "a comprehensive and intensive effort to define a long-term research and development program to begin to achieve our ultimate goal of eliminating the threat posed by strategic nuclear missiles." He called it his "Strategic Defense Initiative."[9] Rarely, if ever, has a major proposal been so distorted and misunderstood by its friends and foes alike. Rarely has a proposal remained so controversial even after it achieved some of its goals.

From his first briefings on strategic nuclear weaponry, Reagan had been deeply disturbed to discover that the United States had no means to defend itself against a missile attack.[10] He found it morally unacceptable that an American president had no defense against nuclear attack aside from acts of vengeance that could spell the end of civilization on earth, if not humanity itself. A defense against weapons of mass destruction would clearly be preferable to retaliation.

The second reason SDI appealed to Reagan was that he wanted to eliminate nuclear weapons, but believed they could be abolished only if an effective defense against them existed. The knowledge of how to make nuclear weapons would not disappear from human minds, and there would always be aggressors tempted to develop them covertly. An adequate defense would be necessary if the world could be induced to outlaw nuclear weapons and abolish existing nuclear arsenals.

Reagan was also aware that the prospect of a defense against ICBMs could provide an incentive for the Soviet Union to reduce its heavy missiles even if the U.S. Congress decided not to deploy a comparable weapon. After all, if strategic defenses made a first strike impossible, there would be no use, even in theory, for large numbers of heavy ICBMs tipped with multiple warheads. He also knew that the Soviet Union was doing more research on missile defense than the United States. If it managed to create a defensive system and retain the full complement of heavy ICBMs, this would increase, not diminish, incentives for a first strike.

Reagan's speech set off alarms among his critics in the United States and among many U.S. allies in Europe. They said SDI was an impossible dream that could not be implemented. Furthermore, it was destabilizing because the Soviet Union would fear that it was part of an offensive strategy. To carry their doubts to the public, they dubbed the whole idea "Star Wars," stimulating images of spacemen fighting with death rays in outer space—a totally false association. Few seemed to notice the incongruity of assertions that strategic defenses were impossible and at the same time threatening.

The Soviet leaders immediately condemned SDI as part of an American attempt to achieve strategic superiority. They ignored the fact that it was complementary to U.S. proposals to make deep cuts in offensive weaponry and that the USSR was ahead of the United States in developing and using defenses against ballistic missiles.

One thing should have been clear from the beginning of the SDI debate: there was no possibility that any country could devise an impenetrable missile-defense shield so reliable that it could be counted on to repel a massive retaliatory attack. The best that any conceivable strategic defense could do was to intercept a small number of missiles, perhaps launched by accident or by rogue governments, or to eliminate a sufficient proportion of a large salvo to make it impossible for an enemy to plan a disabling first strike with confidence. In other words, a successful system might degrade an adversary's offense even if it was less than 100 percent effective. Furthermore, it was not clear in 1983—or, for that matter, twenty years later—that even such a limited system would be feasible at an acceptable cost.

Occasionally Reagan seemed to talk of an impenetrable shield, as when he spoke of "eliminating the threat posed by strategic nuclear missiles."[11] This was hyperbole, and should have been recognized as such.[12] Nevertheless, many of his supporters, most of his critics, and, for several years, the Soviet leaders as well, acted on the assumption that a perfect defensive astrodome over the United States was the goal of the Strategic Defense Initiative.

"Realism, Strength, Dialogue"

GEORGE SHULTZ WAS not consulted when Reagan's speech proposing the Strategic Defense Initiative was being prepared, and he had also been taken unawares by a passing reference to the "evil empire" in an earlier speech devoted largely to domestic issues.[13] Nevertheless, it fell his lot to deal with the negative impact these speeches had on opinion abroad. It was clear that they increased the hostility of the Soviet leaders and—even more worrisome—they produced further strains in the NATO alliance. Within a few months, barring an agreement with the Soviet Union that appeared increasingly unlikely, several NATO governments would be called on to take the politically hazardous step of accepting U.S. nuclear missiles on their territory. Shultz felt that the White House staff ignored these diplomatic realities. The president's national security advisers appeared more interested in blocking steps to improve relations with Moscow than in promoting a dialogue.

This led Shultz to push all the harder for more direct access to the president, for approval of policy initiatives, and for changes in the staff of the National Security Council. He sent the president a memorandum in March outlining his views and began planning major public statements to set forth constructive proposals for dealing with the Soviet Union. One consequence of these efforts was William Clark's request that I join the NSC staff as senior director for European and Soviet Union affairs.

In June, I took up that responsibility in the Old Executive Office Building next to the White House, an ornate building that in simpler days housed the State, Navy, and War Departments. My first major task was to work with Richard Burt, my counterpart in the State Department, and his deputy for Eastern Europe, R. Mark Palmer, on a statement to be delivered by Secretary Shultz to the Senate Foreign Relations Committee. I found the State Department draft consistent with my own views, made a few minor suggestions, and recommended that the president approve it. Reagan endorsed the statement without change.

Shultz made his presentation on June 15. It was the most comprehensive and forward-looking explanation of U.S. policy toward the Soviet Union since Reagan had taken office. The following sentence captured its basic thrust: "Strength and realism can deter war, but only direct dialogue and negotiation can open the path toward lasting peace."[14]

From that time on, we began to describe our approach as one of "realism, strength, and dialogue," which in fact named three fundamental elements in the Reagan approach.

WHEN THE PRESIDENT approved Shultz's testimony, I did not realize that there was anything unusual about the procedure. As I had time to read the files in my office, I found that my predecessors had tended to be much more critical of papers received from the State Department. In truth, the documents submitted were often not what the president needed. Papers from the State Department—and other departments as well—tended to be too detailed, too technical, and outright dull. Draft speeches for the president were never in the language he actually used, and letters to foreign leaders were also devoid of personality—and this for a president whose personality and charm were his greatest assets. These were good reasons to rewrite speeches and letters and to summarize briefing papers, but not to distort recommendations or undermine sound policy advice.

However, the problem was not William Clark, the president's assistant for national security, as Shultz suspected (and alleges in his memoirs),[15] but rather the system of interagency consultation and the president's own ambiguity about many of the issues. From my first day at the NSC, Clark supported my efforts to devise a viable negotiating strategy for the Soviet Union. He knew that was what the president wanted and his job was to get it done. But he also knew that the president was not going to fire those members of his administration who thought it would be heresy to deal with the Soviet Union before it changed its policies. He knew that the president would not give any secretary of state carte blanche to make foreign policy; that would have split his administration wide open. He also knew that, much as the president was eager to deal with the Soviet Union, he was also leery of seeming weak to some of the fire-eaters in his administration. When they felt strongly on an issue, Reagan was inclined to humor them and put off deciding the question unless he could be convinced that procrastination would miss an opportunity. When the Soviet leaders were not budging on any important issue, it was very hard to make a case that delay would hurt.

I was the first foreign service officer named to the NSC staff during the Reagan administration. The exclusion of professional diplomats from the staff before my arrival was an anomaly. Normally, a significant proportion come from the State Department. This was not Clark's doing, for he had inherited most of the staff. Nevertheless, the atmosphere at the NSC was not friendly to the State Department. Most staffers had come from the military services, the CIA or FBI, or the political campaign. Not one of them had lived in the Soviet Union for a significant period of time and, as best I can recall, none had ever worked in an embassy abroad. Most were able to transcend their institutional affiliation to some degree, but still their professional future depended upon their "home" agencies. When these agencies took issue with the State Department, these staffers were easily persuaded to oppose State's position. A few acted simply as mouthpieces for the agencies they came from, never willing to question their agency's preferences.

The State Department indeed needed some friends on the NSC staff, but these "friends" could be useful only if they avoided acting simply as its representatives. An effective staffer works for his or her boss. In this case the boss was the president's assistant for national security. It was my duty to give professional advice, endorsing or criticizing State Department positions on their merits as I saw them, to keep the State Department and other agencies informed of the president's thinking, and to work with colleagues in the various government departments to head off bureaucratic fights whenever possible and to ensure that the documents sent to the White House met the president's needs.

I was lucky to have as my assistants four highly capable specialists: Tyrus Cobb, an army colonel with a Ph.D. in Russian studies, came to the NSC from West Point where he had been teaching. He "covered" Canada and several countries in Western Europe, and provided invaluable help in developing our Soviet policy. Peter Sommer, subsequently U.S. ambassador to Malta, shared the Western European countries with Cobb. Tall, lanky John Lenczowski, a brilliant student of Marxist theory, dealt mainly with public affairs. Paula Dobriansky, who spoke both Russian and Ukrainian, kept an eye on Eastern Europe. Her outstanding work on the NSC staff started her on what became a spectacular career: an assistant secretary of state, head of the Washington office of the Council on Foreign Relations, and then under secretary of state.

My principal interlocutors at the State Department, Richard Burt and Mark Palmer, understood and respected my position. After all, they had encouraged me to take the job. Our offices worked in close harmony throughout their tenure at the State Department, and Secretary Shultz seemed pleased that policy papers were moving through the bureaucracy with less friction. Nevertheless, papers rarely moved with the speed they should have. I soon found that I spent most of my time dealing with agencies other than the State Department, trying to reduce infighting during the interagency process. I cannot say that I achieved much in this respect, but I did acquire a feel for the political forces within the administration and ways they could be mobilized to support the president's goals.

NOBODY OPENLY OBJECTED to the principles of realism, strength, and dialogue in dealing with the Soviet Union, but members of the Reagan administration had different ideas of what each meant and which were most important. Some officials were far more interested in lambasting the Soviet Union than working to increase the strength of our alliances or conducting a useful dialogue with the Soviet authorities. Some thought of strength merely as military force, giving little attention to economic health and political cohesion.

These differences produced constant arguments, but the most serious split was over what was meant by dialogue. Some seemed to be interested only in a monologue: a litany of U.S. complaints about Soviet iniquities. (There was certainly no shortage of them.) The "ideologists" or "propagandists" (as they were termed by "pragmatists"), along with others who conceded the need for negotiations, but only "at the proper time," felt that the Soviet Union had to do something to deserve a dialogue. Until it did, they felt the United States should hold back, to avoid appearing either to ignore or to legitimize Soviet misbehavior.

Those who wished to avoid or withdraw from negotiations rarely argued against negotiations in principle. Instead, they cited some factor that they claimed made negotiation untimely. What Shultz had run into, therefore, was not so much opposition to his specific proposals (though there was some of that) as a belief that the United States would be "honoring" the Soviet Union to deal with its leaders while they were still in Afghanistan, supporting proxy wars elsewhere, encouraging martial law in Poland, and opposing INF deployments in Europe. They wanted the Soviet Union to change *before* we entered into a serious dialogue.

Shultz felt strongly (and I, along with many others, agreed) that communication on political and security issues was necessary whether or not the Soviet Union was changing, and that change would be much more likely if there was a serious dialogue than if there was none. Though Reagan would sometimes waver and procrastinate when the din of opposition was particularly loud, he always came down ultimately in support of dialogue, and so did William Clark and his successors.

MY NEXT MAJOR assignment after working on the testimony Secretary Shultz made to the Senate committee was to write a paper on the pros and cons of summitry with the Soviet leader. The president had begun thinking about a summit meeting, but still was not sure he should go ahead without more signs that something would come of it. The "not-yet-the-right-time" folks were arguing that the public would call the meeting a failure if he did not sign a major arms control agreement, that the position the Soviets were taking made such an agreement impossible, and that the president would be subjected to pressure to sign a bad agreement in order to avoid blame for signing no agreement.

The president seemed to be looking for arguments in favor of a summit, and I supplied them, but was careful to spell out the doubts in the same detail. The paper concluded that the high expectations raised by previous U.S.-Soviet summit meetings need not be a reason to avoid a meeting with the Soviet leader. So long as the president made clear that the purpose of a meeting was to give an impetus to negotiations rather than to make agreements, the public would understand. I believed the president would not be blamed for avoiding bad agreements. He would have to explain only why it was better to have no agreement than the one the other side wanted.

The main benefit of summitry, I argued, lay in the opportunity for direct communication with the Soviet leader and the push such meetings give bureaucracies to work out as many problems as possible in advance. I was in favor of arranging such meetings on an annual basis and without preconditions. They could in time become a part of normal diplomatic communication, which would lower public expectations for spectacular agreements every time the leaders met.

This was the first paper I drafted for the president's personal use. When I received the assignment, I asked how long it should be. My experience had been that presidents wanted such papers in not more than two single-spaced pages.

"Make it as long as you want," Bud McFarlane told me. When I expressed surprise, he noted that it would be for the president's "weekend reading"—the reading he took to Camp David—and suggested that a full discussion would be preferable to summary treatment. I actually wrote six single-spaced pages. Subsequently I learned that Reagan would read, and indeed welcomed, even longer pieces if they were on subjects that interested him.

The president read the paper on summitry with care, making notes in the margin. He obviously wanted to move ahead and create conditions (still not precisely defined) for a meeting with Andropov. We continued work on a U.S.-Soviet agenda, apart from summitry as such, and made considerable progress over the summer. The president approved initiatives on several bilateral issues, from upgrading the hot line to negotiating a new long-term agreement that would increase rather than limit trade in agricultural products.

One cloud hung over thoughts of a Reagan-Andropov meeting. During the Italian investigation of possible accomplices in the attempt on the life of Pope John Paul II in May 1981, evidence had come to light suggesting that Bulgarian intelligence—and, therefore, the KGB—might have been involved. What if it turned out that the KGB had been behind the shooting? How could any American president meet with the former director of the KGB if that organization had tried to kill the pope?[16]

We asked the CIA to examine what was known and make a judgment. Forensic specialists went through the evidence meticulously and advised that it was not conclusive. Mehmet Ali Agça, the would-be assassin, had indeed testified early in the investigation that an officer of the Bulgarian security service had been involved, but he had later changed his story, and many of his early allegations had proven false. The analysts concluded he was a pathological liar. However, none of this proved that the KGB had *not* been involved. Soviet officials were obviously upset when a Polish prelate was elected pope, and they feared his influence on the political situation in Poland. But this was not proof of their involvement in the shooting.

Given Andropov's deteriorating health, of which Washington was aware without knowing how serious his illness was, a Reagan-Andropov meeting probably never would have taken place, even if political conditions had been more favorable. Nevertheless, President Reagan was hoping through the summer of 1983 that a meeting could be arranged. These hopes were finally dashed not by suspicions that Andropov had taken out a contract on the pope, but by an outrage committed by the Soviet air force when it shot down a Korean civilian airliner and plunged 269 people to their death.

KAL: A Big Bump in the Road

IT DIDN'T HAVE to have the impact it had. Tragic as the loss of life was, the Soviet downing of a Korean airliner on the night of August 31, 1983, would have caused only a momentary glitch in U.S.-Soviet relations if the Soviet authorities had acted decently. Acting decently required announcing immediately what had happened, ascribing it to regrettable human error, apologizing, promising steps to avoid a repeat, and offering to pay compensation to the victims' families.

Soviet leaders chose to do none of these things. First, they denied that anything had happened, then they accused the United States of causing the tragedy by using the plane to spy and vowed to repeat the act if so "provoked" in the future. They treated the world's revulsion at what had happened as a calculated American attempt to ruin relations and set the stage for an attack on the Soviet Union. Soviet leaders thus compounded the error with a succession of cover-ups, lies, and fabrications to substantiate an intricate network of utterly groundless accusations.

The Soviet reaction illustrated in microcosm much that hampered normal dealings—even between adversaries—with the Soviet Union. The Soviet leaders had a persistent habit of refusing to admit facts that were embarrassing, of inventing exculpatory circumstances, then insisting that refusal to accept their lies was a hostile act.

Both Shultz and Reagan were outraged by the initial Soviet denials of responsibility and took the diplomatic offensive. The president returned ahead of schedule from his California ranch to chair a meeting of the National Security Council, then delivered a television address to the American people. It was an address he wrote himself, taking the draft I had made as raw material. He called the Soviet action a "massacre," a word that he had chosen himself. Secretary Shultz spearheaded successful efforts at the United Nations to condemn the Soviet Union and persuaded U.S. allies to suspend service by the Soviet airline for a time.

All of these things had unanimous support within the Reagan administration, but there was a sharp difference of opinion over continuing high-level contacts and formal negotiations. Secretary of Defense Weinberger and some members of the White House staff argued that the United States should not resume arms control negotiations as scheduled, and insisted that Shultz refuse to meet Gromyko the following week when both would be attending the concluding session of the CSCE review conference in Madrid.* Shultz felt strongly that the United States should not break off contacts and negotiations, but should actively pursue them. Reagan accepted Shultz's arguments, but instructed him to confine his comments to the Korean airline tragedy and demand that the Soviet government admit error and pay compensation.

Shultz met Gromyko the day after both had made strong speeches at the CSCE meeting. Shultz condemned the KAL shootdown and called for sanctions against Aeroflot, the Soviet airline. Gromyko accused the United States of sending a spy plane over Soviet territory, asserted that the Soviet

---

* The Helsinki Final Act, signed in 1975, provided for periodic conferences to review compliance with the obligations the signatory countries accepted. The United States and many Western European countries used these review conferences to bring pressure to bear on the Communist countries to live up to the commitments they had made to respect the human rights of their citizens.

air defense forces had done what they should, and proclaimed that they would do so again to defend the "sacred territory" of the Soviet Union if there should be further "provocations." Shultz refrained from walking out on Gromyko's speech, but called a press conference to refute it once Gromyko had finished.

Given Gromyko's belligerent stance and the opposition in Washington to any meeting, Shultz took pains to ensure that there would be no pictures of the two shaking hands. When Gromyko arrived at the American ambassador's residence in Madrid for a meeting, Shultz sent Ambassador Arthur Hartman to escort Gromyko inside, out of the view of photographers assembled on the lawn.

Shultz and Gromyko began with a tête-à-tête (joined only by interpreters), as was their custom, at which time Shultz raised several human rights cases with Gromyko, to the latter's annoyance. Then they joined their delegations for the formal meeting. When Shultz announced that he was prepared to discuss only the Korean airliner incident and started to set forth the American position, Gromyko exploded in fury and stood up as if to leave, literally throwing his glasses on the table. The rest of his delegation also rose, apparently uncertain as to whether the boss was on his way out. Shultz, seated across the table from him, also stood, as if prepared to see him out. Gromyko, pacing the floor, started a harangue that went on for a full twenty minutes. In his excitement he frequently interrupted Viktor Sukhodrev, his interpreter, in mid-sentence, so Shultz grasped only snippets of Gromyko's outburst.

Once Gromyko started talking, his colleagues took their seats and began taking notes. Shultz stood with a look of amazement on his face and interjected periodically that he was following President Reagan's instructions. Gromyko thundered that *he*, the foreign minister of the Soviet Union, was not subordinate to Reagan and did not take orders from him. Those of us who were present were glad that a table separated the two. Shultz was outwardly calm, but his cheeks were flushed with anger.

Eventually, both sat down. Gromyko delivered a statement on the arms race that had been cleared with the Politburo, which *inter alia* threatened to "restore parity" if the United States should deploy intermediate-range missiles in Europe. Shultz simply ignored what Gromyko said and returned to the Korean airliner incident, upon which Gromyko retorted that the United States had carried out a "serious and premeditated action against the Soviet Union," which was "a criminal act against the USSR." The meeting broke up shortly thereafter.

Shultz, who rarely showed emotion, was fuming. As soon as Gromyko left the room in Ambassador Hartman's company, Shultz summoned Rick Burt, Mark Palmer, and me and said, "If you fellows ever advise me to see that so-and-so again, you're fired!" We knew he wasn't serious, so we assured him, tongue in cheek, that such a thought would never cross our minds. (Within five months, they met again.)

The meeting was traumatic for both. In his otherwise bland and uninformative memoirs, Gromyko devotes three pages to his encounter with Shultz in Madrid, repeating in a tone of high dudgeon words he had used then. It made no sense to discuss human rights with Shultz, he said, "as it only concerns our internal affairs." And he included his accusation that the Korean airliner had been sent by the United States to spy.[17] When he was in Madrid it is possible that Gromyko did not have a full report on the KAL incident. But the Soviet navy managed to recover much of the wreckage and the plane's black box. By the time Gromyko wrote his memoirs, he should have been informed that there was no evidence that the plane had been on a spy mission. Possibly he never asked and was never told. The Soviet cover story was for him the truth. He would have considered any attempt by Soviet officials to question that version an act of disloyalty.

NORMALLY, GROMYKO CAME to New York for the United Nations General Assembly and, while in the United States, usually went to Washington for a day or two of talks. In 1983, however, Gromyko canceled his visit to New York, not because of anything the administration did, but because the governors of New York and New Jersey denied Gromyko's plane the right to land at airports run by the Port of New York. They were grandstanding. The federal government had not encouraged them to close their airports to the Soviet foreign minister, and in fact offered to allow Gromyko's plane to land at a U.S. Air Force base, but Gromyko took the governors' action as an insult and canceled his visit altogether. He doubtless assumed that Washington had engineered the action by the governors. It was—and remains to this day—difficult for foreigners to understand the propensity some state governors have to dabble in foreign policy.

To judge from the disastrous meeting between Gromyko and Shultz in Madrid and the absence of any change in Soviet policy, Gromyko's cancellation of his trip was no loss to diplomacy. If he had undertaken the visit, it would doubtless have been marked by shrill polemics rather than businesslike negotiation.

Rather than trying to extricate themselves from the public relations disaster their actions had caused, the Soviet leaders raised the stakes on their losing bet by stepping up a counteroffensive based on total fabrications. On September 29, General Secretary Yuri Andropov issued a statement that verged on the hysterical, charging the United States with causing the loss of life on the Korean plane by a "sophisticated provocation, organized by the U.S. special services." By this time he should have been aware that there was not a scintilla of evidence linking U.S. intelligence services with the Korean airliner, yet he stated that American guilt had been "proved."[18]

The statement went on to attack the U.S. position in the INF negotiations. It pulled numbers out of the air to demonstrate that the United States, not the Soviet Union, had been driving the arms race in the 1970s. It also accused the United States of military intervention all over the world—at a time when the Soviet Union was escalating its war in Afghanistan.[19]

Andropov's language was virulent and hardly a word was true, but the White House reaction was calm and avoided polemics. The president approved an immediate statement. It expressed disappointment in Andropov's "failure to address concrete steps to reduce tensions," pointed out that "we know that we must live on the same planet and that peace is imperative to mankind if it is to survive," and invited the Soviet leader to "get down to the task at hand."

The *New York Times* reported the White House comment in full, but the *Washington Post,* always meticulous in covering every Soviet statement, did not even mention it. This was not the only time its editors simply ignored official statements that failed to conform to their preconceptions.

Reagan's critics in the United States and Europe, like the *Washington Post,* ignored his reaction, but seized upon Andropov's comment: "If anyone had any illusions concerning the possibility of an evolution for the better in the policy of the current American administration, events of recent times have thoroughly dispelled them."

"Now see what Reagan has done," the critical chorus swelled. "He has offended Andropov to the point that he won't deal with the United States anymore." But Andropov had only a few months to live. A year after he issued his statement, his successors realized that they had no choice but to deal with the American president.

American Missiles Deployed in Europe

NEGOTIATIONS ON LIMITING INF missiles in Europe continued for several sessions following the abortive walk in the woods in the summer of

1982. In 1983 the United States proposed a compromise, announcing that it would accept equal, verifiable limits on any number between zero and 572 (the maximum number of missiles NATO planned to deploy). Andropov also made proposals, but all would have left the Soviet Union with a monopoly on this type of weapon. U.S. negotiator Paul Nitze continued to try to find some formula that would be acceptable to both sides, but his efforts usually resulted only in public recriminations. A battle was going on for public opinion in Germany, where a large and vociferous segment of the population opposed the impending deployments.

Nitze and other U.S. officials, including Eugene Rostow, the first head of the U.S. Arms Control and Disarmament Agency in the Reagan administration, feared that public opposition in Europe could not be overcome, and therefore sought a negotiated solution. However, Weinberger and other civilian officials in the Department of Defense considered Nitze's formula unacceptable and suspected Nitze and Rostow of dealing behind their backs. Rostow was forced to resign in 1983 largely because of his association with the walk-in-the-woods idea. Paul Nitze survived the storm of resentment from the Defense Department because of Secretary Shultz's strong support and President Reagan's confidence in him.

The predominant opinion in the U.S. government was that it was better to proceed with the deployments than accept any of the deals the Soviet government offered. None of them came close to an arrangement acceptable to NATO; all would have left the Soviet Union with a clear advantage. I have little doubt that President Reagan would have approved a compromise settlement if, by the summer of 1983, the Soviet government had been willing to accept a small number of U.S. ground-launched cruise missiles and to reduce their SS-20s to the same number. It would have left the USSR with a military advantage, since the SS-20s carried three warheads and the GLCMs only one. But an agreement would have avoided the political fights within the basing countries that took place in the fall when the missile deployments were scheduled. It also would have been a step, though a small one, toward Reagan's dream of reducing and eliminating nuclear weapons altogether. If the U.S. and USSR could agree to reduce the number of INF weapons to a common low level, he could hope that together we might soon realize that we did not need the weapons at all.

For this to happen, however, the Soviet reluctance to "trade something for nothing" had to be overcome. In most categories of weaponry they had the advantage of numbers. If there was to be equality, they would have to reduce more than the United States. This was not an unreasonable expectation, since the USSR had consistently produced more weapons than were needed for defense, had used them often to achieve political ends, and could not be rewarded for such practices if there was to be a stable peace.

Those civilians in the Soviet foreign ministry capable of understanding the logic of the U.S. position were unable to stimulate a debate within the Soviet leadership so long as Gromyko sided with Minister of Defense Ustinov, who was unwilling to negotiate away any element of Soviet military superiority. However unbalanced, the existing relationship was labeled "parity" and any reduction had to be one for one. Soviet civilians, even those in high positions, were also handicapped since they were not given the facts about many military programs. The foreign ministry had not been consulted before the SS-20s were designed, built, and deployed, and was not even notified (until the United States complained) about most of the major violations of agreements. Nevertheless, Gromyko never hesitated to defend to the last Soviet diplomat whatever policies his military colleagues devised.

Whatever their ultimate intentions, both the U.S. and Soviet governments understood that they had to *appear* to negotiate seriously on the issue. This is why, after the walk in the woods failed, each frequently announced some revision in its negotiating position: Andropov made periodic public statements, as did Reagan. Increasingly, however, these partook more of public relations gambits than of realistic moves to find a compromise.

MOSCOW'S REFUSAL TO apologize for shooting down the Korean airliner severely damaged the Soviet image in Europe and made it more difficult for those groups attempting to block deployments to prevail in their respective legislatures. Deployments were planned in five countries: Great Britain, Germany, Italy, Belgium, and the Netherlands. However, the key basing country was Germany, where the Pershing IIs were to be located. Despite determined opposition by the "peace movement" in Germany—then joined by the opposition Social Democratic Party, which seemed to forget that its leader, Helmut Schmidt, had been one of the prime movers of the 1979 NATO decision—the German Bundestag voted on November 22, 1983, to approve the deployments. Immediately, American missiles began arriving in Europe at the bases that had been prepared. On November 24, Andropov announced that the Soviet Union was withdrawing from arms control negotiations with the United States, as he had earlier threatened.

Relations seemed to have reached a new low.

U.S. Policy Refined

ALTHOUGH THE KAL incident stalled the gathering momentum for a more serious and comprehensive U.S.-Soviet dialogue, interest in moving relations onto a more positive course remained high in the Reagan White House. Shortly after Andropov's statement that there could no longer be illusions that business with the Reagan administration was possible, we received what appeared to be an officially inspired message that the Soviet leaders would have to hunker down for a few months, but that real business might be possible again in late 1984.[20]

On October 11, Judge Clark called me to his office for a private meeting. He said the president was considering appointing a "close personal associate" as ambassador to Moscow. He hoped that this would be a signal of his seriousness in putting new life into negotiations with the Soviet Union. Since he hadn't yet made up his mind, he needed a summary of the arguments for and against the idea. The paper was to be written in confidence, not cleared with anyone else, and delivered to Clark in single copy.

Clark did not indicate which "close personal associate" the president had in mind, but I suspected it was Clark himself. It was obvious that he was not happy in the thankless job of assistant for national security or with being suspected by Secretary Shultz of thwarting the president's desires.

I could not be sure who the candidate might be, but I doubted that the appointment could work as intended since there was no hope of making much progress in relations with the Soviet Union until the Soviet leadership changed. Nevertheless, I wrote a memorandum with balanced arguments, pointing out that the appointment would call public attention to the president's interest in dealing with the Soviet Union and might be praised in the United States and Europe as a sign of the president's commitment to negotiation. It might also convey that interest to the Soviet leaders, provided it was accompanied by a substantial shift in U.S. policy. In that case, the appointment would help attract attention to the new U.S. proposals, and the proposals themselves would enhance the credibility of the appointee with the Soviet leadership.

I noted, however, that such an appointment would also run serious risks, particularly if it was not accompanied by a policy shift that Moscow deemed favorable. If the new ambassador could not show quick results, he would be accused of failing in his mission. The Soviets might even consider him a political exile. They had a history of naming people to diplomatic posts when they wanted them out of Moscow.

The matter was not pursued further; within a few days Judge Clark was named secretary of the interior when an opening suddenly appeared with James Watt's resignation. Nevertheless, I thought that the idea of appointing a close associate to the Moscow post demonstrated Reagan's eagerness to do something to get U.S.-Soviet relations on a more constructive trajectory. Reagan was not the sort to use important diplomatic posts for political exile, nor would a close associate have accepted a post unless he knew the president really wanted to pursue serious negotiations.[21]

A New Assistant for National Security

BILL CLARK'S RESIGNATION as the president's national security adviser produced a struggle within the administration over his successor. Michael Deaver and George Shultz hoped that James A. Baker III, Reagan's chief of staff, would be named, but William Casey and Caspar Weinberger argued strongly against Baker. They preferred Jeane Kirkpatrick, who was leaving her post as ambassador to the United Nations. Shultz—and others—respected her as a vigorous advocate for her ideas but felt that she was not totally in tune with the president's views and also lacked diplomatic skill.[22] Members of the NSC staff, virtually without exception, hoped that the president would pick Bud McFarlane.

At that time McFarlane was not as well known to the public or to the international community as either Jim Baker or Jeane Kirkpatrick, but he had a greater depth of experience in foreign and defense policy than either. The son of a congressman from Texas, he had graduated from the Naval Academy, served for twenty years as an officer in the Marine Corps (including two tours in Vietnam), and also, along the way, earned a graduate degree in international relations in Geneva, Switzerland. He had served as a military aide on the NSC staff during the Nixon administration, then worked on the staff of the Senate Foreign Relations Committee, as counselor in the Department of State, and for more than two years as William Clark's deputy. What counted with the NSC staff, however, was his commitment to serving the national interest rather than currying favor with superiors or fighting ideological battles in public.

The NSC staff celebrated when the president named McFarlane his assistant for national security on October 17, 1983. Although his earlier assignment had required him to spend most of his time on the complex issues of the Middle East, he was to focus ever more attention on Soviet policy from that time on. Basically, his approach to Soviet affairs was close to Secretary Shultz's—a fact that Shultz at times failed to recognize and appreciate.

Saturday Breakfasts at the State Department

DESPITE HIS IMPATIENCE to get relations with Moscow on a constructive track, Reagan did not seem to be focusing on the substantive issues. Decisions were stalled by squabbles among the various agencies. Shultz noticed this, of course, and tried to break the logjam within the administration by starting a series of Saturday breakfasts for senior officials. Shultz and McFarlane asked me to organize the meetings and act as executive secretary. They wanted to make sure that all the participants could be seated around a single table in a dining room on the eighth floor of the State Department. They also insisted that the fact of the meetings, as well as the content of the discussions, be kept confidential.

When I reviewed with McFarlane the proposed list of participants (including Weinberger, Casey, and their deputies), I noted that Vice President Bush was not included. I suggested that he be invited also. McFarlane questioned whether he would be interested in attending a meeting chaired by Shultz and I told him I thought he would, but in any case the decision should be his. Accordingly, the vice president was invited and he participated actively and usefully in many of the group's meetings.

After the first meeting on November 19, I jotted down some notes on the principles to follow in preparing public statements for the president, his letters to the Soviet leader, and policy guidance for the U.S. government as a whole. I had learned from comments in Shultz's Saturday breakfast group that there was general agreement on American goals. While there were sharp differences regarding the specific steps that should be taken to reach the goals, nobody argued that the United States should try to bring the Soviet Union down. All recognized that the Soviet leaders faced mounting problems, but understood that U.S. attempts to exploit them would strengthen Soviet resistance to change rather than diminish it.* President Reagan was in favor of bringing pressure to bear on the Soviet Union, but his objective was

---

* After the Soviet collapse, several Reagan administration officials have been quoted to the effect that it was Reagan's policy from the outset of his administration to bring the Soviet Union down. (See, for example, quotations in Peter Schweizer's *Victory*.) These statements have either been taken out of context or are the products of rationalization after the fact. If any senior officials held such views at the time Reagan's policy was being made, they were careful to keep them to themselves.

to induce the Soviet leaders to negotiate reasonable agreements, not to break up the country.

U.S. Policy Guidance

Outline Notes of November 19, 1983

Our Agenda: Our principal objectives can be grouped in three interdependent categories:

1. Reduce use and threat of force in international disputes;
2. Lower high levels of armaments by equitable and verifiable agreements; and
3. Establish minimal level of trust to facilitate the first two objectives, including
   a. Compliance with past agreements;
   b. Human rights performance;
   c. Specific confidence-building measures;
   d. Bilateral ties when mutually beneficial.

Our Approach: Attempt to make progress on the following basis:

a. Realism: We recognize that our competition with the USSR is basic and there is no quick fix. We also recognize the nature of the system with which we must deal.
b. Strength: We know that without adequate attention to our strength—military, economic, alliance cohesion, and political will—we cannot deal with the Soviet Union effectively.
c. Negotiation: We are willing to negotiate differences in an honest attempt to find ways to reduce tensions. But we must insist on a real reduction of tension, not agreements which simply cover up real problems and thus mislead the public.

Missing Elements: Our policy should **not** include the following goals:
a. Challenging legitimacy of Soviet system;
b. Military superiority;
c. Forcing collapse of the Soviet system (as distinct from exerting pressure on Soviets to live up to agreements and abide by civilized standards of behavior).

As senior U.S. officials began to agree upon policy goals in respect to the Soviet Union, it was apparent to all, except possibly to Reagan himself, that they had to do more to get both the American public and the Soviet leaders to understand just what our policy was. While Reagan had from the beginning of his administration spoken of the need to negotiate and of the prospects of cooperation if Soviet policy made it possible, the media had focused on his criticism of the Soviet Union. The Soviet leaders obviously believed that his avowed desire to reach settlements was insincere. Events themselves, such as the war in Afghanistan, the military pressures on Poland, the clandestine support of terrorism, the militarization of third world conflicts, the deployment of SS-20 missiles in Europe, and the Soviet treatment of the KAL shootdown, made it impossible to mute American criticism without losing sight of the real issues at stake. Nevertheless, the U.S. approach needed a more reasoned explanation than the piecemeal comments of the past had offered.

This was a task that concentrated minds in the White House and State Department throughout 1984. In fact, the effort began toward the end of 1983, while polemics over the destruction of the Korean airliner were still reverberating and the Soviet Union had withdrawn from nuclear arms negotiations.

IV

————————— ∽ —————————

1984

REAGAN PREPARES;
MOSCOW DAWDLES

*If the Soviet Government wants peace, then there will be peace. Together we
can strengthen peace, reduce the level of arms, and know in doing so we have
helped fulfill the hopes and dreams of those we represent and, indeed, of
people everywhere. Let us begin.*
—RONALD REAGAN, January 16, 1984[1]

A S 1984 WAS a presidential election year in the United States, it was
obvious to all in the Reagan administration that the president's han-
dling of relations with the Soviet Union would be an issue. This led some
campaign advisers to argue against harsh criticism of the Soviet Union and
for more stress on attempts at accommodation. They wished to refute the
charge that Reagan had deliberately increased tensions and was risking nuclear war. Their view was not shared by all advisers. The "ideologists" and
those often identified with the "hard right" thought that a tough line toward
the Soviet Union was politically effective. Given Soviet behavior since the
invasion of Afghanistan, the ideologists were probably correct that Reagan
could have won the 1984 election without any change in the public perception of his attitude toward the Soviet Union.

The shift in focus of the president's statements from late 1983, therefore,
was not motivated primarily by electoral considerations. That shift occurred
because it represented Reagan's aspirations for his record as president. In
his mind, the larger defense budget and his criticism of Soviet actions were

only a prelude to a period of intense negotiation that would set the world on a course of arms reduction. Ending the Cold War seemed too utopian to offer as an explicit objective, though that was Reagan's goal. He was searching for a policy that would outlast his presidency, whether his successors were Republicans or Democrats, and would ultimately achieve what he dared not hope he could do in the five years he would have if he was reelected.

In November 1983, members of the NSC staff and their colleagues in the State Department focused on preparing major public presentations of the president's approach to the Soviet Union: one was the platform *Time* magazine offered by seeking an interview with the president for its "Man of the Year" issue,* and the other was a set speech on U.S.-Soviet relations to be delivered just before Christmas.

I prepared a lengthy briefing paper for Reagan in advance of his *Time* interview. It was approved without change, but it came back with a request for something shorter. Critics would scoff that Reagan was incapable of grasping the details and subtleties of nuanced prose, but this was not true. He understood that communication with a broad public requires a degree of directness, clarity, and—yes—simplicity if it is to be effective. A policy that cannot be conveyed in simple statements is likely to be misunderstood. Furthermore, qualification can dilute the intended meaning of a policy statement and obscure what is most important. Therefore, I provided a few lines that could be typed in capital letters on three-by-five-inch cards, emphasizing Reagan's commitment to negotiating differences with the Soviet Union and his judgment that the world was safer since he took office. These points came across clearly in the interview *Time* published subsequently.

INTERVIEW WITH *TIME* MAGAZINE

Crib Notes for President's Interview
December, 1983

MAIN POINT
—Your commitment to solving problems with the Soviet Union.

BASIC POINTS
—Decline in U.S. strength when you took office.
—Tide of decline reversed.

---

* An "honor" that Reagan shared with Andropov, to the annoyance of Reagan's staff.

—We are committed both to deterrence and to negotiation.

—Arms levels too high, must be reduced.

—We have made serious proposals and will continue to negotiate seriously.

—Future is not more dangerous. World is now more stable in terms of super-power confrontation.

POINTS ON SOVIETS

—Our view on nature of communism and Soviet system is clear, but we recognize that we share the planet and must deal.

—We want to improve and intensify the dialogue.

—Cannot predict what they will do in a specific situation, but believe they share an interest in avoiding war.

—We want to find practical solutions to real problems.

—We prefer cooperation to confrontation if Soviet policies make this possible.

The Speech on U.S.–Soviet Relations

INTERVIEWS HAVE THEIR limits. Since the person interviewed does not control the questions, he cannot be sure that all the thoughts he wishes to convey will be covered. Therefore, Reagan decided to deliver an address that would set forth a detailed explanation of his approach to relations with the Soviet Union. I was instructed to write a draft, with the assumption that the speech would be delivered before the end of 1983. Some on the White House staff felt that the speech was more likely to be dismissed as campaign rhetoric if it was delivered in 1984.

Although my draft was ready by the middle of December, a decision was made to postpone the address until January, so most of the final work on it was done in the two weeks preceding its delivery on January 16.* The draft received much more attention by both staff and the president than most

---

* Those of us on the staff were mystified about the reason for delaying the speech, although I, at least, did not consider the timing critically important. I knew that the Soviet leaders would not respond for months, if then, and also that many American journalists would consider the statement motivated by the reelection campaign, whether it was delivered in 1984 or at the end of 1983. Subsequently, we learned that the delay had not been based on policy considerations, but on the advice of Mrs. Reagan's astrologer friend in California. Whether the timing of the speech played any role in the ultimate success of the policy it announced is an open question, but it is clear that it did no harm.

speeches the president made. Only the annual State of the Union address to Congress occupied more officials in the White House.

I sent my preliminary draft to Mark Palmer in the State Department for amplification, correction, and general vetting, then obtained approval from both Shultz and McFarlane before it went to the president for his review. After reading it, he asked Michael Deaver, deputy chief of staff—and close personal friend of the Reagans—and Richard Darman, Chief of Staff James Baker's assistant, to meet with us and discuss it. Both were associated with the faction in the White House that encouraged the president to establish an active dialogue with the Soviet Union.

Deaver began the meeting by commenting that the president thought the speech had too much material, covered no new ground, and was pedestrian. Darman asked who had drafted the text. With some trepidation, I admitted that I was the main culprit, though I had help from the State Department. Darman then relieved the tension by remarking, "I wondered, because it is the most coherent and reasoned speech draft I have seen in this administration." He went on to say that he could not understand the president's reaction, because if the president found nothing new in it, most people who heard him would, and he was sure it would be eminently newsworthy.

Of course I was disappointed that Reagan found my text pedestrian, since I had tried to make it as appealing as the subject would allow. But it was more important to me to hear that he found "nothing new" in the text. This meant that I had correctly guessed what he wanted his policy to be. In Reagan's mind, the draft contained nothing more than what he had been saying all along. What he didn't understand was the degree to which his intentions had been misinterpreted and misunderstood by much of the public. Therefore, unlike Darman, he was not able to appreciate that it would be considered news by many people.

We decided at the meeting to give the text to the White House speechwriters for some compression and stylistic revision, but not to change the substance otherwise. Simultaneously, I wrote a memorandum to the president to explain why we needed a comprehensive approach, and why it was unwise to include any startling new initiatives. I pointed out that the speech was designed to address four different audiences simultaneously: U.S. opinion makers, Western European governments and people, Soviet leaders, and the Soviet people. There was a message in the speech for each: for the American public, that we were not risking war and were strong enough to negotiate effectively; for Europe, that the United States had a coherent strategy for dealing with the USSR; for the Soviet leaders, that we were willing to deal with them in a cooperative spirit; for the Soviet public, that we were not threatening them and wished them well.

While it was obvious that Reagan wanted to use the speech to announce some grand new initiative, I argued against this. A flashy proposal would distract attention from the presentation of a coherent policy. It would be made at a time when we could be certain the Soviet leaders would not respond. Furthermore, it would continue a tactic we should try to end: making public proposals just for propaganda points. I felt we needed to deal privately with the Soviet government before making proposals public, just as we expected them to do with us. Consulting the other party in advance was the only way to fashion proposals that might be mutually acceptable. The sooner we could move to that practice, the better off we would be.

Aside from the principle of consulting privately in advance, I thought that the initiatives being discussed would not work. One of the favorites—and the most likely to be included in the speech if the president insisted—was a joint U.S.-Soviet project to build a space station. NASA was in favor of making such a proposal, and the State Department was inclined to support it.

I saw nothing wrong with a joint space project and would have supported the idea if I had considered it politically feasible.* However, it was clear that the time was not right. The Soviet leaders would hardly consider it seriously given Reagan's attachment to his Strategic Defense Initiative. Secretary Weinberger would have opposed the idea on the grounds that it would lead to an unacceptable leakage of sensitive American technology. Reagan might well have been persuaded to overrule him, but would probably have not involved himself in the interagency fights that would have ensued if the Soviets had accepted the proposal and we had attempted to implement it. If the president stood aloof, the proposal would be whittled away to inconsequence in a bureaucratic guerrilla war.

Reagan accepted the explanations in my memorandum and we proceeded to work on the text without adding anything of substance. The speechwriters would cut portions, and—if they lost the thread of the argument—we on the NSC would restore words, phrases, or sentences. Finally, a second draft went to Reagan for discussion in his senior staff meeting on January 6. At this point he was generally satisfied with the text, which he promised to work on further over the weekend. He wondered, however, if he really had to use a quotation that I had included from President John Kennedy's American University address of 1963.

---

* I did support the idea, in testimony to Congress, after the Cold War ended.

I explained why I thought it necessary to keep the quote. Kennedy had made the speech in the aftermath of the Cuban missile crisis, as he proposed an agreement to limit nuclear tests. There was thus a historical analogy in going from a period of strain in our relations to a successful agreement. Furthermore, Kennedy had expressed a thought similar to Reagan's when he observed, "If we cannot end now our differences, at least we can help make the world safe for diversity. For, in the final analysis, our most basic common link is that we all inhabit this small planet." Finally, I continued, we want to stress that your policy toward the Soviet Union deserves to be bipartisan.

"That was twenty years ago," Reagan said. "Does anybody really remember what Kennedy said then?"

"Most don't," I conceded, "but they certainly know it in the Soviet foreign ministry, where the same people are working on American affairs as were then. When they analyze the speech for the leaders, they'll point it out. They may not believe you are sincere, but they will understand what you are saying."

Reagan sighed and said, "Well, all right. But make the quote as short as possible."

Reagan himself made the next change in the text when he added a folksy story at the end about an imaginary meeting between an American and a Soviet couple who find that they really have a lot in common and would like to be friends.

This still was not the end of the process. The speechwriters had cut so much of the original draft that key points were lost. Therefore, I rewrote the entire text, restoring some substantive points and fixing up the president's story of Ivan and Anya to make it seem less sexist—originally he had the men talking about their work and the women about cooking and children. Richard Darman then convened a small meeting to go over the text line by line. Bud McFarlane, White House communications director David Gergen, Rick Burt from the State Department, and the speechwriting staff took part. Most of the differences at that point were between the speechwriters and the rest of us. In most instances, Darman favored the substance and overruled the speechwriters.

AFTER EXPLAINING WHY he had considered it necessary to strengthen defenses and the American economy when he came to office, Reagan made clear that this was the means to an end and not the end itself:

. . .[D]eterrence is not the beginning and end of our policy toward the Soviet Union. We must and will engage the Soviets in a dialogue as serious and constructive as possible, a dialogue that will serve to promote peace in the troubled regions of the world, reduce the level of arms, and build a constructive working relationship.

He pointed out that with all our differences, "we do have common interests. And the foremost among them is to avoid war and reduce the level of arms." He went on to formulate U.S. goals as common problems and common tasks, not as U.S. demands:

First, we need to find ways to reduce—and eventually to eliminate—the threat and use of force in solving international disputes. . . . As a first step, our governments should jointly examine concrete actions we both can take to reduce the risk of U.S.-Soviet confrontation in these areas. And if we succeed, we should be able to move beyond this immediate objective.

Our second task should be to find ways to reduce the vast stockpiles of armaments in the world. . . . We must accelerate our efforts to reach agreements that will greatly reduce nuclear arsenals, provide greater stability, and build confidence.

Our third task is to establish a better working relationship with each other, one marked by greater cooperation and understanding. . . . Complying with agreements helps; violating them hurts. Respecting the rights of individual citizens bolsters the relationship; denying these rights harms it. Expanding contacts across borders and permitting a free interchange of information and ideas increase confidence; sealing off one's people from the rest of the world reduces it. Peaceful trade helps, while organized theft of industrial secrets certainly hurts.

He then explained in nonconfrontational terms the meaning of the watchwords "realism, strength, and dialogue." Realism: "We must be frank in acknowledging our differences and unafraid to promote our values." Strength: "Soviet leaders know it makes sense to compromise only if they can get something in return. America can now offer something in return." Dialogue: "We're prepared to discuss the problems that divide us and to work for practical, fair solutions on the basis of mutual compromise."

Throughout the speech, Reagan emphasized the need for cooperation and the U.S. willingness to compromise. He also suggested interconnections among the various problems, pointing out that "greater respect for human rights can contribute to progress in other areas of the Soviet-American relationship."

For most Americans, the most memorable part of the speech was the portion Reagan wrote himself, the Ivan and Anya story. It demonstrated Reagan's respect for the Soviet people, whom he always distinguished from their government, and illustrated one of his fundamental tenets: "People don't make wars, governments do." He then ended the speech with a statement of assurance and a direct appeal:

> If the Soviet Government wants peace, then there will be peace. Together we can strengthen peace, reduce the level of arms, and know in doing so we have helped fulfill the hopes and dreams of those we represent and, indeed, of people everywhere. Let us begin now.

Subsequently, the three "problem areas" Reagan cited in the speech became four when Secretary Shultz decided that human rights was so important that it should be singled out for separate treatment. Thus was born the "four-part agenda" that provided a framework for the negotiations that brought the Cold War to an end.

FORMALLY, THE MOST authoritative policy decisions by the president are incorporated in directives such as NSDD-75, mentioned earlier. In practice, however, such decisions are often vitiated or even undermined by the bureaucracy if powerful elements feel they are unwise. Every statement is, to some degree, subject to interpretation, and this means that arguments can continue even after the president has ruled on an issue.

Public statements are not so easy to circumvent, for if actions by agencies or individuals in an administration seem inconsistent, this is normally noticed by journalists, questions are asked, and bureaucrats do not relish being suspected of resisting the president's policy. Therefore, policy speeches are important not only to explain to the public what a president is doing, but to communicate to officials in the government what the president really wants. Disputes over the concrete application of broad principles continue, but it is much more difficult to attack the principles themselves.

However, the effect of public statements can be undermined by spreading word that they are not serious. This was the tactic employed by persons in the Reagan administration who were uncomfortable with the thought that the president wanted serious negotiations with the Soviet Union. Leaked stories began to appear in the news media that the January 16 speech was merely an election-year tactic; this was also an argument used by Reagan's political opponents.

The president's January 1984 speech worked better with some of its intended audiences than with others. It was generally welcomed in the United States even though some dismissed it as a political maneuver to gain reelection. Its impact in Europe, particularly on allied governments, was greater. German foreign minister Hans-Dietrich Genscher went out of his way to compliment it when he met Shultz in Stockholm on January 18. His aides said that he actually danced for joy as he read the text. The view among U.S. allies in Europe was that, finally, Reagan had the right balance between firmness and negotiability.

The impact on the Soviet government was, however, less than that intended. The White House had gone out of its way to call attention to the speech in advance, alerting Ambassador Dobrynin to it and supplying an advance text to the Soviet foreign ministry in Moscow. In effect, we were saying: "This is special. Whatever doubts you may have had up to now, this is evidence the president is serious." We even explained privately why the president avoided making new proposals: we wished to consult the Soviets in advance, invited them to offer their ideas, and promised our own in the future. We did not expect an immediate favorable reaction—at least not in public—but thought that over the coming months the Soviets might be tempted to "test" the president with new ideas. But Soviet officials failed to use the speech even to make propagandistic proposals, even though some Soviet diplomats detected a new approach on Reagan's part.

Oleg Grinevsky, the Soviet ambassador to the negotiations in Stockholm on confidence building, recorded in his diary that he thought the speech "was not just a maneuver," that it would "require that American diplomats take less extreme positions," and that the Soviet reaction should be designed "to show that is the correct direction to go." However, Gromyko refused to take Grinevsky's advice. He conceded that Reagan's tone was different, but noted the absence of "new moves," and concluded that "we have to continue to support ourselves and our position."[2]

Consequently, Soviet media were directed to treat the speech as nothing new. In a brief statement the official news agency, TASS, labeled it nothing more than propaganda: "Behind the loquacious rhetoric about adherence to limiting the arms race and love of peace, was, in effect, the known position of the U.S. administration. . . . [T]here is no indication of any positive changes in the Reagan administration's approach."[3] Senior Soviet officials dealing with foreign policy paid little attention to the speech. Anatoly

Chernyaev, who was deputy director of the Central Committee's International Department in 1984, commented later that he had been totally ignorant of Reagan's speeches in 1984 and 1985. When he read them more than ten years later, he instantly recognized their significance:

> I was shocked, because I, an international adviser to the general secretary, didn't know about them. I wasn't aware of the existence of these documents in which this [U.S.] agenda was expressed. What they stressed wasn't the arms race; rather, the arms race was moved to the back burner. Instead [in Reagan's speeches] you [the United States] moved to the foreground the desire to have talks, to have human contact, cultural contact, even political contact, and this was said at the end of 1983, beginning of 1984. We didn't know about this.4

It is difficult to determine whether the speech had a significant impact on the Soviet public. Those citizens who listened to foreign radio broadcasts despite the heavy jamming would have been aware of it. However, they were probably already inclined to be more critical of their own government than of the United States, or else they would not have run the risk of listening to foreign broadcasts.

Chernenko Replaces Andropov

WITHIN WEEKS OF Reagan's speech, Yuri Andropov died. The immediate question for the White House was whether Reagan would go to Moscow for the funeral. I favored his doing so if Andropov's successor was named immediately, since this would give him a chance to meet the new general secretary. The successor was not named immediately, however, and Reagan decided not to go. When the question was put to him, he said, "I don't want to honor that prick [i.e., Andropov]." Therefore, he designated Vice President Bush to represent the United States at the funeral, as he had done a little over a year earlier when Brezhnev died.

Four days after Andropov died, February 13, 1984, Konstantin Chernenko was named general secretary of the Communist Party of the Soviet Union. There was no reason to believe that Chernenko had either the mental capacity or tactical skill to change entrenched Soviet foreign policy. Given his reputed weak health, he was likely to be another transitional figure. Nevertheless, the U.S. government proceeded with its game plan. Chernenko would be given every opportunity to engage the U.S. president; if he didn't take it, his successor probably would. Soviet foreign policy was on the defensive everywhere, just as domestic problems were becoming ever more acute.

Therefore, Reagan continued efforts to prepare the ground for a summit meeting and intensified his correspondence with the Soviet leader. He sent a conciliatory letter with Bush to hand Chernenko when they met after the Andropov funeral, and Chernenko replied a few weeks later. Exchanges of letters continued through the winter and spring.[5] Nevertheless, the Soviet tone did not change. This was not surprising, since Chernenko's replies were being written in the same office—Gromyko's—that had drafted Andropov's replies. The Soviet leadership had obviously decided not to deal seriously with Reagan during the 1984 election year lest they inadvertently help his campaign for reelection. The KGB had been given instructions as early as 1983 to mount a covert campaign to prevent Reagan's reelection.[6] Nevertheless, Reagan still hoped that he could induce Chernenko to deal earlier, and pressed his staff to develop a plan for specific negotiations.

By the end of February, I had produced an "action plan" that included initiatives in all four categories on the U.S. agenda. Reagan requested a "close hold" meeting to discuss it, and a group gathered on March 2 in the Treaty Room, located in the central residence portion of the White House, rather than in one of the rooms in the West Wing normally used. The location was chosen to impress on all participants that the meeting, which did not appear on the president's calendar, was strictly private, and that leaks of the discussion would not be tolerated. Nine persons gathered at first—Reagan, Vice President Bush, Secretary of State Shultz, Secretary of Defense Weinberger, National Security Assistant Robert McFarlane, Director of Central Intelligence William Casey, Chairman of the Joint Chiefs of Staff John Vessey, Ambassador to the USSR Arthur Hartman, and I—and we were joined after the meeting started by Chief of Staff James Baker and his deputy, Michael Deaver. By Washington standards it was a small meeting, but it included all the persons Reagan considered necessary to consult regarding the overall thrust of his policy toward the Soviet Union.

Reagan started the meeting by making clear that he wanted to arrange a summit with Chernenko, observing that he needed to show the Soviet leader that he was not the sort of person who would "eat his own offspring." He then let the meeting take its own course. It turned into a desultory discussion of items in the action plan. From time to time Shultz or McFarlane tried to put it on a more purposeful course, but it ended with no concrete decisions made. The president's message was clear, however: he wanted to proceed to summitry as rapidly as possible.

A few days before this meeting, Reagan had received an unyielding response to the conciliatory message Vice President Bush had delivered. I drafted a reply to it that attempted to move away from the mutual accusations that had marked most communication since President Carter's last year in office. In his letter, Reagan observed that he could not understand why Chernenko would accuse him of seeking an advantage, but noted that the important thing was not to debate but to try to understand each other's point of view. He pledged to take account of Soviet concerns, even when he could not agree with them, and invited Chernenko to make further suggestions for solving the impasse on intermediate-range missiles. Regarding the negotiations on strategic arms, still suspended, Reagan acknowledged that Soviet and U.S. forces were structured differently and said he was willing to consider "trade-offs" that would bridge the differences in our respective positions. If Chernenko was not yet prepared to resume negotiations on nuclear arms, Reagan suggested that they concentrate first on an agreement to ban chemical weapons and to establish better communications and procedures to avoid accidents and miscalculations at times of crisis.

Reagan approved the letter as drafted, but—in a typical attempt to make human contact with the Soviet leader—he penned in his own hand a paragraph that recalled the Soviet losses in warfare through the ages. "Surely those losses, which are beyond description, must affect your thinking today. I want you to know that neither I nor the American people hold any offensive intentions toward the Soviet people. . . . Our common and urgent purpose must be the translation of this reality into a lasting reduction of tensions between us. I pledge to you my profound commitment to that goal."[7]

Shultz delivered the letter to Soviet ambassador Anatoly Dobrynin on March 7, and mentioned to him several additional ideas for improvement of bilateral relations and for cooperation on regional issues. He stressed that, while we were prepared to negotiate on the larger issues, we would also take small steps if that was the Soviet preference.

It was to no avail. Chernenko's reply made clear that a summit meeting was out of the question, and showed no give on any of the traditional Soviet positions. Nevertheless, Reagan announced on April 5 that the United States would propose a ban on chemical weapons. Secretary of Defense Weinberger had opposed attempts to limit or eliminate chemical weapons, wishing instead to modernize the U.S. arsenal. However, Reagan accepted Shultz's advice, strongly endorsed by Vice President Bush, to introduce a draft treaty to the Committee on Disarmament in Geneva. The decision was made not only because Reagan believed in arms reduction, but also because we had received informal messages from senior Soviet officials that this might be a promising area for U.S.-Soviet agreement.

Reagan's announcement of what most of us in Washington thought would be taken in Moscow as a forthcoming step evoked only thunderous condemnation. On April 9, *Pravda* carried on its front page a purported interview with Chernenko. The first question asked specifically whether there were any "signs of positive change" in U.S. policy. The answer was unequivocal:

> The situation in the world, unfortunately, is not getting better. It remains extremely dangerous. The reason is that the U.S. administration continues to place its bet on military force, on securing military superiority, on forcing its concepts on other peoples.

So far as INF was concerned, Chernenko ruled out any further negotiations until "the situation that existed before the deployments of U.S. missiles in Europe began" was restored—in other words, until the U.S. missiles were removed. Reagan's announcement of a forthcoming proposal to ban chemical weapons was dismissed as a cynical ploy to obtain funding to expand the U.S. arsenal.

The language of the "interview" was familiar. The words, to a syllable, came from Andrei Gromyko. It should not have been a surprise, therefore, when the Soviet Union announced in May that its athletes would not take part in the summer Olympic Games in Los Angeles. It did surprise President Reagan, however, for he had ordered his staff to meet all Soviet requests for facilities, press coverage, and treatment of Soviet athletes—short only of guaranteeing that there would be no defections by Soviet athletes, a guarantee that he had no legal or moral right to give. Gromyko and his Politburo colleagues probably considered their action retribution for the U.S. boycott of the Moscow Olympics in 1980, despite the fact that Reagan was not responsible for it and, indeed, had criticized it at the time. Gromyko's determination to avoid any impression of improved U.S.-Soviet relations during the presidential campaign in the United States was doubtless an equally weighty reason.

"Back Channels"

IN MARCH, SHORTLY after the president's secret meeting with top advisers, journalists Rowland Evans and Robert Novak wrote in their syndicated column that Weinberger was telling friends that Shultz should resign, and that "conservative Republican senators are convinced of two things: first, that Shultz wants a pre-election U.S.-Soviet arms deal; second, that to get it he and top aides are conducting 'back channel' talks with Soviet leader Konstantin Chernenko, offering him juicy concessions."[8] Neither suspicion was true. As Weinberger knew well from the March 2 secret meeting, it was Reagan who was pushing for a summit. Since Reagan was eager to meet Chernenko, he would probably have approved reasonable compromises in the U.S. position on arms control. He was determined, however, not to sign a bad agreement and not to make one-sided concessions. Soviet leaders were refusing to negotiate INF or START. Secretary of State Shultz was doing nothing more than conducting a policy approved by Reagan, which increasingly focused not on arms control but on the other three categories of the U.S. agenda.

So far as "back channels" and offers of "juicy concessions" are concerned, these were figments of whatever imaginations entertained them. If they were held by "conservative senators," their source was probably elsewhere, among the second-echelon civilians in the Department of Defense. The uniformed military generally stayed out of politicized arguments and rarely resorted to press leaks. Additionally, the Joint Chiefs of Staff were not as opposed to negotiating many of these issues as were their civilian superiors.

Dr. Henry Kissinger's practice of using Soviet ambassador Dobrynin as a "special channel" to reach agreements behind the back of the negotiators officially charged with the negotiation had raised hackles throughout the bureaucracy. From that time on, many U.S. officials experienced a near-paranoid fear that somebody, somewhere in the vast U.S. government, was doing something and keeping them in the dark.

Nevertheless, it was obvious to anyone familiar with the Soviet system and Soviet negotiating behavior that agreements could be facilitated by unofficial contacts to explore possibilities candidly, without obligation, and without publicity. The object would not be to negotiate agreements, but to assist both sides in determining what an acceptable agreement might look like before they locked themselves in an acrimonious public debate. So long as the top policy makers and the official negotiating teams were kept informed of such conversations, they could help. They were most needed at times of high tension, when frank communication in official channels was always difficult and sometimes impossible.

From the outset, the Reagan administration had been willing to establish informal channels of communication with the Soviet leadership. As I have noted, Secretary of State Haig had approved such a channel when I was approached in Moscow in 1981. Then, and at other times, the Soviets had broken off the dialogue in the early stages, perhaps for the same sort of bureaucratic reasons that made such contacts suspect within the U.S. government. The failure of Paul Nitze's attempt at candor during his walk in the woods with Yuli Kvitsinsky demonstrated the obstacles faced by official negotiators if they attempted an unofficial dialogue.

From 1983, Reagan began to ask the Soviet general secretary to designate a contact for off-the-record, unofficial communication. His intent was to share whatever information derived from this contact with a small group of senior officials, including the secretaries of state and defense, his assistant for national security, the U.S. ambassador in Moscow, and the heads of negotiating teams, but with very few others, to minimize the danger of leaks. Each time he made the request, the Soviet leader designated Ambassador Dobrynin and Reagan responded by designating U.S. ambassador Arthur Hartman. Shultz then would arrange a private meeting with Dobrynin to make suggestions, but Gromyko never invited Hartman for an unofficial conversation and continued to prohibit U.S. embassy contacts with members of the Central Committee Secretariat who worked directly for the general secretary.

By the fall and winter of 1983, it was obvious that the United States needed more channels of communication if it was to inject any positive element into the U.S.-Soviet relationship. After Andropov's public statement about the impossibility of doing business with the Reagan administration, it was clear that any U.S. proposal, no matter how well meant, would likely be rejected. By then, Reagan and Shultz had agreed that we should try to move ahead and restore some of the contacts that President Carter had terminated in 1980, notably the agreement on cultural and educational exchanges. However, an official proposal to do so would certainly be rejected as a blatant U.S. effort to divert attention from the INF deployments in Europe. If Moscow publicly rejected the idea, it might take a long time to revive it.

During this time several private citizens with contacts in the Soviet Union approached the State Department or NSC staff with offers to pass any messages we might have to officials in Moscow. Most were told that they should just tell their Soviet contacts that the administration was eager to get on with negotiations and leave it at that. Occasionally, however, the person seemed suited for a more specific task. This was the case when Suzanne Massie, the author of a cultural history of Russia, called me following a trip to the Soviet Union. She was concerned about the tension that had developed and felt that restoring cultural exchanges could do something to relieve it. We agreed, and I asked her to discuss with her contacts in the Ministry of Culture how best to go about getting negotiations started. We asked whether the Soviets were interested in a new agreement and, if so, whether they would respond to a U.S. proposal or would prefer to make one themselves. These were questions that would not ultimately be decided by the Ministry of Culture and even less by the persons who would participate in the exchanges. The Politburo would make that decision, primarily on the basis of Gromyko's recommendation. Nevertheless, it was important to gauge how much support there was among Soviet intellectuals, and to obtain their advice on the best tactics to use to overcome possible obstruction.

Following her trip, Massie reported that there was intense interest (as we had assumed) in renewed exchanges, but no clear message regarding the best tactics to employ. We finally decided to discuss cultural exchanges and other forms of cooperation privately with the Soviet foreign ministry before announcing any proposals. We hoped that this would make it easier for Soviet officials to deal with the questions seriously and, perhaps, even provide an example of the most constructive way to approach other questions.

In late January we received a more significant message. Dr. Lawrence Horowitz, an administrative assistant to Senator Edward Kennedy, asked for a private meeting with John Poindexter and me. He had just returned from a trip to Moscow and reported that on January 19 he had met with Vadim Zagladin, deputy chief of the Central Committee International Department, who had asked him to relay a message to us. (Zagladin had been present at the dinner in Moscow in 1981 when Sytnikov was introduced to me.) His message was that the current state of U.S.-Soviet relations was serious, but that a start might be made in one area to get us back on a negotiating track. That would be to work jointly on a treaty to ban chemical weapons. Zagladin had preceded this message with a vitriolic attack on U.S. policy and President Reagan personally, but at one point made a revealing comment. He said that great powers must give one another "elbow room" at times, implying that the Soviets felt cornered and needed a way out. As an example of what he meant by elbow room, he said that if oil supplies from the Persian Gulf should be cut off at some point, the Soviet Union would understand that the United States had to take action.

Horowitz told us Senator Kennedy considered these matters above politics and would be pleased to cooperate in any way we wished, but would understand if his help was not needed. He asked that our conversation remain strictly private and that we limit knowledge of it to the president, secretary of state, and assistant for national security. Horowitz continued to keep us informed of contacts with Soviet officials, which were always handled responsibly by Senator Kennedy. At a time when other Democrats were telling Ambassador Dobrynin that Reagan was dangerous, Senator Kennedy's quiet coordination with the White House helped convince the Soviets eventually that Reagan was serious about negotiation.

When I accompanied Vice President Bush to Andropov's funeral a few weeks later, I briefed Ambassador Hartman and his deputy, Warren Zimmermann, on the meeting Horowitz had with Zagladin. Then, with the approval of President Reagan and Secretary Shultz, I requested a meeting with Zagladin to respond to the message he had sent through Horowitz. The appointment was granted immediately, and as I entered the forbidding gray Central Committee Building under KGB escort, I realized that I had been trying to establish some sort of contact with the Central Committee staff ever since my first tour in Moscow in 1961. Now, after twenty-three years of trying, I was entering that inner sanctum of the Communist system. The conference room itself was like many others I had seen: rectangular with a table covered with green felt in the center. I sat down on one side and Zagladin, along with a notetaker and Stanislav Menshikov, an economist and son of a former Soviet ambassador to the United States, faced me from the other.

I told Zagladin that we agreed with his comment about elbow room. We thought our actions had been consistent with that principle, but if he had any particular complaints I would let the president know. Perhaps, I suggested, the problem was that they had deprived themselves of flexibility by their own policies. Nevertheless, I assured him that it was not U.S. policy to corner the Soviet Union. I let him know that we would be proposing a treaty on chemical weapons and hoped we could work jointly on it as he had suggested, but this would require Soviet acceptance of on-site inspection. We discussed at some length our respective positions on START and INF, and I suggested that they continue the dialogue with General Brent Scowcroft, who would be coming to Moscow the following month for a meeting of arms control experts. Zagladin agreed that this would be a good idea and assured me that he would receive Scowcroft and, if possible, arrange for him to call on Chernenko. He also proposed that I continue our discussion with Menshikov, who would be coming to New York on UN business in early March.

When I returned to Washington and reported that Scowcroft would be received in the Central Committee to discuss START and INF, we considered this a signal breakthrough in establishing direct communication with the Soviet leaders. Scowcroft was briefed on the administration's position and agreed to conduct exploratory talks, particularly regarding the sort of trade-offs Reagan had in mind in his March letter to Chernenko. However, Secretary Shultz insisted that we ask Gromyko to arrange for Scowcroft to meet Chernenko, ostensibly to deliver a letter from the president. I was not in the meeting when it was decided to handle the visit this way, but when I was asked to draft the letter to Chernenko, I told McFarlane I doubted it would work. In the first place, it was aiming too high. Of course, we hoped that Scowcroft would be able to see Chernenko, but the real communication had to be with members of his staff. And asking Gromyko to arrange the meeting immediately put it in an official context that Gromyko wished to avoid. McFarlane conceded that this might be right, but it was too late to change our approach. Scowcroft was leaving within hours, and he needed a letter from the president.

The result was what I had feared: Gromyko flatly refused to arrange the appointment, but offered a meeting with his deputy, Georgy Korniyenko, which Scowcroft rejected. Then, to make matters worse, the whole incident became public knowledge after Scowcroft returned to the United States. Whoever leaked the story was, in effect, cooperating with counterparts in the Soviet Union who wished to block further negotiation on arms reduction and continue the arms race.

An item in *Newsweek* magazine's "Periscope" section, which followed newspaper stories on the incident, had its own twist, claiming that the Soviet government had refused to give Scowcroft an appointment with Chernenko because the Reagan administration had failed to notify Soviet ambassador Anatoly Dobrynin in advance. The *Newsweek* report, supposedly based on "diplomatic sources," concluded that "[t]he Scowcroft mission was designed to bypass Soviet Foreign Minister Andrei Gromyko because the United States now considers him an obstacle to progress in arms control."[9]

American sources may have been responsible for the original leak, but this item indicated that Dobrynin was not above using his cozy ties with the American press to conduct his own bureaucratic battles. In fact, the White House had alerted the Soviet embassy in advance to Scowcroft's trip and made it clear that he was authorized to discuss arms control issues confidentially. Furthermore, nobody who knew what actually happened would have described the effort to contact the Central Committee staff as an attempt to bypass Gromyko.

The fact was that Gromyko had approved in advance the contact I had arranged, and if Scowcroft had simply asked for an appointment with Zagladin he not only would have had a useful discussion in the Central Committee, but might also have been taken for a meeting with Chernenko. I met Zagladin's assistant Menshikov in New York while Scowcroft was in Moscow. He informed me that Gromyko had approved the arrangements made earlier. When we met, neither of us knew what had happened in Moscow when Scowcroft had requested the meeting with Chernenko. Menshikov assumed that Scowcroft's planned meeting with Zagladin was under way. He also informed me that Gromyko had finally agreed to meetings between members of the NSC staff and Central Committee officials, but still insisted that there be no official contact between the latter and State Department or American embassy officials.

The aim of these contacts was not to bypass anyone except persons inclined to leak confidential discussions to the press. In Washington, we assumed that any arrangements we made would have to be approved by Gromyko, and what was said reported to him. That was fine. We were convinced that he was not getting a straight story from his embassy in Washington. Parallel reporting to his colleagues by U.S. officials directly couldn't hurt, and might even make the Soviet embassy in Washington a little less freewheeling in its interpretation of events. But this was not an easy proposition to sell to zealots in either country.

Despite a promising start in communications with Central Committee staffers, the failure of the Scowcroft appointment and subsequent publicity ended this particular dialogue for several months.

Even though the contacts with the Central Committee staff failed to develop as we anticipated, some of the impressions gained were useful for developing U.S. policy. The United States tested the idea of working together to achieve a ban on chemical weapons by tabling a draft to the UN Committee on Disarmament in Geneva and beginning direct consultations on it with Soviet officials. The White House and State Department also gave considerable attention to the confidence-building talks that had begun in Stockholm in January in the framework of the Conference on Security and Cooperation in Europe. Some of Zagladin's comments on INF led me to believe that there was an assumption in Moscow that the United States was no longer interested in limiting these missiles, but only in completing their deployment. Though I had tried to disabuse him of this notion, it obviously would take more than that to be convincing. Therefore we advised Reagan to continue to stress that the U.S. missiles could be removed if there was an agreement to do so. Thus, the president stated in his speech to the Irish Parliament in June, "I'm prepared to halt, and even reverse, the deployment of our intermediate-range missiles from Europe as the outcome of a verifiable and equitable agreement."[10] But the Soviet position remained firm: so long as the U.S. intermediate-range missiles were in Europe, there could be no negotiations on them.

Trying to Expand Cooperation

TALKS CONTINUED IN regular diplomatic channels, however, as the United States developed an extensive list of bilateral arrangements that would restore most of the pre-Afghanistan interaction, and in several instances improve on it. They ranged from a new agreement for cultural exchanges, to reopening consulates in Kiev and New York, to cooperative agreements for research in environmental protection, housing, health, and agriculture, to agreements on fishing, oceanographic research, and a simulated space rescue mission. In all, the U.S. proposed joint activities in sixteen different areas.

All proposals had been laboriously coordinated within the U.S. government, in many instances in the face of strong opposition from some agencies. Those responsible for counterintelligence were particularly worried about any expansion of cultural and scientific exchanges. Those responsible for controlling strategic exports generally opposed most cooperative projects that might involve advanced technology. The burden of resolving the most acute disagreements fell to the NSC staff, since no government department would willingly give way to another without direction from the White House. Ultimately, President Reagan had to approve every one. Although he rarely went deeply into their details, he had a marked bias in favor of expanding contacts and was usually willing to overrule hypercautious advice from U.S. agencies that could see only danger.

Once the president approved them, the projects were discussed with Soviet diplomats, both in Moscow and Washington, and although their reaction was hardly enthusiastic, none of the American ideas were rejected. By June we felt the negotiations were far enough along to permit public discussion, so we arranged for Reagan to address a conference of American organizations active in exchanges with the Soviet Union. The conference had been arranged, with my support, by David Hamburg, president of the Carnegie Corporation of New York; the eminent historian James Billington, then director of the Woodrow Wilson Center for Scholars (since then librarian of Congress); and Herbert Ellison, one of the most perceptive historians of the Soviet Union who was at the time executive secretary of the Kennan Institute in Washington. They brought together representatives of groups that would be primarily responsible for conducting the exchanges that we in the government might arrange. It was an ideal audience to explain what specific steps the administration had in mind to erode the Iron Curtain.

The president addressed the group in the East Room of the White House. He listed many of the proposals and pointed out that restoring ties broken after the invasion of Afghanistan did not mean that we had forgotten Afghanistan, just as reviving cultural and scientific contacts did not mean that we had forgotten the plight of Andrei Sakharov or the need to support protection of human rights. However, Reagan refrained from castigating his predecessor, who had broken most of the contacts he wished to restore. Instead, he spoke of the dilemma the United States faced when it sought peaceful means to oppose aggressive behavior yet found that these measures hampered the communication necessary to build a peaceful relationship. He stressed, as he had in January, that the people of the Soviet Union were not enemies:

> [O]ur quarrel is not with the Russian people, with the Ukrainian people or any of the other proud nationalities in that multinational state. So we must be careful in reacting to actions by the Soviet Government not to take out our indignation on those not responsible. And that's why I feel that we should broaden opportunities for Americans and Soviet citizens to get to know each other better.[11]

Reagan's audience gave the speech an enthusiastic reception. After all, they were dedicated to the propositions he set forth. Most knew the Soviet Union well, were appalled by its aggressive behavior and assaults on human rights, and understood the dilemma Reagan cited. They saw no contradiction between making clear our problems with the Soviet regime and proposing closer ties with the Soviet people.

Not all journalists were so sophisticated. The *Washington Post* dismissed the speech in an article buried on pages 17 and 27 that concentrated on what the journalist considered a contradiction between "castigating" the Soviets and proposing agreements. The journalist devoted more space to alleged splits in the administration than to what the president actually said.[12] Most other papers also gave it short shrift. Of the major newspapers, only the *New York Times* gave its readers a complete report on the speech and described how it fit within the policy Reagan had declared in January.[13]

The speech was hardly mentioned in the Soviet media. It did not fit the image of Reagan the Soviet leaders were still purveying.

Gromyko Refuses to Take "Yes" for an Answer

JUST AFTER NOON on June 29, the White House received the text of a Soviet statement issued in Moscow inviting the United States to send a delegation to Vienna in September to meet Soviet representatives for talks "to prevent the militarization of outer space." It also offered "to impose on a reciprocal basis a moratorium on tests and deployment of these [space] weapons."

The proposal was obviously directed at Reagan's Strategic Defense Initiative, even though it defined the subject of negotiation in terms so broad that it was hard to determine just what specifically it was intended to cover. There had been no previous discussion of the proposal in diplomatic channels, so the announcement seemed designed for the public rather than policy makers.

Most U.S. officials assumed when they saw the Soviet statement that it would be rejected. I sensed, however, that dismissing it as propaganda—which it surely was—would be a mistake. After all, the United States had criticized the Soviet Union steadily for breaking off negotiations. How would it look if we were to turn down a Soviet proposal, however disingenuous, for talks? I immediately went to Bud McFarlane's office to persuade him that we should find a way to accept. He saw the point instantly (most likely having already come to the same conclusion) and asked me to draft a statement that would accept the proposal, but still make it clear that we also wished to deal with the problems posed by ballistic missiles, which, after all, were important elements in the "militarization of outer space."

By late afternoon, the Senior Arms Control Policy Group, with representatives from all relevant U.S. agencies, gathered in the Situation Room. At first, the sentiment was almost universal: "It's directed straight at SDI. We can't do it. Besides, it's nothing but propaganda." But as we went around the table, opinion began to shift, aided by McFarlane's deft mention, from time to time, of arguments in favor of acceptance. In less than an hour, it was unanimous: the United States should accept, but say that it would also discuss ways to resume negotiations on INF and START. The Soviet Union would not have to agree to reopen those negotiations, but would be placed on notice that the U.S. considered ballistic missiles that travel through space a part of the "militarization of outer space." The statement I had prepared in advance was revised to stress this before McFarlane took it to the president for his approval. Reagan approved it without change and it was issued in time for the evening news on television, and for the following day's papers, which carried both U.S. and Soviet statements.[14] It was probably the most rapid decision ever made by a committee in the U.S. government dealing with arms control.

Most Americans involved believed that the Soviets would agree to the meeting. After all, the United States had accepted their proposal and added only that it would also seek agreement on a related issue. If Moscow was trying to find a way back to the negotiating table on nuclear arms, this would be a face-saving way to do it. I warned McFarlane, however, that this assumption might not be correct. "Gromyko was so sure we would reject the offer, he is probably not prepared for the talks. Besides, he will avoid any show of Soviet-American agreement while the election campaign is going on. He and his colleagues still want to see Reagan defeated at the polls."

My instincts did not betray me. To the amazement of most, the Soviet Union refused to send a delegation to Vienna, even when the White House explained several times that the United States was setting no preconditions.[15] As the British foreign secretary observed, "They refuse to take 'yes' for an answer."

Gromyko Votes for Reagan

WELL, NOT EXACTLY. By September, Gromyko concluded that Reagan was certain to win the November election. The Soviet Union could not afford another four years of confrontation and tension. Gromyko had to find a way back to the negotiating table. The abortive exchange over space weaponry in June suggested an approach that might work, but the Soviet position could not be changed abruptly. The annual meeting of the United Nations General Assembly gave Gromyko an excuse to come to the United States, and he sent word in early September that he would come to Washington during his visit if the secretary of state and president received him. He was immediately assured that he would be welcome.

Foreign ministers, even those of close allies, rarely meet the president when they visit Washington. That privilege is normally reserved for chiefs of state and heads of government. Nevertheless, until 1983 when Gromyko canceled his planned visit to the United States after KAL 007 was downed, the Soviet foreign minister had normally met with the president during his annual visit to the United Nations. Therefore, the meeting in 1984 restored the usual pattern of contact. Reagan went one better: he also arranged for a lunch in the formal dining room at the White House—treatment just short of that normally accorded a visiting chief of state.

Gromyko's call at the White House attracted more interest from the press than visits by foreign kings and presidents. Interest was so intense in getting pictures of the two seated in the Oval Office that photographers were admitted in relays. Each group was given a few minutes, then ushered out to allow another group to enter. This went on for close to half an hour while Reagan and Gromyko engaged in small talk or gave short, usually cryptic, replies to shouted questions. I watched the process with growing impatience, eager to get on with the meeting, but neither Reagan nor Gromyko seemed to mind. Both wanted as much publicity as possible.

The meeting itself and discussion during the lunch that followed solved none of the many problems between the United States and the Soviet Union. However, it established a spirit of direct communication that had been missing since the last year of the Carter administration. Gromyko spoke eloquently on the danger posed by the "mountains of arms" both countries were sitting on. Reagan agreed and insisted that he was determined to reduce them, but said reductions had to produce greater stability and be verifiable. Gromyko still demanded that U.S. intermediate-range missiles be removed from Europe before any negotiations on arms reduction could be resumed. Reagan countered that they could be removed as the result of an agreement, but not before.

There was some verbal fencing over Communist ideology, with Gromyko denying that his country abetted "world revolution," even though he was convinced that "socialism" would triumph in the world of the future. In general, Gromyko showed no interest in discussing anything but arms control. He refused to discuss issues such as human rights or Soviet military activities in third countries on grounds that the United States had no business interfering in such matters.

The most important result of this meeting was psychological. Reagan and Gromyko talked to each other as responsible political leaders who shared an interest in finding a way to end the arms race, even though they could agree on little else. First lady Nancy Reagan did her part. As the luncheon guests were sipping California Chardonnay or orange juice before coming to the table, Gromyko appealed to her to whisper "Peace" in her husband's ear every night. She said she would, and added, "I'll tell you the same." Then, standing on tiptoe, she whispered in his ear, "Peace, peace." Gromyko's initial expression of surprise quickly changed to a most uncharacteristic broad smile. Afterward, he frequently recounted the incident.

Caspar Weinberger, William Casey, and other hardliners in the administration were disturbed by Gromyko's visit and the prospect of renewed arms control negotiations. Their attitude was a mirror image of the Soviet refusal to negotiate on INF and START. Until the Soviet Union changed its policies, they argued, the United States should refuse to "honor them" with a dialogue. Secretary of State Shultz and National Security Adviser McFarlane became the main targets. Hardliners in the administration redoubled efforts to force their resignation, largely through spreading gossip that they were soft on the Soviet Union. Reagan resented the efforts to remove Shultz and McFarlane, because he knew that they were carrying out his policies more faithfully than Weinberger and Casey. He notes in his memoirs:

> Cap [Weinberger] was not as interested as George [Shultz] in opening negotiating with the Russians, and some of his advisors at the Pentagon strongly opposed some of my ideas on arms control that George supported. . . . Cap had allies among some of my more conservative political supporters, who let me know they thought Shultz had gone soft on the Russians and they wanted me to fire him—an idea, I told them, that was utter nonsense.[16]

During October, Reagan and much of the White House staff (though not the NSC) were preoccupied with the election campaign. Nevertheless, those of us responsible for advising on policy toward the Soviet Union understood that General Secretary Chernenko was not in good health and would probably not last much longer. The evidence was that Mikhail Gorbachev was acting as "second secretary" (though he had never been given that title) and was, in effect, in charge of the Politburo. We were eager to make direct contact with him, but it was not obvious how we should go about this. His only government position was as head of a committee in the Supreme Soviet, the nominal legislature.

Since, in terms of power, his real position was roughly comparable to the vice president of the United States, we thought first of trying to arrange a meeting between Gorbachev and Vice President Bush. When Bush decided to go to Geneva in April to present the U.S. proposal to ban chemical weapons, we tried to send a message through the U.S. ambassador to the Committee on Disarmament, Louis Fields, and his Soviet counterpart, Victor Israelyan. Recognizing the delicacy of relations within the Politburo and the danger that the Soviet foreign ministry would take the idea of a Bush-Gorbachev meeting as an American provocation, Israelyan decided not to relay the message to Moscow.

Nevertheless, Bush persisted, meeting privately with Israelyan when he was in Geneva and telling him that he would welcome a meeting with "your next leader, Gorbachev." This time, Israelyan reported the conversation in a private letter to Georgy Korniyenko, Gromyko's first deputy, but even then

refrained from naming Gorbachev, referring only to Bush's desire for an informal meeting with a Soviet leader "at the same level as himself." When he
next visited Moscow, he told Gromyko of the approach. Gromyko listened
intently but made no comment.[17]

Lacking any response from Moscow to the feelers put out in Geneva, we
discussed the possibility of an invitation with congressional leaders and
tried to make contact through Finnish president Mauno Koivisto, who had
called on Gorbachev during a visit to Moscow. We also encouraged the
U.S.-USSR Trade and Economic Council, an organization of private American businesspeople and Soviet foreign trade officials, to urge their Soviet
counterparts to bring Gorbachev to the United States for a planned meeting
of the council in Washington in the spring of 1985.

When we learned that Gorbachev, wearing his Supreme Soviet hat, would
be visiting London in December 1984, Shultz told Soviet ambassador Dobrynin that we would welcome a Gorbachev visit to the United States and
would arrange an invitation in any manner he wished. Dobrynin sent two
telegrams to Gromyko relaying the invitation while the Soviet party was
in London, but Gromyko refused to pass them on to Gorbachev. When
Gromyko next saw Dobrynin, he complained about the messages, saying
that there was no need to involve Gorbachev in U.S.-Soviet relations. Gorbachev was aware that U.S. officials were trying to arrange a visit, but was
unable to respond without seeming, in his words, "overly ambitious" to his
colleagues. He had to wait until he had been elevated to power before he
could contemplate direct dealings with American officials.[18]

Even after the election, the now open rivalry between Shultz and Weinberger did not ease.

In November, Reagan noted in his diary: "[The dispute] is so out of hand
George sounds like he wants out. I can't let that happen. Actually George is
carrying out my policy. I'm going to meet with Cap and Bill [Casey] and lay
it out to them."[19]

Ironically, some in the anti-Shultz cabal bandied the slogan "Let Reagan
be Reagan," as if the president were being hoodwinked by weak-kneed advisers. It was an insult to a president who knew very well what he was doing,
and why.

Despite the rumors spread by Shultz's critics that the president would reverse his policy of seeking accommodation with the Soviet Union now that
he was reelected, Reagan ordered full speed ahead. He had never considered
his speeches and proposals in 1984 an election gimmick.

Negotiations with the Soviet foreign ministry became more intense. In
January 1985, Shultz and Gromyko met in Geneva in a marathon six-hour

session, during which they reached an agreement to revive the suspended arms control negotiations. The United States accepted the Soviet demand to negotiate on weaponry used in strategic defense, while the Soviet Union agreed to resume negotiations on both strategic offensive weapons and intermediate-range nuclear weapons. Gromyko insisted, however, on a double linkage of the areas of negotiation. There could be no agreement on INF, he insisted, without one on START. Additionally, there could be no agreement on either of those weapon types without an agreement regarding "space weapons."

These demands seemed utterly impractical to Secretary Shultz, since the resulting package was so complicated that it was very unlikely everything could be solved at once. Nevertheless, for the United States, the important thing was to get negotiations started again. When the Soviet leaders decided that they really wanted an agreement in one of these areas, they would presumably loosen the straitjacket in which Gromyko had bound the talks.

IN THIS FASHION, the United States and Soviet Union were moving toward a less confrontational relationship even before Gorbachev came to office. There was no fundamental change in Soviet policy, however. The Soviet government wished to negotiate primarily on arms control, ignoring most other issues apart from trade and technical cooperation.

Writing after he was forced out of office, Mikhail Gorbachev described Soviet foreign policy before 1985 as follows:

> These [Soviet] concepts rested on a dogmatic world outlook, not on reality, not on a sober analysis of the situation nor on meeting the real and vital interests of our country and our people. Rather, our foreign policy was oriented toward harsh confrontation with the entire outside world. . . .

> Such was the foreign policy legacy of totalitarianism. By its very nature, . . . totalitarianism cannot exist without a harsh ideological and political system, a set of stereotypes that distort reality and have only one purpose—to serve the interests of the regime, to create conditions for its further entrenchment, and to establish a way of thinking among its " loyal subjects" that is purely to the regime's own advantage.[20]

There was, from 1981 to 1984, no hope for any fundamental change in Soviet policy until a new generation came to power. Even then, it would take a while before it was clear to the Soviet leader how dysfunctional the Soviet system had become. The only way the United States could achieve its aim of reducing confrontation and ending the Cold War was to encourage a more open political system in the Soviet Union.

When Chernenko died, the United States had in place a policy framework that grouped a multiplicity of issues into four categories: two related to the arms race and the use of arms in third countries, and two (protecting human rights and raising the Iron Curtain) directly aimed at changing the Soviet system.

Reagan had prepared for Gorbachev. The Soviet leaders were only beginning to come to grips with Reagan.

V

1985: MARCH–JUNE

GORBACHEV IN POWER

When I became head of state, it was already obvious that there was something
wrong in this country. . . . Doomed to serve ideology and bear the heavy
burden of the arms race, it was strained to the utmost.
—MIKHAIL GORBACHEV, December 25, 1991 [1]

I can't claim that I believed from the start that Mikhail Gorbachev was going
to be a different *sort of Soviet leader.*
—RONALD REAGAN, 1990 [2]

WHEN HE WAS told Chernenko had died in the early evening of
March 10, Gorbachev summoned members of the Politburo who
were in Moscow to an emergency session. Moscow Party boss Viktor Grishin had hoped to succeed Chernenko, but realized that his support was not
adequate. Prime Minister Nikolai Tikhonov had earlier tried to keep Gorbachev out of the limelight, but he, too, realized that he could no longer
block Gorbachev's candidacy. Gorbachev's opponents simply did not have
the votes. Therefore, when the Politburo met, Grishin made a desperate effort to keep his job by suggesting that Gorbachev be the chairman of the funeral commission—a designation that would make him heir apparent. No
one objected, but Gorbachev insisted that the Politburo's formal endorsement be deferred until more members could join them the following day. He
explains in his memoirs that he knew he could not change things with a bare
majority. He needed to be sure of overwhelming support at the outset of his
tenure.[3] Therefore, Gorbachev suggested a Politburo meeting at 2 p.m. the
next day, to be followed by a meeting of the entire Central Committee at

five. Before the Politburo met, he called Andrei Gromyko and asked him to come by his office thirty minutes early. They agreed at that time to "work together."

This way, the stage was set for Gromyko to nominate Gorbachev as the new general secretary when the Central Committee met. Gromyko's proposal passed without dissent—indeed, by all accounts, with genuine enthusiasm. Soviet media immediately announced both Chernenko's death and Gorbachev's election.[4]

There had been guarded hints between Gromyko and Gorbachev before this happened. It would have been hazardous for them to discuss the succession with each other before Chernenko died. If word had gotten to Gorbachev's rivals that the two were "conspiring," these rivals might have used it with their colleagues to derail Gorbachev's candidacy, perhaps even to expel him from the Politburo. Therefore, matters were arranged by trusted emissaries, partly in double-talk. Gromyko sent his son, Anatoly, to Alexander Yakovlev, then head of the Institute for International Relations and the World Economy (IMEMO), with the request to pass on an idea to Gorbachev.

In his memoirs, Yakovlev recalls the conversation as follows:

> "Alexander Nikolayevich," young Gromyko said, "so as not to beat around the bush, I'll explain what I have in mind. If it is not acceptable, we'll consider it nothing more than my personal idea and my own initiative. My father is sure that only Gorbachev can lead the Party in the circumstances that prevail. He, Gromyko, is ready to support that idea and to take the initiative at the future meeting of the Politburo. At the same time, he is fed up with working in the Ministry of Foreign Affairs and would like to change jobs. He is thinking about the USSR Supreme Soviet."

Yakovlev took the message to Gorbachev, who mulled it over while pacing in his office. Off and on he would put a question to Yakovlev, then answer it himself. Finally he composed his answer in his mind and told Yakovlev, "Tell Andrei Andreyevich that it has always been pleasant working with him. I will be pleased to do so in the future, whatever positions we both may hold. Oh, and also say that I know how to keep my promises."[5]

For several years, the Party general secretary had simultaneously held the Supreme Soviet chairmanship. Gromyko's proposal was clear: he would support Gorbachev if Gorbachev would make him chief of state rather than taking that honor for himself. Gorbachev kept his implicit promise when, in July, he proposed Gromyko for the prestigious but largely powerless position of chairman of the Presidium of the USSR Supreme Soviet.

Neither Chernenko's death nor the Gorbachev succession surprised the White House. Chernenko had been seriously ill and Gorbachev had been acting as de facto number two, so both events were expected, even though some intelligence analysts had predicted that Viktor Grishin would prevail in the Politburo infighting. This did not seem plausible to those of us on the NSC staff. The immediate question for President Reagan was whether he should attend Chernenko's funeral. I hoped he would, since I felt that, unlike his two predecessors, Mikhail Gorbachev might turn out to be a serious negotiator. Also, a trip by Ronald Reagan to Moscow would have emphasized the U.S. desire to get on seriously with the effort to improve U.S.-Soviet relations.

I was neither surprised nor dismayed, however, when Reagan decided not to go to Moscow at that time, but to "send George," as he had to Brezhnev's and Andropov's funerals. Reagan knew that any meeting with Gorbachev would be short both in length and substance, and its impact would be diffused by Gorbachev's meetings with many other foreign visitors. He preferred to wait until he could talk to Gorbachev without the distraction of unrelated events.

Thus, once again, Vice President George Bush, accompanied by Secretary of State George Shultz, represented the president at a Soviet leader's funeral. When they met Mikhail Gorbachev they delivered a letter from President Reagan with an invitation to come to the United States. Both Bush and Shultz came away with the strong impression that, finally, a Soviet leader had come to power who might be different from his predecessors. While Gorbachev gave no hint that he would question or change any Soviet policies, he did seem a man who would make up his own mind rather than blindly follow tradition. When the Americans reported to the president, they endorsed Prime Minister Thatcher's view that Gorbachev was a man one could do business with.

Gorbachev was less favorably impressed by Bush and Shultz. Politburo minutes reveal that he commented to his colleagues: "Frankly, the American delegation made a pretty ordinary impression on us. They are not a very serious lot. . . . When I touched on questions that were outside the framework of Bush's text, he became confused."[6]

Gorbachev's true judgment was almost certainly less dismissive than his report to the Politburo would suggest. He was, after all, a new general secretary trying to impress his colleagues with his own competence and firmness. He had not yet removed his opponents from the leadership.

An Unlikely Pair

IT WOULD BE hard to imagine two persons who present a greater contrast than Ronald Reagan and Mikhail Gorbachev in their family backgrounds, their careers, and their political philosophies.

Reagan grew up under far from affluent circumstances in small towns of the American Midwest, was better at athletics than his studies, and made a career as a film actor and trade union leader before entering politics. Gorbachev was born in a Russian peasant family as the country was plunged into turmoil and famine by Stalin's forced collectivization of agriculture, as a child lived briefly under German occupation during World War II, and survived the wartime and immediate postwar hardships that claimed the lives of many of weaker constitution. Nevertheless, his record in school was so promising that he was admitted to the Soviet Union's most prestigious institution of higher education, Moscow State University, where his political career began as a Komsomol (Young Communist) leader.

Reagan's political career began relatively late in life, but with election as governor of his country's most populous state, he was suddenly catapulted to national prominence. Gorbachev entered the Soviet political establishment right out of college, but near the bottom as a local official of the Communist Party's youth wing. Reagan's success in American politics depended on his ability to attract votes. Gorbachev's rise in the Soviet Union depended on his ability to please his superiors, to curry favor with those most likely to prevail in the byzantine infighting of Communist leaders, and—above all—to avoid seeming a threat to those in power. Reagan built his political platform on challenges to the policies of his predecessors; Gorbachev succeeded by conforming to the political system he served, up to the point that he became its master.

Reagan had developed a visceral hatred of communism during the struggle for control of the Screen Actors Guild in Hollywood following World War II. Gorbachev had to behave as a true believer in Marxist-Leninist ideology to survive in the Communist Party of the Soviet Union. Although he was eventually to reject Stalinism, he continued to believe that Lenin had been a great leader.

To describe the difference in the two men's philosophies as that between capitalism and communism is too general to provide much insight. While enormously proud of his country and the capacity of Americans to improve their own lot and be a positive force in the world, Reagan believed that the U.S. government had become too large, expensive, and intrusive and should be trimmed back. He believed that taxes had become so high that they were stifling economic growth and therefore should be reduced. But he was not in favor of dismantling the welfare programs created by Franklin Roosevelt (whom he had supported in his younger years). Though he and his supporters spoke of a "Reagan Revolution," what he had in mind was not a revolution at all but instead marginal changes that would reverse what he viewed as a trend toward bigger and bigger government and an ever weaker private sector.

When he came to power, Gorbachev still believed in the Soviet system as it had evolved. He knew that it had flaws, and serious ones, and recognized that it was working more and more poorly. But he thought that a little tinkering with the mechanism was all that was needed. He was convinced that the instrument to achieve these changes would be the Communist Party itself. Through most of the 1980s, Gorbachev believed in more government rather than less. He was to modify his beliefs during the years between 1985 and 1991 when he was the preeminent Soviet leader, but we should note that when he and the American president began their interaction, Reagan's public rhetoric was the more radical on domestic issues. It is an irony that Gorbachev's policies eventually turned out to be not only more radical, but truly revolutionary, for they ended by destroying the system they were intended to save.

There were some parallels in the two men's experience. Each had mastered the political process in his own country, and some qualities that make for effective political leadership are relevant everywhere. But life in the United States was so different from that in the Soviet Union that they had acquired few, if any, intellectual touch points before they began dealing with each other. In 1985 nobody who knew them could have imagined that personal warmth would be possible.

We can exaggerate their differences; it would be wrong to think that Reagan and Gorbachev stood poles apart in every respect. When they came to power, both had visions of changing the political systems they headed. Each had an abundance of self-confidence and was convinced that he was not simply a victim of blind forces but could make a difference. Both were blessed with happy marriages and wives in whom they could confide. While both talked a lot about ideology, they were more influenced by personal interaction than by theoretical preconceptions. Each was, in his own way, a pragmatist, adept at adjusting erstwhile principles to actual experience.

Nevertheless, these parallels and similarities, such as they were, provided slight grounds for the fruitful personal interaction that ultimately emerged. We can only be astonished that, over the historically brief period from 1985 to 1988, Ronald Reagan and Mikhail Gorbachev managed to find a common language, to build, step by frequently faltering step, a foundation of respect and trust, and on that basis to forge a common purpose that allowed them to transform the political landscape of the entire world.

This happened because Gorbachev was different from the Soviet leaders he succeeded, and Reagan was different from the false image many of his critics—and some of his supporters—fashioned of him.

Delays and New Problems

IN APRIL, EVEN before the U.S. and USSR had agreed when and where their leaders would meet, officials in the State Department wanted to discuss arrangements with their Soviet counterparts. They also wanted to renew the special channel with Soviet ambassador Anatoly Dobrynin. Neither Bud McFarlane nor I thought that these were good ideas. Trying to decide how to conduct the meeting before we knew when and where it would take place would have been pointless. Use of the Soviet ambassador as a special channel would have bypassed our ambassador in Moscow, Arthur Hartman, and blocked our direct access to Soviet decision makers until the meeting occurred.

There were additional reasons to question the State Department's judgment. Although we had made progress in defining the U.S. agenda, the president had not yet focused adequately on the specific content of our proposals. We needed to use the prospect of a summit to encourage him to make some hard decisions. Discussion of modalities rather than substance would be distracting at that point. Furthermore, any attempt to reestablish the Dobrynin special channel would have met the furious opposition of the Department of Defense. It would have exacerbated the bureaucratic infighting that already had reached a dangerously high level, and would have made it much more difficult to persuade the president to approve positions recommended by Shultz but opposed by Weinberger.

President Reagan agreed that it was premature to discuss arrangements for a summit before we knew when and where it would be. He also was determined to do as much business as possible through the American embassy in Moscow. He had the opportunity to discuss the prospects for dealing with Gorbachev when Ambassador Hartman came to Washington for consultations in April. Hartman thought Gorbachev would not be easy to deal with. Hartman said—quite accurately—that Gorbachev would be preoccupied for some time with consolidating his power, leaving him little time to revamp foreign policy, which he was unlikely to do in any case since he was, in Hartman's words, "a narrow fellow, of set views." Secretary Shultz commented that Gorbachev might be more dangerous than his predecessors because he lacked some of their faults. As he noted in his diary that evening, Reagan concluded that "Gorbachev will be as tough as any of their leaders."[7]

Although I knew that Gorbachev would need some time to establish his authority and would be a formidable debater, I thought we had scant reason to predict that he would be as narrow-minded as his predecessors. There was considerable evidence that he was dissatisfied with Soviet economic performance, and also that his thinking was more flexible than that of his predecessors. The Soviet policies he had inherited were not working, and as this became apparent I suspected that he would try to find ways to change them. Unlike many of my colleagues in the State Department, I was not in favor of major alterations in U.S. arms control policies until the Soviet government had demonstrated a willingness to solve some of the other issues on the U.S. agenda. I felt time was working to the advantage of the United States. If there was to be a window of opportunity for major agreements, it would occur after Gorbachev had full command of the Soviet leadership and had come to the conclusion that the Soviet Union required more than arms control agreements to solve its problems. Therefore, throughout 1985 and 1986, I advised Reagan to develop proposals that would encourage Soviet restraint abroad and reform at home and to be patient.

It was not easy to keep attention on the main questions. Unexpected events kept intruding. One of these was the tragic death of U.S. Army Major Arthur D. Nicholson, Jr., who was shot by a guard at a Soviet base in East Germany in late March. Major Nicholson had been attached to the U.S. military liaison mission at Potsdam, but had intruded in an area the Soviet military considered closed. The Soviet guard who shot him refused to allow Nicholson's driver to give first aid.

As with the KAL shootdown, the Soviet refusal to describe what had happened exacerbated the offense. According to Sergei Tarasenko, who at that time worked on the U.S. desk in the Soviet foreign ministry, the Soviet sentry had left his post without authorization, and therefore did not challenge Nicholson when he entered the restricted area. When the guard returned to his post, he spotted an intruder, panicked (since he had violated strict regulations in leaving his post), and fired his rifle. The bullet, as a subsequent autopsy proved, struck Nicholson in the heart and killed him instantly. Prompt medical attention would not have saved him.[8]

However, the United States was never told what had happened, but instead was given a version that mixed fact with fiction to place the responsibility on Nicholson, not the Soviet sentry. The official Soviet explanation was that Nicholson had entered a clearly marked prohibited area, was illegally photographing a Soviet military installation, and when spotted refused the sentry's order to halt. Instead, he tried to escape and was therefore shot. It was this inaccurate version that convinced Weinberger and Reagan that the shooting had been deliberate.[9]

Defense Secretary Weinberger demanded that negotiations with the Soviets be terminated until they apologized and paid compensation to the Nicholson family. The Soviets refused to do either, although they eventually expressed "regret" and Eduard Shevardnadze, their new foreign minister, offered his personal apology to Shultz.

Even if the Soviet claim that Nicholson had deliberately intruded in a restricted area and disobeyed an order to halt had been correct, the Soviet sentry's action was inexcusable. Members of the counterpart Soviet liaison mission attached to the U.S. Army in Frankfurt, West Germany, were caught from time to time in restricted areas. They were not shot, but escorted out, warned, and formal protests were lodged with the Soviet commander.

Soviet officials suggested that the U.S. and Soviet commanders in Germany meet and try to establish procedures that would prevent such incidents in the future. This seemed a reasonable course to the Joint Chiefs of Staff, the NSC staff, and the State Department. However, Weinberger continued to oppose a meeting until the Soviet government met his demands. Reagan rejected Weinberger's advice and backed the position that the commanders in Germany should meet, whether or not the Soviet government apologized and agreed to compensation. The meeting was further delayed, however, when Weinberger blocked a message to this effect, and then, confronted with a direct order from the president, tacked on conditions that had been specifically rejected.[10]

Accounts of a "State-Defense" rift appeared in several newspapers on April 4. They seemed to stem from the office of the secretary of defense. Bud McFarlane's deputy, Admiral John Poindexter, exclaimed, "That troglodyte again!" when he read an article by Bernard Gwertzman in the *New York Times* reporting infighting between the State and Defense Departments. Actually, there was no "State-Defense" disagreement, but a disagreement Secretary Weinberger had with the Joint Chiefs of Staff, the National Security Council, the State Department, and—hardly least—the president of the United States.

In this instance, Weinberger's insubordination was not long lasting. After a few days of bureaucratic arm wrestling in Washington, appropriate instructions were sent to the American commander in Germany, who proceeded to meet with his Soviet counterpart. The commanders agreed on procedures to deal with unauthorized intrusions into restricted areas. From that time, there were no serious incidents at our respective military bases in Germany.

The incident made clear to the NSC staff the problems it would face in trying to implement presidential decisions if the United States moved toward more active negotiations with the Soviet Union. Whereas most departments would obey a decision by the president, one could never be sure that Weinberger would. If he disliked a decision, distorted leaks to favored journalists—perhaps not from Weinberger himself, but obviously from someone in his department—would turn up in the press. The obvious intent was to bring public pressure on the president.

Caspar Weinberger was utterly convinced that there was no potential benefit in negotiating anything with the Soviet leaders and that most negotiations were dangerous traps. He expressed his views most clearly in a book published in 1990 when he observed:

> A recent, rather startling poll indicated that 71 percent of Republicans and 74 percent of Democrats believe that the United States can trust the General Secretary of the Soviet Union [*sic*],* Mikhail Gorbachev. Trust in what sense?
>
> Trust that Mr. Gorbachev will turn his back on the goals of the Soviet state? Trust that he is becoming more like us in economic values? Trust that the Soviet Union will never violate an agreement with the United States (the historical record notwithstanding)? Trust that Mr. Gorbachev is diametrically opposed to the precepts of the Communist Party that he heads (precepts that are, of course, diametrically opposed to Western values and principles)?
>
> All of this is highly unlikely.[11]

Two years before these words were published, it was obvious to unbiased observers that Gorbachev was trying to do all of the things Weinberger ridiculed as unlikely. Whether he would succeed was still very much in question, but it should have been clear that one does not have to "trust" some version of perfection to attempt to influence developments in a favorable direction. If Weinberger's standards were applied literally to any foreign leader, the United States would be left with nobody to negotiate with on anything. After all, negotiation was a tool to test whether Gorbachev meant what he said.

Ronald Reagan's favorite phrase during the last years of his presidency,

* Gorbachev's actual title was general secretary of the Communist Party of the Soviet Union.

"Trust, but verify," was directed not only at Gorbachev—to explain why we needed reliable verification of agreements—but also at those in his own administration who, like Weinberger, persisted in opposing realistic negotiations with the Soviet Union. If Gorbachev had understood this better, he would not have been so annoyed at Reagan's repeated use of it.

When leaks that misrepresented his ideas turned up in the press, most often in the *Washington Times* or in comments by columnists and television pundits Rowland Evans and Robert Novak, Reagan was annoyed, sometimes even infuriated, but he usually tolerated them. He disliked direct confrontation with cabinet members, particularly old friends like Weinberger. He also understood that he would need the acquiescence, if not the active support, of the hardliners in his administration if he was to implement a positive agenda with the Soviet Union. Therefore, when confronted with reports in the press that distorted his views, he would usually just shrug, reiterate his instructions, and expect his staff to see that they were carried out.

By leaving to the National Security Council the hard task of keeping reluctant cabinet members in line, President Reagan encouraged practices which in time would bring his presidency to the brink of disaster.

Perils of Diplomacy in Public

THE NEGOTIATIONS ON nuclear weapons and defensive systems had reconvened in Geneva a few weeks before Gorbachev became general secretary, but they made no real progress during the initial session. Neither side had altered its position sufficiently to interest the other. The Soviet insistence on settling all three negotiations (START, INF, and strategic defense) before any could be resolved reduced any American incentive to propose compromises.

Gorbachev was eager for progress in controlling arms since it was plain that the Soviet economy was suffering from the overwhelming burden of military spending. Given the attitude of his Politburo colleagues at the time, however, he could not justify reining in the Soviet military-industrial complex without agreements with the United States to limit arms. At the same time, he lacked both the authority and the desire to change Soviet negotiating positions. Therefore, his moves had to concentrate more on influencing public opinion in the West than on addressing the real concerns of his negotiating partners.

On April 7, Gorbachev announced, in an interview published in *Pravda,* that the Soviet Union would halt its deployment of further SS-20 missiles in

Europe until November, and would continue a moratorium on deployment if the United States would stop placing Pershing IIs and cruise missiles in Europe. The United States and leaders of other NATO countries immediately rejected the offer. The Soviet Union already had in place 414 SS-20s, each with three nuclear warheads. NATO had at that point only 143 warheads on intermediate-range missiles in Europe. With only slight exaggeration, the Reagan administration charged that Gorbachev wanted to freeze a ten-to-one Soviet advantage in this class of weaponry.* Suspicions of Gorbachev's intent were exacerbated by his failure to discuss his proposal with the U.S. president before he announced it to the public.

In late July, Gorbachev announced another moratorium, this time on nuclear tests: the Soviet Union, he said, would stop all nuclear testing from August 6, 1985, until January 1, 1986, and would be willing to extend the moratorium if the United States would do likewise.

Washington also rejected this idea. U.S. intelligence agencies suspected that Soviet scientists had just completed a series of tests and for a few months had no need for further testing. Many American officials were not confident that the United States could detect low-yield underground tests without instruments near the testing ground. They were particularly wary of unverified moratoria, since Khrushchev had announced one, only to break it suddenly, even though President John Kennedy had halted U.S. testing in response. American officials who were active at that time resolved never to be taken in again. "Fool me once, shame on you, fool me twice . . ."

I was one of those officials, since I was serving in our embassy in Moscow when the Soviet Union suddenly renounced the moratorium it had proposed and the United States accepted. Therefore, while I did not buy the argument that the U.S. needed to continue testing to ensure the safety and reliability of its nuclear weapons, I considered an unverified moratorium that could be broken by either side if it so decided of little benefit, more likely to lead to suspicion and mutual recrimination than a real slowing of the arms race.† A test ban that could be verified, imposed in the context of a substan-

---

* The United States had deployed 63 Pershing II missiles and 80 ground-launched cruise missiles (GLCMs) in Europe, each with a single warhead. The nuclear warhead ratio was, therefore, 1,242 to 143, or 8.69 to 1. The American GLCMs were, however, less capable than the SS-20s and the Pershing IIs.

† Once a weapons design has been thoroughly tested, safety can be assured by close monitoring, testing components, and computer simulations. Over time, reliability would probably decline somewhat with or without periodic testing. However, this would never be sufficient to undermine the capacity of the weapons to deter. A hostile state would no more risk inviting a retaliatory strike of 90 percent effectiveness than one of 99 percent effectiveness!

tial reduction of nuclear arms, would be a different matter, but this was not what Gorbachev offered.

As he had done in April when he offered to freeze INF deployments, Gorbachev proclaimed a test moratorium without prior discussion or even notification. This suggested that Gorbachev had nothing more than propaganda in mind. He was trying to occupy the high ground of public opinion without altering any of the fundamental Soviet policies.

Public opinion was, doubtless, a factor in his decision, but nevertheless Gorbachev had overridden doubts in the Soviet military to make his proposal. He faced substantial opposition in Moscow to a halt in nuclear testing. In retrospect, U.S. agreement to a temporary moratorium while negotiating measures for on-site inspection might have accelerated Gorbachev's rethinking of Soviet positions. If Gorbachev had discussed the idea privately with Reagan, offered deep cuts in heavy missiles, and agreed to some on-site inspection, Reagan might possibly have considered a test ban after a few scheduled tests had been completed. But given past Soviet deception, the proposal's propaganda coloration, and the Soviet refusal to allow monitoring on the nuclear test sites themselves, the moratorium proposal had no chance in Washington. Gorbachev was ill advised to make the proposal the way he did and to persist in considering Reagan's reaction a test of his willingness to reduce weaponry.

ANTICIPATING A MEETING with Gorbachev, Reagan moderated his criticism of the Soviet Union, while holding to the positions he had set out. Gorbachev was less careful. The speech he delivered on May 8 to commemorate the World War II victory in Europe was particularly offensive to Washington and to American allies. Conveniently forgetting about the Nazi-Soviet Pact of 1939 and ignoring the fact that France and Britain went to war against Germany when the Soviet Union was, in effect, allied to it, he charged that the "Western powers" were criminally liable for their "Munich policy" and their "connivance" with Hitler's aggression. Not content with this flagrant distortion, he went on to state that "unfortunately, history is repeating itself," thus implying that the leaders of the NATO countries were the heirs of Hitler.

As for the future, Gorbachev called for a revival of the "process of détente," but only for a transitional period. "Détente is not the final goal of politics," he observed. He then chose his words carefully, but left no doubt as to what he believed would follow this transitional period. "Our allegiance to the policy of peaceful coexistence is evidence of the strength of the new social system, of its faith in its historical possibilities. It meets the interests of all countries and peoples."[12]

Reagan spoke the same day to the European Parliament in Strasbourg, France. While he criticized the Soviet military buildup, particularly the impending deployment of a new ICBM, the SS-24, and noted that the Soviet system "ultimately satisfies neither material nor spiritual needs," his emphasis was on the need for dialogue and radical, verifiable arms reduction. He used the occasion neither to charge that the Communist Party of the Soviet Union was an heir of Nazism because its alliance with Hitler had contributed to the start of World War II, nor to suggest that reducing military confrontations would merely bring about a transition period to a world dominated by the United States.[13]

Some in Washington took Gorbachev's speech as proof that he was "tougher" and more ideological than his predecessors. I gave it little weight, however, since I did not expect to see any modifications of Soviet policy until Gorbachev had dealt with his rivals. Furthermore, I assumed that his speech was a staff-written effort to inspire the faithful, not a considered policy speech. It was, in the Soviet context, the equivalent of a campaign speech by an American political candidate.

Dealing with Allies

SOVIET "ALLIES" WERE not a problem for Gorbachev in 1985. The countries of the Warsaw Pact were controlled at that time by Communist Parties that, with the occasional exception of the Romanian, were conditioned to do Moscow's bidding. In contrast, Reagan could not take his allies for granted. Although governments in the key European NATO countries had resisted public pressure to stop the deployment of INF missiles and had swallowed some doubts about Reagan's willingness to negotiate, all were under domestic pressure to show more "flexibility" in dealing with the Soviet Union. Self-styled "peace movements" were particularly strong in Germany, the Low Countries, and Scandinavia. It seemed most European intellectuals were enamored of the idea of a nuclear freeze. Though Europeans were most directly affected by the Iron Curtain that divided the Continent, there was extreme nervousness, especially in Germany, over any attempt to challenge the territorial status quo. Helmut Schmidt, the leader of Germany's Social Democratic Party, had scolded Secretary of State Haig in 1981 for attempts to "stir up" Eastern Europe, and his doubts about Reagan's policies became more shrill and more public after he lost the election in 1983 to Helmut Kohl.

These pressures were, of course, no secret. The Soviet government had depended on them to thwart the INF deployments, and though it had been disappointed, there was still a conviction in Moscow that key European countries could be used to "moderate" American policy. During Gorbachev's first year in office, he gave more attention to the Europeans than to testing Reagan's intentions.

However, attention alone was insufficient to wean the Europeans from their American alliance. The Europeans considered the Soviet SS-20s a serious threat and Gorbachev initially showed no inclination to eliminate them. The conventional arms balance was so much in favor of the Warsaw Pact as to belie Soviet protestations that they had only a peaceful intent. Soviet negotiators still resisted any idea of reducing their forces to something like parity with NATO. Soviet pressure on Poland to suppress the Solidarity movement by force continued, as did Soviet military intervention in Afghanistan. Much as the Europeans yearned for kinder talk, relaxation, and an end to the arms race, most saw that it was Soviet actions rather than American words that caused most of the tension. Until he changed some traditional Soviet policies, Gorbachev was unlikely to make much headway with the Europeans. Once he was willing to make these changes, they would work equally well with the Americans.

For these reasons, Reagan was never seriously concerned that any key U.S. ally would desert him. He was sympathetic, however, to the political problems friends like Margaret Thatcher and Helmut Kohl faced. It was that sympathy that caused him to agree to Kohl's plea for a joint visit to the military cemetery at Bitburg to symbolize post–World War II reconciliation. Kohl and Mitterrand had earlier visited the cemetery at Verdun to bury the hostile emotions wars had produced in Germany and France, and Kohl saw the visit to Bitburg as a counterpart act that would bring closure to the hostile emotions of World War II. Neither Kohl nor Reagan was aware that some bodies of Waffen SS troops* were buried at that cemetery when they agreed on a joint visit.

When this fact became known, there was a storm of opposition to the Bitburg visit in the United States. Critics argued that the visit would somehow "honor" the Nazis and downplay their atrocities. Many of Reagan's domestic advisers urged him to cancel the visit, but Reagan refused to do so. He felt he

* Unlike the regular SS, who were volunteers and vicious Nazi enforcers, the Waffen SS was made up of conscripts late in the war when the troops buried at Bitburg would have been killed.

owed the gesture to Kohl, who had held steadfast on INF deployments and re-jected the feckless criticism of the United States purveyed by his opponents in Germany's Social Democratic Party. Of course, neither Kohl nor Reagan went to the Bitburg cemetery to honor the Nazis in any way, and Reagan never understood why anyone could think they did. Reagan's speech there, and his visit to the former death camp at Bergen-Belsen—added to the itin-erary after the controversy over Bitburg arose—made his attitude crystal clear.[14]

Reagan was also aware that none of his European or Canadian friends were enthusiastic about SDI, and that Thatcher and François Mitterrand, the French president, loathed his talk of abolishing nuclear weapons. They felt that his dream gave comfort to the domestic elements that opposed nuclear weapons in Britain and France. Though their doubts did not change his mind about the desirability of SDI or of a nuclear-free world, it stimulated him to cast about for ways to give the allies a stake in SDI. Officials in the State De-partment, Department of Defense, and the National Security Council agreed that some of the research required could be conducted in allied countries. Reagan endorsed the idea with enthusiasm and instructed his staff to work with the State and Defense Departments to develop a proposal to discuss with other governments.

I supported the idea, but with two caveats. First, I thought that we needed to make sure, before we made an offer, that the Department of Defense would be willing to let a substantial number of contracts to allied firms. U.S. defense contractors would lobby to minimize foreign participation and their supporters would argue that we should not share sensitive technology with foreign countries. The proposal could be controversial in Congress, which would have to appropriate the funds. It was important to consult congres-sional leaders and the chairmen and senior members of the Armed Services Committees as we developed a proposal. Second, we needed to consult the allied governments before making a public announcement. The issue would be politically difficult for them. We would need to explain what we had in mind and estimate the value of contracts to be let. If other governments were interested, we would need their advice on how best to make the announce-ment in order to achieve the purpose we had in mind: a shared interest in SDI.

Just as staff work got under way, however, Secretary Weinberger made a public announcement offering to share SDI research with the allies. The State Department and NSC were inundated with inquiries and protests from allied governments. What do you have in mind? Why weren't we consulted?

Don't you realize that this is a delicate issue at home? Oh, and by the way, how much of the research do you plan to share if we go along?

We were unable to answer a single one of these questions. My superiors on the NSC and colleagues in the State Department were convinced that Weinberger had gone public precisely with the intent to kill the whole idea, while professing to be carrying out the president's wishes (and his own earlier recommendation). Maybe so. Or maybe he just wanted to step into the limelight. Nevertheless, my earlier premonitions turned out to be accurate: though both the NSC and the State Department pressed to get the Defense Department to specify what sort of SDI research contracts it would conclude with allied firms, there was never a clear answer. The incident, in the end, heightened rather than reduced allied reservations about the whole SDI concept, even though agreements were eventually signed with Britain and Germany.

During the spring another issue with the Soviet Union and with U.S. allies loomed. It had to do with the unratified SALT II treaty. Although the treaty had not come into force, both countries had continued to abide by the restrictions it placed on the number of strategic weapons.* But the time came when a new U.S. nuclear missile submarine (one of the "Ohio class") was scheduled to be commissioned. If the United States failed to retire one of its older, Poseidon-type submarines, it would exceed the limit specified by the treaty. The navy had designated a submarine for the scrap heap, having no need or desire to keep it in service, and this would have kept the United States in compliance.

However, civilian officials in the Defense Department objected. Supported by Secretary Weinberger, they wished to violate the SALT II limits in order to make a political point. They were dubious of the value of arms control treaties in general and wanted the United States to free itself from as many treaty restrictions as possible. They also thought the Soviet Union was acting contrary to some treaty provisions, most importantly in developing two missiles of a new type when the treaty permitted only one. The U.S., they argued, should make a point of demonstrating that it was not bound by provisions of the SALT II treaty.

U.S. allies did not see it that way. For them it was not a question of legal

---

* According to international law, states are obligated to abide by the terms of treaties pending ratification so long as they intend to ratify the treaty. However, the SALT II treaty had been withdrawn from the Senate by the Carter administration and Reagan had announced early in his term that he would not seek ratification since he considered the treaty "fatally flawed." The United States was, therefore, not legally bound to observe the limits it set.

rights but political and military logic. They might have been persuaded that the U.S. was entitled to violate the numerical limits of an unratified treaty if the USSR had exceeded the limits or if there had been a military reason for the step. In this case, however, there was no military necessity. The navy had no use for the old submarine once the new one was in service. Why would the United States willfully violate an agreement, the Europeans asked, if it was committed to ending the arms race? If the United States refused to stay within the SALT II limits, it would play right into the hands of Soviet propagandists, who were arguing that the Reagan administration was not interested in arms control, but only in using negotiations as a cover to develop military superiority—and perhaps even to unleash a nuclear war.

After weeks of hesitation, Reagan decided to decommission the old submarine and stay within the SALT II limits. However, he tried to appease the hardliners in the Defense Department by describing Soviet treaty violations in his public statement and promising "appropriate and proportionate responses to Soviet non-compliance."[15] European allies applauded the decision, but were uneasy about the direction Reagan's policy might take in the future. In Moscow, Soviet officials cited the decision as "proof" that Reagan had no genuine interest in limiting arms.

Communication in Private

THE PUBLIC DIALOGUE was marked more by debate and accusations than by genuine communication. Nevertheless, Reagan and Gorbachev entered into an exchange of lengthy letters in which they explained their positions in detail. The tone of the correspondence was invariably respectful, even when they disagreed on the matters discussed. Gorbachev reiterated traditional Soviet positions and harped on his suspicion that SDI (which he called "space weaponry") was a cover for an offensive, maybe even first-strike, strategy. Reagan stressed the need to build trust, reduce weapons to a common low level, and deal with regional issues and human rights. He defended SDI as a purely defensive strategy and warned that he would not under any circumstances terminate the research program he had initiated.

In addition to the direct correspondence, there were many indirect contacts. Speaker of the House Thomas P. "Tip" O'Neill led a delegation of congressmen to Moscow in April. When the group met with Gorbachev, they delivered a letter from Reagan. Secretary of Commerce Malcolm Baldrige made the trip in May for a meeting of the revived U.S.-USSR Trade and Economic Council (its first since the invasion of Afghanistan) and spent over two hours with Gorbachev.[16] He, too, brought a letter from Reagan. Traditionally, presidential letters carried by congressmen and cabinet members other than the secretary of state are more ceremonial than substantive, serving as little more than letters of introduction. In these instances, Reagan used the letters to make specific points, such as the need to improve the political relationship before trade could expand. But most discussion of disputed issues took place in the private correspondence.

Renewed U.S. attempts to establish a regular private channel for informal discussion of issues came to naught. Before I came to Moscow in May with Secretary Baldrige, I asked the U.S. embassy in Moscow to make an appointment for me with Vadim Zagladin, still deputy head of the Central Committee International Department, while I was there, as it had the previous year when I was in Moscow during Andropov's funeral. Zagladin had seemed to me a better listener than our normal interlocutors in the foreign ministry. By discussing with him the issues that might come up at the summit, we hoped to get a better fix on Gorbachev's priorities and to provide an explanation of U.S. policy not filtered through the Soviet embassy in Washington or the Ministry of Foreign Affairs in Moscow. However, the American embassy requested the appointment not for me alone, but for Ambassador Arthur Hartman and me together. Since Gromyko insisted that Central Committee staffers not deal with Western ambassadors, Zagladin was not permitted to make an appointment to see both of us. He explained his situation to an American businessman who was in Moscow at the time and asked him to let me know that he could receive me alone, but not with Hartman.

When I explained the situation to Hartman, he was adamant that I should not call on Zagladin alone. "We shouldn't let them play that game," he observed. I did not understand what "game" he had in mind. Certainly, it was not one to divide counsels in the U.S. government, since President Reagan wanted me to see Zagladin, and Hartman would have been fully informed of what was said. The fact was that we had several indications that Zagladin's thinking, and that of others in the Central Committee Secretariat, was less rigid than Gromyko's.* We presumed that Gorbachev would replace Gromyko as soon as he could and would turn to the Central Committee staff for advice

* On this point we were not mistaken. In his memoirs, Gorbachev comments: "It is noteworthy that in drafting foreign policy documents and statements two trends were clearly discernible. One originated with the Central Committee international department . . . ; the other was that of the Ministry of Foreign Affairs. The former contained an invitation to negotiate, seek agreements, liberalize and upgrade relationships. The latter was more rigid and, one may say, locked in concrete" (Gorbachev, *Memoirs* [New York: Doubleday, 1996], p. 166).

on foreign policy issues. It seemed only prudent to make sure that the advisers closest to Gorbachev were aware of American attitudes and proposals without the spin the Soviet foreign ministry might put on them.

Hartman's attitude was hard for me to understand since I had briefed him fully before and after my previous meetings with Central Committee personnel and had kept him informed of other unofficial contacts, such as that by Lawrence Horowitz, Senator Edward Kennedy's assistant. There could be no question of something being done behind his back. If I had chosen, I could have obtained the president's approval to go to Zagladin's office alone. I decided not to seek such instructions, however, since I believed that ambassadors should have the final say on all official activities in the countries where they are accredited.

Though for a time we were deprived of direct contact with Central Committee officials, we did receive frequent reports from private Americans who met with Zagladin and his colleagues. James Giffen, an American businessman who was then American co-chairman of the U.S.-USSR Trade and Economic Council, frequently reported to us on his meetings. Larry Horowitz also briefed us on his frequent contacts.

Their correspondence and the indirect contacts gave both Reagan and Gorbachev a better idea of each other's positions than the polemics exchanged in public, but a lengthy meeting between Shultz and Gromyko in Vienna in May seemed a wearisome repeat of earlier encounters. Gromyko, who knew that he would soon be replaced as foreign minister, trotted out the same outworn arguments the United States had been rejecting for years. It seemed that his only objective was to goad Shultz into making a suggestion for a date and place for Reagan and Gorbachev to meet.

Finally, a Place and Date

AS GORBACHEV DELAYED setting a date and place for his meeting with Reagan, American officials began to debate whether a location other than Washington would be acceptable. Self-styled hardliners, uncomfortable with the president's desire to have a face-to-face meeting with the Soviet leader, kept insisting that the summit be held in Washington if it was to take place at all. They argued that protocol required this because American presidents had been twice to the Soviet Union (Nixon to Moscow and Ford to Vladivostok in 1974) since a Soviet leader had come to the United States. However, their real reason was to create an image of a Soviet leader begging for concessions. Reagan understood the protocol argument but did not consider it the decisive factor. He had a different reason to prefer an American venue: he wanted to show the Soviet leader the United States in order to convince him that America was a country of peaceful intent, and furthermore a flourishing democracy worthy of emulation. He would often speak of how he would like to take Gorbachev on a helicopter to get a good look at American farms and suburbia from the air. Exposure of that sort to "the real America," he believed, would shake the Marxist faith of any thinking person.

Secretary of State Shultz also preferred to have a summit in Washington, but was convinced that Gorbachev, still new in office, could not take the political risk of coming to Washington without advance assurance that he could sign a major agreement. This was obviously not in the cards. Therefore, Shultz favored meeting in a third country.

My own judgment differed from both the "nowhere-but-Washington" and the "Geneva-is-best" advice. I thought that there were distinct advantages to a meeting in Moscow, as Gorbachev, probably tongue in cheek, suggested. A Reagan trip to Moscow would convey his willingness to go the extra mile to reach agreement. I knew him well enough to be confident that he would not make unwarranted concessions, but his going to Moscow would encourage doubts in Gorbachev's mind about the advice he was getting, which held that Reagan had no desire to solve difficult issues. I also knew that Gorbachev would have to allow Reagan to deliver a nationwide television address if he visited Moscow. This would undermine the Soviet propaganda claim that Reagan was threatening to start a war. The Russian sense of a host's duty would require soft-pedaling anti-American propaganda, and Gorbachev's desire to trumpet "concrete results" would make him more amenable to concessions than he would be if the meeting occurred outside the country. In brief, I felt that a meeting in Moscow would be more promising than one either in Washington or a third country.

As his diary entries show, President Reagan was nearly convinced that he should accept Gorbachev's invitation to meet in Moscow. If Secretary Shultz had agreed, he almost certainly would have done so. But Gromyko was maneuvering to have the meeting in a third country. When he and Shultz met in May, he raised the question in a private conversation following the formal part of the meeting. He did so in a curious, roundabout manner. According to the interpreter's notes, Gromyko put it this way: "Please tell the president that, in my informal, personal opinion, the general secretary is thinking along the lines of November, most likely the second half. As for the place, the general secretary will not be attending the UN General Assembly, and thus the meeting could be held in the Soviet Union. This invitation stands, and if the president wishes, we would be prepared to host him in the Soviet Union. If for some reason that did not suit him, the meeting could be held in some mutually acceptable European country." Shultz's recollection of the conversation differs slightly from the interpreter's notes, but the essence is the same.[17]

I was not convinced that this represented Gorbachev's final position. We had received several reports of comments by Central Committee staffers who indicated that Gorbachev personally wished to come to the United States and was trying to find an acceptable way to do so. And why, if Gromyko had been expressing Gorbachev's view, did he specify that it was *his* "informal, personal opinion"?

I urged McFarlane to suggest that the president make one more attempt to convince Gorbachev to come to the United States, and to accept the invitation to Moscow if he should refuse, rather than agreeing on a third country. After all, it was still May, and if the meeting was to be as late as November, we had time to talk about the best place for it. I thought Reagan's reply should go something like "It's our turn to host you here in America, and I really want to. But if you have reasons not to come, I will accept your invitation to meet in Moscow with pleasure, since I really want to see your country. In that case, of course, I assume you will give me the opportunity to reciprocate next year. I believe that we should start doing business in our respective countries rather than imposing on a third country as if we don't trust one another to be a proper host. Nevertheless, if you find neither of these arrangements acceptable, I will certainly agree to meet you in a third country. The most important thing is for us to get together. We must stop looking for excuses not to meet."

Secretary Shultz had a different opinion. He was so apprehensive that a summit meeting might somehow slip away that he urged Reagan to agree to a meeting in Geneva without further ado. Reagan, eager, above all, to go head-to-head with the Soviet leader, accepted Shultz's advice. And so on July 1 it was settled: the meeting would take place in Geneva in November.

It was clear in Washington that the meeting could not produce a major arms control agreement such as the ABM Treaty that Nixon and Brezhnev had signed in 1972, or the abortive SALT II treaty that Carter and Brezhnev had signed in 1978. Therefore, part of the preparation had to be to lower expectations in both countries for spectacular results. In order to prepare the public not to expect an orgy of treaty signing, which had been the hallmark of the Nixon-Brezhnev summits, McFarlane insisted that we refrain from calling the upcoming encounter a "summit," but rather refer to it as merely a "meeting." Shultz misread his intent, suspecting that the NSC was trying to "downplay" the event.[18] That was not McFarlane's purpose, and his effort to avoid using the word "summit" turned out to be futile. The media and the public were accustomed to calling any meeting between the Soviet and American leaders a summit, and were not about to discard the term. Nevertheless, it was important to make clear in advance that the main goal of the Geneva meeting was not to sign agreements but to open up direct communication between the American president and the Soviet leader.

If there was to be any result other than getting acquainted, the U.S. and Soviet governments needed to improve communication at all levels. With this in mind, Reagan had proposed, in a speech to the United Nations in 1984, regular consultation on regional conflicts by specialists on the various regions in both countries. The Soviet foreign ministry accepted the proposal and offered meetings on most of the regions of the world, including Afghanistan, the Middle East, and Central America. However, the State Department surprised me when it delayed approving consultations on some regions. Secretary Shultz had endorsed the president's proposal, but when the opportunity materialized, some of his assistant secretaries balked. Elliott Abrams, the assistant secretary for inter-American affairs (that is, Latin America), was strongly opposed to discussing Nicaragua or other Western Hemisphere issues with his Soviet counterpart. As a result, Shultz was reluctant to approve all of the consultations the Soviets offered.

I argued that regular consultations by regional specialists would be useful in the long run, if only to give both countries a clearer view of what the other was up to. By late summer, Shultz agreed and instructed all his regional assistants to establish a regular dialogue with their counterparts in the Soviet foreign ministry. Although it took until 1987 and 1988 for these meetings to have results, eventually they achieved spectacular success.

I also felt that it would be useful to initiate regular meetings of senior U.S. and Soviet military officers. It would have been particularly helpful to have Soviet and U.S. generals compare their threat assessments and discuss their reasons for them. Each exaggerated the capability of the other and tended to make their plans on a worst-case analysis. They were unlikely to convince their counterparts that their fears were totally unfounded, but discussion would sensitize both to the particular concerns of the other and mitigate Soviet paranoia.

President Reagan thought meetings of American and Soviet military officers would be a good idea, as did Bud McFarlane and John Poindexter on the NSC staff, the chairman of the Joint Chiefs of Staff, and Soviet specialists in the State Department. The idea was not implemented for several years, however, because of rivalries in Washington—and probably also in

Moscow. Secretary Weinberger did not like the idea and refused to approve any high-level military contacts unless and until he personally met the Soviet minister of defense. Given Weinberger's public attacks on the Soviet Union, his Soviet counterpart never proposed a meeting. Secretary Shultz opposed Weinberger's direct involvement in Soviet affairs, and Weinberger himself did not want to be seen talking to Soviet military leaders. He feared any warmth in the relationship would diminish support for his defense budgets in Congress. Furthermore, there always seemed to be some particular incident, such as the KAL shootdown or the Nicholson killing, that could be used to avoid a meeting of defense ministers. Actually, such incidents could have been used to justify a meeting if there had been a desire for one.

Meanwhile, in Moscow . . .

GROMYKO HAD APPARENTLY decided to leave the foreign ministry on the assumption that his first deputy, Georgy Korniyenko, would succeed him as minister. If that had happened, he could continue to lead the ministry from his new position. He had worked closely with Korniyenko for many years and had picked him to be his principal deputy. He had every reason to expect Korniyenko to keep him informed of developments and to take his views seriously.

Gorbachev had other ideas, but he held his cards close to his chest. It was mid-June before he telephoned Eduard Shevardnadze, the Party boss in Tbilisi, to alert him that he would be offering him a job in Moscow. He didn't say what it would be, only that it would be extremely important. Shevardnadze wrote later that he tried to discourage the idea of a transfer, but Gorbachev insisted. On June 30, Gorbachev telephoned again and told Shevardnadze he wanted him to be minister of foreign affairs; he should come to Moscow the next day for the Politburo meeting that would confirm his selection.

Shevardnadze wrote subsequently that he had often said this was "the greatest surprise of my life." His head swam. He wondered if he had misunderstood, but he hadn't. Gorbachev persisted, and when Shevardnadze protested that he had neither the knowledge nor the experience needed for international diplomacy, Gorbachev told him, "Well, perhaps that's a good thing. Our foreign policy needs a fresh eye, courage, dynamism, innovative approaches."[19]

When Gorbachev told Gromyko he wished to name Shevardnadze foreign minister, Gromyko was stunned, but he knew better than to oppose the

general secretary. Therefore, he did not object openly, even though he considered the appointment a slap in the face, an implicit rejection of his han-
dling of Soviet foreign policy.[20] Alexander Bessmertnykh, one of his
deputies and later Soviet foreign minister himself, recalls the time Gromyko
and Korniyenko returned to the ministry from the Politburo session on
July 1, 1985. As they met the senior staff to convey the news, Gromyko's face
was flushed with rage and Korniyenko's white as a sheet. They had both
been dealt a severe blow.[21]

They should not have been surprised. It should have been clear that Gorbachev chose an outsider, a person who had not been involved in foreign affairs earlier and who was not associated with any clique in Moscow, in order
to bring foreign policy under his direct control.

VI

~∞~

1985: July–October

ENTER SHEVARDNADZE

The contrast between him and Gromyko was breathtaking. . . . He could smile, engage, converse. He had an ability to persuade and to be persuaded.
—George Shultz, 1993[1]

When it has been drilled into you for decades that the peaceful coexistence of countries with different social systems is "a specific form of class warfare," . . . it is incredibly difficult to accept something different immediately, in a flash.
—Eduard Shevardnadze, 1991[2]

EDUARD SHEVARDNADZE DID not have the manner of an autocratic leader. Soft-spoken, invariably courteous to colleagues and subordinates, he moved into Gromyko's office with hardly a ripple. He brought only two staffers from Tbilisi, a bodyguard and the bilingual (Georgian and Russian) journalist Teymuraz Stepanov, who served as his speechwriter. Otherwise he accepted the professional staff in the Ministry of Foreign Affairs that Gromyko had assembled and trained. Insiders feared a purge when he was named, but it did not occur. Shevardnadze established his control of the ministry gradually, giving increasing attention and responsibility to those he found in accord with his views. It was not his habit to dismiss senior staff, but in time some, like First Deputy Minister Georgy Korniyenko, left the ministry when they realized that Shevardnadze was paying more attention to the views of colleagues their junior.*

---

* In his book about his father, Anatoly Gromyko charges that Shevardnadze conducted a purge of the foreign ministry after he took over (*Andrei Gromyko: v labirintakh Kremlya: vospominaniia i razmysh-*

Shevardnadze was an unknown in diplomatic circles. He had been educated and spent his entire career in his native Georgia, holding both Party and government positions. For the thirteen years preceding his appointment to the foreign ministry, he had been the Party boss in Georgia. He was considered less corrupt than most other provincial Party officials, but his public statements were notable for their sycophancy to Moscow. However, he and Gorbachev were personal friends, and Gorbachev knew something about him that outsiders—and even most insiders—could not: Shevardnadze shared Gorbachev's impatience with the way the Soviet system was operating and was eager to change it.

Since the end of the Cold War, the Central Intelligence Agency has been subjected to severe criticism, much of it unfair, for its analysis of the Soviet Union. It is worthy of note, therefore, that its assessment of Shevardnadze was accurate. A paper prepared for Secretary Shultz described him as a man with "flamboyant style, courageous, decisive, intelligent, and with an imaginative approach to problem solving." It predicted that Shevardnadze "will eventually leave a distinctive mark on Soviet foreign policy and the conduct of diplomacy."[3] At first, however, his impact was more on the style than the substance of Soviet policy.

George Shultz first met Shevardnadze at the end of July when both were in Helsinki for a meeting to mark the tenth anniversary of the Helsinki Final Act. As was his habit, Shultz used their initial private meeting to make an appeal to correct some specific human rights abuses—a practice he followed every time he met his Soviet counterpart. Shevardnadze was offended, though he did not show it to Shultz. Instead, he asked if he should criticize race relations in the United States, to which Shultz replied, "Be my guest!" Nevertheless, Shevardnadze told his staff afterward that he resented Shultz's action in putting him on the spot in their first meeting.

His annoyance was not evident when he and Shultz were joined by their delegations. After some preliminary pleasantries, Shevardnadze suggested that they concentrate on the "major, central questions," which were "in the security area." Shultz agreed, but with the caveat that human rights issues could affect security questions since President Reagan would be influenced

---

leniia syna [Moscow: Avtor, 1997], p. 116). Most of the departures of senior people, such as Ambassador to the U.S. Anatoly Dobrynin and First Deputy Minister Georgy Korniyenko, occurred well after Shevardnadze became minister. Dobrynin was shifted from his post in Washington to the potentially powerful position as head of the International Department in the Party Central Committee; Korniyenko subsequently joined him there as his deputy. Life at the foreign ministry probably became uncomfortable for Korniyenko after the Geneva summit in November 1985 when Shultz accused him of blocking agreements and Gorbachev personally reversed some of the positions the first deputy minister had taken in the negotiations.

by the Soviet treatment of its people. Shevardnadze countered that the "fundamental human right is the right to live," and therefore "security issues are the core issues."

Shevardnadze made the initial presentation, often reading from notes. His words were essentially those Gromyko would have used—at least when he was in his infrequent succinct mode—but they were delivered calmly, without the supercilious tone that often permeated Gromyko's arguments. Shevardnadze's smiles were frequent and seemed spontaneous. His humor was soothing rather than caustic. When he finished his catalog of the Soviet view of the main issues, he apologized for taking so long. Shultz assured him that they should take whatever time the subjects required, and added that he might need even more. Shevardnadze countered with a laugh, "I won't mind if you don't answer each and every question!"

The meeting concluded with both parties holding to the positions they brought to the room. But the atmosphere contrasted sharply with what had prevailed in Shultz's meeting with Gromyko in Vienna just weeks earlier. A problem-solving spirit had replaced the confrontational tone. Shultz and Shevardnadze agreed that, in their next meeting in September, they would concentrate on those issues most ripe for solution before Reagan and Gorbachev met in November. At the end, Shultz suggested that they agree what to say to journalists about their meeting. (Gromyko had often warned that if Shultz said they made any progress, he would contradict him.) They then agreed that they would say they had a productive meeting during which they discussed intensively the whole range of issues in a frank and businesslike manner.

Bland? Of course. But it was a true statement.

Education of a President

EVEN BEFORE IT was decided when and where Reagan and Gorbachev would meet, Bud McFarlane asked me to think about how we could see that the president had more and better knowledge of the Soviet Union before he faced the Soviet leader. Dealing as he did with Reagan every day, he was struck by the president's spotty command of historical facts. Reagan had had very few contacts with Soviet officials and still tended to base many of his judgments more on generalities, even slogans, than on a nuanced understanding of Soviet reality. To his credit, the president was acutely aware that there were serious gaps in his knowledge of our adversary, and always welcomed thoughtful discussions and well-written articles that provided insights into the country and its people.

I suggested a series of papers for the president to read and then discuss. Together they would cover the ground of a college textbook on the Soviet Union, but with particular emphasis on the Soviet leaders and the way they thought. These briefing papers would be supplemented by periodic meetings with specialists from inside and outside the government, with some recommended books and films, and with video presentations of appropriate topics—such as, for example, Gorbachev as a public leader.

Soviet Union 101

WE BEGAN WORK in early June on what came to be called "Soviet Union 101," as if it were a college course. I suggested twenty-four individual papers, most eight to ten single-spaced pages long, organized to give a rounded picture of the country and its people. The first section, entitled "Sources of Soviet Behavior," included three papers covering topics such as psychology, the Soviet view of the country's place in the world, and whether the Soviet Union was Russian or Communist (I said it was both). The second segment included nine papers on "The Soviet Union from the Inside," and others went on to cover foreign policy, national security, and U.S.-Soviet relations in Soviet eyes. Finally, two papers assessed Gorbachev the man and his aims for his meeting with Reagan.

If I could have located a published book that covered these subjects adequately and in lively fashion, I would simply have sent it in to the president. But there was none; we had to create the "course" from scratch. The simple and normal method would have been to turn the job over to the "intelligence community" and have it submit "coordinated papers" by a certain date. However, I knew very well that this would not work. Any "coordinated" intelligence product would likely put any but a bureaucratic infighter to sleep, and would be so balanced in its judgments that nobody could make out what they had to do with policy decisions. What Reagan needed was the work of well-informed individuals capable of writing clearly, not negotiated pap from interagency committees.

I called my friends Morton Abramowitz, director of the Bureau of Intelligence Research in the State Department, and Robert Gates, deputy director of the CIA, and asked each to assign his most knowledgeable analyst to write a paper on each of the topics I listed. These were to be sent to me, with no more than minor stylistic editing, with the name of the author. I reserved the right to select the paper I considered best, or to combine elements of both drafts, but any product sent to the president would bear the name of the author and not be the responsibility of the agencies where the analysts worked. In effect, I asked them to show which agency had the best specialist on the topic in question and promised to give credit to that individual for his or her work.

Twenty-one papers came in on time—I had assigned to myself the first three—and the quality of those sent to me was very high. In only two instances did I feel a need to rewrite the paper, combining elements from both drafts. Each agency was roughly equal in its "success rate," even though the CIA had more analysts than the State Department.

Reagan read these papers with care, often jotting notes in the margins. Sometimes, at his morning staff meeting, he would pass one around and recommend that everyone read it. We organized meetings for him with some of the authors so that he could discuss the questions raised in whatever detail he desired. We also arranged for him to meet specialists from outside the government and to read some of their writings. Nina Tumarkin of the Russian Research Center at Harvard University did a paper on the image of Lenin, and Suzanne Massie, author of *Land of the Firebird,* a cultural history of Russia, had several meetings to discuss the Russian character. Reagan found their advice helpful as he considered ways to approach Gorbachev personally. He also enjoyed Massie's book, which he was still reading in Geneva as he prepared for his meeting with Gorbachev.

By mid-October, general education gave way to discussion of concrete issues, sometimes as we prepared public statements, and then as Reagan reviewed specific talking points for his upcoming meetings. Reagan would usually review detailed suggestions from the State Department and then comment on them, sometimes ordering changes. I would alter them according to his instructions and then summarize the points so that they would fit on a few three-by-five-inch cards. Material from the State Department was always too voluminous for the meetings, but sometimes it dealt with key issues that the president needed to master in depth. He did not need, however, extensive discussion of secondary questions that were unlikely to arise—indeed, in some cases, were all but certain *not* to arise. Too often material sent from the State Department ignored this consideration and was bloated with minutiae that even the secretary of state had no need to read.

Actually, so far as specific talking points were concerned, Reagan needed little prompting by the time he left for Geneva. He had firmly in his mind what he wanted to say and how he would say it. Furthermore, he went through a rehearsal in Geneva the day before he met Gorbachev the first time. I played Gorbachev, speaking Russian to give Reagan the feel of working with an interpreter and a familiarity with the arguments Gorbachev was expected to make. Since Gorbachev had discussed many of his ideas on television during an earlier trip to France, I was able to voice his arguments accurately and even imitate his gestures.

Education of a General Secretary

GORBACHEV'S "EDUCATION" WAS more haphazard. It was not focused on an intense study of the United States or of Reagan personally, and had no overall plan. He had begun to think about the need to change the style of Soviet foreign policy, as his selection of Shevardnadze showed. He commissioned papers by specialists outside the Soviet foreign ministry, and welcomed other studies sent to him spontaneously by scholars or by officials in the Party apparatus whose views had been suppressed for more than a decade. However, new thoughts were not absorbed into Soviet policy before the Geneva summit; inertia of the old thinking was too great both in the Politburo and in the bureaucracy to permit much deviation from traditional policy.

Nevertheless, as soon as he became general secretary, Gorbachev not only consulted but also began to promote "Party intellectuals" who had been developing ideas for bringing the Soviet Union into the modern world. Their unorthodox thoughts began during Khrushchev's "thaw." None of these officials had become open dissidents, but their personal views were closer to those of critics of the system such as Andrei Sakharov than to those of the leaders in power before Gorbachev became general secretary. In particular, they deplored the class-struggle ideology that divided the world into opposing camps, condemned (at least in their own minds) the Brezhnev Doctrine used to justify military intervention in other countries, and hoped that the Soviet Union could eventually become part of Europe as a social democracy under the rule of law.4

Alexander Yakovlev was the most influential of these "Party liberals" about to come out of the closet. A scholar and philosopher by inclination and training, Yakovlev had been in the first group of Soviet exchange students to study in the United States after Dwight Eisenhower concluded an agreement with Nikita Khrushchev for academic exchanges. After he returned to Moscow, Yakovlev worked on the staff of the Party Secretariat, but ran into difficulties after he published an article warning about the dangers of "great-power" (i.e., Russian) chauvinism. To escape the hostile atmosphere he sensed in the Party apparatus, Yakovlev requested transfer to a diplomatic post in an English-speaking country and was sent to Ottawa as Soviet ambassador. He remained there for ten years, during which time he had the further opportunity to observe and reflect upon the way a democratic society works. It also gave him the possibility of escorting Mikhail Gorbachev, then a Central Committee secretary in Moscow, on an extended visit to Canada.

In 1983, Gorbachev had arranged Yakovlev's appointment to head the prestigious Institute for International Relations and the World Economy, better known by its Russian initials IMEMO. Shortly after he became general secretary, Gobachev put Yakovlev in charge of propaganda in the Party Central Committee. This gave him the authority to assemble a group of unofficial advisers and also, subsequently, to place freethinking journalists from the "liberal" 1960s in charge of key newspapers and magazines.

Yakovlev had doubtless been influenced by his exposure to North America. Other scholars and officials developed similar ideas in Soviet satellites in Eastern Europe. Oleg Bogomolov's Institute of the Economy of the World Socialist System sheltered several freethinking scholars such as, most notably, Alexander Tsypko, who had studied for his Ph.D. in Poland, made friends with Solidarity leaders there, and returned to Moscow in 1981 eager not only to encourage acceptance of Solidarity by the Soviet leadership, but also to discredit Marxism as a philosophy. Several Party officials who had been sent to work on the Communist journal published in Prague came back to jobs in the Central Committee Secretariat with "revisionist" views they had to keep to themselves until Gorbachev became general secretary.

It would be wrong, however, to imagine that Gorbachev was, in the first instance, persuaded and "educated" by these "establishment liberals" (for want of a better term). He drew on their ideas, listened to their advice, and used them to draft his speeches and correspondence, but he himself was the main driving force behind what came to be called "new thinking" in Soviet foreign policy. Where did he get these ideas, then? Alexander Bessmertnykh, who, as Shevardnadze's deputy and immediate successor, worked with him closely, noted that Gorbachev had been an avid reader of translated foreign political literature distributed in limited editions to senior Soviet officials. They were known as the "white books" issued by Progress Publishers, the distribution of which was strictly controlled as classified information. Other Politburo members generally ignored them, but not Gorbachev.

Gorbachev has called certain of these books crucial in his intellectual development during the 1970s. The ones he has mentioned include several by West European Communists, a collection of essays on the Prague Spring, and also articles by European social democrats Willy Brandt and François Mitterrand.[5]

All of these challenged the traditional Soviet view of events, most from the perspective of revisionist Marxism. Though he has not mentioned them publicly, he may also have read works by anti-Marxist Sovietologists, since translations of these were also issued in the white book series.

WHILE GORBACHEV AND Shevardnadze were both intrigued by "revisionist" ideas, they were not convinced that more than cosmetic changes were required for Soviet foreign policy. They were willing to replace Gromyko's scowl with a smile and to pay court to America's European allies, but considered it neither necessary nor politically feasible to make major policy changes at that time.

The fact is that many of Gorbachev's Politburo colleagues, along with some scholars like Georgy Arbatov, head of the USA-Canada Institute, thought it was a mistake to try to deal with Reagan. He would use negotiations, they argued, only to avoid agreements. Since Reagan was bent on achieving military superiority over the Soviet Union, they held, negotiations with him would be a sham. Such skeptics felt that the only safe policy for the Soviet Union was to refuse to take part in a charade of high-level meetings. They felt this would bolster their argument that the United States was threatening to destroy civilization with its aggressive policies.

Just as their American counterparts demanded changes in Soviet policy before they would support realistic negotiations, Soviet hardliners wanted an American commitment to an arms control agreement before the leaders met.

Fine Print for an Agenda

REAGAN HAD SET forth in his public statements and described in his correspondence his views on some key issues, and also had described the contours of an overall policy in the four broad areas he proposed for the U.S.-Soviet agenda. However, except for the positions taken in the arms control negotiations and a few specific negotiations such as those on a broadened exchanges agreement, the United States had no detailed proposals regarding the way to reach the goals it had enunciated. Despite Reagan's eagerness to get on with a dialogue, each question seemed to bog down in an endless interagency process. Even issues that the State and Defense Departments agreed on (such as expanding exchanges) could meet opposition from other agencies. For example, the FBI was reluctant to approve any measure that would bring more Soviet citizens to the United States. FBI agents believed, with some justice, that these programs could be used by the Soviet government as a cover for spying.

The upshot was that meeting after meeting was held with very little result. It was clear to McFarlane and to Shultz that something had to be done to streamline the process if the Geneva summit was to have any concrete results at all. Soviet and American positions on most nuclear weapons issues were so far apart that nobody expected a breakthrough there. But if we were serious about ending our involvement in regional conflicts and eroding the Iron Curtain, this was the time to make significant proposals. They would test Gorbachev's willingness to curtail Soviet military activities abroad and open up his country. If they worked, they could start building the trust required for significant agreements in the military field.

In August, Reagan issued a directive establishing a coordinating committee for the Geneva summit. I was designated chairman of the committee and charged with developing recommendations for the president in all areas except arms control.* I established subgroups to work on various aspects of the summit, including plans for public relations and liaison with journalists. Aware that Shultz was still suspicious of the NSC staff, I designated Mark Parris, the director of Soviet affairs in the State Department, as executive secretary of the coordinating committee.

In some areas, such as the physical plans for the meeting, which were handled with great skill by the White House advance office, no great supervision was needed. However, the established mechanisms were not very useful for generating new ideas. Therefore, I created two small groups of staffers from the State Department and NSC to work out new proposals for two areas of the president's agenda. One developed a step-by-step approach for a mutual withdrawal from conflicts in third areas, the other a set of proposals to expand citizen-to-citizen contacts and improve the flow of information.

---

* Arms control issues continued to be coordinated by the Senior Arms Control Policy Group, which included representatives from the Defense and State Departments, the Joint Chiefs of Staff, the CIA, the Arms Control and Disarmament Agency, and the NSC staff.

Once these ideas were developed and had the approval of Secretary Shultz and Bud McFarlane, I cleared them with Secretary Weinberger and CIA director William Casey. Weinberger sent word that he thought they were a good idea since they would "deflect attention from SDI." Casey told his deputy, Bob Gates, that he doubted they would produce anything, but he had no objection. Reagan then instructed the State Department to present the ideas to Soviet diplomats and invite their suggestions for additional problems we might work on jointly. They responded with additional suggestions, such as for developing computer software for use in education and joint experiments to see whether thermonuclear power stations were possible.

Reagan was particularly eager to expand contacts between American and Soviet citizens. In addition to traditional programs for the exchange of exhibits, performing artists, and graduate students, he proposed that large numbers (thousands or tens of thousands) of high school students and college undergraduates spend time and go to school in the other country. Up to then, the Soviet government had resisted exchanges of high school and college students, limiting such programs to a few dozen "graduate students." Most of those sent to the United States were middle-aged scientists in military-related specialties. The Soviet government did not generally allow its young people to study or make home stays in countries outside the Communist bloc.

Preparations in Moscow for the meeting concentrated much more heavily on arms control issues. Staffing on them was done by an interagency group of five senior officials, one each from the Ministry of Defense, Ministry of Foreign Affairs, Party Central Committee, the KGB, and the government's Military-Industrial Commission. This group, called "the Five" or "the Big Five," had been established to backstop negotiations on SALT II. During most meetings the heads of agencies were represented by their deputies. These included, for most of the period up to 1986, Marshal Sergei Akhromeyev of the General Staff, Gromyko's (and, for a time, Shevardnadze's) first deputy, Georgy Korniyenko, and Lieutenant General Nikolai Detinov of the Central Committee Department of Defense Industries. All recommendations by this group were forwarded through the Central Committee Secretariat for approval by the Politburo.[6]

The Soviet positions in the renewed nuclear and space talks contained several nonstarters so far as the United States was concerned. Soviet negotiators still linked agreements on both strategic and intermediate nuclear missiles with a ban on "space-strike weapons." Reagan told Gorbachev repeatedly that he would not give up SDI, though he assured him that he would keep the research program within the bounds allowed by the ABM Treaty.

Furthermore, Soviet negotiators continued to insist that they be allowed to retain at least as many INF missiles in Europe as the nuclear missiles in British
and French arsenals. Also, they were still resisting deep cuts in their heavy
ICBMs, considered by the United States potential first-strike weapons.

By 1985, several of the Soviet members of the Big Five understood that
the Soviet proposals were not realistically negotiable, and that they were
blocking achievement of the Soviet government's prime goal—to reduce the
number of American weapons that could strike the Soviet Union. Nevertheless, the Politburo was not yet willing to approve a radical change, and Gorbachev still hoped that, with the help of the peace movement, he could force
Reagan to back down.[7]

Warm–up: Dealing with Shevardnadze

WE HAD ALREADY presented many of our ideas for increased contacts
and cooperation to Soviet diplomats when Shevardnadze came to Washington for lengthy meetings with Reagan and Shultz on September 27, 1985.
He came from New York, where he had addressed the United Nations General Assembly. It was his first trip to the United States.

Reagan prepared for the meeting with the intensity usually reserved for
the head of a major allied government. He studied a set of lengthy position
papers in advance, held several discussions of critical questions, and, on the
day of the visit, met for an hour with State Department and NSC officials before Shevardnadze arrived for his ten o'clock appointment. The two-hour
meeting continued over lunch in the White House formal dining room. It
was one-thirty before Shevardnadze returned to the Soviet embassy on Six-
teenth Street. Two and a half hours later he came to the State Department for
a follow-up meeting with Secretary of State Shultz.

Although Reagan had been given suggested talking points on small cards,
he referred to them hardly at all. He needed no notes for the things he
wanted to say. He opened the meeting by observing that the Geneva summit
should be used to "get beyond the stereotypes" that had plagued the U.S.-
Soviet relationship. In particular he felt that, despite the differences in our
philosophies and political systems, we "live in the world together" and must
"handle our competition in peace." He could not understand why the Soviet
Union should feel threatened by the United States, but he wanted to go beyond explanations and to share his hopes and plans with Gorbachev. He then
mentioned in general terms the four areas of the U.S. agenda: to find a way
to withdraw from violence in third countries, to reduce weaponry and de-

velop defenses against nuclear missiles, to expand contacts and cooperation, and to provide more effective protection for human rights.

Shevardnadze presented a letter from Gorbachev that outlined new proposals for the arms control negotiations (which, however, contained only minor changes in previous positions). He said that Gorbachev believed that their meeting in Geneva could produce a mutual understanding on preventing nuclear war, and put in a plug for "ending the arms race on earth and preventing it in space"—that is, renouncing the Strategic Defense Initiative. He then described the Soviet approach to the arms control negotiations in familiar terms and made a brief mention of discussion of "international issues" (mainly conflict in third countries) and of possible bilateral agreements.

Then he shifted to the topics that fascinated Reagan most: motives and attitudes. He scoffed at the idea (which he attributed to the press, not to Reagan) that the Soviet Union could be exhausted economically by competition from the United States. In fact, he said, the Soviet Union was not only strong economically, but had a moral and political unity that was as important a source of strength as nuclear weapons. As for creating a favorable atmosphere for the summit in Geneva, he warned that the "barrage of unfounded accusations" from American officials poisoned the atmosphere. He joked that when Reagan referred to an "evil empire," they thought he had the "old empire, not the one of today" in mind.*

Other comments, not always by Reagan himself, were damaging, however, such as accusations that they had more weapons, were stealing technology, and—particularly—criticisms of Lenin. For them, Shevardnadze pointed out, Lenin was like God is for a religious believer. Criticism of him, in Soviet eyes, was tantamount to blasphemy.

Reagan took up the debate with gusto, but without arrogance. He welcomed the statement that the Soviet Union would accept on-site inspection of some arms control agreements and appealed for deeper cuts in nuclear weapons than the Soviet proposal envisioned. As for U.S. charges that the Soviet Union had more weapons, he pointed out that the United States had reduced its nuclear forces in the 1970s, after parity had been declared, while the Soviet Union continued to build up its arsenal, to the point that it now seemed to have an offensive rather than defensive purpose. And, of course, in conventional forces the Soviet Union and its Warsaw Pact allies had far

---

* When he said this, I thought he had misspoken when he implied that the Soviet Union was an empire. Later I learned that he considered the Soviet Union an empire. From 1991 on, his characterizations were even harsher than Reagan's.

more weapons than the United States and NATO. Reagan defended SDI as research in full conformity with the ABM Treaty, and said that the world was unlikely to eliminate nuclear weapons, as he devoutly wished, unless it developed a defense against them. Both countries should continue their research and, if an effective system became feasible, should consult about what to do. "Today," he observed, "it is uncivilized to say we can only maintain peace by threatening innocent people."

As for his reference to the evil empire, Reagan explained that he was perhaps just responding to Soviet charges that America was a country of bloodthirsty imperialists. He agreed that we should stop talking so much about each other and start talking more to each other. As for his Lenin quotes, maybe all were not letter perfect, but the idea of the destruction of the "bourgeois world" underlies all of Lenin's philosophy. But when all was said and done, he concluded, we had to live in peace and we had to cooperate more. We could get together and stop some of the regional wars, and he also hoped that the Soviet Union would find a way to withdraw its forces from Afghanistan.

The debate continued over Soviet violations of agreements and the legality of SDI research, but was conducted mainly by Shevardnadze's deputy, Georgy Korniyenko, Shultz, and McFarlane. Both Reagan and Shevardnadze seemed content to leave the details of arguments to subordinates. In fact, Reagan wanted Shultz and McFarlane to deal with the details. In contrast, Shevardnadze was sensitive to being upstaged by his deputy; though he did not show it openly, he resented Korniyenko's injecting himself into the discussion, and this resentment played a part in their subsequent estrangement.

Polemics ended during lunch, when conversation was relaxed. Reagan, Shevardnadze, and the others around the table conversed with one another as fellow human beings with much more in common than the political tension between their governments would imply. A year before, when Gromyko dined in the same room, there was an overall feeling that our countries were locked in a zero-sum game. This year, that mind-set was no longer so pronounced. We were still at odds on most key issues, but somehow these disputes seemed more tractable than they had appeared the year before.

Later in the afternoon Shevardnadze and Shultz set about making a list of the issues that might be ripe for some agreement in Geneva. Shevardnadze pushed hard for U.S. adherence to the moratorium on nuclear tests Gorbachev had declared, and also proposed a zone free of chemical weapons in Europe. Shultz countered that any test ban would depend on verification, and that only a global prohibition of chemical weapons would be effective. After all, chemical agents can be easily moved around in secret. Shultz spent most of his time describing U.S. proposals for cultural and educational exchanges and cooperative projects. Before they broke up, Shultz and Shevardnadze agreed that their staffs would continue to work on a draft communiqué—the normal procedure before earlier U.S.-Soviet summit meetings.

When Reagan saw the report on this meeting, he was annoyed—not by what was said on the issues, but by the idea of working on a joint statement in advance. He had remarked earlier that he did not want a "pre-cooked" summit, with everything decided beforehand. He wanted the meeting in Geneva to be *his* meeting; he believed any statement should be composed after he met Gorbachev, and should reflect what happened. Shultz either did not understand the intensity of Reagan's feelings on this point or felt that the normal diplomatic preparations did not conflict with them. Any statement could easily be adjusted at the meeting to incorporate what the leaders agreed.

However, Reagan ordered that any official discussion of a joint statement cease forthwith. Officials in the State Department were outraged, and blamed the NSC staff for "interference." (Actually, McFarlane had tried to convince Reagan that exchanging draft statements in advance was appropriate.) Soviet negotiators complained equally vehemently; they had instructions to produce a document, and Reagan's order made that impossible. They suspected that this was an indication that Reagan intended to stonewall Gorbachev and then blame him for failure to reach any agreement at all.

Despite appeals, Reagan stood his ground and insisted that there should be no discussion of any "concluding document" or joint statement until he and Gorbachev decided personally what to put in it.*

At the time I felt that Reagan was behaving unreasonably. Any draft document could be modified if the principals so decided, and key items could be left blank until they had been agreed. Negotiating a statement on points agreed could reassure Soviet negotiators that the United States was serious about its proposals. In retrospect, however, Reagan was probably right. It was fine to negotiate specific agreements in advance, such as a renewal of educational and cultural exchanges, but a negotiated report on the

---

* Officials in the State Department never understood that this instruction came from Reagan. They suspected intrigues by the NSC to cut them out of the picture. They had exchanged drafts with Soviet negotiators before Reagan had ordered them to desist, and therefore were able to discuss many of the questions informally.

meeting as a whole would constrain the principals. Any draft statement would have to be cleared widely in both governments and any subsequent changes would be difficult for the leaders to impose without stimulating talk of wins and losses, something neither wanted. If we were to move away from the confrontational psychology that had marked relations up to then, it was better not to tie the hands of our leaders, even loosely, before they met.

This, of course, made bureaucracies on both sides nervous. The very idea! Reagan was insisting that they do what he and Gorbachev decided! In the mind of bureaucrats in both countries, neither had the knowledge and experience to be trusted with decisions. But the fact was that our respective bureaucracies had spun their wheels for years without tangible result. It was time for the president and general secretary to take charge.

SHULTZ MET WITH Shevardnadze several more times before their bosses met in Geneva: in New York in October and in Moscow in early November. Even though the American negotiators were forbidden to talk about a joint communiqué for the Geneva summit, they discussed the various topics that might go into such a document. The meetings with Shevardnadze concentrated on a systematic review of the proposals each had made. Shultz invariably organized his presentation in accord with the four-part agenda the United States had developed, starting with human rights in a private session. Though Shevardnadze continued to spend most of his time on arms control issues and resisted commitments regarding the human rights cases called to his attention, more and more "bilateral" items were placed on the schedule, proposals for cooperative projects as well as cultural, educational, and information exchanges. By early November, it was clear that the two countries not only would restore most of the contacts and joint projects that had existed before the Soviet invasion of Afghanistan, but would expand them substantially. The negotiations with Shevardnadze proceeded without serious leaks or public controversy.

The meeting Shultz had with Gorbachev in Moscow on November 5 was more confrontational, however. Gorbachev spent most of his time complaining that the military-industrial complex in the United States dictated American policy and accusing the U.S. of an attempt to use SDI to achieve an advantage over the Soviet Union. Shultz tried to explain that developing defenses allowed by the ABM Treaty could not be an aggressive strategy if accompanied by a sharp reduction of offensive weapons, but Gorbachev summarily rejected the argument. "We know what's going on," he declaimed. ". . . If you want superiority through your SDI, we will not help you. We will let you bankrupt yourselves. But also we will not reduce our offensive missiles."[8]

Shultz was not disturbed by Gorbachev's pugnacious approach, since he assumed that Gorbachev would be less combative when he sat down with Reagan. He was surprised, however, by the extent to which Gorbachev had a distorted image of the United States and an inaccurate grasp of Reagan's policy. For the first time, perhaps, he was forced to recognize that explaining something to Soviet ambassador Anatoly Dobrynin did not ensure that Gorbachev would get an accurate report of what was said. Though Shultz had approved some attempts to create a private channel, he had been skeptical of the concept and indeed had at times insisted on conditions that caused the efforts to fail. Now he had experienced the result firsthand, and that made him all the more eager to educate the Soviet leaders about the United States and developments in the world economy. It was obvious to him that global economic trends would require fundamental changes in the Soviet system if the Soviet Union was not to fall disastrously behind the advanced capitalist countries.

Informing the World

FEW QUESTIONS RECEIVED more attention in the Reagan White House than public relations and the use of imagery to convey the president's message. Therefore, those of us who planned the Geneva meeting spent as much time thinking about presentation and appearances as we did about the issues themselves. It was important, of course, to keep the American public and its Congress on our side. But we also wanted to achieve a breakthrough in communicating with the Soviet public. The Voice of America and Radio Liberty were still jammed in the Soviet Union—as were the BBC and the German Deutsche Welle—so access to the Soviet information media became a high priority.

Though few American commentators were sympathetic to the Soviet Union, Soviet leaders had ready access to the American media whenever they desired. Whatever they said was newsworthy and would be carried. Newsmagazines and television producers vied for the opportunity to interview any Soviet general secretary. Before Gorbachev came to power, however, such interviews were rare. During the early 1980s the elderly Brezhnev, the infirm Andropov, and the incompetent Chernenko were incapable of holding their own with Western journalists and their handlers wisely shielded them from any but the most controlled and formal contact. If "interviews" appeared in the Soviet press, they were not the result of spontaneous questions and answers but the product of staff writers in the Central Committee apparatus.

Gorbachev was different. Able to speak at length and in detail without notes, well dressed and photogenic, he was a godsend to journalists. All major publications and television networks clamored for interviews. In Washington, White House aides could grit their teeth and grumble about the unfairness of it all, but there was no way the administration could discourage news coverage of what the Soviet leader said. All they could do was request, on the grounds of elementary fairness, that major Soviet publications carry at least one extensive interview with the president before the meeting in November.

When Gorbachev's office granted an interview to *Time* magazine, we were told that the Soviet government newspaper, *Izvestiya,* would carry an uncensored interview with President Reagan. The White House agreed to the same rules that had been arranged for Gorbachev's interview: questions would be submitted in advance, to which written answers would be given, after which a panel of three journalists would question the president on the record. This was to be the first interview with an American president specifically for the Soviet press since Nikita Khrushchev's son-in-law Aleksei Adzhubei interviewed President John Kennedy in 1961.

When we received the Soviet questions, I was assigned the duty of drafting answers. Recognizing that Soviet readers would be unfamiliar with many ideas in Reagan's answers, I provided much more detailed replies than I would have done if I had been suggesting answers for an American or Western European newspaper. I also kept in mind how the answers would read in Russian; I remembered the difficulty I had experienced in 1981 in making Lincoln's words about a government of, by, and for the people comprehensible in Russian. Concepts that seemed simple to Americans had to be described in greater detail. Reagan read my draft and called a meeting to discuss it. His first comment was that he agreed with the answers but found them "awfully long." Then he turned to me and said, "Jack, you've taken each question like it was the subject for an essay!"

"Yes, sir," I agreed. "The answers are small essays. But let me tell you why."

After discussion, Reagan conceded with some reluctance that the lengthy replies were justified in that instance. When the Soviet journalists questioned him directly, his answers, delivered spontaneously, were not much shorter.

As agreed, *Izvestiya* ran both the oral and written parts of the interview. They did not run them in full, however, but left out some important passages. The editors also appended editorial comment almost as long as Reagan's answers in an attempt to refute some of his statements. The cuts we found annoying, but the refutation did not bother us. We knew that most Soviet readers would be more impressed by what the American president had to say than what Soviet propagandists might say about it.

Gorbachev's interview in *Time* magazine was unquestionably successful from his point of view. He left the impression of a person who genuinely wanted to end the arms race. Even more important for the American public, he came across as a personality. Finally, the Soviet Union seemed to have a human leader rather than a mere mouthpiece of an all-powerful bureaucracy.

Up until the meeting in Geneva, however, Gorbachev paid more attention to Europe than to the United States. He made a trip to Paris a few weeks before he met Reagan and was lionized by the French media. The long interviews carried on French television were invaluable material for those of us who were preparing Reagan for the Geneva meeting. Gorbachev explained on camera his objections to SDI and other issues in terms he was likely to use even in private meetings with Reagan. The CIA used extensive clips from the television coverage of Gorbachev's trip to France when it compiled a video presentation of Gorbachev the man.

In planning for the meeting itself, the White House staff tried to leave nothing to chance. One of our jobs was to think through what headlines we wanted to see in the American and European press each day, and to plan activities that were likely to produce them. (They turned out almost precisely as we anticipated.) William J. Henkel, who headed the advance team to Geneva and had long experience in arranging for effective campaign appearances, looked to every detail of imagery: where the press pool would be located so as to present Reagan in the most favorable light, what would be in the background of photographs, how to position Reagan to be seen as the dominant partner in the dialogue. The villa where the first meeting was held had a comfortable boathouse on the edge of Lake Geneva. It was Henkel's idea to have a fire in the fireplace when Reagan invited Gorbachev to stop in for a private chat during their planned walk around the grounds.

The Soviet advance people were obsessively protective of their leader's status. It was important to them that Gorbachev at all times be viewed as Reagan's equal. However, not having run election campaigns and with little experience dealing with Western journalists, they were no match for their American counterparts when it came to setting the stage to make their man look good.

VII

1985: NOVEMBER

GENEVA: THE FIRST SKIRMISH

*We viewed the Geneva meeting realistically, without grand expectations, yet
we hoped to lay the foundations for a serious dialogue in the future.*
—MIKHAIL GORBACHEV, 1996[1]

*I believed that if we were ever going to break down the barriers of mistrust
that divided our countries, we had to begin by establishing a personal
relationship. . . . I wanted to convince Gorbachev that we wanted peace.*
—RONALD REAGAN, 1990[2]

WHITE HOUSE EFFORTS to convince the public that the Geneva
summit could be successful without a major arms control agreement
finally paid off. At the end of October, a poll indicated that 69 percent of the
Americans questioned did not expect an arms control agreement, but that 83
percent favored the summit anyway.[3] Judging by editorial comment, European publics had more ambitious expectations in September and early October, but by November few expected dramatic results. The leftist press
continued to blame Reagan for the arms race, but comment from the center
and right tended to agree that Gorbachev's "initiatives" were an inadequate
basis for a breakthrough on arms reduction.[4]

The Soviet government dispatched a team of briefers to Geneva a week
before Reagan and Gorbachev were to meet. The spokesmen attracted much
attention, particularly in Europe, in the days leading up to the meeting, and
there was talk of the United States being placed on the propaganda defensive. The mood in the president's party as it headed for Geneva was optimistic, however, despite publication of a letter from Weinberger warning the

president not to compromise on SDI or to commit himself to abide by the ABM Treaty. It was a flagrant attempt to steal the limelight and Reagan's aides were furious. They reported that Reagan, too, was angry, as he should have been since the letter was a public display of Weinberger's lack of confidence in the president's judgment. When someone mentioned the letter during a briefing session with his staff, Reagan responded, as he often did, with a rhetorical question: "Doesn't everybody know what Cap thinks?"

Those of us in Reagan's entourage were encouraged that Gorbachev seemed more willing than his predecessors to accept a major expansion of contacts. If these contacts helped open the closed Soviet system, they would facilitate changes in Soviet behavior. I personally believed that what happened internally in the Soviet Union was of more importance than the rapid conclusion of an arms control agreement. Most of my colleagues in the State Department were convinced that, unless the United States made significant concessions in its negotiations on arms control, nothing else would happen. Many of us thought that Gorbachev could be convinced that SDI was not a danger to the USSR if the number of nuclear weapons was cut sharply. Once Reagan made clear that SDI was not negotiable, we believed, Gorbachev would come to understand that it was not in his country's interest to delay arms reductions because of a long-term research program.

We knew that Gorbachev would not change his position at the Geneva meeting. He was too committed politically for that. Even if Gorbachev drew the conclusions we anticipated, we understood that he would have to return home and prepare the ground for a policy shift. We did not realize, however, that it would take him until 1991, when President George H.W. Bush signed a START agreement on terms Reagan would have accepted, to reach that conclusion.

Reagan's Mood

SHORTLY BEFORE HE left Washington for Geneva, Reagan dictated to his secretary his thoughts about Gorbachev and the upcoming meeting. He read the text, made a few amendments with his ballpoint pen, and gave it to Bud McFarlane for comment. McFarlane gave it to me, saying that he saw no problems, but if I did, we would need to work some corrective advice into our briefings.

"I believe Gorbachev is a highly intelligent leader totally dedicated to traditional Soviet goals. He will be a formidable negotiator and will try to make Soviet foreign and military policy more effective," the comment began.

"He is (as are all Soviet General Secretaries) dependent on the Soviet-Communist hierarchy and will be out to prove to them his strength and dedication to Soviet traditional goals." So far, so good, I thought as I read. Subsequently, the president acknowledged that Gorbachev did not "want to undertake any new adventures" but would be "stubborn and tough about holding what he has." He believed that Gorbachev's major goal would be "weaning our European friends away from us" by "making us look like a threat to peace."

As for arms reduction, he believed that Gorbachev wished to "reduce the burden of defense spending that is stagnating the Soviet economy," and that "could contribute to his opposition to SDI" since "he doesn't want to face the cost of competing with us." He also recognized that Soviet "military planning differs from ours" and a more defensive orientation would require a costly "revamp."

On the Soviet military threat he made a curious statement that I would have tried to correct if he had not amended it in handwriting when he saw his words in print. It ran, ". . . Our recent PFIAB* study makes it plain the Soviets are planning a war. They would like to win without it and their chances of doing that depend on being so prepared we could be faced with a surrender or die ultimatum." Actually, Reagan had not been advised that the Soviets were planning to start a war, but that they were planning so that they could fight one and prevail (which was true). When he read his statement, Reagan apparently understood that what he had said was misleading, marked the phrase about planning a war for deletion, and added words to make his sentence read, "They would like to win by being so much better prepared we could be faced with a surrender or die ultimatum." The worry that the Soviet leaders could use a real or perceived military superiority for blackmail was a major factor in his insistence on improving U.S. military strength.

Reagan then turned from substance to public opinion:

In the world of P.R. we are faced with two domestic elements. One argues that no agreement with the Soviets is worth the time, trouble or paper it's written on so we should dig in our heels and say "nyet" to any concession. On the other side are those so hungry for an agreement of any kind that they would advise major concessions because a successful Summit requires that.

My own view is that any agreement must be in the long-term interest of the United States and our allies. We'll sign no other kind.

---

* The President's Foreign Intelligence Advisory Board, a group of prominent private citizens, independent of the CIA.

He did not note that the first "element" he described was well represented in his own administration, but his comment made clear that he did not adhere to it. He was in favor of agreements, so long as they were in the U.S. and allied "long-term interest."

His comments on human rights occupied a full page of the four-and-one-half-page double-spaced typescript. He regretted that "we are somewhat publicly on record about human rights. Front page stories that we are banging away at them on their human rights abuses will get us some cheers from the bleachers but it won't help those who are being abused." Then he quoted Richard Nixon's comment that he had encouraged a rapid expansion of Jewish emigration from the Soviet Union by dealing with Brezhnev privately after they had reached the agreements signed in 1972. Soon after Congress passed the Jackson-Vanik amendment to the Trade Act of 1974, tying emigration to trade issues, Jewish emigration plummeted. It was almost totally prohibited when Reagan came to office in 1981.

In this connection, Reagan commented: "We must always remember our main goal and his [Gorbachev's] need to show his strength to the Soviet gang back in the Kremlin. Let's not limit the area where he can do that to those things that have to do with aggression outside the Soviet Union." "Our main goal" in this instance was helping people, not making propaganda points.

His concept of linkage crops up several times in the statement. He recognized the intense Soviet interest in American technology and expanded trade. Since trade was more important to the Soviet Union than to the United States, Reagan considered it a "bargaining chip" and asked rhetorically, "But how about just hanging back until we get some of the things we want instead of giving consideration up front to what they want?" Increased trade was not part of the four-part agenda precisely because Reagan wanted to see some political change before the United States permitted the export of items incorporating advanced technology.

He noted that we must convince the Soviet leader to stop supporting armed conflicts "in Southeast Asia, the Middle East and Latin America" if Congress was to approve any trade or arms control treaty.

Thus, the linkage he had mentioned in his first press conference was not a rigid "You must do *x* before we do *y*," but a more general attitude that improvement of relations in one area could not get far ahead of improvement in others.

He welcomed the prospect of agreements on cultural exchanges, consulates, and some economic cooperation, but called them "window dressing" so far as public perceptions were concerned. The "main events" in his mind were "security issues like arms control, the regional areas of conflict and the prevalent suspicion and hostility between us." He thought he should tell Gorbachev in private that "failure to come to a solid, verifiable arms reduction agreement will leave no alternative except an arms race and there is no way that we will allow them to win such a race."

In conclusion, he noted that agreeing to future meetings would be an important result since it would "set up a process to avoid war in [and?] settling our differences in the future." He thought of going to Moscow in 1986 if Gorbachev wished and having Gorbachev come to the United States in 1987. Referring to his orders to the State Department not to negotiate a communiqué in advance, he observed that he was willing to discuss "a frank statement of where we agreed and where we disagree." But, he concluded, "Let there be no talk of winners and losers. Even if we think we won, to say so would set us back in view of their inherent inferiority complex."

I have quoted from this memorandum at length because it is one of the few statements that Reagan dictated spontaneously to explain his views. He was, in effect, thinking out loud about his meeting with Gorbachev and then asking his staff to tell him if he had anything terribly wrong.

Some might question his statement that Gorbachev was "totally dedicated to traditional Soviet goals." After all, didn't he discard many traditional Soviet goals? Yes, he did. But that was later. In 1985, Gorbachev had not modified Soviet goals. Gorbachev himself remarked after he left office, "At first, as the general secretary . . . , I spoke of our country's unchanging foreign policy course, stating that there was no need to change it."[5]

Perhaps the most interesting aspect of the statement was its repeated reference to Gorbachev's need to impress his colleagues in the Kremlin. Obviously, it was important to the new general secretary not to seem weak or incompetent to those who had put him in office. But the sentiment Reagan ascribed to Gorbachev applied to Reagan as well: he, too, was determined not to seem weak to his more hardline supporters. They understood this and played on it to head off negotiations or slow them down. After Reagan began his direct interaction with Gorbachev he exhibited progressively less concern on this score than he had earlier.

Reagan's concern for his own image aside, the statement illustrates his habit of concentrating on the biggest issues, thinking about how to negotiate them given the personality and political needs of his interlocutor, while simultaneously taking account of probable public reaction. He did not think in neat, analytical categories, but in a general, almost impressionistic way. Yet he managed to grasp simultaneously the various dimensions of an activity: goals, tactics that work and don't work, the mind-set and political needs of his interlocutor, and the public reaction to his proposals.

Gorbachev's Mood

WE HAVE NOTHING comparable to Reagan's dictated statement to judge Gorbachev's thoughts as he went to the meeting in Geneva. But the memories of his assistants and declassified records show that his image of Reagan was more distorted than Reagan's image of Gorbachev. He suspected that Reagan was interested only in stringing him along with sweet talk and no substance, using the meeting as cover for an American drive to secure military supremacy. He was still being advised that any real agreement with Reagan would be impossible, and that the only prudent course for the Soviet Union was to continue its confrontational policies until U.S. allies woke up to the dangers and pressed Reagan or his successor to act more rationally.

Gorbachev had received conflicting advice regarding Reagan's favorite dream, the Strategic Defense Initiative. Soviet scientists advised against trying to match the U.S. program since they were dubious that it would work. Soviet generals and the managers of Soviet military industries were of a different opinion, however. They claimed that the scientists underestimated the capability of American technology, that SDI was clearly an offensive strategy since it would permit the United States to attack the Soviet Union with impunity and furthermore was probably a cover for placing offensive weapons in space, weapons such as lasers that could destroy targets on earth. "If the Americans do that," they argued, "we must match them."

As noted earlier, the Soviet Union had not given up the idea of developing weapons to counter ballistic missiles. It maintained ABM defenses around Moscow. Soviet scientists had also tested an anti-satellite weapon and some powerful land-based lasers. They had enough elements of a defensive system to suggest that the USSR had undertaken a comprehensive project to develop strategic defenses even before Reagan announced his SDI.*

---

* In October 1985 the Departments of State and Defense jointly published an unclassified report entitled "Soviet Strategic Defense Programs." In a preface signed jointly by Shultz and Weinberger, it highlighted six "recent Soviet activities in strategic defenses," including upgrading the ABM system around Moscow, research on laser and particle-beam weapons, maintenance of an anti-satellite system, and improvements in "passive defenses" such as shelters. In his discussions with Reagan, Gorbachev consistently ignored Soviet efforts to develop missile defenses.

Gorbachev decided that if he was to resist demands to pour additional resources into the military-industrial complex, precisely when the country needed to transfer more resources to civilian needs, he had to stop SDI. His main goal at Geneva was to persuade Reagan to back off and trade SDI for reduction of offensive weapons. He still thought that American accusations of treaty violations were mainly propaganda, designed to provide a pretext for avoiding new agreements, and was determined to resist any American intrusion into Soviet domestic matters, such as the regime's treatment of its citizens. Unlike his predecessors, however, he was willing to consider expanded contacts with the outside world and to agree—at least in principle—to further meetings.

While Gorbachev knew that the meeting in Geneva would not produce an arms control agreement, he was looking for reassurance that Reagan was a man he could do business with. The only business that really mattered to him at that time was stopping the arms race. But he was mistakenly convinced that the arms race would continue unless the United States agreed not to explore the possibility of defenses against nuclear missiles.

The Meeting

BOTH REAGAN AND Gorbachev were determined to make their meeting look like a success. In their public appearances they were smiling, shaking hands, or chatting amiably before getting down to work. When the summit ended, they appeared onstage together to announce that it had important results and that more would follow.

For once, the public imagery and the carefully massaged announcements were accurate. In fact, their conversations in Geneva accomplished more than the minimum each expected, though less than both had secretly hoped.

They met in working sessions for some eight hours on November 19 and 20, half of which time they were alone, with only interpreters present. In addition, they had dinner together with their wives and senior members of their delegations both evenings. Although Gorbachev had not yet explicitly endorsed the four-part agenda Reagan had been proposing for nearly two years, he accepted a schedule that allowed time for Reagan to introduce each of the topics.

Their first private meeting was scheduled for fifteen minutes, but it lasted an hour. Reagan used it to reassure Gorbachev of his desire for peace and an end to the arms race, explaining in the process why, from the point of view of the United States, there was tension and mistrust in the relationship. He made it clear that he was not demanding a change in the Soviet system, but that Soviet support to "socialist revolutions" was a source of mistrust since it undermined the right of self-determination.

Gorbachev seemed uncomfortable discussing the sources of tension and urged Reagan to concentrate on a formula that would lead to an end of the arms race. He conceded that there were many problems in the world, but denied that the Soviet Union was "exporting revolution." He called for co-operation rather than confrontation in dealing with regional conflict, but avoided any comment on Reagan's specific proposal for a step-by-step process to end Soviet and U.S. involvement in these conflicts.

When they joined their delegations, Gorbachev led off with a strong pitch for increased trade and observed that the United States was losing an important market because of its restrictions on exports. He appealed to Reagan to join him in giving a new "impulse" to the nuclear arms negotiations so that resources could be released for both countries' civilian economies. He also cautioned the president not to entertain "delusions" about the Soviet Union: the Soviet economy was not, he said, in a perilous state and thus subject to the leverage of an arms race; it was not lagging behind in high tech-nology; the Soviet Union did not seek military superiority.

I observed him from across the table with growing disbelief. Here was a man reputed to be a formidable debater. I had witnessed his vigorous and clever debating style when Secretary of Commerce Malcolm Baldrige had called on him in May. But now he was leading with his chin. By stressing the importance of trade, he reinforced Reagan's determination to withhold any trade concessions until some U.S. requests (particularly regarding emigra-tion and human rights) were granted. Furthermore, his attempt to character-ize his economic problems and laggard technology as delusions not only called attention to these real problems, but also cast doubt on his denial that the Soviet Union sought military superiority. He obviously had not been briefed on American, and particularly Reagan's, psychology as carefully as Reagan had on Soviet thinking, Gorbachev's in particular. This is not to say that Reagan had a perfect understanding of Gorbachev, but he would not have made the elementary negotiating mistake of highlighting well-known weaknesses by denying their existence.

When it was Reagan's turn, instead of commenting on Gorbachev's pre-sentation, he reverted to the topic he wanted most of all to discuss, the causes of distrust. He noted that there had been U.S.-Soviet cooperation in the past (which proved that it was possible), but that he had seen no desire to cooperate on the part of Gorbachev's immediate predecessors. He could not understand why the United States was being accused of seeking military superiority when the Soviet Union maintained much larger forces—5.4 million men under arms as compared to 2.4 million American servicemen. Soviet armed forces had been in Cuba for years, and now they had turned up in Afghanistan and as advisers in Ethiopia, Angola, and Yemen. He said this not to argue, but to explain why there was a lack of confidence between our countries. And, he added, referring to Gorbachev's meeting with Shultz in Moscow, "You are mistaken about the influence of the military-industrial complex. We spend more on social needs than on defense, and two thirds of the defense budget is for salaries. We have no economic interest in continuing a military buildup."

As for American fears, they were, perhaps, not that the Soviet Union would attack, but that it could force the United States to grant political concessions if it had military superiority. Violations of previous agreements also undermined confidence, but he was prepared to meet Soviet concerns if the Soviet Union would meet American concerns. The main thing, Reagan stressed, was that the United States had no hostile designs.

After a lunch break, Gorbachev took the floor. Once again he wanted to focus on "solutions," not causes. He denied that there was a Soviet plan for "world domination," but observed that since World War II the third world was asserting its independence. This, he claimed, was an "objective process," and the Soviet Union did not involve itself other than to oppose "counterrevolution." He then made a brief mention of Afghanistan, stating that he supported "regularizing the process around that country" and accusing the United States of trying to keep Soviet troops there as long as possible.* As for the Soviet military buildup Reagan had mentioned, he said it was only to reach parity with the United States.

Gorbachev then turned to his main point, one that he repeated countless times: SDI, he alleged, made sense only if used to permit a country to deliver a first strike, then defend its people from retaliation. He quoted Caspar Weinberger as having said that if the Soviet Union developed strategic defenses first, it would be a threat to the United States. "If you fear our having these defenses, why should we not fear your having them?" he asked. If the U.S. proceeded with SDI, he thundered, "We will build up in order to smash your shield." As for Reagan's comment that the Soviet Union had its own program of research on defense against nuclear weapons, Gorbachev claimed, "The Soviet Union is not doing the same. All our research is for

---

* Secretary Shultz remarked later that the president should have picked up on this; actually, I saw nothing new in the statement since Gorbachev had spoken not of the situation *in* Afghanistan, but *around* it. In other words, it was the traditional Soviet position that if only "outside interference" ended, there would be no opposition to the government in Kabul and Soviet troops could leave.

peaceful purposes." He then stated with emphasis: if the United States continued its work on "space weapons," there would be no reduction of offensive weapons and the Soviet Union would respond.

Whoops, I thought. He made a clever point quoting Weinberger—who was speaking of Soviet defenses combined with a large offensive force, not what Reagan was proposing—but then he blew it. But the Soviet Union had more programs under way to develop and use missile defenses than the United States. Denying the obvious hardly strengthened his argument. And why, I asked myself, does he paint himself so far into the corner regarding the Soviet reaction? It did not seem prudent, no matter what he thought of SDI.

Reagan did not reply immediately to the latter point. He was expecting it. I had delivered it almost verbatim when I impersonated Gorbachev during our mock session the day before. The words came right out of Gorbachev's interview for French television. Instead of raising his voice, as Gorbachev had begun to do, Reagan observed that Gorbachev had illustrated what he meant by a lack of trust. He gave further figures on the number of weapons the Soviet Union had acquired since the SALT I and SALT II treaties were signed and pointed out that the USSR had deployed thousands of additional nuclear weapons while the U.S. was reducing its arsenal. If there was parity in 1972, as both Nixon and Brezhnev declared, how could one claim that the U.S. was seeking superiority when it had not even matched the Soviet buildup?

Then Reagan turned to SDI. Its goal, he insisted—as he would repeatedly in this meeting and subsequent ones—was to determine whether or not defense against nuclear missiles is possible. As both countries conducted research, they should reduce offensive weapons by 50 percent. If they then found that a defense would be possible, they should share it and eliminate nuclear weapons altogether. If offensive weapons were reduced, neither side would have a first-strike capability.

Gorbachev grew more excited, and Reagan (as had been planned) suggested a walk outside. He and Gorbachev put on their coats and strolled down toward the lake, accompanied only by interpreters and bodyguards, the latter walking just out of earshot. The air was cold and provided some relief from the stuffy room and the heat their arguments generated. At the lakefront they paused and Reagan invited Gorbachev into the boathouse with the fireplace.

When they settled down before the fire, Reagan pulled out a sheet of paper with the outline of proposals for the nuclear arms negotiations. They had been typed in Russian so that Gorbachev could read them directly. Reagan asked Gorbachev to consider the paper a "draft compromise" and "a seed for possible instructions" to negotiators. Such instructions could provide the impulse Gorbachev had called for.

Gorbachev read the outline carefully, then commented that he could accept the proposal for a 50 percent reduction in strategic nuclear weapons, but that two major propositions in the paper were unacceptable: there was no provision to prevent an arms race in space, and the proposal on INF (to limit U.S. launchers in Europe to the number of Soviet SS-20s deployed at the end of the year—which would give the USSR a three-to-one advantage in warheads) did not take into account British and French nuclear systems or cruise missiles launched from aircraft or submarines. He asked whether Reagan planned to limit SDI to research. Reagan replied that some testing would be necessary to prove the validity of research, but he would agree that no country would have a monopoly if defenses were feasible.

Gorbachev asked why he should have confidence in such a commitment, and Reagan assured him that he would make a formal undertaking to conduct all research with inspectors from the other side ("open laboratories") and, if successful, to share the benefits. Gorbachev was not buying. He insisted that both agree to refrain from research, development, testing, and deployment of "space weapons," and only then proceed to a 50 percent reduction in nuclear arms. Reagan asked why he kept referring to space weapons and pointed out that there would be nothing in space that would threaten targets on earth.

Gorbachev never explained precisely how he defined the term, but reiterated his threat to counter SDI in every possible way, including by increasing the number of offensive weapons. Reagan urged him to reconsider, but Gorbachev held firm. (In his memoirs, Gorbachev describes Reagan's proposal as a "take-it-or-leave-it" proposition.[6] Actually, Reagan had said explicitly that it was a framework for discussion.)

They put on their coats and started back. When they got to the parking lot next to the villa, Reagan invited Gorbachev to come to the United States. Gorbachev accepted and invited Reagan to Moscow to reciprocate.

When Reagan reported this to his delegation, he pretended to be pleasantly surprised by Gorbachev's ready acceptance of further meetings. Actually, he had received assurance in advance from Soviet ambassador Dobrynin that Gorbachev would agree to further meetings.

That evening the Reagans dined with the Gorbachevs in a villa on the grounds of the Soviet diplomatic mission in Geneva. Neither attempted to continue discussion of the matters that had held their attention all day. In fact, their conversation was as amiable as it had been tense throughout the afternoon. They spoke of their families, about the Soviet film industry, and Russian history, with Gorbachev explaining that Russia had historically shielded Europe from the Mongols and had suffered repeated invasions from both east and west, but had always come back with added strength following a reverse. When Mrs. Reagan asked about social problems, Gorbachev claimed, as he later must have had reason to regret, that his anti-alcohol campaign was a huge success with much grassroots support.

Both raised toasts to closer relations, and Reagan recalled that the Soviet counterattack on German positions at Stalingrad had ended forty-three years ago on the same day. He hoped that their meeting would mark another turning point for mankind. It was a gracious reference to the Soviet effort in World War II, and the fruit of the diligence of researchers on his speechwriting staff. But it was not a hypocritical pose. Reagan was capable of understanding and recognizing the positive contributions the Soviet peoples had made to the world, even as he branded the political system under which they lived an evil empire.

WHILE THE REAGANS and Gorbachevs chatted, U.S. and Soviet negotiators began working on what would be a concluding statement if their bosses decided to issue one. Alexander Bessmertnykh, the longtime head of the USA division in the Soviet foreign ministry who was now a deputy to Shevardnadze and point man for dealing with Americans, headed the Soviet team. Shultz selected his new assistant secretary for European affairs, Rozanne Ridgway, to lead the American group.

Although comparatively new in the job, Roz Ridgway was one of the most capable negotiators in the American Foreign Service. She had negotiated a series of highly technical fisheries agreements with several other countries when Congress extended U.S. control to two hundred miles from the U.S. coastline. She had also settled a highly complex issue of gold claims by Czechoslovakia and U.S. claims for compensation for the American property that had been nationalized by the Communist regime. The issue had eluded solution for thirty-five years. Two earlier negotiated agreements had been rejected by Congress, but Ridgway was able to get from the Czechoslovak government commitments that satisfied most claimants and the Congress: 100 percent compensation, plus some interest—virtually unheard of in settling nationalization claims. She then served as ambassador to the German Democratic Republic (East Germany), which gave her additional experience dealing with Communists. She was an ideal choice to make sure that negotiated agreements during the Reagan administration did not have the sort of flaws found in the agreements Nixon and Kissinger negotiated with Brezhnev and Gromyko. If there was to be another relaxation of tensions (détente), it could not be a one-way street; Roz Ridgway would see to that.

ON NOVEMBER 20 the site of the meetings shifted to the Soviet mission. Once again Reagan and Gorbachev closeted themselves with interpreters for a private session. Once again they ignored the quarter hour schedulers had allotted and continued for seventy minutes. Reagan, as guest, took the lead and immediately launched his pitch on human rights, explaining that it would be much easier for him to get congressional approval for cooperation, trade, and other beneficial agreements if the Soviet government would allow refuseniks to leave the country and stop dividing families by refusing exit permission to one of the spouses. Gorbachev denied that there was a real problem; a spouse of a foreigner was temporarily denied permission to leave only if he or she had been involved in secret work.

Reagan persisted, mentioning specific cases as well as the standards set by the Helsinki Final Act and repeating his previous assurances that if cases were solved, he would never attempt to take public credit. He tried to give Gorbachev an out by saying that he knew it was hard to keep track of what bureaucrats were doing because he had experienced problems with unauthorized discrimination when he was governor of California.

Gorbachev countered that the United States had used accusations of human rights violations for ulterior political purposes, and this had to be rejected. The U.S. had its own problems, but each country should live by its own system without throwing stones at the other. He would examine individual cases that Reagan brought to his attention, but he implied that this was merely a goodwill gesture. Enforcement of Soviet laws and regulations he considered an internal matter, not subject to negotiations with other countries.

Some half hour into this conversation, Gorbachev became impatient. "We've each had our say," he remarked several times. "Now let's move on and join the others." But Reagan was not to be denied, and continued to cite specific cases and explain how they affected opinion in Congress. His irritation rising, Gorbachev finally blurted out that he knew well that the president could do what he wished; all his talk of pressure from Congress and "small pressure groups" was just a pretext. As they moved into the room with their delegations, Reagan shook his head as he remarked, "You sure are wrong about an American president's power!"

The formal discussions that followed amounted to a repeat of the exchanges the day before, with only slight variations but even more intense emotion on Gorbachev's part. Reagan offered suggestions for the nuclear negotiations similar to those he had made in the boathouse, and Gorbachev had the same reaction. As they repeated their respective comments on SDI, Gorbachev's temper rose, and his face flushed with anger. "Do you take us for idiots?" he asked, red-faced, when Reagan for the nth time explained that he was not proposing that defensive weapons be added to existing offensive arsenals, but to reduce offensive weapons by 50 percent while conducting research to see if defenses were feasible. Reagan, still calm, replied that he had shown no disrespect and had never considered the Soviet leaders naive. But he could see no logical argument against a research program if safeguards prevented any country from acquiring a defensive monopoly.

When the delegations gathered in the afternoon, they began to discuss how to wind up the meeting. Ridgway and Bessmertnykh had been discussing a concluding document, even though Reagan still had not agreed to one. After discussion, Reagan and Gorbachev agreed that they would issue a document that described what they had agreed. Now Ridgway and Bessmertnykh could work officially rather than informally.

REAGAN AND GORBACHEV reassembled with their wives for another dinner, this time at the villa where the Reagans were staying. Once again the arguments of the day were set aside in favor of general table talk, of relatives, of letters from constituents, of religion in the Soviet Union and the influence of Islamic fundamentalism. In their toasts, both agreed that they had "made a start" toward a new relationship. They then left the table and went into the study.

As soon as the group had settled, Shultz turned to business, suggesting that both Reagan and Gorbachev make public statements the following morning as they signed whatever documents were prepared. Apparently fearing that Reagan might say something that would embarrass him, Gorbachev was dubious at first, but finally agreed, provided the statements were kept very short. At that point, Roz Ridgway called Shultz out to report that the working group was stalled; the Soviet negotiators were haggling over language and, she felt, reneging on some agreements made earlier. If that kept on, she warned, there might be no agreed document for the ceremony the next morning.

Shultz was furious. He came back into the room, told Gorbachev and Reagan that things were not going well with the statement, and placed the responsibility on Georgy Korniyenko, who was among the group at dinner but had presumably given Bessmertnykh instructions as to his approach. Gorbachev said that he was sure they could work things out. When he left the dinner, he conferred with Bessmertnykh, convinced himself that the differences that had emerged were trivial, and gave orders to stop haggling and finish the document. Thus, after midnight, work proceeded rapidly and a joint statement was drawn up for presentation to journalists the next morning.

I WORKED THROUGH the night to help prepare the speeches Reagan would make the following day. Several were required, all important: a brief statement at the concluding ceremony in Geneva; a report to the North Atlantic Council (the leaders of NATO governments) in Brussels, where Reagan would stop on his way back to Washington, and then a report to the nation, scheduled to be delivered before a joint session of Congress just after Reagan's return to Washington that evening. It would be a long day: everything would be packed in the twenty hours from our working breakfast with the president at eight o'clock Geneva time to the end of his address in Washington at about 10 p.m. eastern standard time. Nevertheless, there was no time for rest: we had to make sure everything was ready before the president went onstage with Gorbachev at ten the next morning.

It didn't help that our negotiators worked with the Soviet team until the wee hours to get an agreed document, but that was not the main problem. We could write drafts of the various speeches and statements on the assumption that certain things would be agreed; if we turned out to be wrong on some particular points, we could easily correct the details when we had the final text. The more serious problem came from the White House speechwriting staff. They had never been comfortable with talk about cooperation with the Soviet Union and resented having been bypassed when some of Reagan's key policy statements were prepared. Several of the speechwriters were constantly in a preachy, confrontational, anti-Soviet mode. When Patrick Buchanan replaced David Gergen as White House director of communications, a restraining hand was removed, and from that point almost every speech on foreign affairs was preceded by pitched battles between the NSC staff, determined to carry out the president's desire to pave the way for negotiation, and the speechwriters, intent on using every occasion for verbal attacks on the Soviet Union.

All of the initial speech drafts were larded with disparaging statements about the Soviet Union and communism, and even contained slighting references to Gorbachev. I would mark them out and explain that the president considered this meeting a success; to use his report on his meeting with Gorbachev to attack the Soviet Union would be inconsistent with his judgment and would strike the public as proof that he had no intention of trying to improve relations. Attacks on Gorbachev personally would be even more out of place; Reagan hoped to prepare the ground for working with him and needed to give our public and our allies some hope that he could.

Such explanations were usually met with charges that I was being "soft" and urging "defeatist" attitudes. Sometimes there were even hints that any talk of cooperation or compromise (both words Reagan loved) was somehow pro-Soviet, maybe not outright treasonous, but definitely "détentist," and therefore suspiciously "leftist."

With Bud McFarlane's strong support, I managed to expunge most of the anti-Soviet rhetoric from the speech drafts and, when the text of the agreed joint statement arrived, to make such factual adjustments as it required. There were still three passages in one of the speeches that worried me, however: they would be read as direct personal insults by Gorbachev. I knew that was not what the president wanted, but Peggy Noonan, who had written them, and Pat Buchanan, who supervised the preparation of speeches, were adamant. They refused to take them out.

By 4:30 a.m. everyone except the speechwriters, who had had nothing to do in Geneva up to then, was dead tired. The draft had to be put in a form for the president to review when he got up. I saw that further argument was hopeless, so I agreed that they should send him the draft as it was. "Do you want to mark the passages you don't like?" I was asked.

"No," I replied, exasperated with what seemed to me the obtuseness the speechwriters were exhibiting. "You act as if I'm trying to put something over on the president. That's ridiculous. Send in your draft without any indication that the NSC objects, and we'll see what happens."

We gathered for breakfast with Reagan a few hours later. He came in, speech draft in hand, with the three passages I had questioned marked out. Turning to Buchanan, he said, "Pat, this has been a good meeting. I think I can work with this guy. I can't just keep poking him in the eye!" Then he glanced over at me with a quizzical expression, as if to say, "How the hell did you let that stuff slip through?"

THE REST OF the long day went well. Before an auditorium packed with journalists, Gorbachev and Reagan made brief, polite statements about the start they had made on the road to a peaceful world, then retired with their aides to a side room for a departure toast. I chatted with Andrei Alexandrov-Agentov, the foreign affairs adviser whom Gorbachev had inherited from his three predecessors and I had known since Brezhnev days. Urbane and often witty, he joked that his boss was known at home as the "mineral secretary," a sly reference to the anti-alcohol campaign Gorbachev had bragged about at dinner the night before. (In Russia, soda water is often called "mineral water," or simply "mineral," rhyming, as it does in English, with "general.") In this case, Gorbachev's glass was filled with a French champagne of respectable vintage. He sipped it gingerly, as if it were a duty that gave him scant pleasure, and probably was thankful that there were no television cameras in evidence. He was, however, in a buoyant mood, as was Reagan. They indulged in no more heavy argument, just small talk laced with promises to meet again soon.

Reagan's report to the North Atlantic Council in Brussels received strong applause. Allied governments had been so concerned by the U.S.-Soviet confrontation that any meeting that did not break up in mutual recrimination would have been judged a success. When Reagan walked into the chamber of the House of Representatives that evening to address a joint session of Congress he was greeted as a conquering hero.

Press coverage in the United States, Europe, and the rest of the world was overwhelmingly positive. It was as if the world breathed a deep sigh of relief.

A Balance Sheet

MY FIRST JOB after returning from Geneva was to review the summaries of the various meetings and to analyze the results. In general, the United States valued action and concrete agreements more than proclamations of general principles. However, one of the principles incorporated in the joint statement was important, as much for the way it was phrased as for what it said. It was that "a nuclear war cannot be won and must never be fought." In the past, the Soviet Union had always insisted that others endorse "peaceful coexistence," but this was an ideologically loaded term. It was applied only to "states with different social systems," leaving the door open for one "socialist state" to use force against another, as the Soviet Union did in Hungary in 1956, Czechoslovakia in 1968, and Afghanistan in 1979. At Geneva, Soviet negotiators accepted for the first time a flat, nonideological statement. In fact, it was a statement Ronald Reagan had made in several speeches before he went to Geneva.

Curiously, as Gorbachev, Shevardnadze, and Alexandrov-Agentov all mention in their memoirs, the Soviet officials in Geneva considered this statement and the one that followed about the "importance of preventing any war between them [the U.S. and USSR], whether nuclear or conventional," as achievements of Soviet diplomacy. This showed that they had not been paying attention to what Reagan had been saying—or, more likely, had been paying attention to just part of what he said. But it was a good thing. We Americans were pleased that the Soviets had taken ideology out of war and peace (at least in principle); the Soviets were pleased that the United States would pledge efforts to prevent a war. That statement obviously did not and could not eliminate mutual suspicion, but it is relevant to note that the hysterical accusations that the U.S. was planning a nuclear strike, so prominent in Soviet propaganda in the early eighties, virtually disappeared following the Geneva summit.

Though issues in all four areas of the American agenda had been discussed in Geneva, there was no perceptible movement in two of them, human rights and regional conflicts. On the first, although Gorbachev agreed to review individual cases, he was not willing to grant that protection of human rights was a legitimate subject for international attention. He had little to say of local and regional strife except for the fighting in Afghanistan (which he considered a problem caused by the interference of countries other than the Soviet Union), and had pointedly avoided discussing Reagan's proposal for dealing with regional turmoil where the U.S. and USSR backed opposing groups.

The clearest success was in the area of cultural and other exchanges and cooperation on joint projects. All the useful projects that had been jettisoned by the Carter administration after the invasion of Afghanistan were restored and even expanded. Airline service between the two countries would resume; there would be cooperation to ensure aircraft safety in the North Pacific, which would prevent another disaster with a Korean or any other civilian airliner. Cultural, educational, and athletic exchanges would be expanded and include younger persons than before. The American goal in all of this was to erode the Iron Curtain; Gorbachev's willingness to cooperate—still to be tested in practice—would tell us how serious he was about bringing his country into the modern world.

For most Soviet officials, many American officials, and the world at large, nuclear weapons were the central issue. Despite the sharp disagreement regarding SDI, there was unmistakable progress in closing some gaps between the U.S. and Soviet positions. Gorbachev had now agreed to a 50 percent reduction of strategic nuclear weapons, a prime American goal. (In

1977, Gromyko had run Secretary of State Cyrus Vance out of town when he came to Moscow with a proposal for "deep cuts" amounting to a mere 35 percent.) Reagan had substantially modified the U.S. position on INF, making clear that he would not insist on total elimination. Both sides agreed in principle to comprehensive on-site inspection, something the Soviet Union had always resisted.

Encouraging as these changes were, one could not be sure how meaningful they would be until specific treaty language was drafted. As in many areas of life, when it came to arms control, the devil was in the details. It had always been difficult to reach agreement on what, concretely, general principles meant. Therefore, we could not be sure that we would both understand a 50 percent reduction in the same way, or that the Soviets would agree to as much on-site inspection as the United States considered necessary. Nevertheless, there could be no progress at all until views converged on these broad questions, and therefore the movement in the positions of both countries was something to be welcomed.

As I reflected on the heated exchanges on SDI, I was struck not so much by the fact that Gorbachev condemned SDI with as much vigor as Reagan used to defend it—this we had expected—but by the number of statements Reagan made that went far beyond the thinking of the Defense Department, State Department, and his own NSC staff. He not only offered to share missile defenses, but was willing to formalize a commitment to do so in a treaty and to provide guarantees that no single country would have a monopoly of them. He offered to open U.S. laboratories to inspection by Soviet scientists. He offered on-site inspection to verify that SDI research did not involve development of offensive weaponry. He did not demand a right to deploy missile defense systems, but only to conduct research and testing to determine their feasibility. Although he would insist on a right to conduct some testing, he said nothing about a right to test components or to develop weapons based on "other physical principles" cited in the ABM Treaty. An attentive listener would have detected a number of openings that Gorbachev could have explored, if only to put Reagan on the spot and call his presumed bluff.

However, Gorbachev had not been an attentive listener, nor had he provided a coherent explanation of the Soviet point of view. At times he sounded as if he would ban research altogether, even that which the ABM Treaty explicitly permitted; at others he implied that he would draw the line at testing. He insisted on calling strategic defenses "space weapons" (in theory, at least, they might or might not be) and denying that the Soviet Union had any, when the ABM system around Moscow comprised land-based interceptors designed to destroy incoming missiles in space. This was a "space weapon" according to the definition Gromyko had offered in 1984, as was the anti-satellite (ASAT) weapon the USSR had tested, but Gorbachev bridled when Reagan mentioned them, objecting that they were permitted by the ABM Treaty. They were, and Reagan never claimed otherwise, but this was irrelevant to the point he was making.

In fact, Gorbachev could have molded Reagan's position without making commitments himself just by asking a few questions. When Reagan spoke of sharing, he could have asked what specific guarantees Reagan was willing to undertake and how he would make them enforceable. He could have asked for more details on "open laboratories" and whether the idea should be applied to offensive weapons research and development as well. He might have asked whether Reagan would accept a joint SDI program. My guess is that, in many of these areas, Reagan would have been willing to make some far-reaching commitments in order to gain Gorbachev's acquiescence to SDI research.

That does not mean that a treaty would have been easy to conclude even if Gorbachev had shown more curiosity and flexibility. There would have been hell to pay in Washington when Reagan returned and word got out about what he had promised.

"Share? He's crazy! This is sensitive technology! We can't do that!"

"Open labs? He's gotta be kidding. I won't have the rooskies snooping around my lab and picking up ideas!"

Yes, there would have been some intense fights, but Reagan's critics might well have found him as stubborn as Gorbachev did. Once he had an idea in his head, it was mighty hard to dislodge it. Sharing SDI was one of those ideas, and it was just about as immovable as the idea of SDI itself.

Given the intense opposition throughout both the Soviet and U.S. governments to sharing technology, Reagan and Gorbachev probably could not have forced their governments at that point to agree to open laboratories and to share defensive weaponry. But if Gorbachev had picked up on the ideas Reagan threw out in Geneva, Reagan would have tried to make them work. Gorbachev's adamant refusal to consider SDI in any form was a strategic error even more profound than Andropov's refusal to make a deal on INF before American deployments started in Europe. The more rigid his opposition, the more necessary the program seemed and the more leverage hardliners who opposed any accommodation with the Soviet Union would have over Reagan's thinking.

———

REAGAN RETURNED FROM Geneva with respect for Gorbachev. In fact, he liked the man. When Gorbachev got excited, he didn't act like Gromyko, who always seemed to be putting on a calculated act, working himself up in a lather just for effect. (A professional actor is pretty good at spotting an act.) Gorbachev seemed to say what he thought, even if he kept in mind what the folks at home would think. Yes, Gorbachev had gotten hot under the collar when it was a question of SDI, and had not been very forthcoming when it came to human rights and settling regional conflicts or withdrawing from Afghanistan. But he did seem genuinely interested in reducing arms and he clearly had problems at home that would limit his capacity to change Soviet policy overnight. But unlike the other Soviet leaders Reagan had dealt with or heard about, Gorbachev was a human being, not some ventriloquist's dummy that just repeated set phrases. He seemed to be a man Reagan could reason with. Maybe Gorbachev's rejection of SDI was a ruse; obviously no sensible person would claim that missile defenses would give a country that reduced nuclear weapons in advance a first-strike capacity. Maybe Gorbachev just needed to go home and massage a few egos.

Gorbachev's reaction to Reagan seems to have been more complex. In his memoirs he writes that at times during his meetings, "Reagan appeared to me not simply a conservative, but a political 'dinosaur.' "[7] He also found him, as he reported to the Politburo later, stubborn and ill informed. Nevertheless, there was something intangible that attracted him. Reagan treated him with respect. Reagan's appeals that the two were responsible for world peace struck home; he seemed to consider Gorbachev, at least when it came to war and peace, as a partner. Reagan's charm and openness served to compensate, to some degree, for his intransigence. Reagan, too, was struggling with problems at home and probably couldn't get everything he wanted from the military-industrial complex and the fire-eaters in his administration. Maybe Andropov had been wrong that the man was impossible.

Follow-up

AFTER THE MEETINGS in Geneva, Reagan flew out to his ranch near Santa Barbara for Thanksgiving. He was still there when I was asked to draft a letter to Gorbachev following up on the discussions in Geneva. Eager to avoid the delays of interagency consideration and bickering between Shultz and Weinberger, Reagan intended to copy my draft in his own handwriting.

He felt that his cabinet officers were less likely to pick it apart if he presented it that way.

I sat down at my word processor and had a text ready in a few hours. Poindexter read it, approved it, and sent it to McFarlane, who was with the president in Santa Barbara. The president liked it, copied it out in his own handwriting, and sent it back to Washington to show to Shultz and Weinberger. They read it hurriedly and made no objections. On November 28, just a week after we returned from Geneva, the letter went out to Ambassador Hartman for delivery in Moscow. If we had followed normal procedure, with a draft by the State Department, clearance by an interagency group, then checking and revision at the NSC, the process would have taken weeks if not months, Reagan would have rejected the cautious, prolix product, and I would have ended up drafting the same letter before he would have agreed to send it.

Instead of cataloging all the issues on the agenda, this letter selected two questions for immediate attention: Gorbachev's perception that the United States was seeking a strategic advantage, and a political settlement in Afghanistan. On the first, Reagan suggested that our negotiators discuss frankly what developments each country would find threatening and explore ways to avoid them. Specifically, he proposed to focus on measures that could eliminate the possibility of a first-strike strategy by either side, in order to find a solution to Gorbachev's principal objections to SDI. Regarding Afghanistan, Reagan pledged "to cooperate in any reasonable way to facilitate . . . a withdrawal," and noted that he understood "that it must be done in a manner that does not damage Soviet security."[8]

A few days after the letter was dispatched, Secretary Shultz proposed to Soviet ambassador Dobrynin that Gorbachev come to Washington in June 1986. Both Reagan and Shultz were eager to fix a date for the next meeting.

McFarlane Resigns

JUST A FEW days after Reagan wrote out his letter to Gorbachev, while the two were still in California, Bud McFarlane gave the president a letter of resignation. In his memoirs, he explains that he was fatigued, desperately wanted more time with his family, and was fed up with bickering in the administration and Chief of Staff Donald Regan's attempts to deny him direct access to the president.[9] In addition, he had been involved in a secret effort to make contact with moderate elements in Iran by supplying arms to defend the country from Saddam Hussein's Iraq, which had attacked Iran. McFarlane felt that this effort was becoming little more than an arms-for-hostages deal—Iran was the main backer of the group that was kidnapping Americans in Lebanon—and should be ended. He doubted however, that Reagan would agree to end the operation given his determination to do everything possible to free the American hostages in Lebanon.

As soon as he read the letter of resignation, Reagan pressed McFarlane to reconsider, but when McFarlane insisted that it was time for him to return to private life, Reagan acquiesced. Within days, McFarlane regretted his action, feeling that he was copping out rather than finishing the task he had set out to do. But it was then too late to change his mind.

McFarlane recommended that Rear Admiral John Poindexter, his deputy, be named to replace him, and Reagan agreed. Poindexter had then been on the National Security Council staff since 1981, working as the third-ranking official under William Clark and then as McFarlane's number two. He was thus the most experienced senior official available. His quick selection avoided a fight within the administration such as that which followed Clark's resignation. Members of the NSC staff were shocked and saddened by Bud McFarlane's sudden departure, but—if he had to go—were pleased that the president named John Poindexter as his successor.

Poindexter, a career naval officer with a Ph.D. in nuclear physics, had worked harmoniously with McFarlane for several years and agreed with him on all key policy matters, but they had different views of the role the national security assistant should play. Both understood that their primary responsibility was to the president, but McFarlane was comfortable in continuing the tradition Dr. Henry Kissinger had initiated of briefing the press often—usually "on background," that is, not for attribution—but often also on the record. He also was diligent in consulting with key members of Congress.

In contrast, Poindexter felt that he could best serve the president by staying in the background, avoiding press briefings and consultations with Congress when he could. His concept of the role was, therefore, closer to that followed by national security assistants before Kissinger. It was not suited to building cozy relations with journalists or an image with the public at large, but for a time it kept Poindexter out of public bickering over policy.

John Poindexter was popular with his staff. As a good military officer, he understood the importance of loyalty down as well as loyalty up. His loyalty to President Reagan was total and he was more reluctant to "teach" the president than McFarlane had been. In regard to the Soviet Union, he had been an early supporter of the Strategic Defense Initiative, but as a scientist he understood that strategic defenses could never be perfect and therefore did not make sense as an offensive strategy. He also was coming to understand that space-based strategic defenses were unlikely to prove feasible. While he was a firm believer in using a threat to create them as a means of inducing the Soviet leaders to reduce their heavy ICBMs, he did not have Reagan's romantic attachment to SDI and did not share Weinberger's view that any limitation on the program would kill it.

Gorbachev Stonewalls

IT TOOK NEARLY a month for Gorbachev to reply to Reagan's letter, and when he did, he said nothing about a meeting date and rejected Reagan's attempt to find ways to meet the concerns he had expressed in Geneva. He was certain, he said, that SDI could be only an offensive strategy, even if Reagan himself did not consider it so. The only thing to do was to ban any effort to build "space-strike weapons." Gorbachev also disputed Reagan's reference to the advantage the Soviet Union held in weapons suitable for a first strike, citing American submarine-launched ballistic missiles (SLBMs) and the Pershing IIs in Germany.[10]

His answer was discouraging since he continued to make flat statements that misrepresented the situation and made no effort to explore ways to avoid the dangers he imagined. So far as first-strike weapons were concerned, the United States did not believe that its SLBMs would be effective against hardened missile silos since they did not have the accuracy of the land-based ICBMs. Also, it was absurd for Gorbachev to claim that the Pershing II was a potential first-strike weapon. It did not have the range to come anywhere near most Soviet ICBM silos. In fact, as already noted, it could not even reach Moscow from its bases in Germany.

There was a big question in our minds in Washington when Reagan received this letter. Did Gorbachev really believe some of the things in his letter? If so, he was being misinformed, but this did not seem likely. He had apparently decided not to discuss the relationship of defensive and offensive weaponry but to force Reagan to accept a highly symbolic political defeat, which, for Reagan, was much more than symbolic.

Though it was not yet apparent to American officials, the overdue reassessment of Soviet policy had begun. Much later, Gorbachev himself wrote that March to December 1985 "was an extremely important period, marked by an intense search for new policy approaches leading to conclusions that became the core of the new thinking."[11] The fruits of that rethinking would not emerge for some time, but on one important point Gorbachev and Reagan were already in agreement. In Gorbachev's words, "Because of the prevailing mistrust between East and West, only specific measures could contribute to establishing trust. And without trust even the slightest improvement in world affairs would be impossible to achieve."[12] Reagan, too, had described "the prevalent hostility and suspicion between us" as one of the three "main events" in U.S.-Soviet relations, and had been waiting, largely in vain, for evidence that the Soviet leaders would reduce armaments equitably and refrain from using force to achieve political objectives outside their borders.

Both Reagan and Gorbachev were convinced that trust was a fundamental issue, but they had different ideas of what it would take to build trust. Gorbachev wanted signs that Reagan would cool the arms race. Reagan wanted signs that Gorbachev would change Soviet attitudes and practices. Each looked for a "reliable partner" without, as yet, fully comprehending what he had to do to convince the other that he could be trusted.

VIII

1986: January–August

GENEVA RECEDES; COMPLICATIONS MOUNT

The Americans continued to proclaim in public their readiness for serious arms control negotiations, but in reality they were again undermining the talks.
—MIKHAIL GORBACHEV, 1996[1]

Although I agreed with the goals of Gorbachev's proposal, there were enormous problems to be solved before we could work out an agreement.
—RONALD REAGAN, 1990[2]

THE YEAR 1986 began auspiciously for a new spirit in U.S.-Soviet relations, as President Reagan and General Secretary Gorbachev each sent televised New Year's greetings to the people in the other country. Americans, occupied with other matters on New Year's Day, paid little attention. Soviet citizens were less blasé. The image of Ronald Reagan, scourge of the "evil empire," on their television screens was a revelation. Reagan radiated goodwill and an interest not just in peace, but in the welfare of Soviet people. They also saw Gorbachev's message to Americans. They could relax. Nuclear war was obviously not about to break out, as they had been encouraged to believe in 1983 and 1984.

People in the Soviet Union were not mistaken in that conclusion, but, so far as arms reduction was concerned, 1986 turned out to be a year of recurrent hope followed by disappointment. The war in Afghanistan continued, as did other regional conflicts. Soviet authorities allowed some divided spouses to leave the country, released Anatoly Shcharansky in a trade for Communist bloc spies held in West Germany, and in December permitted

Andrei Sakharov to return to his residence in Moscow. Nevertheless, Gorbachev had not yet acknowledged that protection of human rights was a legitimate subject for negotiation; the number of Jewish refuseniks continued to grow, and most of the political prisoners arrested in the 1970s and early 1980s remained in labor camps.

The only consistently encouraging trend in the U.S.-Soviet relationship that year had to do with people-to-people contacts, crucial for eroding the Iron Curtain and exposing the Soviet public to the realities of the outside world. At Geneva, Gorbachev had accepted ambitious goals for cultural, educational, scientific, and athletic exchanges. The United States moved promptly to press for a rapid expansion of contacts that had been nearly strangled following the Soviet invasion of Afghanistan. Charles Wick, the energetic head of the United States Information Agency, was given responsibility for implementing what we called the "president's initiative," in reference to the proposals Reagan had signaled in June 1984 and had presented formally to Gorbachev before the Geneva summit meeting.

Recognizing that the existing bureaucracy might not give this program the attention it required, Wick established a special office to work out agreements with the Soviet government and American sponsors to expand contacts in as many areas as possible. He recruited Stephen H. Rhinesmith, the former head of the American Field Service, to manage the effort and obtained for him the rank of ambassador in order to give him access to senior Soviet officials. Rhinesmith's rank, equivalent to that of U.S. arms control negotiators, was also intended to call attention to the importance the United States attached to the expansion of private contacts. Wick and Rhinesmith traveled to Moscow early in 1986 and arranged with several Soviet ministries and public organizations an ambitious schedule of visits in both directions. These grew rapidly during 1986 and, by 1987 and 1988, had reached an unprecedented scale.[3]

Cognitive Disjuncture

REAGAN AND GORBACHEV both left Geneva determined to press ahead for verifiable agreements to reduce nuclear weapons and to reverse the arms race in general. However, they had quite different ideas of the way that objective could be achieved.

President Reagan wanted to negotiate the key elements personally. He was encouraged that Gorbachev had accepted his invitation to come to Washington, and for him the most important next step was to set a date for that meeting. He also felt that agreements on arms reduction could not stand alone; they should be accompanied by substantial progress in other areas of the agenda he had set forth. In particular, it would be difficult for him to conclude a major arms control agreement unless the Soviet Union took steps to reverse its most serious violations of previous agreements and had realistic plans to withdraw its troops from Afghanistan.

However, General Secretary Gorbachev felt that he could not go to the United States for a meeting unless he was assured in advance that one or more significant arms control agreements could be reached. Furthermore, he wished to get these agreements without any understandings regarding Afghanistan, regional disputes, treaty violations, or protection of human rights. For him, any acceptable agreement to reduce nuclear weapons had to contain severe limits on testing and developing strategic defenses. He was also still insisting that the United States agree to a moratorium on nuclear testing before the Soviet Union would consider on-site verification.

Reagan had moved more quickly than Gorbachev to capture the "spirit of Geneva." The letter he sent a week after he returned from Geneva made concrete proposals that could have formed the basis for agreements at the next summit. Reagan had not expected Gorbachev to agree to them without further consideration, but was disappointed that Gorbachev avoided even discussing them. As for the date of Gorbachev's visit, there was only silence. By February and March 1986, Soviet diplomats, and then Gorbachev himself, started telling people that he would not set a date until he was sure that agreements could be reached. One "get acquainted" meeting was all right, his people explained, but a second one without concrete results would be considered by the public in both countries as a failure.

On that point, he was probably right, but if that was the case he should not have accepted the invitation Reagan extended during their walk in Geneva without mentioning the condition. He could have said, "I'll be pleased to come next year if we can reach some significant agreements." But that is not what he said. Reagan interpreted his reluctance to set a date as a blatant attempt to extract a price for the meeting. This encouraged Reagan to hold firm until he knew when Gorbachev would come to Washington. Gorbachev, in turn, interpreted Reagan's stance as an effort to lure him to a fruitless meeting.

Gorbachev's "January Initiative"

ALTHOUGH GORBACHEV HAD gone along with the traditional Gromyko-devised policies throughout 1985, he had been dissatisfied. He wanted an innovative policy and started pressing the foreign ministry to come up with new ideas. In particular, he wanted something new following his meeting with Reagan in Geneva. Two officers in the foreign ministry's USA division, Sergei Tarasenko and Georgy Mamedov, had earlier drafted a proposal which they thought would make a propaganda splash and also contain some elements that could move negotiations in the right direction. A proposal to abolish nuclear weapons by the year 2000, though unrealistic, would attract public attention; the first step, a 50 percent cut in strategic nuclear weapons, would be useful even if subsequent stages were not possible. They passed their draft to Viktor Komplektov, then head of the USA division in the ministry.

The draft never came back to them, and subsequently Tarasenko asked Komplektov what had happened. Komplektov advised him to forget it; as far as he and Mamedov were concerned, it no longer existed, but "belonged to others." But it was almost identical to the proposal that Georgy Korniyenko, Shevardnadze's principal deputy, and Sergei Akhromeyev, chief of the Soviet General Staff, recommended to Gorbachev following the Geneva summit. Korniyenko had presumably brought Akhromeyev into the picture because he knew that the Ministry of Defense would oppose any proposal made by the Ministry of Foreign Affairs alone. Akhromeyev accepted it because he believed the United States would reject it and thereby relieve the Soviet military from pressure for more limited concessions.[4]

When the proposal was given to him, Gorbachev liked it. It seemed to be just what he was looking for, an "initiative" that would leave the impression that the Soviet Union, unlike the United States, was serious about ending the arms race. He put it in a proposal to Reagan and other Western leaders, and instructed the Soviet information media to publicize it.

Gorbachev's message was received in Washington the morning of January 15. John Poindexter, still in his first weeks as assistant to the president for national security, called me out of a meeting elsewhere in Washington and, after I rushed across town to his White House office, showed me the text and asked whether I thought Gorbachev was serious. "Have they put it on TASS yet?" I asked.

Poindexter telephoned the duty officer in the Situation Room and was informed that the text was coming over the newswires at that moment. For nearly a year we had followed the practice of making our proposals in private and giving the Soviets time to react privately before publicizing them. Gorbachev's action in announcing his proposal to the world even before we had a chance to read it carefully raised the suspicion that he had nothing more than propaganda in mind. I pointed this out to Poindexter.

"I think you are right," he said, "but the president has already looked at it and likes the part about getting rid of nuclear weapons. He believes it's the first time a Soviet leader has suggested a certain date." (Both countries had been on record for years favoring the ultimate elimination of nuclear weapons—or, in the Soviet case, "general and complete disarmament"—but nobody took that seriously because no date was set as a goal and neither country had described a realistic process to reach it.) "Of course," he continued, "there are several things we can't accept. Gorbachev is still trying to kill SDI before we make the initial cut in nuclear weapons, and there are other problems with it, such as the insistence on an immediate moratorium on nuclear tests." It was also obvious to us that Britain, France, and China were unlikely to agree to phase out their nuclear forces the way the Soviet scheme would have required.*

Most U.S. government agencies considered Gorbachev's proposal nothing more than smoke and mirrors and advised a flat rejection. Reagan did not want to seem negative, however, and insisted on a positive statement. His public reaction was that Gorbachev's proposal was "at first glance constructive" although it contained certain elements that caused the United States "serious concern." He promised to give the proposal careful study. This was considerably more forthcoming than Gorbachev's reaction to Reagan's proposals had been. Gorbachev had not even accepted the idea of having U.S. and Soviet military specialists meet to compare and discuss their respective threat assessments. Unlike the United States, Britain and France refused even to discuss the Gorbachev proposal. Prime Minister Margaret Thatcher called it "pie in the sky."

Though specialists on both sides considered the idea impractical, this proposal had an important psychological effect on both Reagan and Gorbachev. It fitted Reagan's dream of putting the world on the road to abolishing nuclear weapons. As for Gorbachev, it seems to have marked a shift from the tactic of bringing pressure to bear on Washington through American allies in Europe to dealing directly with Reagan.[5] However, this is apparent only in retrospect; many of Gorbachev's actions in early 1986 continued the tactics adopted in 1985.

---

* Gorbachev proposed elimination of nuclear weapons in three stages, the first to constitute a 50 percent cut in strategic weapons by the U.S. and USSR, followed by two further stages of reduction that would include the other nuclear powers (Britain, France, and China). This would permit, in the year 2000, a "universal accord that such weapons should never again come into being." Everything was conditioned on an immediate moratorium on nuclear testing and banning "space-strike weapons" from the start.

A Key Appointment

ON FEBRUARY 1, Gorbachev called Anatoly Chernyaev and invited him to become his assistant for foreign affairs, replacing Andrei Alexandrov-Agentov. Chernyaev had worked for Boris Ponomarev in the Central Committee International Department since returning to Moscow from an assignment in Prague on the staff of the international Communist journal. Gromyko, a rival of Ponomarev's, had for years resisted the involvement of the International Department in the key issues of East-West relations. Gromyko insisted that Ponomarev's staff deal only with foreign Communist Parties, and sometimes non-Communist parties, rather than with foreign governments. Staffers in the International Department chafed under this restriction and were privately critical of Gromyko's approach. It would be wrong to think that they were in any way pro-American in their attitudes—they were not—but they deplored the rigidity of Gromyko's diplomacy, the militarization of Soviet foreign policy, and the Soviet opposition to "revisionism" in European Communist Parties. Their views were close to those of the Euro-Communists, particularly the Italians. Of this group, Chernyaev was probably the most critical of traditional Soviet foreign policy. He tells us in his memoirs that he wrote in his diary when he heard that Brezhnev had died that Brezhnev's successor should make radical changes in Soviet policy:

> Goal: Feed our people and restore an incentive to work.
> Methods and chief problems:
> 1. Root out the Brezhnev infrastructure—all those relatives, hangers on, favorites, and cronies dragged in from Moldavia and Dnepropetrovsk. . . .*
> 2. Leave Afghanistan.
> 3. Tell Jaruzelski that it is up to him to get out of his mess and give everyone to understand that there is no way we are going to intervene in Poland.
> 4. In regard to the socialist countries, make a declaration similar to the one Khrushchev made in 1956 (which he immediately violated in Hungary). Renounce the principle that we must control everything. Let them do what they wish.
> 5. Remove the SS-20s from Europe.

---

* Brezhnev had brought to Moscow a number of cronies from his earlier assignments in Kishinev and Dnepropetrovsk. Their sycophancy and intrigues had stimulated much hostility among other Party officials and civil servants.

6. Rein in the military-industrial complex. Defy American blackmail and cut the armed forces to a quarter of what we have now.
7. Put the foreign ministry under the control of the Central Committee. . . . Name a Central Committee secretary to supervise foreign affairs. (But not Boris Ponomarev!)
8. Let all dissidents, first of all Sakharov, leave the country, including those Andropov imprisoned as well as those he hasn't yet managed to put inside.
9. The same thing regarding all Jews who want to leave. At the same time outlaw anti-Semitism. Treat Jews at least with the same respect as Armenians in the system of "people's friendship."

[Points 10 to 15 were of a purely domestic import.][6]

Obviously, if Chernyaev was thinking these things in 1982, he would have had to keep his mouth shut or lose his job. He was able to start expressing some of them only after his personal relationship with Gorbachev solidified. Nevertheless, the diary entry shows that it was possible, even under Soviet conditions in Brezhnev's time, to see that many Soviet policies were not serving the Soviet interest.

Chernyaev wrote that Gorbachev gave him no instructions when he asked him to become his personal assistant. Chernyaev himself defined his priorities as "disarmament, Soviet-American relations, regional crises, Jewish and other emigration issues, and forming a 'security council' (using Washington as an example)."[7] Two of these, regional crises and emigration, were issues from which Gorbachev still tried to exclude the United States. Chernyaev never managed to develop a staff as extensive and well equipped as the National Security Council in Washington, but over time he exercised a strong influence on Gorbachev's view of the world.

One of Chernyaev's early assignments was to help draft the foreign policy section of Gorbachev's report to the upcoming Communist Party Congress. His subsequent observations pinpoint the contradictory elements in Gorbachev's thinking in 1986.

Judging by this speech, and by the words and actions that distinguished Gorbachev from our previous leaders, he'd already formed an idea of "new thinking." But it was still contaminated by ideological and class mythology, and influenced by an outdated view of the situation even at that moment. And most important—it was hampered by old commitments to friends and allies as well as the duties of "proletarian" and "socialist" internationalism. The CPSU [Communist Party of the Soviet Union] saw itself as the mainstay and guarantor of that internationalism and considered it one of the main sources of our strength as a superpower. Hence the mixture of new and old, the imaginary and real, the contradictions and inconsistencies in Gorbachev's views that I constantly encountered when reading my notes of his conversations.[8]

The contradictions and inconsistencies Chernyaev mentioned were, of course, obvious to President Reagan and his staff. And although Reagan considered his own views totally consistent, his reaction to what he considered Gorbachev's jockeying for advantage caused him to make decisions that convinced Gorbachev that he was not sincere. These were the factors that lay behind the frustration experienced by those of us on both sides who were trying to end the arms race but were confronted by a succession of events that could only encourage it.

The Issues

THE SAME ISSUES that had plagued relations throughout 1984 and 1985 persisted through 1986 in spite of efforts to tackle some of them. Furthermore, new irritants arose: in April, Gorbachev blamed the United States unfairly for using the nuclear catastrophe at Chernobyl for propaganda; in May, there was a battle of words over U.S. military action against Libya; in September, Soviet authorities charged an innocent American journalist with spying. Most of the other issues were carried over from 1985.

Afghanistan, Regional Conflict, and Terrorism

GORBACHEV'S FAILURE TO engage Reagan in a discussion of the terms on which the Soviet Union would withdraw its forces from Afghanistan contradicted the general impression of candor that Gorbachev had conveyed at Geneva. He had sidestepped discussion of the issue when they met and had not responded at all to the potentially forthcoming proposal Reagan made in his letter following the Geneva meeting. Despite his occasional talk of the desire for a political settlement and reference to the war there as a "bleeding wound," Soviet forces had actually intensified the fighting.

On January 20, 1986, just five days after he had received Gorbachev's proposal for the elimination of nuclear weapons, Reagan received a group of Afghan resistance fighters who came to Washington with several small children who had been maimed in the conflict. The president was deeply moved. Photographs taken on that occasion show him visibly fighting back tears. The instincts of a teenage lifeguard came to the surface of his emotion. These were people who needed to be saved from the ravages of a war thrust upon them. Why was Gorbachev, if he was the man he pretended to be, so callous? It was not his war, but by not ending it he was making it his own.

In Moscow, Anatoly Chernyaev and others were asking themselves the same question. Gorbachev was not prevented by internal forces from scheduling a withdrawal from Afghanistan. Soviet military leaders did not want to be seen in defeat, but they would have welcomed a withdrawal that did not carry that stigma. They had never been happy with the decision to intervene in Afghanistan. Politically, Gorbachev had a relatively free hand, but he did not make use of it. On this point the "old thinking" still had him in its grip.

The fighting in Afghanistan continued through 1986 and 1987 to weigh heavily on the U.S.-Soviet relationship. It delayed the development of that measure of confidence between Reagan and Gorbachev necessary for accommodation in many other areas of the relationship.*

Cuban involvement in the civil war in Nicaragua, possible only because of Soviet military and financial support, was also an important issue that Gorbachev avoided. Reagan's proposal for both countries to end military involvement in local conflicts could have provided a framework for disengagement if Gorbachev had been willing; eventually that is what happened. But in 1986 the old Soviet commitments and the faith Gorbachev still placed in "proletarian internationalism" stood in the way of his cooperation.

Given Soviet unwillingness to end the Cuban interference, Reagan was determined to keep the Nicaraguan opposition—the so-called Contras— active. The majority in Congress had other ideas and refused to continue funding. This led some members of the NSC staff to undertake an operation to finance the Contras that was to have an effect on U.S.-Soviet relations, though not until late in the year.

The Reagan administration had complained about Soviet support for terrorism from the beginning of its term in office, but the issue became more acute in 1986 with a series of terrorist incidents staged from Libya. Years earlier, in 1981, the U.S. Navy had scheduled maneuvers in the Gulf of Sidra adjacent to Libya to substantiate the U.S. claim that these were international waters. Libyan planes challenged the task force, which shot down two of

---

* Since the withdrawal of Soviet troops from Afghanistan in 1989, some scholars have written that Gorbachev had tried from the beginning of his tenure to find a way to leave Afghanistan and that the refusal of the United States to cooperate served to prolong the war there. This is utter nonsense. It ignores the many efforts the United States made, beginning in 1981, to find a face-saving way for the Soviets to withdraw. In fact, it was late in 1987 before Soviet officials were willing to discuss withdrawal terms seriously with the United States. The first constructive comment Gorbachev made to Reagan occurred only in December 1987.

them. Subsequently, a series of kidnappings and terrorist actions were traced to Libya. On April 5, 1986, a bomb was set off at a discothèque in West Berlin frequented by U.S. servicemen. Two people were killed and two hundred injured. For President Reagan, this was the last straw. He ordered F-111 fighter-bombers from bases in Great Britain to strike targets in Libya in retaliation.

The Soviet government had complained about the maneuvers in the Gulf of Sidra, failed to condemn the terrorist act in West Berlin, and protested the U.S. bombing of Libyan targets. Shevardnadze had been scheduled to come to Washington the day after the raid to work on an agenda for the next summit meeting, but he abruptly canceled the trip to protest the U.S. attack on Libya. Gorbachev added injury to insult by assuring Libyan leader Qaddafi that the Soviet Union would "fulfill its commitments in terms of further strengthening Libya's defense capability."

Since Libya was suspected of being one of the most active supporters of terrorism, Reagan resented the Soviet stance. Soviet actions seemed to belie the claim that the USSR was opposed to terrorism. Apparently Soviet leaders were opposed to terrorism only when it was directed against them. With this in mind, Reagan took Gorbachev severely to task in one of his letters:

What are we to make of your sharply increased military support of a local dictator who has declared a war of terrorism against much of the rest of the world and against the United States in particular? How can one take Soviet declarations of opposition to terrorism seriously when confronted with such action? And more importantly are we to conclude that the Soviet Union is so reckless in seeking to extend its influence in the world that it will place its prestige (and even the lives of some of its citizens) at the mercy of a mentally unbalanced local despot?[9]

These were sharp words, and the hint that the United States would not be deterred from attacking terrorist bases by the presence of Soviet personnel was unmistakable, but Gorbachev never answered the rhetorical questions directly. Since Soviet leaders normally were uneasy about military aid to people they could not control, the last sentence may have struck home. Soviet propaganda support for Libya became more muted and reports of Soviet aid to terrorist groups began to diminish.

Arms Reduction

IN THE PRIVATE correspondence and public statements, nuclear arms reduction attracted more attention than any other topic. Reagan continued to try to find ways to reassure Gorbachev that there was nothing to fear from SDI as the United States conceived it. Gorbachev simply ignored his arguments and implied that if Reagan was unwilling to ban "space-strike weapons" and enter into a moratorium on nuclear testing, nothing else would be possible. In June, Gorbachev even proposed a summit meeting in Europe to talk exclusively about a ban on nuclear testing. Of course, this was unacceptable to Reagan—the more so since Gorbachev announced it as a public challenge rather than a suggestion conveyed in private. Reagan still felt that Gorbachev's moratorium was a trick, called when the Soviet Union had completed a cycle of testing and designed only to interfere with tests the United States had scheduled. Furthermore, he was not sure that all tests could be monitored without on-site inspection. Given the many other misunderstandings that persisted, Gorbachev's concerted effort to link everything to a test moratorium merely exacerbated Reagan's suspicions of Gorbachev's motives.

Nevertheless, Reagan kept making suggestions of ways to reassure Gorbachev on SDI. In July he offered a treaty commitment to share strategic defenses if they should prove feasible. He also offered to enter into an agreement to liquidate and ban all offensive ballistic missiles before any strategic defenses would be deployed. This was an important proposal that has received little attention from arms control specialists. It originated with Defense Secretary Caspar Weinberger and subsequently, after considerable discussion and reflection, was endorsed by both Secretary Shultz and Admiral Poindexter, then approved by the president. Some might have suspected that Weinberger's motivation was to scuttle any agreement, and maybe it was, but like the zero/zero option for INF, it made a lot of sense.

By their very nature, ballistic missiles are surprise weapons. They have a short flight time and are most effective against fixed targets. They have little use against mobile military targets once a war starts, but can ravage a country's civilian population and infrastructure. They would be the weapons of choice to start a war, and they are the only plausible vehicles for a disarming first strike in a nuclear war. They are dangerous even if they do not have nuclear warheads since they can be used for surprise attacks with conventional warheads and also can deliver chemical and biological weapons. Eliminating ballistic missiles would remove any possibility of a first-strike strategy that Gorbachev claimed had to be behind the Strategic Defense Initiative.

Elimination of ballistic missiles is not the same thing as elimination of nuclear missiles. Cruise missiles and bombs from aircraft would still be permitted (though limited by agreement). But if there were no ballistic missiles, this would prevent the "militarization of outer space," which had been an avowed Soviet objective since 1983. After all, ballistic missiles, unlike aircraft and cruise missiles, travel through space.

Gorbachev simply ignored both these proposals and continued to argue against "the militarization of outer space" by banning "space-strike weapons."* He also continued to ignore U.S. grievances over violations of treaties signed earlier. Treaty violations had been important irritants from the beginning of the Reagan administration, and from 1984 Congress required the president to report periodically on any Soviet violations that continued. The U.S. Arms Control and Disarmament Agency issued one of its regular reports in March 1986. On the basis of careful assessment of the facts, it reported that there had been nine outright violations of treaty or political commitments and a few potential, probable, and likely violations. In some suspicious instances, the intelligence community found that the evidence was ambiguous. In only two cases was there evidence that action had been taken to correct a probable violation.[10]

Gorbachev reacted to the publication of this report as if it were a calculated provocation, with no purpose other than to disrupt arms control negotiations. He ignored the fact that the president was responding to a reporting requirement imposed by Congress, and that the findings were issued with an explanation that the United States intended to continue to try to negotiate new agreements with the Soviet Union, even if they were violating existing ones.

In fact, the covering letter to the "noncompliance report" refuted the argument of those officials in the administration who believed that the United States should not negotiate new arms control agreements while the Soviet Union was in violation of any existing agreement. "New arms control agreements, if soundly adhered to, can serve U.S. interests," ACDA director Kenneth Adelman stated in his letter to Congress that accompanied the report.[11] Reagan, who would have preferred to deal with the compliance issues in diplomatic channels, insisted on that language when he approved the report. But he resented Gorbachev's accusation that SDI research, which was not different from that conducted by the Soviet Union, violated the 1972 ABM Treaty. The Soviet Union was clearly violating that treaty by constructing a prohibited radar near Krasnoyarsk in Siberia. Reagan also objected to demands that the United States continue to observe the limits set by the unratified SALT II treaty signed by President Carter when the Soviet Union was in violation of at least four of its provisions.

---

* His attitude was not based on a careful analysis of the proposal. According to Alexander Bessmertnykh, the Soviet military advised, without careful study, that the proposal was unacceptable. Soviet generals felt that the Soviet Union had advantages in ballistic missiles and assumed that Reagan's proposal was a propaganda trick, not a serious proposal.

These violations influenced Reagan's several decisions regarding U.S. compliance with the unratified and thus nonbinding SALT II treaty. As in 1985, in the spring of 1986, Reagan was once again confronted with a decision whether to destroy old nuclear weapons as new ones were introduced and thus stay within the limits specified by that treaty, or whether to exceed these limits by a small amount to demonstrate that the United States did not consider itself bound by it. In the spring he decided to keep within the SALT II limits, appealing to the Soviet Union to take corrective action. In December, when the Soviet Union had still not acknowledged or corrected its violations, Reagan decided to exceed the SALT II ceiling by a small amount.

Gorbachev criticized all of these decisions, and Soviet propagandists claimed that they proved Reagan was hostile to arms control in principle. The decisions did not, however, affect the military balance, and eventually they became moot when the treaty to reduce strategic nuclear weapons was concluded in 1991.

Gorbachev's refusal to address these compliance issues was a sign that he had not yet put all elements of the "old thinking" behind him. He was more interested in 1986 in covering up violations than in recognizing and correcting them. Not all Soviet officials were so inclined. Arms control specialists in the Ministry of Foreign Affairs were increasingly disturbed by the evidence that treaties had been violated. (Decisions had often been made by the military without consultation with or notification to civilian officials below the Politburo level.) In a memo to Gorbachev in the spring of 1986, Anatoly Chernyaev observed: "We cannot simply deny accusations that we are violating these agreements [SALT II and the ABM treaties]." But even he suggested that the Soviets get something from the Americans in return for compliance.[12]

Arguments continued over the interpretation of the ABM Treaty, not only with the Soviets but within the United States. The officials who had negotiated the agreement said that they considered the "narrow interpretation" correct—that the treaty prohibited testing and developing ABM components regardless of type. This had been their testimony to the Senate when the treaty was submitted for ratification. However, senior Soviet officials had made public statements shortly after the treaty was signed that implied a "broad interpretation": that "Agreed Statement D" to the treaty gave both countries the right to conduct research, testing, and development—but not deployment—of strategic defenses based on "other physical principles."

In 1985, when Bud McFarlane had first described the broad interpretation in public, the U.S. government was divided on the issue, but in 1986, step by step, the Reagan administration came to endorse the broad interpretation. An analysis of the treaty by the State Department's legal adviser, Abraham Sofaer, concluded that the negotiating record supported it.[13] Although President Reagan continued to stress that all SDI activity under way conformed to the narrow interpretation of the treaty, he maintained that the United States should have the right in the future to conduct activities permitted by the broad interpretation if it chose.

Gorbachev flatly rejected the broad interpretation and insisted that Reagan commit himself to the narrow interpretation as part of any subsequent agreement on strategic nuclear weapons. This argument continued well beyond 1986 and was a major factor in preventing any agreement on strategic defenses and delaying an agreement on offensive strategic weapons until 1991.

The negotiations on nuclear arms were bilateral between the United States and the Soviet Union, and they attracted the most attention by both the public and governments. Nevertheless, at the same time several other negotiations were under way in broader forums that were to help end the arms race. The Conference on Security and Cooperation in Europe sponsored negotiations in Stockholm on confidence-building measures, mainly a set of agreements for transparency in military operations such as inviting foreign observers to major military exercises and notifying other governments in advance of troop movements. Countries belonging to NATO and the Warsaw Pact were negotiating in Vienna on reductions of conventional weapons in Europe—an issue that would become very important after the INF Treaty was concluded in 1987. A treaty banning chemical weapons was under negotiations in Geneva under the auspices of the United Nations Committee on Disarmament.

All of these negotiations were making little progress during the first half of 1986. In Stockholm, the Soviet Union resisted opening up its military operations to foreign observation. In Vienna, the Warsaw Pact, following the Soviet lead, resisted reducing its forces to levels comparable to NATO's. In Geneva, Soviet negotiators opposed on-site inspection (except by invitation) for chemical plants, which was required to verify a ban on chemical weapons. Even as he entered his second year in office, it seemed that Gorbachev was dragging his feet in all the negotiations related to arms and military operations until he could get his way on his nuclear testing moratorium and SDI.

Chernobyl

THE EVENT THAT was to have the greatest impact on Soviet attitudes toward nuclear weapons did not occur at negotiating tables, in high-level correspondence, or in public statements by political leaders. The accident at the nuclear power plant at Chernobyl, Ukraine, in the early hours of Saturday, April 26, caught the attention of the world, embarrassed the Soviet leadership, and changed the attitude of the Soviet military toward nuclear weapons. It provided an impetus both for internal reform in the Soviet Union and for more urgent efforts to reduce the danger nuclear weapons posed to mankind as a whole.

Radiation from the accident was detected in Scandinavia a few hours after the accident occurred, well before Moscow announced to its own people what had happened. It caught the Soviet leadership totally unprepared for an emergency of that type and magnitude. The Politburo was so poorly informed of the destructive potential of radioactive fallout that it dithered for days. Corrective measures were tardy and often inappropriate. The Soviet leaders came across as both inept and callous.

So far as Gorbachev's own performance is concerned, he seems not to have been responsible for the delays in keeping people informed. In fact, he instructed Soviet authorities to give full information about the catastrophe from the very beginning. However, the Soviet bureaucracy blocked the flow of timely information, even to the Politburo.[14]

When Washington first learned of the accident, President Reagan was in Japan on an official visit. I had remained in Washington, but I sent an urgent message to John Poindexter, who was traveling with the president, asking if the United States should offer assistance. The reply came back in minutes that the president wanted us to offer assistance without delay. We did so, in messages through both the Soviet embassy in Washington and the American embassy in Moscow. The offer was rejected. Moscow said everything was under control and they were quite capable of dealing with whatever emergency might exist. The tone was actually accusatory, as if, in offering to help, we had insulted them.

President Reagan also instructed us not to "propagandize" the issue. He felt we should keep politics out of it, try to help if that was needed, keep our own people informed of what we knew, but avoid hysteria about the danger of nuclear power plants. He was in favor of nuclear power plants if they could be kept safe.

It was not easy to restrain anti-Soviet statements by U.S. officials. Propagandists in the administration were eager to use the catastrophe to berate the Soviet government (which it deserved), but they were ordered in writing to clear all comment with the NSC. At the same time, the NSC instructed the Environmental Protection Agency to set up a task force to follow the situation and keep the public informed of the facts and of precautionary measures that should be taken outside the Soviet Union. Radioactive fallout had affected agricultural land and livestock in several countries. For several days the Soviet authorities released so little information that people had to depend on foreign experts for facts necessary to protect their own health. The U.S. task force held its first press conference on April 30; Soviet media did not begin to provide facts about the accident until May 4 and offered the first detailed press conference a full ten days after the accident occurred. Gorbachev made his first speech on the subject even later, on May 14.

Given our strenuous efforts to avoid making political hay out of the accident, we were astounded when Gorbachev accused the United States of an "unrestrained anti-Soviet campaign" and the Western media of building "a mountain of lies."[15] If information about the accident reported abroad contained some inaccuracies, that was an inevitable result of the Soviet cult of secrecy and the tendency of Soviet institutions to avoid embarrassing exposures. Yet Gorbachev took objective information as hostile propaganda, just as his predecessors would have done.

Gorbachev's pique was short-lived. Despite his pugnacious outburst, he drew many of the right conclusions from the catastrophe. It spurred him to get on with reforms and probably made him less confident of much of the advice he was receiving from the Soviet bureaucracy. It provided a telling example of the danger nuclear radiation can pose to human life. The Soviet high command also sat up and took notice. This was an accident outside their jurisdiction, but Dmitri Yazov, who became minister of defense the following year, often said in private that until the accident at Chernobyl he had believed the Soviet Union could prevail in a nuclear war. Chernobyl taught him, and presumably most of his colleagues, that there could be no winners. A country could be devastated even if nuclear weapons were not used. A hostile power would only have to bomb nuclear power plants!

Recurrent Doubts

PRESIDENT REAGAN HAD been energized by his meetings with Gorbachev in Geneva. Even during his Thanksgiving vacation on his ranch in 1985 he was thinking of how to prepare for Gorbachev's visit to the United

States. When Gorbachev did not respond either to his proposals or the invitation, he was puzzled. Nevertheless, he welcomed Gorbachev's proposal in mid-January to abolish nuclear weapons by 2000. If Gorbachev had proceeded to take up some of Reagan's ideas as a basis for negotiation and agreed, even conditionally, to a meeting date during the summer, they might have been off and running, though the concrete negotiations would doubtless have been arduous.

This didn't happen. When Soviet negotiating positions showed little change, weeks went by without a date for the next meeting, and as Gorbachev continued to insist on ideas Reagan had rejected, Reagan's perplexity gave way to annoyance and annoyance to heightened suspicion. It was in this mood that he made several of the decisions that troubled Gorbachev— those on SALT II "interim restraint," the ever firmer defense of the broad interpretation of the ABM Treaty, and a refusal to modify nuclear testing schedules. The president was determined not to be jerked around by an adversary who tried to force him to make compromises without offering any significant accommodation in return.

By late winter and early spring, the effort Reagan had put into proposals to meet Gorbachev's principal objections began to wane. He found it difficult to focus on controversial decisions unless some upcoming event made delay impossible. Without a date for another meeting with Gorbachev, he could see little reason to change U.S. negotiating positions. The State Department began to pepper him with suggestions for this or that minor modification of some arms control proposal, intended as a stimulus to negotiation. Every time the idea was discussed with him he would ask, "What have the Soviets offered?" When informed that there had been no significant change in the Soviet position on that particular matter, Reagan would say, "Well, let's wait until there is. Then we'll see what we can do."

Secretary Shultz grew increasingly restive and tended to blame Admiral Poindexter and the NSC for the president's hesitation. In fact, the NSC was not the problem. Its staff was trying, even more energetically than Shultz's colleagues in the State Department, to keep the process of negotiation moving. But aside from Shultz personally, the State Department was not helping. Once Rick Burt and Mark Palmer left the Bureau of European Affairs,* their successors seemed out of tune with President Reagan's thinking. They were convinced that Gorbachev would move on nothing on the American agenda until he got something on the "central issue" of nuclear weapons. While they

* In 1985, Burt had been sent to Bonn as ambassador and Palmer to Hungarian language training in preparation for appointment as ambassador to Hungary.

never directly questioned the president's objectives, their advice and actions often implied that U.S. policy was largely responsible for the continued deadlock in the arms control negotiations, and therefore it was up to Reagan to be more forthcoming in order to prove that he was "reasonable." Their proposals, which either focused on details and technicalities or were merely procedural, were never adequate to make a decisive impact and usually did not fit the president's sense of timing. When I tried to explain to my State Department colleagues what the president expected, they complained that I was not providing the support I should for their views.

The spring and summer of 1986 was a trying time for all of us working on Soviet affairs in Washington. Both Gorbachev and Reagan were holding stubbornly to positions the other would not accept. Though there was plenty of communication—by letter, diplomatic representatives, and through third parties—both seemed to be talking past each other. Yet I was convinced that both were genuinely committed to bringing the arms race under control. But so far nothing was working, in part because both lacked the means to discuss frankly the ways various stalemated negotiations could be unblocked.

From May, my discouragement grew. I had hoped at the beginning of the year that things would move much faster. Interagency squabbling was growing ever more vicious and I was fed up with spending most of my day trying to resolve turf battles among the various government departments. Interagency disagreement meant that many decisions that should not have required the president's attention were passed to him for decision. But without a date for meeting Gorbachev to spur him on, Reagan had trouble making up his mind and the disputes continued to rage. Periodically some of the parties, most often those opposed to any negotiation with Gorbachev, fed their favorite journalists one-sided accounts of these bureaucratic battles.

AT THIS TIME Gorbachev was not plagued with leaks to the mass media, but he worried that his meeting with Reagan had not produced a breakthrough in controlling the arms race. His "initiatives" had not brought easier relations but new arguments. He thought Reagan was primarily at fault, but seemed at a loss as to how to bring him around. By late spring, as Reagan became less decisive, Gorbachev began more actively to search for ways to break the stalemate. He also began to supplement the advice he was getting at home with some from foreign political leaders.

Chernyaev began, after only a few weeks as Gorbachev's foreign policy adviser, to prod his boss to take a more realistic look at Soviet negotiating positions. He pointed out in memoranda written in late April and early May that the positions taken by Soviet negotiators in the negotiations in Stockholm, Vienna, and Geneva were not yet in accord with Gorbachev's wishes. Gorbachev then took up the matter in the Politburo, accusing the bureaucracy of undermining his directives.[16]

In May, Gorbachev called a conference of Soviet ambassadors and senior foreign ministry officials to argue against previous thinking on national security. He rejected both the idea that only military strength counted and the insistence that the Soviet Union maintain forces equal to all its potential enemies combined. "The hypertrophy of that military might," Shevardnadze wrote later, "its unrestrained growth, had reduced the state to the position of a third-rate country and had stimulated processes that had brought it to the brink of catastrophe." He had in mind the low standard of living, poor food supply, shortage of consumer goods, deteriorating public health, and other social ills that were becoming more evident each day.[17] He and Gorbachev thus made it clear that they wanted new ideas, and that they would not necessarily support every position taken by the Soviet military establishment.

So far as dealing with Reagan is concerned, Gorbachev was influenced by meetings with foreign political leaders, particularly French president François Mitterrand and former U.S. president Richard Nixon. Mitterrand visited Moscow on July 7 and 8, just after he talked to Reagan in New York on July 4. He told Gorbachev that he would get nowhere with Reagan if he insisted the United States give up SDI (which Mitterrand did not like) before there could be an agreement to reduce nuclear weapons. Reagan was sincere, he explained, in his desire to reduce nuclear weapons but would not abandon SDI to do so. When Gorbachev said he was convinced that what Reagan feared most of all was the economic development of the Soviet Union, Mitterrand told him that he was not so sure of that, and added, "Notwithstanding his political past, Reagan has the intuition that the current tension must be ended. He is not a machine. He likes to laugh, and more than the others is influenced by the language of peace."[18] Gorbachev describes this meeting in his own memoirs, but does not cite this passage. He also makes it seem that Mitterrand was more in agreement with Soviet policy than the French record and Chernyaev's account indicate.[19]

According to Chernyaev, Gorbachev commented, "This is extremely important, and I am taking special note of it." In this way, Chernyaev observed, "the French president played a major role in eroding the major stereotypes in Gorbachev's 'new thinking.' "[20] Ten days later Gorbachev received former president Richard Nixon, who told him that Reagan viewed the U.S.-Soviet relationship as his personal responsibility, that Reagan had been impressed by his conversations with Gorbachev in Geneva, and that Reagan believed there could be agreement if Gorbachev would work with him.[21]

AS THE STALEMATE persisted into the summer, I felt that at least three things were needed: a better means of informal communication, a better understanding on Reagan's part of the pressures on Gorbachev, and more thought about U.S. objectives and the way the various issues on our four-part agenda might be related.

Despite the various direct and indirect channels of communication between Reagan and Gorbachev, they were still not agreeing on anything concrete. It was all very well for various legislators, businessmen, and foreign statesmen to shuttle back and forth and assure Gorbachev that Reagan really wanted to deal with him, and to tell Reagan that Gorbachev really wanted to find a way out of the impasse. This had a certain effect. But it did little to determine just how the discordant perceptions of each could be reconciled enough to start building confidence. For that we needed something else. I urged further efforts to establish an informal channel to Gorbachev's immediate staff, keeping the key senior people on the American side fully informed of any dialogue.

Secretary Shultz remained skeptical, but not totally opposed, and was willing to have Paul Nitze go to Moscow to discuss arms control issues informally. President Reagan was enthusiastic and suggested that I accompany Nitze to interpret and to discuss the issues on the U.S. agenda other than arms control. Vadim Zagladin sent word through Larry Horowitz that Nitze would be received in the International Department of the Central Committee, by Anatoly Chernyaev, and most likely by Gorbachev personally, and that the Soviet Ministry of Foreign Affairs would be kept informed. The latter was important reassurance, since we did not want to appear to be going around Shevardnadze. We simply wanted to communicate as directly as possible with Gorbachev and were willing—even eager—to say the same things to senior people in the foreign ministry.

Before arrangements were final, distorted accounts of the idea began to circulate in the U.S. bureaucracy, in large part as a result of indiscretions by Nitze's assistant. Demands began to be made by every agency in town to be represented. Eventually, the proposed group grew to eight persons, a totally unwieldy delegation that wags referred to as "Snow White and the Seven Dwarfs" (Nitze's hair was white). Not one spoke Russian well enough for a relaxed conversation. The whole effort thus became a ludicrous exercise that was damaging to the United States since it conveyed unmistakably that the administration was divided and that the various agencies trusted neither one another nor the president. That was an accurate conclusion, but it missed one important point: President Reagan was not a prisoner of any of these factions and was capable of overruling any and all if he saw fit.

What sort of things would have been discussed in a properly organized private channel? Essentially, it could have been used to convey frank explanations of political hang-ups on both sides and thus to stimulate thinking about ways they could be surmounted. For example, the American representative could have explained why Gorbachev's moratorium on nuclear testing was a nonstarter; whatever theoretical advantages it might have had, it was not going to be accepted as Gorbachev had proposed it. Therefore, Gorbachev should not have been encouraged to continue extending it in the hope that it would bring pressure to bear on Reagan. It would have been far better for the Soviet Union to resume some nuclear tests and accept the U.S. proposal to calibrate instruments for on-site verification.* If the Soviets had been willing to do this, they probably could have obtained a commitment to ratify the two treaties limiting underground explosions that had been signed but not yet ratified. Further limitations on nuclear testing could follow as part of a nuclear arms reduction agreement. The point of the informal discussion would be to convince Gorbachev that the only way to limit nuclear testing eventually would be to drop his moratorium proposal and permit testing of devices that would enhance verification of a ban.

At the same time, Gorbachev's advisers could have been encouraged to look more seriously at the sort of agreements that would ensure their security but permit SDI research and the testing of technical concepts to go forward. An explanation could have been given of the reasoning behind Reagan's proposals to ban ballistic missiles and to share the benefits of successful research on strategic defense. Furthermore, the Americans could, without undue offense, stress the importance of moving more rapidly in acknowledging and correcting treaty violations, scheduling a withdrawal from Afghanistan, and enforcing the commitments in the Helsinki Final Act to protect human rights.

The point would be to find approaches to these controversial issues that could produce solutions that would avoid a public "defeat" for either leader. Purely private consultation was still impossible in 1986, however. By then,

---

* Most private American arms control experts were urging Gorbachev to continue the moratorium. However, this actually delayed progress toward an agreement to ban nuclear testing.

Gorbachev was probably ready for such a dialogue, but Washington was unable to get its act together.

Although efforts to establish an unofficial dialogue failed, we found a way to reduce Reagan's suspicion of Gorbachev's motives. At John Poindexter's suggestion, I drafted two spoof memos—clearly labeled as such—supposedly from Anatoly Chernyaev to Gorbachev, purportedly giving advice on how to deal with Reagan. They were interlaced with jokes and anecdotes. My point was not to guess what sort of advice Chernyaev was actually giving—that, I did not know. Rather it was to convey my understanding of the political position Gorbachev found himself in. I thought that he was not trying to strong-arm Reagan into bad agreements (as most of Reagan's advisers argued), but that he desperately needed some agreements in order to get on with the reforms he understood the Soviet Union needed. But to do this Gorbachev had to be able to convince his people that Reagan was willing to wind down the arms race without demanding military superiority over the Soviet Union.

Reagan loved these fake memos and even asked for extra copies to share with friends. They amused him, but they also helped him understand that Gorbachev was a fellow politician forced to deal with a lot of domestic pressures, even though his political system was quite different from Reagan's. If Gorbachev really wanted to reduce weaponry and save his country from an arms race—even if it was to make the Soviet economy stronger—Reagan was willing to help. But to tap this latent willingness, Gorbachev had to start using the language of accommodation rather than defensive polemics and accusations of bad faith.

There was little progress during the summer in dealing with the third problem, defining the interrelationship between the various elements on the U.S. agenda. It was, of course, very difficult to predict with any degree of precision just what impact a withdrawal from Afghanistan would have on some of the arms reduction negotiations or what the president would be willing to do to loosen trade restrictions if the Soviet leaders allowed more people to leave and released political prisoners. Clearly, improvements in some of these areas would bolster confidence in tackling some of the others, but precise predictions were normally impossible. There were, in most cases, no obvious trade-offs.

Nevertheless, I thought it would be helpful to define U.S. objectives in a more comprehensive way than we had. Gorbachev's January proposal for a three-stage reduction of nuclear weapons to zero had gotten a lot of attention and even impressed Reagan, but it did not provide a realistic scenario for radical reduction of nuclear weapons (much less their elimination) because it dealt only with the weapons themselves and ignored the political context in which they had been created. It was, perhaps, conceivable that there could be a 50 percent cut in strategic weapons, or the elimination of intermediate-range nuclear missiles without much else changing in the relationship, but further progress in arms reduction would depend on much more than the arms themselves. This was the whole point of the U.S. four-part agenda, but there was a tendency to discuss and negotiate each issue as if it could be solved in isolation from the others. We needed more thought about how we could link those elements of primary interest to Gorbachev to those of primary interest to Reagan. I requested that the State Department do some thinking about the interrelationship of the items on our agenda, and suggested to John Poindexter that the president incorporate in his forthcoming speech to the United Nations some ideas about the ways political issues related to arms reduction. They were:

> (1) The United States and Soviet Union agree to move toward a world free of nuclear weapons. (2) The first step would be to achieve a radical reduction of nuclear weapons. (3) As nuclear arsenals become smaller, other factors will determine how much more they can be reduced; circumstances must be created to permit the elimination of nuclear weapons. (4) These include reduction and control of conventional weapons, ending the practice of using and threatening force to settle disputes, opening up society so that neither country need fear the other, and creating effective defenses, if science can devise them.

Two days after I sent this note, a new crisis was thrust upon us.

IX

―――――――――――――

1986: SEPTEMBER

A CRISIS AND A NEW PROPOSAL

Gorbachev's response to my letter was arrogant and rejected my statement
that Daniloff was no spy. I'm mad as hell.
—RONALD REAGAN, September 7, 1986[1]

We have to assume that it is possible to achieve positive results. . . . But we
certainly cannot prepare something that is sure to provoke a refusal. . . . We
also have to take their interests in account and not expect to get 100 percent of
what we want.
—MIKHAIL GORBACHEV to the Politburo, September 22, 1986[2]

THE PROBLEM THAT preoccupied President Reagan and Secretary
Shultz throughout September 1986 started in August with a seemingly
routine memorandum from the FBI. It requested authorization to arrest and
prosecute Gennady Zakharov, an official in the United Nations Secretariat.
Over three years, he had recruited an employee of a defense contractor to
spy for the KGB. Unknown to Zakharov, his recruit had been cooperating
with the FBI. Although that particular relationship posed no danger to the
national security, the FBI was eager to prosecute Zakharov in order to deter
Soviet use of the United Nations Secretariat as a cover for intelligence
agents. The USSR had by far the largest mission to the United Nations in
New York, and a significant portion of the "diplomats" assigned to it were
spies. They had diplomatic immunity, and if they were caught breaking the
law they could only be expelled from the country, not jailed. Unlike members of the Soviet mission, Zakharov, as an employee of the UN Secretariat,
did not have immunity from legal prosecution for acts not part of his UN duties.

198 / Reagan and Gorbachev

The plan to arrest Zakharov was developed at a time when Soviet espionage operations in the United States were receiving greater attention than normal. Several Americans had been arrested and charged with spying for the Soviet Union. Richard Miller, an FBI counterintelligence officer, was convicted in 1986. John A. Walker, Jr., his son, Michael, his brother Arthur, and his friend Jerry Whitworth were arrested in 1985 and, following a highly publicized trial, convicted in 1986 of selling secret navy ciphers to the KGB over nearly two decades. In November 1986, Ronald W. Pelton, an employee of the supersecret National Security Agency, was arrested, tried, and subsequently convicted of espionage.

In early 1986 the State Department had ordered the Soviet government to reduce the size of its mission to the United Nations in stages, with a reduction of twenty-five positions due in October. The purpose of the order was to make it more difficult for the Soviet Union to send large numbers of professional spies to its UN mission in New York. The personnel restriction could be circumvented, however, if the KGB and the GRU (the Soviet military intelligence service) placed more operatives in the UN Secretariat. It was important to make it clear that if they did so, their spies would face trial and imprisonment if caught in illegal acts.

The FBI proposal to arrest Zakharov had been approved by both the State Department and the CIA when it reached my desk. It surprised me that the State Department made no objection to the arrest since retaliation against an American was likely to follow. I commented to John Poindexter that I thought he should not oppose the arrest since no agency objected, but we could expect the KGB to arrest an American without diplomatic immunity in the hope of forcing a trade. If they did so, it would be important to react as President John Kennedy did when Yale professor Frederick Barghoorn was arrested in a comparable situation: Kennedy insisted that Barghoorn be released before he would discuss the status of the Soviet official accused of spying in the United States. Nikita Khrushchev complied with his demand. However, subsequent incidents were not handled that way and this would complicate matters, I warned. Both the Nixon and Carter administrations had negotiated trades under analogous circumstances, which doubtless had convinced the KGB that the way to spring Zakharov was to grab an American on trumped-up charges.

On August 23 the FBI arrested Gennady Zakharov as he paid the FBI's double agent a substantial sum of money for a package of classified material. Zakharov was arraigned in the Federal District Court of Brooklyn and held without bail for subsequent indictment and trial. On August 30 the KGB arrested Nicholas Daniloff, an American journalist in Moscow, on charges of espionage. I had known Daniloff for years, having met him during my first tour at the embassy in Moscow when he was working for United Press International. I knew very well he was not a spy but a legitimate journalist. President Reagan immediately asked CIA director William Casey whether Daniloff had any connection with the agency. Casey certified to him that Daniloff was not and had never been employed by the agency, although he had once delivered to the American embassy in Moscow an envelope addressed to the embassy that had appeared in his mailbox. Inside that sealed envelope, there was another envelope addressed to the CIA station— something Daniloff could not have known. Accordingly, Reagan sent a message directly to Gorbachev attesting to Daniloff's innocence. Gorbachev refused to accept this and subsequent assurances.

Reagan was furious. He made diary entries almost every day Daniloff was incarcerated, and his account of efforts to free Daniloff takes up nearly eight pages in his autobiography.[3] When Gorbachev refused to release Daniloff, I recommended that we notify the Soviet government, without public announcement, that the United States would expel three members of the Soviet mission to the United Nations each week Daniloff continued to be held, would refuse to issue visas for replacements, and would respond disproportionately to any retaliation against U.S. diplomats in the USSR. The FBI and CIA both agreed to this, even though the FBI preferred much more extensive expulsions. I also recommended that we refuse to discuss Zakharov's situation until Daniloff was released, but that we continue all other negotiations, making it clear that there would be no progress in any, and certainly no summit meeting, so long as Daniloff was being held. When I checked with the State Department, however, my colleagues there objected.

"The secretary wants to negotiate this," I was told by the director of Soviet affairs over the secure telephone. "We mustn't do anything precipitous!"[4]

"I don't think this is precipitous," I countered. "The sentiment over here [in the NSC] is to use the Daniloff arrest to expel as many Soviets from the United States as possible. Weinberger wants to do that and suspend all negotiations until Daniloff is out and we have an apology and compensation for Nicholson. The FBI would like to send out more than a hundred, and you can imagine what that would do to the relationship, not to speak of the risk to our people in Moscow. The president is hopping mad, increasingly at Gorbachev personally, and is not going to let the KGB get out of this unscathed. Despite all of that, I have persuaded everybody to agree to a much gentler approach. Periodic small expulsions, aimed directly at the KGB presence, is the least precipitous thing we can do."

"Gorbachev is tough, not somebody we can push around," I was told.

"Push around? How can you say that? His people have arrested an innocent man and he's trying to push *us* around," I replied, trying not very successfully to control my temper. "Gorbachev has insulted the president," I added, "which isn't going to help one bit to build the confidence we need for arms reduction agreements. Don't forget that Gorbachev needs us more than we do him. He will try to do the KGB's bidding if he can, but he has bigger fish to fry and will overrule the KGB if he has to. Maybe he won't even have to do that. If the KGB sees that holding Daniloff is going to damage its operations here, and that the longer he is held the more damage will be done, it may soon agree to Daniloff's release."

"They've got a lot of evidence on Daniloff. The agency really screwed up. Maybe they really think he is guilty," my interlocutor speculated. He was referring to the fact that a CIA officer had made an indirect reference to Daniloff during a telephone conversation monitored by the KGB.[5] This was a serious operational mistake, but not evidence that Daniloff had wittingly done anything illegal.

"The Soviets know very well Daniloff was set up," I said. "At least the KGB does, and if the KGB is misleading Gorbachev the sooner he finds out the better for him and everybody else. Basically, Daniloff's guilt or innocence is irrelevant to his arrest. He was set up simply to add some surface plausibility to the operation. Nobody says the secretary shouldn't talk to Shevardnadze about this," I continued. "Of course he should. But he should demand Daniloff's release before we negotiate anything regarding Zakharov. Given what has happened in the past, it is extremely important not to equate the two cases. Any hint that we would negotiate a deal before Daniloff is released will convince Soviet officials who don't know the full story—which means all of them except those on the top level of the KGB—that Daniloff is guilty. If we delay any retaliation while we negotiate, the Soviets will assume that we blame the CIA for the whole mess and they will hold Daniloff until they have a trade. If small expulsions go forward periodically, it will strengthen the secretary's hand and reinforce the point that Daniloff is innocent."

"The secretary won't buy it," I was told. "He wants to work it out himself, and he wants you guys to stay out of it. He'll talk directly to the president on this." The receiver clicked.[6]

I reported to Poindexter that problems had arisen with the State Department. "What do they propose?" he asked.

"Nothing except an offer to negotiate. Shultz wants to handle it with Shevardnadze," I replied.

"Do they understand that if they don't do what you have suggested there will be mass expulsions?" he asked.

"I tried to tell them, but they don't seem to understand the mood here, or in the rest of Washington, or for that matter how the president feels. They just want us to step aside and let Shultz handle it, and that would be all right, but I don't believe they are reading the Soviet mentality accurately. If we do it their way we are going to convince Gorbachev that we refuse to treat him as an equal because we won't agree to a one-for-one trade. He would not negotiate if the shoe was on the other foot and his man was innocent, and he wouldn't think he had to offer a lot of proof if he told the president, in an official message, that his man was not a spy. He would expect the president to accept his word and release the Soviet citizen under arrest. Then he would make sure nothing terrible happened to the American spy they had caught. Gorbachev understands that our countries have matters to deal with that are much more important to him."

Poindexter wondered if Gorbachev could really believe that Daniloff was guilty. I told him I couldn't be sure, but I suspected that the KGB told him they had plenty of evidence on Daniloff and he had not asked for details. If we held firm on the president's assurances I thought Gorbachev might well question the KGB in more detail regarding its evidence. Of course, if we acted as if we doubted Daniloff's innocence, Gorbachev would likely conclude that the president lied and the only acceptable resolution would be a direct trade.

Secretary Shultz met with Reagan the next morning, with John Poindexter present. When the meeting ended, Poindexter called me to his office. "The president agreed for Shultz to try to get Daniloff released so long as he doesn't propose a trade. As for the expulsions, Shultz wants none until Daniloff is released. But he agreed that we can expel as many as we wish as soon as Daniloff is out."

I had trouble believing what Poindexter had said. "Are you sure Shultz agreed to that? That is the worst possible way to go about it. Gorbachev will assume that the matter is closed when he releases Daniloff—which he will before long, one way or the other. He needs a summit and knows the president won't meet him while he's holding Daniloff. If we retaliate after he releases Daniloff, particularly in a massive way, it will seem like a calculated provocation. It could involve hundreds of people, provoke retaliation against our embassy in Moscow, and seriously delay everything else."

"Shultz understood what he agreed to, all right," Poindexter explained, "but he didn't discuss the implications. He acted as if he hadn't thought through the repercussions. He just blames the whole mess on CIA incompetence and FBI grandstanding. It's almost as if he thinks we are in the wrong rather than Gorbachev. The president prefers the tactics you worked out, but he doesn't want to cross Shultz. He is going to insist on one thing: if we don't retaliate now, we will later. He made that very clear and Shultz agreed."

Poindexter then handed me the memorandum Secretary Shultz had brought to the president. The recommendation he had received from the State Department's Bureau of European Affairs was attached. I was curious about the way my colleagues had described my proposal, so I read it carefully. I saw to my amazement that my plan had not been described at all. There was not even a hint as to what the proposal was, much less a discussion of its advantages and disadvantages. The memorandum to Shultz simply stated that "the NSC plan" would not work. It contained no cautionary words about the dangers of retaliation after Daniloff's release.

I had been both annoyed and disturbed by my conversation the day before, but assumed that the secretary of state had considered the action I had proposed and decided against it. But now it turned out that Shultz did not know what my proposal was.

I was incensed. I could have accepted being overruled after a discussion of the options available to us, though I did not believe that would have happened. But my proposal had been dismissed without consideration, and on spurious grounds, since it predicted that Daniloff would "rot in jail" unless some trade was arranged. Most of the memo discussed how to keep a trade from being obvious. Furthermore, the memo did not alert Shultz to the likelihood that the president would require retaliation, the magnitude of which would increase with every delay, or explain the potential damage if the United States ordered expulsions after Daniloff was released. Instead, it dwelled on the CIA's "mistakes," as if these justified the KGB running agents out of the UN Secretariat or framing an American journalist.

I called the director of Soviet affairs to warn that the course Shultz had urged contained a time bomb that, at the very least, could result in crippling retaliation against the American embassy in Moscow. I could not conceal my anger when I told him that the information provided Secretary Shultz was incomplete and misleading.

"The secretary has instructed us not to discuss this matter with you," he said, and hung up.

Chautauqua in Latvia

MONTHS BEFORE NICHOLAS Daniloff was arrested, plans had been made for an unprecedented U.S.-Soviet "citizens forum" in the resort town of Jūrmala, near Riga, Latvia. During its 1984 and 1985 summer seasons, the Chautauqua Institution in upstate New York had sponsored a week of debate between Soviet and American scholars and officials. In response, the Soviet Union of Friendship Societies invited the Chautauqua Institution to bring speakers, entertainers, and listeners for a similar week of debate and musical entertainment in the Soviet Union in 1986.

John Wallach, the foreign editor of the Hearst newspapers, organized a group of American speakers to participate in the debate, while the Chautauqua Institution chartered a plane for the speakers and over two hundred of its members who signed on to go as spectators. Wallach wanted a no-holds-barred exchange of views, not the sort of lovefest that some self-styled peace organizations arranged. Representatives of each government would explain directly their view of just what had produced the tension between the United States and the Soviet Union and how it might be reduced. If the Soviet government allowed the debate to be aired, it would be the first time the Soviet public would be exposed to an uncensored explanation of American policies. The Soviet sponsors assured Wallach that the speeches would be covered by the national media and televised locally in full.

Wallach asked me to head the group of American speakers, which was to include a number of reputed hardliners, such as Richard Perle, the assistant secretary of defense; Jeane Kirkpatrick, the former ambassador to the United Nations; and Alan Keyes, then an assistant secretary of state. Bud McFarlane also agreed to join the group. I was intrigued by the idea and, with John Poindexter's support, said I would do it. It seemed to fit perfectly one of the objectives on the American agenda, to erode the Iron Curtain by increasing people-to-people contacts and the flow of information.

Everything seemed to be in order for an unprecedented public debate when Nicholas Daniloff was arrested. Most American participants felt that they should not go to the Soviet Union while Daniloff was held in prison, even though it was not obvious that canceling the meeting would help him. After all, the Soviets were running some risk in exposing their people to the American debaters. Nevertheless, nobody wanted to seem to ignore Daniloff's plight.

Although he had originally endorsed the idea, Secretary Shultz took an equivocal stance regarding the Jūrmala conference following Daniloff's arrest. He spoke to the group of Chautauqua regulars who had come to Washington for the charter flight, but refused to advise them whether to go or not. His main comment was that Daniloff's arrest showed that any American might be picked up and charged with espionage. Since there was no reason to believe that any member of the Chautauqua group ran that risk, the comment was not relevant to the decision that had to be made.

When Daniloff was released in the custody of Ambassador Hartman as part of a deal Shultz and Shevardnadze had negotiated, leaders of the Chautauqua group told me that they would proceed with the trip and debate provided I would accompany the group. (I was the most senior U.S. government official invited to speak.) If I could not go, they would cancel the meeting. We had to decide within hours; the charter flight had already been delayed for two days. I called Secretary Shultz's personal assistant and asked him to find out what Shultz wanted me to do. He called back an hour later to say that Shultz considered me a "grown man" capable of making up my own mind. This was a most uncharacteristic stance for Shultz, who normally expected foreign service officers to take instructions from him. I then asked Poindexter to find out how the president viewed the matter. He called me a few minutes later and said, "He thinks you ought to go. This is an opportunity to reach the Soviet public that we shouldn't pass up." A few hours later over two hundred "Chautauquans" and about fifteen speakers and entertainers boarded a Pan American charter flight to Leningrad, where they were to change to a Soviet plane to Riga.

Richard Perle, Jeane Kirkpatrick, and Alan Keyes pulled out of the speakers group at the last minute. They said releasing Daniloff from prison was not enough; they would not honor the Soviet Union with their presence unless Daniloff was allowed to leave the country without a trial. I pointed out that the meeting could be used to call greater attention to Daniloff's plight, but to no avail. Bud McFarlane withdrew for other reasons; he explained to me that he was involved in a "sensitive mission" for the president that would require travel to a different location that week. Nevertheless, Wallach was able to keep together a group of prominent Americans willing to talk straight about problems in the U.S.-Soviet relationship, including R. Mark Palmer, who had been named U.S. ambassador to Hungary; Helmut Sonnenfeldt, who had played a prominent role in the Nixon and Ford administrations; journalist Ben Wattenberg; and Senator Charles Robb of Virginia.

In my opening speech, which was carried in full on local television, I read a few paragraphs in the Latvian language before switching to Russian. Aside from my protest of Daniloff's detention, my main message was that the

United States had never recognized the incorporation of the three Baltic countries into the Soviet Union. This came as a surprise to most Latvians, Lithuanians, and Estonians, who tended to believe that they had been forgotten by the United States and the West. According to leaders of what became the Latvian National Front, that speech provided the first impulse for an organized independence movement, one that secured a restoration of Latvian independence without extensive bloodshed before five years had passed.[7]

I HAD TO return to Washington before the conference in Jūrmala ended in order to take part in meetings in Washington with Shevardnadze, scheduled for later that week. But the evening after my speech, Georgy Korniyenko invited me to a private meeting in the hotel where we were staying. He had recently left the foreign ministry to become Anatoly Dobrynin's deputy in the Central Committee International Department; since he was not a speaker at the Chautauqua meeting, he seemed to have come to Riga specifically to confer with me. I had known him since the early 1960s, and he had been my principal interlocutor in the Soviet Ministry of Foreign Affairs when I was in charge of the American embassy in 1981.

We relaxed with nothing stronger than mineral water to lubricate our conversation (this being at the height of Gorbachev's anti-alcohol campaign) and talked for some ninety minutes in Russian. Korniyenko began by remarking that our positions were so far apart on the most important questions that he wondered whether agreements were possible before the end of the year. I told him that I believed some agreements would be possible if Daniloff was allowed to leave the Soviet Union without further delay.

As for the most promising areas, I cited INF, provided the Soviet government dropped its demand for compensation for British and French nuclear systems. Regarding strategic arms, I told him I thought we were close. An overall reduction by half was acceptable, but the United States would insist on adequate verification measures and some sublimits on specific systems to prevent either side from having a first-strike advantage.

Korniyenko observed that it would be difficult for his government to drop any link between INF and British and French systems, but he didn't say it was impossible.* So far as START was concerned, he agreed that the ceilings proposed were close, but stated that no agreement in this area would be

---

* Actually, Gorbachev signed a letter to Reagan the following day that dropped the insistence on compensation for British and French nuclear systems.

possible without one on "space weapons"—that is, one to end or limit SDI. I pointed out the various ways Soviet concerns might be addressed—Reagan had made numerous suggestions in his letters to Gorbachev—but Korniyenko gave me no encouragement that any had received serious consideration. He made an argument that seemed more pro forma than sincere for the United States to agree to Gorbachev's repeated offer of a nuclear test moratorium, but I told him that it was a nonstarter, for the reasons we had explained repeatedly.

When I turned the conversation once more to the necessity of releasing Daniloff, Korniyenko said, "The way you have handled this matter has convinced me of his guilt." I told him that we knew very well Daniloff had not been a spy and that our willingness to treat Zakharov and Daniloff in the same way by releasing both in custody of their ambassadors was based exclusively on our desire to get an innocent man released from prison as soon as possible. It did not mean that the United States would accept any further parallelism in the cases, since essentially they were quite different. The longer Daniloff was held, I predicted, the more intense would be the attention Congress and the American public directed to the Soviet abuse of the United Nations for espionage against the United States.

Korniyenko did not respond to the last point, but observed that they "had a lot of evidence on Daniloff."

The next day I flew from Riga to Moscow, on my way back to Washington, and spent the evening with my old friend Richard Combs, who was in charge of the embassy during Ambassador Hartman's vacation. Ruth and Nick Daniloff, then staying at the embassy, had dinner with us. I found Nick in good spirits, grateful to President Reagan for the strong support he had given, and most concerned with leaving the Soviet Union without being tried. He was, after all, a Russian specialist and a descendant of a Russian family. A conviction for espionage, however trumped up, would probably prevent his subsequent return to the country, and he naturally wished to avoid this if at all possible.[8]

When the Daniloffs left the Combs's apartment, I tried to determine whether the embassy was aware that the United States was likely to expel a substantial number of Soviet officials. Knowing that his apartment might not be free of KGB listening devices, I wrote short notes, then tore them up and burned them in the ashtray after they had been read. Combs replied in similar fashion. It turned out that the State Department had told the embassy nothing of the disputes that had emerged in Washington, and in particular nothing about Shultz's agreement to subsequent large expulsions of Soviet agents. Obviously, embassy management needed to be aware of the situation

oviet leaders instructed the KGB to conduct a covert campaign to prevent Reagan's reelection. By
eptember 1984, however, it was clear that Reagan would probably be in office for another four years,
nd Foreign Minister Andrei Gromyko decided it was time to put relations back on track. Here he is in
he Oval Office telling Reagan it was time for both sides to stop building "mountains of weapons."
hite House photo

eptember 1985: Eduard Shevardnadze's first visit to Washington. Reagan received the new foreign
ninister in the Oval Office even though meetings this large were often held in the Cabinet Room.
hevardnadze is seated on Reagan's left because Reagan heard better out of his left ear than his right.
   Persons seated in the picture, from left to right, are: Dmitri Zarechnak, Reagan's interpreter; on the
ouch: Georgy Korniyenko, Anatoly Dobrynin, and Teymuraz Stepanov; in chairs: Oleg Sokolov
minister-counselor of the Soviet embassy in Washington), Sergei Tarasenko, Robert McFarlane, Jack
Iatlock, and Arthur Hartman; on the couch on the right: Donald Regan, George Shultz, and George
I.W. Bush; at the extreme right: Pavel Palazchenko, Shevardnadze's interpreter. *White House photo*

Street-side entrance to the Chateau Fleur de l'Eau, the site of the first Reagan-Gorbachev meeting in Geneva. At the time, the building was up for sale, which made it possible to arrange for it to be used for the meetings Reagan hosted without disturbing the normal residents.
Photo by Jack Matlock

November 19, 1985: Journalists and photographers gathered in makeshift bleachers outside the Chateau Fleur de l'Eau on Lake Geneva to catch a glimpse of Reagan and Gorbachev when they first met. I grabbed a shot of them with my tiny Minox 35 just before Gorbachev's ZIL pulled up.
Photo by Jack Matlock

November 19, 1985: Reagan stands without overcoat and hat as Gorbachev's limousine pulls up at the Chateau Fleur de l'Eau for their first meeting. I shot the photograph through a window from inside the chateau. *Photo by Jack Matlock*

November 1985, Geneva: The "fireside chat" in the boathouse at the Chateau Fleur de l'Eau. When Gorbachev read Reagan's arms reduction proposal, he stopped smiling. *White House photo*

March 1986: Following up on his meeting with Gorbachev in Geneva, Reagan meets with Charles Z. Wick, director of the U.S. Information Agency, and Stephen H. Rhinesmith, his envoy to negotiate an agreement to expand citizen exchanges with the Soviet government. Reagan gave close personal attention to this effort, which was aimed at penetrating the Iron Curtain by increasing the travel and contact of private citizens in both countries. *White House photo*

Höfdi House, the site of the 1986 Reagan-Gorbachev meeting. It was one of several houses imported from Norway as building kits in the early 1900s, Iceland being devoid of timber at that time. Offered by the Reykjavík government for the summit, the house was not equipped as a conference center. Some of the secretarial work was done in a bathroom, since there was no other space for the word processor and copier. *Photo by Jack Matlock*

The first, "private" meeting of Gorbachev and Reagan at Reykjavík. I put "private" in quotation marks since the two were joined by interpreters and I was present as note taker. *White House photo*

Reagan and Gorbachev leaving their final meeting at Reykjavík. Their faces tell the story. (Pavel Palazchenko is walking between them.) *White House photo*

Flying back from Reykjavík on Air Force One following the meeting with Gorbachev in October 1986, Reagan was given a selection of letters addressed to him; he often answered such letters in his own hand. One, in Russian, was from a man named Yuri Orlov, a former political prisoner in the Soviet Union who had been allowed to emigrate to the United States. Reagan walked back to where I was sitting and asked me to translate it for him. The White House photographer caught me with my mouth open and Reagan bowing his head to hear me over the engine noise. *White House photo*

The National Security Council's Senior Directorate for Europe and the USSR upon my departure in December 1986 to go to Moscow as U.S. ambassador. Unfortunately, Stella Brackman, my executive secretary, who kept us all organized, was recuperating from an injury and thus is not in the picture. *White House photo*

December 1987: Gorbachev and Reagan chat in the White House. Pavel Palazchenko (standing) and William Hopkins (seated) are interpreting. Anatoly Dobrynin and Alexander Yakovlev seem to be trying to listen in. *White House photo*

Washington, December 1987: Gorbachev and Reagan sign the INF Treaty in the East Room of the White House. *White House photo*

The Reagans arrive in Moscow on May 29, 1988. Before leaving Air Force One, the president asked me how to pronounce the Russian proverb "Rodilsya ne toropilsya" (I was born but didn't rush it). It was among the remarks he made when he descended the ramp and accepted Andrei Gromyko's welcome. The proverb suggested that there would be no new arms control agreement during his visit. The agreement's birth could not be rushed. *Author's private collection*

When he and his wife, Lidia, met the Reagans upon their arrival in Moscow on May 29, 1988, Andrei Gromyko proved what many until then had doubted—that he could in fact smile. Gromyko, widely known as "Mr. Nyet" when he was Soviet foreign minister, was at that time the chairman of the Presidium of the USSR Supreme Soviet, the titular head of state. He thus outranked Gorbachev in protocol, though not, of course, in power. *Author's private collection*

May 29, 1988: This Soviet family, like most others, watched on Soviet television as the Reagans called on the Gorbachevs. *Author's private collection*

The "photo op" before one of the official sessions. By May 1988, the smiles were genuine. *Author's private collection*

Reagan and Gorbachev, surrounded by their delegations, chat after signing and exchanging the instruments of ratification of the INF Treaty. When photographers showed up, everybody tried to get into the picture.

Recognizable faces, left to right, are: Jack Matlock, Rozanne Ridgway, Colin Powell, Reagan, Alexander Yakovlev, Pavel Palazchenko (back to camera), and Minister of Defense Dmitri Yazov; behind Yazov (faces partially obscured), Alexander Bessmertnykh, Anatoly Chernyaev, and Yuri Dubinin; behind Gorbachev, Eduard Shevardnadze and William Hopkins; and at right, George Shultz and Anatoly Dobrynin. *Author's private collection*

Reagan delivers a toast at the state dinner in the Hall of Facets in the Kremlin, a building that was finished a year before Columbus discovered America. It was normally not open to tourists, but was reserved for the most formal state occasions. The atmosphere in the banquet hall was totally un-Soviet, since the walls were covered with carefully restored religious frescoes and quotations from the Bible in Church Slavonic. *Author's private collection*

Gorbachev turned out to be a well-informed tour guide! *Author's private collection*

This time it was Gorbachev's joke that broke them up. Pavel Palazchenko, Gennady Gerasimov (press spokesman of the Soviet foreign ministry), White House chief of staff Howard Baker, and Thomas Simons of the U.S. State Department are standing behind Reagan and Gorbachev. *Author's private collection*

When Reagan went out of Spaso House, the American ambassador's residence, for an unannounced stroll on the Old Arbat, he was quickly surrounded by surprised Soviet citizens seeking a handshake or at least a glimpse. His Secret Service detail and their KGB colleagues had to hold off the friendly crowd with their bodies to prevent the Reagans from being crushed. Nancy Reagan did her best to hang on to her husband. *Author's private collection*

In May 1988, the Reagans went to see monks at the Danilov Monastery in Moscow. The Russian Orthodox patriarch, Pimen, had insisted that Reagan not meet with some Orthodox priests who were campaigning for democratic reforms. Since Reagan was unwilling to allow the patriarch to dictate whom in the church he could see, he decided to visit the monastery rather than paying a formal call on the patriarch. *Author's private collection*

Moscow, May 31, 1988: The Reagans, poised to greet the Gorbachevs
before joining them in the presidential box at the Bolshoi Theater.
Photo by Rebecca Matlock

Nancy Reagan's table when the Reagans entertained the Gorbachevs at Spaso House. While the Soviets seated everyone following strict protocol at official dinners, the Reagans tried to make the conversation interesting by mixing writers, athletes, and scholars with others of comparable rank at each table. When the Russian novelist and literary critic Tatyana Tolstaya (in white) grilled Gorbachev regarding his real intentions for reform, Gorbachev took it in good stead, to the apparent amusement of the poet Andrei Voznesensky. Librarian of Congress James Billington, a noted specialist on Russian history, was in a strategic position to take it all in. *Author's private collection*

Governors Island, New York, December 7, 1988: Although they all smiled for the camera, Gorbachev was worried by reports of a serious earthquake in Armenia. He cut his visit short and rushed back to Moscow. When he reported to the Politburo on his meeting with Reagan and President-elect Bush, he said he believed that Bush was more cautious than Reagan and that Bush's advisers were still mired in Cold War thinking. *White House photo*

During Reagan's visit to Moscow in September 1990, the publisher of the Russian edition of Reagan's *Speaking My Mind* presented a copy of the book to him and obtained his autograph. *Photo by Rebecca Matlock*

The Reagans leave Spaso House following their September 1990 visit to Moscow. Both are carrying their own hand luggage—which never happened when he was in office. *Photo by Rebecca Matlock*

since it could be subjected to counterretaliation and, if the expulsions mounted, to a loss of its Soviet employees. Advance planning would be necessary to avoid disruption of the embassy's essential services.

It was impossible to explain the situation in brief notes, and I did not want to be accused of bypassing the State Department in communicating with the embassy. For those reasons, I suggested in my final note that Combs send a classified message to the State Department inquiring about the possibility of future expulsions. He did so, but his colleagues in Washington left him in the dark. Thus there was no advance planning to help the embassy cope with the Soviet retaliation against it that took place a few weeks later.

The Daniloff affair dominated the news for weeks. But other events that occurred in September and October 1986 were to have a much more profound effect on the subsequent course of history.

A Proposal to Meet Again

AS THE SUMMER wore on, the stalemate in the negotiations on nuclear arms was even more worrisome to Gorbachev than it was to Reagan. Gorbachev had been general secretary for over a year and the changes he had introduced in economic and social policy were not making the Soviet economy work better. He had to get Soviet relations with the United States on a more even keel if he was going to undertake more fundamental reform at home. But so far as he could tell, Reagan wasn't responding. Therefore Gorbachev sent instructions to the Ministry of Foreign Affairs to draft a new policy initiative to shake Reagan out of his stubbornness, which Gorbachev believed resulted from pressures by the American "military-industrial complex." In August he proceeded to the Crimea for his annual vacation.

Chernyaev, the only senior aide who had accompanied him, delivered the ministry's draft as Gorbachev sat in shorts on the balcony of his dacha, taking in the sun. Gorbachev read it and asked Chernyaev what he thought of it. "It's not what you need," Chernyaev advised. Gorbachev agreed with him emphatically, even calling the ministry's effort the Russian equivalent of bullshit. He then asked Chernyaev to take down a memo and dictated his instructions: "Urgently prepare a draft of a letter from me to the President of the United States of America with a suggestion to meet in late September or early October either in London or"—and after a slight pause—"Reykjavík."

"Why Reykjavík?" Chernyaev asked, surprised at the suggestion.

"It's a good idea. Halfway between us and them, and none of the great powers will be offended," he explained.9

The idea emerged in the letter Eduard Shevardnadze delivered to President Reagan when they met on September 19. When it was delivered, Daniloff was still forbidden to leave the USSR. Gorbachev began the letter with accusations that the "Zakharov-Daniloff" affair had been exaggerated out of all proportion and used by the "American side to unleash a massive campaign of hostility." It was, Gorbachev suggested, enough to create the suspicion that the whole thing was a deliberate attempt to worsen relations and increase tension. He then criticized the American position on three arms control issues: the ABM Treaty, INF, and a nuclear-testing moratorium.

"These [negotiations] will get nowhere if you and I do not involve ourselves personally," he wrote, and added that he thought the two of them could find solutions if they dealt with the questions directly.

His concrete proposal appeared in the final paragraph of his three-page letter:

> This is why the thought came to me to propose to you, Mr. President, that, as soon as possible, putting off all other matters, we meet one on one close by— for example, in Iceland or in London—maybe for just a day, for a completely confidential, closed, frank conversation (possibly only in the presence of our ministers of foreign affairs). The result of that conversation—we wouldn't get into details, its rationale and meaning would be in a demonstration of political will—would be instructions to our appropriate departments for draft agreements on two or three questions that you and I could sign during my visit to the United States.

As soon as Shevardnadze left the White House, I went to John Poindexter's office and read the Russian text of the letter. Of course the president should accept, conditional on Daniloff's release without a trial, I advised. Gorbachev would not propose the meeting unless he intended to bring some significant concessions to it, I reasoned, but cautioned that we shouldn't talk dates until Daniloff was out of the Soviet Union. It was obvious to me that Gorbachev's desire for the meeting he proposed meant that he would quickly find a way to release Daniloff. If we had stuck to a demand for his release before negotiation on Zakharov, Gorbachev probably would have resolved the question before he sent the letter. Now that we had treated Zakharov and Daniloff the same, the only question was how much we could get for a trade and how to disguise it so that we could pretend it was something else.

Another aspect of the letter struck me. Its style was very personal, more like Reagan's and quite unlike the usual product from the Soviet Ministry of

Foreign Affairs. The informal, almost colloquial language was somewhat obscured in the official English translation but came through clearly in the Russian original.

"My guess is," I told Poindexter, "Gorbachev tossed the draft he got from MFA into the wastebasket, called in his stenographer, and straight-out dictated the letter. The man is serious. He knows he needs a deal, and he'll try not to let the bureaucrats screw it up." The approach Gorbachev took in the letter was totally consistent with the thinking I had tried to convey in my "spoof" memos a few weeks back. For the first time since January, I began to feel optimistic that U.S.-Soviet relations might be on the verge of a sudden turn for the better.

An Arms Control Breakthrough

HARDLY NOTICED BY the public in all the clamor over spies, nuclear weapons, and projected summit meetings, the CDE conference in Stockholm* began to show encouraging progress during the summer of 1986. This conference, designed to produce greater transparency of military operations in Europe, and therefore greater confidence between East and West, had been sputtering along since January 1984, stymied by Soviet hypersecrecy in its military movements and exercises. However, Gorbachev's pressure on the foreign ministry for new ideas produced new instructions to the Soviet delegation.

During the summer of 1986 the Soviet Union finally accepted key Western demands, the most important being on-site observation of large military exercises. The change in the Soviet position permitted the conference to end successfully on September 22.[10] The agreement represented an important step in penetrating the veil of secrecy the Soviet military had habitually drawn over its military operations. It required advance notification of maneuvers of a significant size and the admission of foreign military observers to them. This was the first significant evidence that Gorbachev had indeed modified the traditional Soviet rejection of on-site verification.

The success in Stockholm suggested to some policy makers in Washington that Gorbachev might indeed begin to come to terms on some additional negotiations.

* The full name was the Conference on Confidence- and Security-Building Measures and Disarmament in Europe.

The Zakharov–Daniloff–Orlov Trade

ALTHOUGH GORBACHEV'S PROPOSAL for another meeting was convincing evidence that he would find a way to release Daniloff, he had not yet
done so, and the American demand for the American journalist to be freed
unconditionally had been vitiated by the State Department's negotiating tactics. From the start, arrangements made by the State Department implied
mirror-image situations, such as the mutual release in the custody of their
ambassadors. Then, just three days before Reagan received Gorbachev's letter proposing another meeting (actually, the very day Gorbachev signed the
letter), Shultz instructed Assistant Secretary Rozanne Ridgway to give information to Soviet Chargé d'Affaires Oleg Sokolov about the way the CIA
station in Moscow had implicated Daniloff in one of its recruitment efforts
without Daniloff's knowledge.[11] The information was correct, but the move
was ill advised since it suggested to the Soviet government that the State Department was blaming the CIA for Daniloff's arrest, and therefore would
look for a deal rather than a vindication of Daniloff.

Meanwhile, pressures on the president to retaliate grew as his own anger
at the treatment of Daniloff intensified. Consequently, on September 17 the
Soviet government was given a list of twenty-five members of its mission to
the United Nations who were required to leave the United States. As noted,
the Soviet Union had been ordered earlier in the year to reduce its UN mission by twenty-five by October 1986, but this time the order cited specific
names, all believed by the FBI to be intelligence agents. Simultaneously, the
KGB was warned privately that the United States would not tolerate retaliation against the American embassy in Moscow, which was not a counterpart
to the Soviet UN mission. Should there be any retaliation, KGB representatives were told, the United States would reduce the size of the Soviet embassy in Washington and consulate general in San Francisco to the same size
as the American counterparts in the Soviet Union.

When Shultz and Shevardnadze met September 19 and 20, then subsequently in New York, they spent almost as much time dealing with Daniloff's
detention as they did preparing for the upcoming meeting in Reykjavík. Secretary Shultz describes his negotiations at great length in his memoirs.[12] In
the final analysis, what he got was a thinly disguised trade, not directly of
Daniloff for Zakharov, but of Daniloff and imprisoned Soviet dissident Yuri
Orlov for the Soviet spy. This allowed both Shultz and Reagan to argue that
Daniloff was not part of the trade since Orlov was released in exchange for

Zakharov. But, of course, this was not the way Soviet officials viewed the transaction.

Gorbachev Prepares a Surprise

AS SOON AS Shevardnadze reported to Moscow that Reagan accepted the invitation to Reykjavík, Gorbachev called a meeting of the Politburo to discuss Soviet aims. He reported that the United States had expelled twenty-five persons and had demanded that several Soviet citizens, including Sakharov and Orlov, be allowed to leave the country to settle the "Daniloff affair." He said he would respond to the list of twenty-five (that is, retaliate), but not in full and not all at once. He also said that they would announce a halt in grain purchases from the United States, to show they had leverage, and would "make some propaganda" about the listening devices found in the Soviet embassy in Washington. These were clearly minor matters in his mind, however, mere posturing, according to Anatoly Chernyaev, to convince his own people that he was firm as he prepared to make major concessions.[13]

His main goal was to force Reagan to meet and to begin easing the burden of military expenditure, essential if his domestic reforms were to proceed. Therefore, after huffing and puffing, he lectured the Politburo on the need to be realistic, to stop proposing things that would not be accepted, and to understand that American interests had to be taken into account. "We cannot," he said, "expect to get a hundred percent of what we want."[14]

A few days before he left for Reykjavík, Gorbachev received a suggested position paper for his meeting with Reagan. It had been drafted by Yuli Vorontsov of the foreign ministry, Sergei Akhromeyev of the defense ministry, and Georgy Korniyenko of the Central Committee International Department. Anatoly Chernyaev found it inadequate and sent it to Gorbachev with a covering memorandum proposing a different approach:

> The main goal of Reykjavík, if I understood you correctly in the South [i.e., during his vacation], is to sweep Reagan off his feet with our bold, even "risky" approach to the central problem of world politics. . . .
>
> This draft does not satisfy your plan either in form or content. . . .
> 1. We should make strategic weapons, not nuclear tests and space, our first priority. . . . In contrast to our former position, we should not make reductions here conditional upon a space agreement [i.e., SDI]. Otherwise it will be another dead end. . . .

2. On medium-range missiles [INF]: . . . Liquidate all medium-range missiles in Europe, ignoring the British and French arsenals. . . .

3. The ABM issue should be combined, I believe, with banning nuclear tests. . . .[15]

Gorbachev used Chernyaev's suggestions in his presentation to the Politburo, ridiculing as he did so the drafts he had received from the bureaucracy. "If we are still trying to conquer the entire world, then let's discuss how to defeat the Americans in the arms race. But then we can forget all we have said about our new policies," he exclaimed at one point, according to Chernyaev's notes. As for INF missiles, he suddenly endorsed the zero/zero option (without, of course, alluding to its provenance): "We want Europe to be completely free of these weapons because the Pershing II missiles are like a pistol held to our head."

Then, in concluding comments to his Politburo colleagues, Gorbachev demonstrated that he had grasped one of the most important points Reagan had wished to convey the year before in Geneva:

> We are by no means talking about weakening our security. But at the same time we have to realize that if our proposals imply weakening U.S. security, then there won't be any agreement. . . . If we don't back down on some specific, maybe even important, issues, . . . we will lose in the end. We will be drawn into an arms race that we cannot manage.[16]

Thus, the proposals Gorbachev brought to Iceland were slapped together at the last minute, and were quite different from the ones Soviet officials had recommended initially. They resembled Chernyaev's ideas much more than those of the foreign policy establishment. Unfortunately, however, Gorbachev did not take all of Chernyaev's proposals; he continued to link the reduction of strategic nuclear weapons with limits on SDI. Also, he continued to ignore all the areas of the American agenda except arms reduction. He went to the meeting in Reykjavík with nothing new on treaty violations, Afghanistan, regional conflict, or human rights.

Reagan Readies for Reykjavík

AMONG THE UNFOUNDED myths about the meeting in Reykjavík, none has been more persistent than the one that Gorbachev came thoroughly prepared and surprised an unwary, naive American president who had given little advance thought to the meeting. The meeting brought surprises from both participants, but, if anything, Reagan came better prepared than Gorbachev, who had cobbled together his proposals at the last minute.

Reagan's direct preparations for the meeting in Reykjavík were concentrated in a few weeks rather than the months he had spent to prepare for Geneva. But he went into the meeting with a clear idea of what he wanted: an understanding regarding one or two major agreements that would permit Gorbachev to come to the United States for a full-fledged summit. He had concluded that INF presented the most likely subject for an arms control agreement and was willing to accept several variants of a compromise as the first step toward eliminating this class of weapons. He also hoped to settle on a framework for a strategic arms agreement if Gorbachev dropped the linkage with SDI and agreed to reduce his heavy ICBMs by 50 percent. In addition, he came with a radical proposal, already mentioned in his correspondence, to eliminate and ban all offensive ballistic missiles before strategic defenses, if found feasible, could be deployed.

Another charge made after the meeting was that Reagan had not consulted his allies before making commitments that affected their security. This also had no foundation. He sent a detailed outline of his proposals, including the proposal to eliminate ballistic missiles, to the presidents or prime ministers of key NATO allies. In their written replies, none objected to any of the positions Reagan outlined. However, most did not consult extensively within their own governments since Reagan had asked them to keep his ideas strictly confidential. Therefore, many allied officials may not have been aware that consultation had taken place over their heads. Furthermore, Reagan did not indicate in advance that he might agree to eliminate nuclear weapons totally. This was not part of what he proposed going into the meeting.

In contrast to Gorbachev's intent to "sweep Reagan off his feet" with unexpected proposals, Reagan wished to build upon positions already taken and explained. Only that way, he felt, could he begin to instill confidence that he was steadfast in his purpose. He thought circumstances would eventually force Gorbachev to see their merit. Therefore, his proposals were designed, for the most part, to be incremental rather than radically new. The proposal to eliminate ballistic missiles was the only exception.

In the initial preparations for the meeting in Reykjavík, I gave one piece of advice that I subsequently came to regret. Gorbachev had proposed that it be purely a working meeting, and I advised the president to go without his wife so that there would be no temptation to include purely social or ceremonial events. I assumed that Gorbachev would follow suit if we informed the Soviet government that Mrs. Reagan would not attend. President Reagan took my advice, but my assumption proved wrong when Raisa Gorbacheva turned up at Reykjavík and went through a heavily publicized round of activities. Nancy Reagan was not happy and her husband was, if anything, more annoyed.

I was not the only one surprised by the decision to include Raisa in the Soviet delegation. When the Soviet foreign ministry sent Gorbachev a draft schedule of activities that omitted any mention of her, Gorbachev returned it with the comment, "You have reserved no time for me to consult my wife."

"He was unable to make decisions without her advice," a senior Soviet official commented subsequently. All of us were learning.

X

REYKJAVÍK: WRESTLERS IN THE RING

At Reykjavík, my hopes for a nuclear-free world soared briefly, then fell,
during one of the longest, most disappointing—and ultimately angriest—days
of my presidency.
—RONALD REAGAN, 1990[1]

[O]ur generals and even some people in the Foreign Ministry . . . were
doubtful. They were firmly stuck in a logic of antagonism.
—MIKHAIL GORBACHEV, 1996[2]

AIR FORCE ONE touched down at Keflavík, Iceland, just after 7 p.m. on
Thursday, October 9, 1986. President Reagan was not scheduled to
meet Gorbachev until Saturday morning, but whenever he had to absorb a
significant time difference he usually traveled soon enough to have a day to
adjust and prepare for the meetings to come. Iceland's stunning president,
Vigdis Finnbogadóttir, and her prime minister, Steingrimur Hermannsson,
were on hand to greet him as he stepped down his plane's ramp. The arrival
ceremony was brief—perfunctory, in fact, since Reagan was to call on both
the following day for a more leisurely chat. With barely time for the American staff to scramble into the cars assigned, the presidential motorcade
dashed out of the airport and began the drive to Reykjavík, three quarters of
an hour away.

It was already dark in Iceland, but moonlight revealed the contours of the
barren lava flows along the highway, leaving the impression of a jaunt along
the surface of the moon itself. The bleak landscape had an austere attraction

and the American party was in a mood to be pleased. The Daniloff affair had ended without damage to the overall U.S.-Soviet relationship (or so it was thought at the time), and Gorbachev's eagerness to meet implied that he would bring a negotiable proposal. Most American officials assumed that Gorbachev would open the door to an agreement on INF that could be signed during a summit in Washington within a few months.

While in Reykjavík, Reagan stayed in the American ambassador's residence, a pleasant cottage adorned with numerous plants. In contrast to the palacelike mansions ambassadors inhabit in the larger European capitals (and the chateaux on Lake Geneva used the year before), the Reykjavík residence was comfortable rather than pretentious. Reagan's meetings with his staff and the briefings before and during the sessions with Gorbachev took place there and its ambience helped relax the participants. There was little of the frenetic hyperactivity usually evident during preparations for presidential meetings.

The Gorbachevs arrived the following day, by air from Moscow. Since facilities in Reykjavík were limited, they and the Soviet delegation stayed on a Soviet ship in the harbor. Even before the Gorbachevs arrived, however, a team of Soviet spokesmen was on hand to brief the journalists from many countries who had gathered for the event. In contrast to their behavior before the Geneva summit, the Soviet briefers spent more time describing Gorbachev's goals for internal reform than they did attacking U.S. policy.

The American party also arranged for a lengthy "background" briefing by Assistant Secretary of State Rozanne Ridgway and me. Although we thought that the meeting was likely to result in an agreement for Gorbachev to come to the United States, we were careful not to set that as its goal. There were several reasons for this, the most important being that Gorbachev suspected Reagan of wanting a meeting in the United States for its own sake, just to propitiate those who doubted that he wanted to reduce arms. To say that the primary American goal was to set a date for Gorbachev to come to Washington would have made it more difficult to achieve that objective. Furthermore, summit meetings in themselves were useful only if they reduced tension and eased negotiation of difficult issues. Therefore, they always should be described as efforts to solve problems, not as ends in themselves.

Official briefings followed this approach. State Department and NSC officials learned in Reykjavík, however, that Chief of Staff Donald Regan was telling American reporters that the meeting could be considered successful if no more was accomplished than agreement for a Reagan-Gorbachev summit in Washington. He doubtless did so thinking that it was all but certain that a date would be agreed and that it would be politic to lower expectations for anything else. Nevertheless, it was the wrong approach and illustrated, once again, Regan's penchant for meddling in foreign policy issues that he scarcely understood, behavior that had contributed to Bud McFarlane's decision to resign the year before.

President Reagan held several meetings with his staff on Friday. They dealt mainly with issues other than arms control, which had been thoroughly aired in the briefings in Washington. Saturday morning, at the breakfast table, we did another warm-up for his meeting. As at Geneva, I played Gorbachev. This time, however, I did not try to anticipate what Gorbachev would propose on arms reduction—that had been easy the year before, but this time we were not sure what approach Gorbachev would take. Therefore, I concentrated on Gorbachev's manner of argumentation on other questions likely to arise. These included SDI, nuclear testing, Afghanistan, human rights, and charges that the United States was trying to dominate the world. After all, the idea was not to rehearse a script (which had not been written and could not have been written), but to provide a warm-up, just as a baseball pitcher exercises his arm with a few throws before he goes to the mound in a real game.

Two Intense Days

THE GOVERNMENT OF Iceland, proud that its country had been chosen for the meeting, placed at the disposal of the Soviet and American delegations its official guesthouse, called Höfdi House. There were meeting rooms on the ground floor and space for staff conferences upstairs. Each delegation was allocated an upstairs wing with two rooms to rest and confer. A room between the two wings could be used by representatives of both countries for informal conversations.

Saturday Morning

GORBACHEV AND REAGAN were scheduled to arrive simultaneously at 10:30 Saturday morning, pose for photographers outside and inside the building, and then begin their initial private session at 10:50. Things started precisely as planned, and Reagan and Gorbachev went into their first meeting close to the appointed minute. Reagan's talented Russian interpreter, Dmitry Zarechnak, and I, assigned to take notes, accompanied him into the small room reserved for the private meetings.

Reagan and Gorbachev agreed immediately that they would alternate private sessions with meetings that included foreign ministers Shevardnadze and Shultz. There would be no "plenary sessions" of entire delegations as there had been at Geneva. Reagan then said there were a number of issues "left open" when they met in Geneva: INF (intermediate-range nuclear missiles), the ABM Treaty, space arms, and nuclear testing. The United States, he continued, was "especially interested in strategic arms proposals," and added that "both the U.S. and USSR would like to see a world without nuclear missiles" and the world would like to hear whether this could be achieved.[3]

Gorbachev agreed that this was the "main issue" and suggested that they discuss the general situation and then invite the foreign ministers to join them, after which he would outline his proposals. He added that "regional issues, humanitarian issues and bilateral relations" could be taken up in the afternoon following their discussion of strategic arms reduction—thus, for the first time, organizing his agenda around the four points of the American agenda.* The only difference was that he spoke of "humanitarian questions" instead of human rights.

Reagan picked up on Gorbachev's mention of humanitarian issues and observed that it was most important to make progress in this area if they were to reduce arms and improve relations in other respects. He realized that human rights were not an appropriate subject for formal agreements, but Gorbachev needed to understand that an American president would have difficulty convincing the U.S. Congress to go along with other agreements if Soviet restrictions on emigration were not eased. If there was improvement, the United States would never try to take credit for it.

Gorbachev proposed that they proceed with their evaluations of the situation that had developed since they met in Geneva, but Reagan continued to explain why improvement in protection of human rights would be necessary if they were to achieve their goals in other areas.

Gorbachev listened for a while with evident impatience, then interrupted to say, "We'll talk about human rights later. But now I'd like to tell you in general our impression of what has happened in the world since Geneva." Reagan agreed, but continued his explanation of the political importance of human rights in U.S.-Soviet relations. Obviously annoyed, Gorbachev said petulantly, "Mr. President, following what we agreed about how to organize this meeting, I want to bring to your attention the view of the Politburo and

* This proposal was omitted from the Soviet notes.

myself personally of the Reykjavík meeting in the context of the situation in the world and the condition of Soviet-American relations." He then observed that it was important that their dialogue, difficult as it had been, was continuing. But, he added, some people—many people, in fact—"believe that the meeting is a chance for each of them to promote their personal ambitions." Gorbachev firmly rejected this idea since he believed the meeting was "evidence of the commitment both of us have to the people of our countries and the whole world."

As I listened to what he said about suspicion of "personal ambitions," I thought he might be referring to opposition at home to his having taken the initiative to arrange the meeting and, perhaps, to the proposals he would be making. However, his words could have referred to the suspicion that Reagan had come to Reykjavík not to make an agreement but just for show. In any event, Reagan did not ask what Gorbachev meant. Instead, he endorsed the thought that the two had the power to decide whether there would be war or peace in the world, and therefore they had to find a way to bolster confidence and reduce suspicion between them.

When Gorbachev deplored the stalemate that continued in the arms control negotiations and observed that they needed a "new impetus," Reagan readily agreed and launched into a discussion of numbers. The United States had proposed reduction to 4,500 warheads, he pointed out, while Soviet negotiators wanted a higher number, something in the range of 6,400 to 6,800. Why not split the difference and settle for 5,500, Reagan asked, bearing in mind that this would be a step toward the goal of completely eliminating strategic nuclear weapons.

He was getting ahead of Gorbachev, still intent on confining himself to generalities until he made his own proposal. Ignoring Reagan's suggestion, Gorbachev assured him that the Soviet Union was in favor of reducing nuclear weapons in a manner that preserved a strategic balance at each step of the process. Reagan said that was fine, but noted that it would be vital to devise adequate verification procedures for the agreements reached. He had already learned the Russian proverb "Doveryai no proveryai" (Trust but verify) and used it on this occasion, as he would continue to do for the rest of his presidency. Gorbachev assured him that the Soviet Union would agree to whatever measures were needed to guarantee that the agreements they reached would be observed faithfully.

When Gorbachev started to talk about his expectations for their future meeting in the United States, Reagan suddenly blurted out, "By the way, could we talk about the date for your visit? Are you going to suggest one, or do you want me to?" Whoops, I thought. He's making the same mistake Gorbachev did in Geneva when he talked about the importance of trade. Clearly, Gorbachev was not going to talk dates until he had a clear idea of what sort of agreement would be reached. We had briefed Reagan repeatedly on this point, advising him to play it cool and not appear to want a meeting without results. He would always agree, but at that moment in Reykjavík his eagerness to show Gorbachev the United States got the better of his judgment.

Gorbachev turned the question aside, saying, "Let me finish my thought," and explained once again that they would be condemned in both countries if he came to Washington and was unable to conclude and sign a significant agreement to limit arms. It was in the interest of both to make sure that this would happen before they made concrete plans.

Reagan said that they should try to do this. Recalling his earlier reference to numbers of strategic nuclear warheads, he noted that there was an additional matter he should mention, namely that they had to limit not just numbers of warheads, but throw weight as well. Gorbachev assured him he would deal with that question too, and suggested that they invite Shultz and Shevardnadze to join them.

When they did, Gorbachev outlined his proposals. As for strategic arms, he offered a 50 percent reduction overall,* with a "substantial" reduction of Soviet heavy missiles, but not specifically 50 percent as the United States had proposed. Regarding intermediate-range nuclear missiles, he dropped the earlier Soviet demand for the right to match the number of British and French nuclear missiles. He now proposed that all INF systems be removed from Europe and negotiations begin on limits in Asia. He also wanted a commitment not to withdraw from the ABM Treaty for at least ten years, during which time research and testing of strategic defenses would be permissible only in laboratories. Also, he would prohibit all anti-satellite weapons and conclude a ban on nuclear testing.

When he had finished describing the proposals, he gave Reagan a written description of them.

Reagan said that he was encouraged by Gorbachev's proposals although in some respects they differed from U.S. ideas. For example, the United States had proposed that INF missiles be eliminated everywhere, not just in

---

* At the meeting in Geneva, Gorbachev had spoken of a 50 percent reduction of nuclear weapons, but this included all weapons capable of reaching the Soviet Union, such as those on carrier-based aircraft. In Reykjavík he accepted the American definition of strategic weapons as the basis for the reduction.

Europe. Those in Asia could be moved easily to Europe since they were mobile. If any were kept, then perhaps each side should retain a hundred in Europe until all could be eliminated. Furthermore, he was in favor of eliminating all strategic offensive weapons. He proposed replacing the ABM Treaty with an agreement that would allow both countries to continue research and testing within the limits set by the ABM Treaty. If either country considered it necessary to go beyond those limits, it would be obligated to invite specialists from the other country to observe the testing. If, subsequently, it turned out that strategic defenses were feasible, the country that developed the technology would be obligated to share it with the other and to eliminate all remaining strategic offensive missiles in two to three years.

Reagan explained that he made this proposal because the two of them "would not be here forever." Some future leader might wish to cheat, or another madman like Hitler might come to power. If both countries had a defensive system they could "rid the world of strategic nuclear arms" without endangering the security of their countries.

Gorbachev was obviously disappointed that Reagan did not show greater enthusiasm for his proposals. "We'll consider your reaction preliminary," the Soviet leader said, explaining that he had made entirely new proposals while Reagan kept repeating the old ones. Reagan had even gone back on his own "zero" proposal for INF, Gorbachev claimed. (Here, Gorbachev got carried away by his own rhetoric; he knew very well that Reagan's original proposal was a global zero, not zero in Europe alone, and Reagan had just reminded him of this.) The Soviets knew very well, he reiterated, that SDI was an offensive strategy, and if the United States deployed "a three-layered system" of strategic defense, the USSR "would find an answer." In sum, he hoped that the president would study the Soviet proposal carefully and give him a point-by-point reaction.

Reagan agreed to continue the discussion after lunch, but once again explained why his proposals on SDI could not logically be considered part of an offensive or first-strike strategy. How could that be if strategic defenses could not be deployed until both sides had eliminated their offensive nuclear weapons? he asked, and added that we all kept our gas masks after World War I even though the use of poison gas had been outlawed.

Gorbachev replied that the Soviet Union had studied the Strategic Defense Initiative carefully, and he had explained their position.

They broke for their separate lunches.

Saturday Afternoon . . . and Evening

THE AMERICAN DELEGATION considered Gorbachev's proposals during the lunch break and prepared counterproposals for Reagan to make when the meeting resumed in the afternoon. Reagan immediately took the floor and discussed them in detail—in fact, in even greater detail than Gorbachev had presented his ideas that morning. Gorbachev pressed him as to whether the United States would accept a 50 percent cut in each type of strategic nuclear system, implying for the first time that he would accept a 50 percent cut in his heavy ICBMs, the SS-18s. Reagan was not sure, but did not discard the idea out of hand, suggesting that a joint working group convene that evening to discuss it.

Gorbachev then turned to INF, pressing Reagan to accept zero in Europe. After explaining several additional times that the U.S. proposal was for a global zero, Reagan conceded that he could accept zero in Europe if Gorbachev would accept limits in Asia. After extensive discussion, their positions on nuclear testing moved closer, with Gorbachev agreeing to try a step-by-step approach. But they remained at loggerheads regarding SDI and the ABM Treaty. When Reagan, for the nth time, explained his logic and offered a treaty commitment to share the benefits of any defensive system that might be developed, Gorbachev finally exploded.

"Excuse me, Mr. President," he said, voice rising, "but I cannot take your idea of sharing SDI seriously. You are not willing to share with us oil well equipment, digitally guided machine tools, or even milking machines. Sharing SDI would provoke a second American revolution! Let's be realistic and pragmatic."

On this note, the substantive discussion ended, but both had agreed to have two working groups convene and confer as long as necessary in an effort to produce some understandings that could be adopted the next morning. One group, led by Paul Nitze and Marshal Akhromeyev, worked on the arms control questions while another, led by Rozanne Ridgway and Alexander Bessmertnykh, dealt with questions regarding regional conflicts, human rights, and improving contacts and communication.

Both working groups convened at eight that evening, one in the ground-floor conference room in Höfdi House, and the other in the upstairs common room. Discussion in the Ridgway-Bessmertnykh group, in which I participated, went little beyond summaries of what had been discussed earlier. The discussion of human rights was devoid of acrimony but resulted in no concrete commitments by the Soviet representatives. Americans were somewhat surprised that Yevgeny Primakov, then head of the IMEMO think tank, was tapped to lead the discussion of the Soviet position on the Middle East. Up to then, all such discussions had been only with foreign ministry officials; it was most unusual that a quasi-academic would be authorized to present the Soviet position on a subject as important as Israel's relations with its Arab neighbors. Incidentally, Primakov explicitly denied, for the first time that I could recall, that the Soviet government was following a "no war, no peace" policy in the Middle East as American officials suspected. He assured us that the USSR would welcome real movement toward peace.

Although the group made little progress in solving the problems discussed, it did agree on a list of cooperative projects that might be undertaken. Also, for the first time at a summit-level meeting, the Soviet delegation had explicitly accepted a framework for discussion based on the American four-part agenda.

The group dealing with regional conflict, human rights, and cooperative projects finished its work a little after midnight, but participants in the arms control working group were not so lucky. They continued to work through the night with occasional short breaks. We were all eager to learn whether they were getting close to an understanding. During one of the breaks American participants reported that they were making some progress, but that they were "not there yet." I was sitting in the upstairs common room, trying to get my notes of the working group session in order, when Alexander Bessmertnykh came in. His face betrayed deep concern.

"I don't understand what's going on," he confided. "We thought we were offering you everything you really wanted, including the 50 percent cut in heavy ICBMs, but your guys aren't moving. They are haggling over every point. Gorbachev has gone out on a limb to get an agreement, and it won't be good for any of us if he has to go back to Moscow empty-handed."

I told him I sensed that we were close enough on INF to get an agreement there even if the other elements didn't fall into place.

"But our proposal was a package," he said. "We can't just let you pick those parts you want and throw the rest away!"

The arms control group was still in session when I turned in about 4 a.m.

Sunday Morning

ACCORDING TO THE original schedule, this was to be the final session. Reagan and Gorbachev were supposed to wrap up their meeting by twelve-thirty, have lunch, and fly home. Staff members were instructed to send their baggage to the planes right after breakfast.

Reagan started the session by remarking that he was generally disappointed with the report by the arms control working group, although he conceded that it contained some encouraging points. He then discussed the issues in detail. The main progress regarding strategic nuclear arms was an agreement to cut each element of the strategic forces by 50 percent; thus, Reagan now accepted the suggestion Gorbachev had made the day before.

Regarding intermediate-range missiles, Reagan explained why he could not agree to eliminate them in Europe and leave them unconstrained in Asia. He suggested an interim agreement whereby each side would have a hundred INF warheads in Europe and not more than a hundred in Asia and on U.S. territory.

Following an extensive to-and-fro on the INF proposals, Gorbachev made a frantic appeal for a more forthcoming approach: he was offering the United States, he said, a unique opportunity. The "major compromises" he had offered had not been available to him the year before and were even further out of the question before that. He could not guarantee that he could make the offer again; if they could not come to terms there in Reykjavík, the window of opportunity could close once again.

After further discussion of INF issues, Gorbachev finally asked if Reagan would accept zero in Europe if Soviet INF missiles in Asia were cut to a hundred, and Reagan agreed. At this point it seemed that an agreement that would justify Gorbachev's trip to Washington was in sight. All Gorbachev had to do was untie this issue from the others.

The working group had agreed on procedures to begin negotiations on nuclear testing but could not agree on what to call them. Reagan asked what was wrong with simply saying that negotiations would start on questions regarding nuclear testing with the goal of banning all tests when nuclear weapons were eliminated. Gorbachev insisted that it had to be clear from the outset that the negotiations were about a comprehensive test ban, though he no longer objected to the concrete steps the United States had proposed. After much discussion, the two finally agreed on wording close to Reagan's original idea.

So far, so good. They were closing the gap on some of the most contentious issues in the U.S.-Soviet relationship. But that progress came to a complete halt when the two went over the tediously familiar ground of SDI and the ABM Treaty. The exchanges seemed almost a replay of Geneva, except that Reagan was now suggesting a complete elimination of all ballistic missiles before strategic defenses could be deployed. Gorbachev would not move off his demand that SDI research be confined to laboratories and that the United States commit itself not to withdraw from the ABM Treaty for ten years. The discussion became more and more heated, and Reagan began explaining (as he had at Geneva) why the United States thought the Soviet Union had expansionist goals based on Marxism-Leninism, and why Gorbachev should trust the United States not to seek military superiority (it had not used its nuclear monopoly in 1945 to threaten the USSR).

Gorbachev was determined not to get bogged down in a squabble over history and ideology. Borrowing a phrase Reagan had used in one of his presidential debates, Gorbachev parried, "There you go again, talking about Marx and Lenin. . . . A lot of people have tried to refute [them]. . . . None of them had any luck, and I advise you not to waste time and energy trying." He then charged that Reagan had spoken of the Soviet Union as an evil empire and called for a crusade that would relegate it to the ash can of history. In contrast, the Soviet Union recognized "the right of the American people to their own values." Reagan countered that there was a Communist Party in the United States, but no parties but the Communist Party in the Soviet Union.

As the discussion of the ABM Treaty continued without any element of agreement, Shevardnadze made a desperate attempt to salvage something on the issue. He asked whether they could drop the other details and just talk about a time period during which the parties would undertake not to renounce the treaty. Before either Reagan or Shultz could comment, Gorbachev said that if that time period was ten years (i.e., what he had already proposed), he would accept it. And then, in a clear rebuke to Shevardnadze, he added, "I made a specific package proposal, and I would ask you to treat it as such."

Reagan argued against the linkage Gorbachev continued to apply. The United States believed, he pointed out, that the Soviet Union was in violation of the ABM Treaty, implying but not yet saying that the U.S. had grounds for leaving the treaty rather than accepting a further limitation as Gorbachev was demanding.

Before Reagan finished his thought, Gorbachev interrupted with a comment that implied that he was prepared to pack up and go back to Moscow:

> So, we now have the same position on two questions [START and INF]. On the others we have had an interesting exchange of views, but without coming to terms. I believe we can end our meeting with that. Even so, it has not been useless. It didn't have the results that were expected in the Soviet Union and in the United States, and that I expected, but we have to deal with reality. The reality is that we have not been able to work out agreed positions on these questions. We spoke of major reductions of nuclear arms, but if the fate of the ABM Treaty is not clear then the whole concept collapses and we are back where we were before Reykjavík.[4]

Reagan pointed out that they agreed on a 50 percent reduction of strategic arms, on INF, on considering what to do about the ABM Treaty, and on nuclear testing. With so much agreement, he asked plaintively, "Can we really leave with nothing?"

Gorbachev countered, "Unfortunately, yes, we can." But then he pointed out that they had not yet discussed "humanitarian questions" and asked whether they should take them up, as well as regional questions and the other issues considered in the second working group.

Reagan agreed that they should, then read from the text of subjects upon which the Ridgway-Bessmertnykh group had agreed. They concerned mainly cooperative and bilateral projects that had been negotiated earlier, during Shevardnadze's and Bessmertnykh's visits to Washington. Gorbachev listened impatiently—after all, he too had received a copy of the report.

When Reagan finished reading the draft, he reiterated some of his statements the previous day about the necessity for progress in protecting human rights if he was to go as far as he would like in cooperation with the Soviet Union.

Gorbachev said that it was unfortunate that they did not have time to deal with humanitarian questions in more detail. He claimed that the Soviet government had some real concerns over the "condition of human rights" in the United States and he wished he had time to lay them out. But he did have one concrete proposal regarding the flow of information: if the Soviet Union stopped jamming American-sponsored radio stations, would the U.S. agree to Soviet broadcasts to the United States from American or nearby territory?

At first, Reagan did not reply directly but commented that the United States recognized the right of the individual to hear all points of view. Americans would see Gorbachev's press conference after their meeting, but Soviet citizens would not see Reagan's.

Gorbachev reminded Reagan that he had made a specific proposal to remedy this situation. Would Reagan cooperate to make the flow of information reciprocal? Reagan answered that he would take the matter up as soon as he returned to Washington and that he had a favorable attitude toward the proposal.*

Gorbachev then asked about motion pictures. "We are for equality," he

---

* The proposal was to allow the Soviet Union to make medium-wave radio broadcasts from a station in Cuba or somewhere in the United States. Reagan favored this in principle, but the proposal was not feasible since the Soviet broadcasters wanted to utilize a frequency that had already been allocated to American broadcasters.

said, but half the foreign films shown in the Soviet Union were American and almost no Soviet movies were shown in the United States.

"We don't keep the theaters from showing your movies," Reagan replied. "They can if they want to. We can't dictate to a private business."

"I see that the president is diverting the question to one of business," Gorbachev said with a chuckle. Reagan replied with a short lecture on the difference between private and state property, and reminded Gorbachev that the Soviet government had every right, if it wished, to set up a sales and rental office for its films in the United States.

Gorbachev said he had another example of the lack of reciprocity: "telebridges" involving Soviet and American citizens were shown on nationwide networks in the Soviet Union but not at all in the United States.

"But you can control what your networks carry because your government owns them; I can't do the same because our government doesn't own ours," Reagan answered, then added that Soviet performing arts groups like the Kirov Ballet attracted many people when they toured the United States.

Gorbachev said that he could point to more instances of lack of reciprocity but would add only one: why did the United States refuse to issue visas to officials of the Soviet trade unions?* Reagan said he would look into these matters, but had a question for Gorbachev: "How am I to explain to our farmers why you have failed to buy the grain you agreed to buy?"

"It's very simple," Gorbachev parried. "The money we would have used is still in the United States, or maybe Saudi Arabia, because of the fall in oil prices." Reagan remarked that American oil companies had also suffered from the fall in prices, but Gorbachev turned the comment aside, saying, "We know who started beating down oil prices, and who benefits from it!"

Reagan demurred, asserting that the problem with the petroleum market was the attempt by OPEC to control it. But then he shifted to another matter he had promised to take up with Gorbachev: would the Soviet authorities allow Mstislav Rostropovich's relatives to travel abroad for two months? Rostropovich had invited them to his sixtieth birthday party and had written Gorbachev asking him to assist.

Gorbachev said he had received Rostropovich's letter and the relatives had already been notified that they could travel. He then turned to Reagan and said, "Well, Mr. President, the H hour has come. What are you going to do?"

---

* It had long been U.S. policy to refuse visas to officials of Soviet trade unions who wished to travel to the United States on union business. The AFL-CIO was strongly opposed to such visits since it considered the Soviet trade unions instruments of the Communist Party and not representatives of Soviet workers.

Shevardnadze intervened to ask whether he and Shultz were to remain "unemployed," or whether the leaders had any instructions for them.

Shultz said he had put down some words that reflected what he believed had been said about INF and space, recognizing that there had been agreement on one and lack of agreement on the other. As for the areas of disagreement, he proposed the following: "The President and General Secretary discussed questions related to the ABM Treaty, the prospects for strategic defense and its relationship to the levels of offensive ballistic missiles. The discussion was intensive and substantive. They instruct their delegations in Geneva to use the record of their discussions to further progress in their work."

Gorbachev said that was not acceptable and proposed that they take a break and ask Shultz and Shevardnadze to work on a proposed statement. "You and I can stick around awhile longer," he observed. "If you don't object, we'll adjourn until three."

Sunday Afternoon

SHULTZ AND SHEVARDNADZE, accompanied by Nitze, Akhromeyev, and a few other arms control specialists, met during the break to draft language that might satisfy both. They came close. They agreed on principles for an INF Treaty and for a cut of half the strategic nuclear weapons over an initial five-year period. The United States was willing to commit itself not to withdraw from the ABM Treaty for ten years. There were only two major points of difference: (1) the Soviet delegation still insisted on limiting SDI research and testing to laboratories—a restriction that was not part of the ABM Treaty; and (2) the U.S. delegation proposed to eliminate all ballistic missiles in the second five years of the ten-year agreement while the Soviet team insisted on eliminating the remaining strategic nuclear weapons.

Before Reagan and Gorbachev resumed their meeting—at 3:25 rather than three—the American delegation reviewed the state of play. It seemed almost certain that an agreement could be reached, either by somehow bridging the gap on the remaining differences or by deciding to conclude a treaty to achieve the reductions that had been agreed while continuing negotiations on the disputed points.

Even so, there was one problem. When Reagan briefed allied leaders on his plans for Reykjavík, he had told them he was willing to compromise on INF missiles and agree to a hundred warheads on each side in Europe. He had not told them that he would agree to zero in Europe while the Soviet Union retained mobile intermediate-range missiles in Asia. Therefore, he asked us to send urgent messages to our ambassadors in allied countries instructing them to track down their presidents or prime ministers on that Sunday afternoon to inform them about the terms of the INF agreement that seemed imminent. He did not want them to learn for the first time in the Monday newspapers that the agreement differed from the one he had told them he was willing to reach.

WHEN REAGAN, GORBACHEV, Shultz, and Shevardnadze reconvened, Gorbachev read the language his team had worked out. It included an obligation not to withdraw from the ABM Treaty for ten years, no testing in space of SDI components outside laboratories, a 50 percent reduction of "strategic offensive weapons" by the end of 1991, and elimination of the remaining strategic offensive weapons by the end of 1996.

Reagan countered with a more complicated formula: Both sides would "confine themselves to research, development and testing which is permitted by the ABM Treaty for a period of five years . . . during which time a 50 percent reduction in strategic offensive arsenals would be achieved." The remaining "offensive ballistic missiles" would be eliminated by the end of a second five-year period. After ten years, with all offensive ballistic missiles eliminated, "either side would be free to introduce defenses."

Gorbachev immediately objected that Reagan's formula would undermine rather than strengthen the ABM Treaty. He argued that ten years in laboratories would not harm Reagan's dream of strategic defense; all he was asking was that testing not be carried out in space for the ten-year period. In this argument, Gorbachev had a point: ten years in laboratories would not have killed SDI, but Reagan had been convinced by Caspar Weinberger, among others, that Congress would not fund SDI if it was limited to laboratories. So far as I know, Shultz never contradicted Weinberger's assessment, with the result that "laboratories" became in Reagan's mind nothing more than a backdoor way to destroy his dream.

Gorbachev also objected to the statement that both countries would be free to deploy strategic defenses after a ten-year period, pointing out that there was no need to agree to that now; the Soviet Union would be willing to negotiate on the question following the ten-year period.

Reagan said both sides would need defenses if they had eliminated all their own ballistic missiles, as he had proposed. Their defenses would protect them against other countries that might have retained or developed ballistic missiles.

Gorbachev countered that the Soviet Union wanted to eliminate strategic nuclear weapons in ten years, not ballistic missiles, and repeated his argument in favor of confining SDI research to laboratories during that time. Reagan answered that he had made a major concession when he agreed to abide by the ABM Treaty for another ten years, particularly since the Soviet Union had violated it, and continued to violate it, with the radar station it was building near Krasnoyarsk. The United States was in full compliance, and would stay in full compliance, but he could not accept Gorbachev's attempt to make the treaty more restrictive than it was.

Gorbachev sidestepped the reference to treaty violations and observed that if Reagan would think about the Soviet proposal, he would find in it elements taken from both approaches. He went on to say that his proposal would not bind their countries after ten years; at that time all "nuclear weapons" would have been eliminated and the U.S. and USSR could negotiate on what they should do in regard to defenses.

From this point, things got confused as to what precisely Gorbachev was proposing. Up to then he had spoken of eliminating within ten years all "strategic offensive weapons" or "strategic nuclear weapons." This would have left many nuclear weapons: those on a hundred intermediate-range missiles in Asia as well as all tactical and short-range systems. When Gorbachev had spoken earlier of eliminating nuclear weapons altogether, he had referred to his proposal in January, which had elements that differed from the proposals he made in Reykjavík. For example, it called for elimination of nuclear weapons not by 1996 but by the end of 1999, and that only after agreement with the other avowed nuclear powers—all three of which had rejected the idea.

However, Reagan did not press Gorbachev on this point. He still could not understand why Gorbachev would oppose deploying strategic defenses after the two countries had destroyed all their nuclear weapons or all ballistic missiles. "If we eliminate our nuclear weapons," he asked, "why would you be bothered if one of us wanted to protect his country against other countries that might still have them when we don't have any ourselves?"

Gorbachev avoided a direct answer, but continued to argue that his proposal would let Reagan have his SDI if he wished, and that the agreement had to be such that neither would be a winner or a loser. Reagan agreed that there should be no winners or losers and suggested that they leave the question as to what kind of research, development, and testing was allowed by the ABM Treaty to further negotiation during Gorbachev's visit to the United States.

Gorbachev was firm. "Without that, we don't have a package," he said. "All the elements are interrelated."

Reagan said he was still perplexed. How could Gorbachev object to building defenses if both sides had eliminated their ballistic missiles? He proposed a recess to review "what is keeping us apart."

When they reconvened, Reagan presented a slight revision of the formula he had introduced earlier.

Reagan asked Shultz to explain the differences in the Soviet and American approaches. Shultz said he saw two differences: first, regarding what type of testing would be permissible in the ten-year period when both were obligated not to withdraw from the ABM Treaty; and second, the question of how long the parties would be required to adhere to the ABM Treaty. The Soviet proposal implied that it would be in force for an indefinitely long period, while the United States had agreed to keep it in force for ten years.

Gorbachev objected that Shultz's understanding was not quite right: The Soviet position was that both sides should decide after ten years what to do about the ABM Treaty. The United States would be free to withdraw on six months' notice if it chose.

Then he recalled the incident when the two were at dinner in Geneva and Shultz had reported that the Soviet delegation was not cooperating. Reagan had challenged him, "Why don't you just pound on the table and insist they come to an agreement?" In fact, he had met with his people and in fifteen minutes the problems were solved. "If we call a break now," Gorbachev concluded, "and you go back to your delegation and in ten minutes convince them to agree, you'll have beat me at that game!"*

Shultz questioned Gorbachev regarding the way he visualized the reductions taking place, and then added that there was an additional difference in the U.S. and Soviet positions: the United States, he pointed out, was proposing to eliminate offensive ballistic missiles in the second five-year period, while the Soviet proposal involved strategic offensive weapons.

Gorbachev replied that the compromise he had made, to reduce all categories of strategic offensive weapons at the same rate, had been a difficult one. Since these weapons would be cut by 50 percent in the first five years, it was logical to eliminate these types in the second five years.

With that explanation, they called a break and returned to their delegations. It was then four-thirty in the afternoon.

* A literal translation of his Russian would be, "you can consider yourself the victor!"

———

WHILE THE PRESIDENT was closeted with Gorbachev, Shultz, and Shevardnadze, some dozen U.S. officials waited in their parlor in Höfdi House
for him to emerge from the meeting to brief them on the outcome. Paul
Nitze, who had worked most of the night on the arms control issues, napped
on a couch. Donald Regan reviewed for those who were interested Republican prospects in the races for the U.S. Senate. Congressional elections were
fast approaching, and Regan considered the prospects favorable for Republicans in some of them, though not, probably, in enough to retain a majority
in the Senate.

The small talk and brief respite granted exhausted negotiators masked
a feeling of tension and anticipation. Euphoria lurked, barely concealed,
under the surface of emotions. The U.S. and USSR seemed to be on
the verge of the most sweeping commitments in history to reduce mankind's most destructive weaponry. Negotiations on other topics had produced little that had not already been agreed, but suddenly Gorbachev
seemed to be offering most of what Reagan had requested regarding nuclear
arms reduction.

When Reagan and Shultz emerged and briefed the group on the differences that remained, someone suggested that since both Reagan and Gorbachev were getting tired, perhaps they should prolong the meeting for
another day and let their delegations work on language overnight. Reagan's
face fell; he winced and blurted out, "Oh, shit!"

If he had been pressed to stay, he probably would have agreed, but nobody had the heart to insist. I remembered bitterly my advice to leave Nancy
Reagan in Washington. If she had been in Reykjavík, he probably would
have been content to continue the meeting another day. Gorbachev was not
the only leader who seemed lost without his wife. But that was not the only
reason members of Reagan's staff hesitated to push him to stay. The Americans could not be sure that prolonging the meeting would help. Gorbachev's
attitude that morning seemed to be that he would rather go home without
agreement on anything if he couldn't get his way on SDI. That was the one
thing—at that point the only thing—he was not going to get, however long
the meeting lasted.

The situation seemed far from hopeless, however. It was difficult for any
of the American officials to believe that, given the progress that had been
made up to that point, either leader would break off the talks in complete
disagreement. If Gorbachev had dropped his insistence on limiting SDI re-

search to laboratories, Reagan would have accepted Gorbachev's position regarding what would happen to the ABM Treaty after the ten-year non-withdrawal period was over. Reagan was also prepared to accept elimination of strategic nuclear weapons as a ten-year goal if the Soviet Union had been willing to eliminate ballistic missiles (many of which were neither of strategic range nor nuclear) at the same time. In fact, if the only issue remaining had been whether to eliminate ballistic missiles or strategic nuclear weapons in the second five-year period, Reagan would have accepted the Soviet position. So far as he was concerned, the only make-or-break issue left was Gorbachev's attempt to limit SDI research to laboratories. It was difficult to believe that the Soviet leader would let that word stand in the way of an agreement he needed. If, however, he couldn't live with the idea that Reagan would be the "winner" on this point, he could have gotten what he needed most by untying his package and agreeing that the two countries could proceed with an INF agreement and a 50 percent cut in strategic nuclear weapons while continuing to negotiate on what would happen after that. Even this would have exceeded most expectations of what their meeting might achieve.

At five-thirty, when Reagan and Shultz joined Gorbachev and Shevardnadze for their final session, they had in mind the potential compromises that would solve the remaining contentious issues once Gorbachev dropped "laboratories" from his proposal. In fact, Shultz introduced some of the U.S. fallback proposals before Gorbachev did so. He asked whether Gorbachev would be willing to eliminate both strategic nuclear weapons and offensive ballistic missiles in the ten-year period. Even though Gorbachev gave no clear answer, Reagan indicated that he would agree to include all nuclear weapons in the group to be destroyed. At one point he went so far as to say that if they could agree to eliminate all nuclear weapons, they could turn it over to the negotiators in Geneva for them to draft an agreement for Gorbachev to sign during his visit to the United States.

Gorbachev's reply was conditional, however: "Well, OK. That is one way we can agree. But another matter concerns me greatly."* And he went on to argue that reduction and elimination of nuclear weapons depended on "strengthening" the ABM Treaty, and that depended on keeping SDI research in laboratories for ten years.

Reagan explained that, in his view, even the strictest interpretation of the

* From the Soviet notes. The U.S. version reads: "Gorbachev agreed. He continued that he now wanted to turn to the ABM Treaty. He was apprehensive about this."

ABM Treaty would not require research to be limited to laboratories. Furthermore, the U.S. aim was to deploy defenses, provided they were feasible and cost-effective, only after the U.S. and USSR had eliminated the missiles that could be used to attack the other. Nations that pledged not to use poison gas didn't object if others had gas masks.

Gorbachev replied with a tone of contempt in his voice, "Yes, I've heard about gas masks and maniacs maybe ten times from you. But you still haven't convinced me."

Reagan commented that he had been talking about only one possibility of what could happen after ten years. He couldn't be sure that strategic defenses would turn out to be technically feasible, though he thought they would be. Even if they were, they might be too expensive. Also, they would not necessarily be space-based, as Gorbachev seemed to assume. However, his objective was to make sure that the possibility of developing defenses against a missile attack could be researched and tested. If they both wanted to reduce nuclear weapons, they should proceed to do so and not let a theoretical possibility become a bone of contention.

Gorbachev said there would be no bone of contention so long as SDI research was confined to laboratories for ten years.

Even Reagan was beginning to lose patience. "I am not asking for the right to deploy an ABM system in space," he said. "I am speaking only of research permitted by the ABM Treaty." Then he added, "And, by the way, the Soviet Union is not above reproach. I have in mind the radar near Krasnoyarsk. It is a fact that we interpret the ABM Treaty differently."

Gorbachev answered that keeping SDI research within the confines of laboratories was, for the Soviet Union, a question of principle. He was not being stubborn or hardheaded. The Soviet Union would not accept any SDI research or testing if it was conducted in the atmosphere or space.

Reagan made clear that he could not accept this limitation because he would be violating a pledge he had made to the American people to find out whether strategic defenses were feasible. Gorbachev did not have to contend with a free press or a Congress dominated by the opposing political party, he observed, but he, as U.S. president, did, and he could not break his promise.

Gorbachev argued that the Soviet concessions had been such that Reagan would be a hero at home if he made an agreement possible by limiting SDI research to laboratories. If Reagan couldn't do that, he added, "we may as well go home and forget about Reykjavík. There is no other possibility. In any case, I know that for me there is no other way." He went on to speak at some length about his earlier belief that they could come to terms, that he had made major concessions, but that he could see the Americans were unwilling to make any concessions of importance.

Shevardnadze intervened at that point to say that they had gotten very close to a historic agreement. "When future generations read the transcripts of this meeting, they will not forgive us if we let this opportunity pass," he observed. He seemed to be appealing to both Reagan and Gorbachev.

Reagan explained, as one politician to another, that if he were accused of giving up SDI to get weapons cuts, it would do him great harm politically.

Gorbachev said abruptly, "Well, then, let's bring the meeting to an end. We will not accept what you propose. I've said all I have to say."

Reagan was incredulous. "Can you really mean that you would turn down a historic opportunity because of a single word? After all, we have made very clear that we will abide by the ABM Treaty!"

"You say that it is the question of a single word," Gorbachev replied. "But for us it's not the word that counts, it's the principle." Taking a leaf from Reagan's political argument, he added that if he returned to Moscow with an agreement that permitted the United States to test weapons in space so, after ten years, it would be in a position to deploy them, he would be considered "a fool, an irresponsible political leader."

Reagan continued to plead, pointing out that after their meeting in Geneva he had thought they understood each other. But now, when he asked for one little favor that could greatly influence their future relations, Gorbachev had refused.

Gorbachev countered that "there are favors and favors." If Reagan had asked him to buy more grain because his farmers needed the money, he could arrange that. But to ask him to allow the United States to develop a space defense system while offensive weapons were being eliminated was to ask too much. It would not even be in the U.S. interest, he argued, because SDI only created nervousness and suspicion.

One final time, Reagan asked why, if both sides eliminated their nuclear weapons, they should care whether one side or the other deployed defenses subsequently. He was willing to guarantee that there could be no deployments for ten years. As for who made the concessions, he pointed out that he had accepted every Soviet position except the use of the word "laboratories." He appealed to Gorbachev at least to offer another word.

Gorbachev refused and added, "Even though our meeting is ending this way, I have a clear conscience. . . . I did everything I could."

Reagan said he was sorry they were parting that way when they had been so close. Apparently Gorbachev just didn't want an agreement after all. He regretted that.

Gorbachev said he was also sorry that it had turned out that way, but he had done all he could.

When they came out of the building at 6:50, their somber faces told the story. Marshal Sergei Akhromeyev looked at Paul Nitze and said ruefully, "It's not my fault." It was Gorbachev, not his military, who had made the word "laboratories" a stumbling block.

XI

──────── ⮕ ────────

1986: November–December

REYKJAVÍK: RECRIMINATIONS

*I realized he had brought me to Iceland with one purpose: to kill the Strategic
Defense Initiative. . . . I was very disappointed—and very angry.*
—RONALD REAGAN, 1990[1]

*With Reagan, we had to struggle in Reykjavík not only with a class enemy but
with an extraordinarily primitive one, a feeble-minded cave man.*
—MIKHAIL GORBACHEV to the Politburo, October 14, 1986[2]

IMMEDIATELY AFTER REAGAN and Gorbachev parted in front of
Höfdi House, Reagan's motorcade rushed a few blocks away to the
American ambassador's residence. Reagan took a short rest before starting
home. Secretary Shultz convened a meeting of the American delegation.
"I've never been so proud of our president as I was this afternoon," he announced. "Gorbachev tried to kill SDI, but the president would have none of
it. He held firm. We should all be proud."[3]

When Shultz had finished his brief, which consisted largely in justifying
Reagan's rejection of Gorbachev's package, I asked, "Did Gorbachev accept
our proposal to eliminate ballistic missiles?" (I had been a notetaker earlier,
but Thomas Simons of the State Department had taken the notes in the final
session.)

"Yes, he did," Shultz replied, and then rushed off to his press conference.
He still had to fly to Brussels that evening in order to brief the North Atlantic
Council the following morning.

I felt crushed. Ten years in laboratories would not have killed SDI; it could have preserved the concept since there was at least that much research needed to determine what technologies were most promising. If Gorbachev had agreed to eliminate ballistic missiles as part of the package, there would have been a breakthrough more significant even than a 50 percent reduction of nuclear weapons.

I rushed to the car assigned me in the motorcade and sank into the rear seat in a blue funk. How could Shultz have let this happen? He was in the final meeting, and neither Poindexter nor I was. Ten years in labs for SDI and elimination of strategic nuclear weapons and ballistic missiles would have been an agreement totally in the U.S. interest. If Shultz had told Reagan that, Reagan might have accepted it. Why had Shultz been so obtuse? When all this came out, I thought Reagan would be the loser in public opinion.

While these morose thoughts were swarming in my mind as the motorcade sped to Keflavík, Secretary Shultz was holding a news conference. According to journalists who attended, he did not need to say a word. The expression on his face, like that of Reagan's as he emerged from the meeting, read failure—FAILURE, in fact. Right up to the end, everyone had been expecting a date for Gorbachev to visit Washington, and there was none. For many in the press, that was all that mattered.

Gorbachev said that he had intended to put a positive spin on the meeting since he felt that the progress made had been significant, but that Shultz's press conference made that difficult.[4] If the American secretary of state implied that the meeting was a failure, how could Gorbachev speak even of qualified success? As it was, during his press conference in Reykjavík, he still gave the meeting a more positive treatment than did Shultz. When he reported to the Politburo in Moscow, however, his condemnation of Reagan was crude and unequivocal, as the quotation in the chapter epigraph indicates.

I did not know how either of these press conferences had gone when I took my seat in Air Force One to return to Washington. I tried to sort out just what had happened, since I knew I would be responsible for preparing the record of the meeting. I had notes on all but the final meeting, so I reviewed it with Dmitry Zarechnak, Reagan's interpreter. The first thing I established was that, contrary to what Shultz had told me, Gorbachev never accepted the idea of eliminating ballistic missiles, even as part of a package that included all strategic offensive weapons. The second was that, in fact, Reagan had spoken of eliminating all nuclear weapons in ten years. His willingness to speak of abolishing all nuclear weapons by 1996 scandalized many of Reagan's associates, who didn't want to admit it. They forgot that Gorbachev's refusal to ban ballistic missiles made the whole question moot. SDI was not the sole issue that separated the two. Reagan was not the only one who balked at what many would have considered a world-transforming arms control agreement.

Aside from ballistic missiles and laboratories, however, the leaders had apparently agreed on every other key issue regarding nuclear weapons and strategic arms. The extent of agreement on key points was unprecedented. The list I made of contentious issues that seemed to be agreed filled a page of my yellow legal pad. I took it to Chief of Staff Donald Regan and John Poindexter, who were sitting together in a forward cabin, and pointed out that Reagan and Gorbachev had solved more problems than any of us had expected of the Reykjavík meeting. When they looked over my list, both agreed. Poindexter rushed back to the press section of Air Force One to explain what had really happened. Unfortunately, most journalists had already filed stories calling the Reykjavík summit a bust.

Debating What Happened

WHEN REAGAN REPORTED to the nation in a televised address, naturally he defended his insistence on continuing research and testing of strategic defense concepts. Public opinion in the United States soon rallied to his support.* Public opinion in Western Europe was not so easily influenced. The general opinion, among the news media at least, was that Reagan had rejected a world-transforming arms control agreement for an impractical dream of making the United States invulnerable to attack. However, key European government leaders were shocked not by Reagan's refusal to agree to Gorbachev's terms, but by the concessions Reagan offered. They were relieved that his devotion to SDI—however misplaced that was in their view—had prevented his agreeing to what Gorbachev wanted. West German chancellor Helmut Kohl rushed to Washington to protest Reagan's willingness to eliminate all intermediate-range nuclear missiles in Europe while the Warsaw Pact held a decisive advantage in conventional weapons. British

---

* A poll conducted by the *New York Times* and CBS News on October 14 and 15 found that 44 percent of the respondents felt that Gorbachev was more to blame than Reagan for the "failure" of the meeting, while only 17 percent felt that Reagan was more to blame. At the same time Reagan's overall approval rating rose to 73 percent from the 64 percent recorded in a poll a week earlier. *New York Times,* Oct. 16, 1986.

prime minister Margaret Thatcher and French president François Mitterrand were scandalized by Reagan's hatred of nuclear weapons. It seemed none understood why it would be desirable to eliminate ballistic missiles, even though they had not objected when Reagan had informed them before he went to Reykjavík that he would make the proposal.

Opposition to some of the provisions was not limited to Europe. The chairman of the Joint Chiefs of Staff informed Reagan that eliminating ballistic missiles would "pose high risks" to U.S. security.[5] He and his staff could not think beyond preserving the "nuclear triad" as a deterrent force. Apparently they did not take into consideration the way the threat to the United States and its allies would be transformed if there were no Soviet ballistic missiles.

Meanwhile, Gorbachev accused Reagan of denying that he had agreed to eliminate all nuclear weapons by the end of 1996. American officials, many of whom were aghast that at one point Reagan had put this in the package he proposed, avoided confirming what he had said rather than explaining the context in which it had been said. Reagan obviously had in mind that he would agree to eliminate all nuclear weapons if Gorbachev accepted the American proposals, including elimination of all ballistic missiles and acceptance of the broad interpretation of the ABM Treaty.

Gorbachev's complaint was effective with many people—and lives on today in much commentary—even though it was fundamentally illogical. He blamed Reagan's stubbornness for the lack of agreement at Reykjavík, but if Reagan had gone so far as to agree to eliminate all nuclear weapons as part of a package, was not Gorbachev the one responsible for scuttling the agreement on grounds that were ultimately frivolous? After all, the only thing Reagan asked was for Gorbachev not to insist on modifying the ABM Treaty, which the Soviet Union was itself violating. Since confinement of SDI research to laboratories for ten years would not have killed SDI (even though Reagan was convinced it would), Gorbachev could have gotten agreement on everything he sought at Reykjavík by abandoning a demand that in no tangible way served Soviet interests!

It was a mistake by Reagan and his advisers not to present from the outset a full explanation of the give-and-take at Reykjavík, but, even so, those who were persuaded by Gorbachev's charges failed to detect the logical inconsistency in his accusations. Both Reagan and Gorbachev had been stubborn on the one issue each considered a matter of principle when, in fact, that issue was not of critical importance. Of the two, Reagan had been more flexible and more eager to look for solutions not in his earlier proposals. Gorbachev came to the meeting with a number of "concessions" (all of which were consistent with Soviet interests), but would not budge on a matter that was substantively inconsequential.

Leaving aside the question of who was most responsible for the disagreements at Reykjavík, is it fair to say, as many have, that either Reagan's or Gorbachev's stubbornness blocked "the most sweeping and important arms control agreement in the history of the world," or, in Gorbachev's words, "a historic chance"?[6]

Hardly. Those who have accused Reagan of passing up a unique opportunity to rid the world of nuclear weapons must assume that, once there had been a broad agreement in principle, a treaty would have been forthcoming—automatically as it were—and that this treaty would have been ratified by the legislatures of both countries and then faithfully implemented regardless of other events or the policies of other countries. Nothing in the history of U.S.-Soviet relations up to then would have provided any encouragement for such expectations. They were based on wishful thinking, not a sober appraisal of the likelihood that the agreements Reagan and Gorbachev nearly made in Reykjavík could have been implemented.

In the past, general agreements on principles had proven extremely difficult to put into acceptable treaty form. The understandings that Gerald Ford and Leonid Brezhnev reached in Vladivostok in 1974 were not incorporated in a treaty until 1978, and then only with substantial modifications. Even so, the U.S. Senate refused to ratify the resulting treaty (SALT II), in part because it opposed some of the terms, but most decisively because of the Soviet invasion of Afghanistan. It is simply not plausible to think that the much more radical changes that Reagan and Gorbachev discussed in Reykjavík, some of which were vehemently opposed by powerful interests in both countries and by America's closest allies, could have been put in acceptable treaty language, ratified, and implemented in the short period of time they postulated. The program in its entirety was too ambitious to be practical. It was a mistake for either Reagan or Gorbachev to assume that both countries could undertake such a rapid and radical degree of disarmament unless a lot of other things fell into place, many of which were beyond their control.

Parts of the agreement were feasible, nevertheless: The 50 percent reduction of all strategic nuclear weapons in five years could have taken place and would have improved both countries' security. It was also possible to eliminate intermediate-range nuclear weapons without linkage to any other issue except effective verification. If there had been an INF agreement along the lines Gorbachev demanded in Reykjavík, however—with a hundred Soviet missiles left in Asia—it would have militated against his aim of improving relations with China and Japan.

What the meeting did do, and this was of profound importance, was con-vince Gorbachev eventually that Reagan genuinely desired to end the arms race. However, this was not a conclusion that Gorbachev reached immedi-ately. Emotions were too raw, and the mutual feeling of betrayal too intense, to permit calm judgment. Relations were to take a severe beating for several months to come.

The Other Shoe Drops: Diplomatic Expulsions

ON OCTOBER 19, barely a week after Reagan and Gorbachev parted in Reykjavík, the USSR expelled five diplomats from the U.S. embassy in Moscow in retaliation for the earlier expulsion of twenty-five from the So-viet UN mission—precisely what the United States had warned the KGB not to do. Two days later, the United States ordered fifty-five additional Soviet diplomats out of the United States and imposed personnel ceilings on the Soviet installations that prevented replacing the persons who were expelled. The Soviet government responded by removing overnight the 260 Soviet citizens who were employed in various support functions at the American embassy in Moscow and the consulate general in Leningrad.* Eventually they were replaced by a much smaller number of security-cleared American citizens who much improved services at the embassy, but embassy person-nel went through a stressful winter and spring in 1986 and 1987 since they had to wait for the replacements to be recruited and trained. Although the State Department had been pressed for years by the NSC and other federal agencies to reduce its reliance on Soviet employees in Moscow, it had re-sisted the pressure and had no plans in place to send Americans to do these jobs until it suddenly had no choice.

Both Shultz and Shevardnadze have since described their negotiations over Daniloff's detention as among the most difficult of all their negotia-tions. Finding a solution bolstered their confidence in each other. The world can be thankful for this. But it would have been better if the growing confi-dence had resulted from solving other problems. The fact is that Shultz's tactics put Shevardnadze in the middle of a dispute not of his making and, by implying that the United States was at least in part responsible for the

---

* Normal services were not easily or reliably available in Moscow and the embassy had to maintain its apartments and vehicles with its own employees. Therefore, such "local employees" included carpen-ters, plumbers, mechanics, painters, drivers, maids, and cooks, as well as clerical personnel in non-sensitive areas such as the consular and public affairs sections. No Soviet citizens worked in the areas of the embassy that dealt with classified materials.

situation, made it difficult for Shevardnadze to extract from the KGB the concessions necessary to make the trade deniable. The United States should have emphasized from the start the Reagan-Gorbachev relationship and pressed Gorbachev to release Daniloff without preconditions.

In retrospect, this incident was mishandled by all who made the key decisions: the FBI, by prosecuting (instead of simply expelling) a minor spy whose contact was under FBI control and therefore could not do substantial damage; Gorbachev, by refusing to release Daniloff on the basis of Reagan's assurances; Reagan, by allowing Shultz to negotiate a trade; Shultz, by employing tactics that prolonged and even heightened the confrontation. The only real winner was the KGB. It managed, once again, to free one of its agents by arresting an innocent American citizen.

This was a short-term victory, however, for at the end of 1986 the KGB was destined to last less than five years. Subsequent events make clear an additional misperception that prevailed in Washington in 1986. American officials assumed that an important message passed to the KGB would have gone to Gorbachev as a matter of course. Any significant message from Moscow received by the CIA would have been instantly conveyed to the White House. Yet it seems that one of the problems in 1986 was that the KGB did not tell Gorbachev or Shevardnadze of the U.S. warning about the consequences of retaliatory expulsions. As a result, they both considered the U.S. expulsions sudden and unreasonable.

This was evidence of a deeper problem that American officials did not understand in 1986: Since Stalin's time the general secretary did not really exercise full control over the KGB except, perhaps, when its former chairman, Yuri Andropov, held the top office. It had become an agency with close to complete autonomy. Its chairman was in a position to report what he pleased to the general secretary. There was no mechanism to make sure that the reports were honest or complete. By 1991 this became clear when KGB chairman Vladimir Kryuchkov conspired against Gorbachev. But in 1986 neither Gorbachev nor the U.S. government suspected that this could be possible.

Further Frustration: Shultz and Shevardnadze in Vienna

THE EXPULSIONS OF diplomats and arguments over what was said by whom in Reykjavík dominated the news for a time, but American officials hoped that negotiations could be put back on track quickly. Secretary of State Shultz and Foreign Minister Shevardnadze were both scheduled to attend a conference in Vienna during the first week of November, and they agreed to meet while they were there to review the results of the Reykjavík summit and discuss ways the remaining differences could be bridged. To assist the process, State Department officials prepared a set of papers setting forth their understanding of what had been agreed and what they understood the Soviet position to be on those points that had not been settled. Shultz gave Shevardnadze the papers and invited him to have his staff check them for accuracy and tell him whether they described the Soviet position accurately.

Shevardnadze spent most of the time in the first meeting trying to persuade Shultz to "admit" that Reagan had agreed to eliminate all nuclear weapons by 1996 and to confirm that this "commitment" was still valid. Shultz replied that Reagan considered the elimination of nuclear weapons an ultimate goal, but not necessarily one that could be reached in ten years. He pointed out that both sides at Reykjavík had spoken of various possibilities in various contexts, but Gorbachev himself had made clear that nothing was agreed until everything was. Reagan had felt that the meeting in Reykjavík had made substantial progress and had instructed Shultz to try to move the negotiations forward by exploring ways in which the questions that were not decided might be settled. For this, however, both of them needed to have a clear understanding of what was agreed and what not. After hours of inconclusive discussion, Shultz and Shevardnadze appointed two working groups to continue the talks, through the night if necessary. One dealt with arms-related questions and the other with the remaining three categories on the four-part agenda.

To the amazement of the Americans, neither Viktor Karpov, the arms control negotiator, nor Viktor Komplektov, who had been delegated to deal with the other issues, would discuss the American papers—or offer any of their own. They protested that the papers were one-sided and misstated the Soviet position. The Americans replied that they had done their best to be accurate, but of course would revise the papers to reflect the Soviet position if the Soviet delegation would only let them know what they wanted changed. If that was unacceptable, they invited the Soviet delegation to describe its position in its own paper. "We are not trying to tell you what your policy is," I told Komplektov. "We are just trying to make sure that we understand it correctly. How can we possibly settle our differences if we don't know what they are?"

The crux of the Soviet position seemed to be, "Admit that your president is committed to eliminate all nuclear weapons by the end of 1996 or we will

not talk about anything else." Appeals to logic were of no avail. Both working groups broke up early without any clarification of what the Soviet government really wanted, and Shevardnadze did nothing to set things straight
in his meeting with Shultz the next day.

The Soviet stance left the American negotiators utterly perplexed. They
could not understand any rationale for the Soviet behavior except perhaps a
desire to embarrass the American president by making it seem that he had
been reckless in his dealing with Gorbachev. How this was going to facilitate agreements with the United States that the Soviet government seemed to
want and certainly needed was a mystery. After all, if it was true that eliminating all nuclear weapons by the end of 1996 had been a realistic possibility and Gorbachev had turned it down just to make sure that SDI research
stayed in laboratories for ten years, then he, not Reagan, had been the fool.

Shevardnadze compounded the American disappointment when he told
the press upon his return to Moscow that the discussion papers Shultz had
provided "actually canceled everything achieved by the sides in Reykjavík."7 Such accusations, coupled with the acrimony surrounding the expulsions of diplomats, lasted well into the following year.

The United States Loses Key Players

EVEN BEFORE THE disastrous Shultz-Shevardnadze meetings in Vienna,
I had been instructed to draft a letter for the president to send to Gorbachev
in an attempt to solve the impasse that had occurred at Reykjavík. Initially,
Reagan wanted to preserve the ultimate goal of eliminating both nuclear
weapons and ballistic missiles, but recognized that this process was going
to take longer than the ten years cited at Reykjavík. Poindexter was convinced that Reagan could accept some period of time to keep SDI research
in laboratories—seven years perhaps—if that would help Gorbachev accept
the broad interpretation of the ABM Treaty, which would be necessary eventually if SDI was to remain a viable program within that treaty's restrictions.

I worked out a conceptual schedule for reductions that integrated the four
elements of the U.S. agenda into each stage of the arms reduction process.
During the first phase of nuclear reductions, conventional weapons in Europe would be reduced to equal levels and both countries would withdraw
military support for regional conflicts. Further reductions of weaponry
would be coupled with reforms within the Soviet Union, such as better protection of human rights and removal of barriers to travel and the flow of in-

formation. Eliminating ballistic missiles before strategic defenses could be deployed remained an offer, but not a requirement for continued reduction of nuclear weapons. Total elimination of nuclear weapons would be an ultimate goal, but would require the cooperation and agreement of the other nuclear powers.

A totally unrelated event sidetracked these efforts. Just as Secretary Shultz was traveling to Vienna for his futile meeting with Shevardnadze, the news broke that the United States had sold arms to Iran in an effort to establish communication with moderate forces in that country and encourage the release of American hostages held in Lebanon. This quickly developed into a major scandal. When it was learned that some of the proceeds from arms sales to Iran had been secretly used to finance supplies to Nicaraguans fighting the Sandinista regime, Reagan's advisers convinced him that he would have to replace his national security team in order to avoid critical damage to his presidency.

On November 24, I sent John Poindexter a lengthy memorandum that set forth my recommendations for building on what had been agreed at Reykjavík, including a draft of a letter the president might send to Gorbachev. Unfortunately, Poindexter never had time to read it; the next morning he sent members of the NSC staff a message that he was resigning. A few hours later, President Reagan announced that Poindexter had resigned and that NSC staffer Oliver North had been fired.

I was appalled that the president had been persuaded to part with a key official who could have kept our policy toward the Soviet Union on course. That evening, I noted in my personal journal, "Frankly—since there was apparently no diversion of U.S. funds [to personal use], and no suspicion that anyone profited personally, I'm not sure why this is such a big deal. No doubt the press and Congress will make it so, however."

The Iran-Contra scandal cost Reagan the people who were key to maintaining momentum in negotiations with the Soviet Union. Their replacements, Frank Carlucci as national security adviser and General Colin Powell as his deputy, were highly competent, experienced officials. But they had not been part of the team that had fashioned the four-part agenda or had participated directly in the negotiations leading up to the meeting in Reykjavík. Carlucci did not agree with the president's proposal to destroy ballistic missiles or with his aspiration to eliminate nuclear weapons. Carlucci's initial attention was absorbed in the task of "cleaning house" at the National Security Council, which had been accused unfairly of running amok.

Subsequently, both Carlucci and Powell played key roles in getting relations with the Soviet Union back on track. When he replaced Weinberger as secretary of defense in 1987, Frank Carlucci, a former professional diplomat, immediately established personal contact with Soviet defense minister Dmitri Yazov and authorized broad contacts between American and Soviet military officers. As national security adviser in 1988, Colin Powell played a key role in obtaining Senate ratification of the INF Treaty without crippling amendments. Subsequently, as chairman of the Joint Chiefs of Staff during the first Bush administration, he cultivated a personal relationship with his Soviet counterpart that eased the way to the agreements that brought final closure to the Cold War. But, initially, the replacement of Poindexter caused a delay of several months in implementing the U.S. agenda.

The change of personnel at the NSC was not the only factor that delayed a rapid presidential follow-up to the Reykjavík meeting. While the expulsions of spies and diplomats following the Daniloff arrest and release were still fresh in people's minds, the president was informed that the U.S. embassy in Moscow had been penetrated by the KGB. A former marine guard, Sergeant Clayton Lonetree, had confessed that he had been recruited by the KGB. Following intense interrogation, another marine who had been at the embassy in Moscow signed a statement that he had cooperated with Lonetree to allow KGB agents to enter the embassy building at night when both were on guard duty.

This disturbing report came to the president almost simultaneously with news from the CIA that virtually all of its agents in the Soviet Union had been arrested and that many technical intelligence collection projects had been compromised. When he briefed the president, CIA deputy director Robert Gates speculated that a former junior CIA officer, Edward Lee Howard, had betrayed these agents and the secret technical devices when he had escaped FBI surveillance and defected to the Soviet Union a few months earlier.

That was not all so far as the spy business was concerned. As these revelations were made public, key congressional leaders seized on the discovery of parts of a listening system in the outer walls of the uncompleted U.S. embassy in Moscow. Before thorough studies were made of the situation, several senators declared that the embassy was unusable and should be demolished. The atmosphere was not conducive to rational public discussion, particularly since many of the facts were highly classified. Unsubstantiated allegations, if made by powerful congressional figures, were allowed to stand without challenge.

The upshot was that, for the president and other senior U.S. officials, the fallout from Iran-Contra and the various spying and bugging accusations involving the Soviet Union prevented a prompt and forthcoming follow-up to the Reykjavík near agreement. Of course, Shevardnadze's behavior in his meetings with Shultz in Vienna provided no encouragement that new proposals by Reagan would be treated seriously in Moscow. In late December, my draft of the letter from Reagan to Gorbachev that John Poindexter had been eager to send had still not been read in the NSC front office.

Second Thoughts in Moscow

SEVERAL PROMINENT SOVIET scientists, including Yevgeny Velikhov, director of the Kurchatov Institute in Moscow who accompanied Gorbachev to Reykjavík, and Roald Sagdeyev, who headed the civilian space program, had advised Gorbachev before he went to Reykjavík that the United States was most unlikely to devise a strategic defensive system that could not be penetrated. Indeed, they did not see how one would be technically possible. Therefore, there would be no need for the USSR to match U.S. efforts if it proceeded with Reagan's Strategic Defense Initiative. They had the impression that Gorbachev would not make SDI a stumbling block if Reagan accepted his other proposals. Therefore, they were surprised when Gorbachev did just that.

Subsequently, Sagdeyev commented to colleagues in the Academy of Sciences that if Gorbachev had wanted to keep SDI research and testing out of space, he had been poorly advised to seek a limitation of research to laboratories. The Soviet Union had put laboratories in space and had bragged about it publicly.

Shevardnadze, too, had been uneasy that Gorbachev had staked so much on keeping SDI research in laboratories. When his arms control negotiators informed him of Sagdeyev's comments, he invited Sagdeyev to explain the point to him directly. When Sagdeyev did so, Shevardnadze asked him to go to Washington and explain that there could be laboratories in space. He did so, and was quoted by the American press to that effect, but was severely criticized by Soviet military officers when he returned home.[8]

By 1987 the Soviet position shifted. Laboratories were no longer mentioned. Instead, Gorbachev focused his effort on getting Reagan to confirm the narrow interpretation of the ABM Treaty. Although the U.S. SDI program was still being conducted in accord with the narrow interpretation, Reagan was convinced that the United States had a legal right, under the broad interpretation of the treaty, to test and develop components of a system based on, in the treaty's words, "other physical principles." He feared that if he renounced that right it would foreclose the possibility of determining whether strategic defenses were feasible. Congress was unlikely to fund an illegal program. He was well aware, however, that even the broad interpretation of the ABM Treaty would not permit the United States to *deploy* these weapons.

Reykjavík, SDI, and the End of the Cold War

IT WAS GOOD that the meeting did not reach the understandings on arms reduction that Gorbachev had proposed and to which Reagan had come close to agreeing, not because Reagan was right to believe that ten years of laboratory research would kill SDI, but because the agreements would not have worked. Negotiating the details would have led to more acrimonious debates and delayed implementation of agreements in other areas, precisely those that were most important for building confidence between the two leaders.

Reagan refused to come to terms at Reykjavík because of SDI; Gorbachev because he did not want to eliminate ballistic missiles and insisted on confining SDI research to laboratories for ten years. But what both were proposing for the second five years of reductions was impractical unless many other things changed in the relationship. The U.S. four-point agenda had been designed to put in balance the various elements of the U.S.-Soviet relationship that had to change if the Cold War was to end. Reagan should have refused to go beyond eliminating INF missiles in Europe and cutting strategic weapons in half until Gorbachev showed that he would move on other parts of the agenda. The following year, Gorbachev did accept the whole agenda and the arms control issues were eventually settled on terms close to the original U.S. positions. The main impact of the "failure" at Reykjavík, therefore, was to persuade Gorbachev that he had to begin reforms at home if he was going to end the arms race with the United States.

All the participants eventually came to see that the Reykjavík summit had positive results. Shevardnadze remarked in 1991, "Looking back, I believe today that perhaps it was good that the meeting in Reykjavík ended as it did."[9] Gorbachev later called it "a real breakthrough,"[10] and Reagan considered it "a major turning point," as noted in his memoirs.[11]

Without the impasse at Reykjavík, the Cold War almost certainly would not have ended as rapidly as it did. Looking back, we can see that the Reykjavík summit marked a psychological turning point. But it took months for tempers to cool, for Gorbachev to embark on genuine internal reform, and for American and Soviet officials to engage seriously in a constructive dialogue across the full spectrum of issues that divided East and West.

XII

1987

A COMMON AGENDA

As difficult as it is to do business with the United States, we are doomed to do it. We have no choice.
—MIKHAIL GORBACHEV to the Politburo, February 1987[1]

Our policy did not change until Gorbachev understood that there would be no improvement and no serious arms control until we admitted and accepted human rights, free emigration, until glasnost became freedom of speech, until our society and the process of perestroika changed deeply.
—ANATOLY CHERNYAEV, 1998[2]

THE YEAR BEGAN with Gorbachev still in a sulk and Reagan distracted by the Iran-Contra scandal. To make clear his discontent, Gorbachev refused to continue the practice, started only the year before, of televised New Year's greetings to one another's country. Nevertheless, Reagan sent a warm radio message to the Soviet people through the Voice of America.

By February, however, Gorbachev realized that time was not on his side and that something had to be done to break the post-Reykjavík impasse. He called two Politburo sessions to discuss foreign policy and the strategic situation. Anatoly Chernyaev's notes give us valuable insight into Gorbachev's thinking at the time. Gorbachev told his colleagues that he felt Reagan was diddling him, pretending to want to reduce nuclear weapons only in order to placate his public and keep SDI alive for his successor. Reagan would get by with it, Gorbachev mused, if the Soviet Union kept insisting on linkage. Maybe they should call Reagan's bluff and propose sharp reductions without tying them to SDI.

Gromyko suggested that they might take the SS-20s "out of the package" presented at Reykjavík, and Yegor Ligachev, then Gorbachev's number two in the leadership, agreed, pointing out that this would not weaken Soviet defense capability. Defense Minister Sergei Sokolov complained that the British and French would still have nuclear missiles. Gorbachev ridiculed the comment, saying, "There is not going to be a war with Britain or France; it's impossible. Removing our medium-range missiles doesn't change a thing."

He then asked Anatoly Dobrynin if they could "trade" their medium-range missiles for an agreement on Afghanistan. Dobrynin replied that it wouldn't work since the Americans didn't want an agreement on either issue. (This illustrates that, for all his diplomatic skill and affability, Dobrynin totally misconstrued American policy. Reagan would have been delighted with an agreement on both questions, as he had indicated to Gorbachev in his private letter just after returning from their Geneva meeting.)

In an earlier Politburo discussion Gorbachev recognized that the only way to end the fighting in Afghanistan was to withdraw, but he was unwilling to do so at that time because he thought it would undermine Soviet prestige and give veterans the sense that they had fought for nothing. He did want to move on INF, however, and proposed that they invite Secretary of State Shultz to come to Moscow and also announce that they were withdrawing the linkage of INF with SDI and strategic weapons. Gorbachev had already authorized a resumption of nuclear testing and thought that delinking INF would moderate foreign criticism of the forthcoming tests.

Gorbachev's sense that the best way to break the negotiating standoff with the United States would be to conclude an agreement on INF was accurate, but his suspicion that only public pressure would keep Reagan from backing out of the Reykjavík deal was unfounded. Some allies and the American commander of NATO forces in Europe were dubious (to put it mildly) about the wisdom of eliminating U.S. intermediate-range missiles in Europe while the Warsaw Pact held an overwhelming advantage in conventional arms. But Reagan never questioned the desirability of eliminating that class of nuclear weapons. When he agreed at Reykjavík that each country might retain a hundred warheads outside Europe, he considered this a concession to Gorbachev, not the ideal solution.

During this period I was preparing to go to Moscow as U.S. ambassador. In December 1986, President Reagan had asked me to replace Arthur Hartman, whose tour in Moscow was ending, and by February I was going through the confirmation process with the Senate and calling on cabinet members to get their thoughts on our Soviet policy. When I met with Secretary of Defense Caspar Weinberger, he told me that his highest priority was to persuade Gorbachev to drop the linkage and allow an INF agreement to go forward. It was almost uncanny, more than a decade later, to read Chernyaev's Politburo notes and realize that Gorbachev was telling the Politburo about the same time that this was what the Soviet Union had to do. Fulfilling Weinberger's priority wish turned out to be the easiest item on my "to do" list. Gorbachev announced his decision to drop the linkage a few days before I arrived in Moscow.

Gorbachev's thinking moved an important step further when British prime minister Margaret Thatcher visited Moscow toward the end of March. Rather than mincing words and avoiding the hard issues as so many visitors did, she made a point of explaining to Gorbachev why the West considered the Soviet Union a threat to the peace. When Gorbachev took her to task for a speech she had made a few days before leaving London, Thatcher stood her ground. As she recalls in her memoirs:

> I said that there was one point which I did not make in my Central Council speech but which I would make now. This was that I knew of no evidence that the Soviet Union had given up the Brezhnev doctrine or the goal of securing world domination for communism. We were ready to fight the battle of ideas: indeed this was the right way to fight. But instead we in the West saw Soviet subversion in South Yemen, in Ethiopia, in Mozambique, in Angola and in Nicaragua. . . . We saw Afghanistan occupied by Soviet troops. We naturally drew the conclusion that the goal of worldwide communism was still being pursued. . . . We had to ask ourselves whether [Gorbachev's internal reforms] would lead to changes in external policies.[3]

During their meeting Gorbachev vigorously refuted Thatcher's charges, but her words left their mark. He subsequently wrote in his memoirs, "I must admit . . . that our policy towards developing countries had been highly ideological and that, to a certain extent, Mrs. Thatcher had been right in her criticisms."[4] A few weeks after her visit, he was even more categorical when he told the Politburo that the Soviet Union had to reduce its conventional weapons in Europe. Chernyaev's notes summarizing Gorbachev's comments to the Politburo on May 8 include several striking passages:

> Remember, I told you about my meeting with Thatcher. She said they were afraid of us, that we invaded Czechoslovakia, Hungary and Afghanistan. This perception is widespread among the public there. It persists in the minds of many people. Anti-Soviet propaganda is based on it. We should strengthen

our policy for the humanization of international relations with our actions. We should let them know that we are not just sitting or lying on our military doctrine, but that we are trying to find a way to make the world more stable.

He demanded that the Soviet Union come clean about the predominance of Soviet arms in Central Europe. "We told half truths for thirteen years, and we have to admit it now," he lectured his colleagues. "We are raising the issue of disarmament but at the same time are trying to avoid it ourselves." Meanwhile, in the guise of achieving "parity," the Soviet Union had created a bloated military-industrial complex. "We are stealing everything from the people and turning the country into a military camp," he thundered, and added that the West was trying to ruin the Soviet Union by luring it into another round of the arms race. The point was, he concluded, that they had to tell the truth about the number of their troops in Europe, and that meant they would have to reduce them at some appropriate time in the future.[5]

Nineteen months were to pass before Gorbachev announced a major reduction of Soviet armed forces. However, his attitude toward Reagan and American policy was already evolving. Immediately following the Reykjavík meeting, he had believed that Reagan was a prisoner of the American military-industrial complex. While he did not abandon his belief in its heavy influence on United States policy, he was beginning to see that there were additional explanations for American actions. The Americans and the West in general really had grounds for worrying about a Soviet threat!

Mr. Shultz Goes to Moscow

WHEN GORBACHEV DECIDED to invite George Shultz to Moscow, he could not have imagined the opposition the trip would arouse in Washington. This controversy had nothing to do with arms reduction or the other issues Shultz would discuss, but with the belief that the KGB had penetrated the American embassy in Moscow and had tried to bug the new building, still incomplete.

It should have surprised nobody that the KGB would try to plant listening devices in the new U.S. embassy. American security agencies preferred to let Soviet workers build the shell of the building rather than risk KGB recruitment of some of the hundreds of American construction workers that would have had to go to Moscow to build the embassy complex from scratch. When the shell was completed, American guards were to secure the building, the devices were to be located and removed, and the interior of the building completed by American workers—U.S. Navy Seabees. In case some listening devices in exterior walls eluded detection, there would be rooms within rooms, shielded to prevent any communication outside the inner room. Presumably the Soviet government made the same assumptions since they hired an American contractor to erect their building in Washington. There was no reason to believe that planned countermeasures were not adequate to foil any attempt to extract sensitive intelligence from secure areas of the new embassy.

As for Sergeant Lonetree, he had undertaken some tasks for the KGB, for which he deserved punishment, but working alone, the damage he could do to U.S. interests was slight. Marine guards served in pairs when on duty, and the pairings were constantly shifting. The marine guards did not have access to the most sensitive areas of the embassy, such as the communications center. They did not have combinations to the safes where classified material was stored. About the only thing a single marine could do was extract some material of low classification from the burn bags he and his partner collected from offices at night. (The most sensitive material was shredded or pulverized before it was placed in the heavy paper bags the marines removed from offices and destroyed in an incinerator.)

It was, of course, necessary to examine the new embassy's outer walls with sophisticated instruments in order to locate and remove the unwanted devices before completing construction of the embassy. It was also necessary to investigate carefully what Sergeant Lonetree had done at the KGB's bequest, assess the damage, and adjust procedures to reduce the vulnerability of embassy personnel to KGB recruitment. All of this could have been done quietly, with little if any disruption of embassy functions. Since, in these instances, the Soviets had done no more to us than we, if given the opportunity, would have done to them, there were no reasonable grounds for turning these incidents into political issues.

Anyone who imagines that these routine problems could have been dealt with calmly and rationally would be ignoring three facts of American life: the propensity of politicians to grandstand, the eagerness of the media to create sensations whenever there are hints of sex and spying, and the viciousness of bureaucratic infighting. As soon as news leaked that U.S. investigators had discovered cleverly concealed parts of a listening system in the embassy's outer walls, prominent members of Congress declared that the building was utterly unusable because it was honeycombed with listening devices. Never mind that the system was incomplete, not present at all in the floors where sensitive activities were to take place, and, even if it had been complete and had worked, could not have extracted information from the rooms within rooms. A procession of lawmakers descended on the overworked and harassed embassy staff, eager to show the folks back home that, if it were not for their vigilance, the Republic would founder.

One should not make members of Congress or the media culprits in the matter, however. Both were seriously misinformed by government officials who were determined to find a scapegoat for the loss of U.S. intelligence assets in the Soviet Union. In 1985 and 1986 the United States lost every covert intelligence source it had on Soviet territory. Security officials were desperate to explain the loss, and the discovery of bugs and of Sergeant Lonetree's recruitment set them on a frenzy of speculation. Each agency came up with various worst-case scenarios, whether they made sense or not, and when there were insufficient facts to substantiate the fears, persons could be found to fabricate them. For example, the president and Congress were informed that Lonetree had worked in concert with another marine and that the two of them had allowed the KGB access to the embassy in Moscow at night. When we checked the logs recording which marines had been on duty at which time, we found that the two had never been on duty together. The sensitive areas of the embassy had been protected by fail-safe devices unknown to the marines; none of these showed any evidence of tampering or of unauthorized entry. When these discrepancies were reported, it turned out that the Naval Investigative Service had extorted a confession from the second marine by methods just short of torture and had written his "confession," which he signed under duress and repudiated immediately.

This was a flagrant case of deceit for which nobody, to my knowledge, was punished. Most of the other allegations about the penetration of the embassy and the consequent loss of important secrets turned out to have as little basis. Searching for listening devices in the new embassy building and certifying that the old embassy had not been penetrated and was safe for confidential work took months and cost the U.S. taxpayer close to, if not more than, a hundred million dollars—more than the total cost of a secure new embassy. Every piece of sensitive equipment was shipped back to the United States under guard and examined in minute detail. None had been touched by any nonauthorized person. Congress would supply unlimited funds to look for nonexistent devices, but not a cent to complete the embassy.

Many years later, when the Cold War was over and there was no more Soviet Union, it was discovered that the U.S. intelligence assets in the Soviet Union had been betrayed by moles in Washington, Aldridge Ames in the CIA and Robert Hanssen in the FBI.

BUT LET US return to the situation in March and April 1987. During all the hue and cry over the Soviet "penetration of the American embassy," the usual suspects in the Reagan administration argued that the secretary of state should not go to Moscow for meetings with the Soviet leadership because he could not be confident that his communications with Washington would be private. (Why he would need to communicate with Washington in order to explain American policy to the Soviet leaders was never asked; after all, he was not negotiating final agreements and could easily report his conversations upon his return to Washington if there had been any doubt about the security of communication.) A Senate resolution advising the secretary of state not to go to Moscow at that time received an overwhelming vote. Prominent figures outside the administration also argued that Shultz should not travel to Moscow. For example, Dr. Henry Kissinger—conveniently forgetting that when he was in office he had never hesitated to conduct negotiations in places without secure communication facilities, and ignoring the fact that even if Shevardnadze had been willing to meet Shultz outside the Soviet Union, Gorbachev could hardly have been expected to do so—argued that Shultz should insist on meeting on neutral ground, such as in Helsinki. It was Gorbachev, in the first instance, Shultz needed to reach.

As usual, Reagan favored contacts and communication, and encouraged Shultz to travel to Moscow in order to get negotiations back on track. Shultz went to great lengths to demonstrate that he could consult Washington in confidence, arranging for a secure communications unit, called the "Winnebago" (it was in a bus-sized motor home), to be flown to Moscow and stationed in the U.S. embassy's garage area. President Reagan arranged an unscheduled press conference to reassure the American public that he was taking the "breach of security at our Moscow embassy" seriously and had undertaken steps to correct it.[6]

Shultz's meeting with Gorbachev began with a discussion of intelligence collection. When, at the outset of the long meeting, Gorbachev referred to a "shortage of trust," Shultz remarked that the intelligence scandals undermined trust.[7] Gorbachev responded that they should not behave like "naive girls" (implying that both countries operated in similar fashion when it came to spying), and that to a certain degree espionage had a constructive aspect since it could contribute to "stability."* When Gorbachev remarked that there had not been a Soviet penetration of the U.S. embassy, Shultz asked

---

* In his *Turmoil and Triumph,* Shultz comments that Gorbachev spoke "disingenuously" (p. 890). My impression at the time, reinforced by subsequent comments by Gorbachev in the same vein, was that Gorbachev was sincere in this comment. Espionage, after all, is one means by which governments verify that agreements are being kept. Gorbachev had trouble understanding why there was so much pub-

him directly if he could tell President Reagan "that it is against your policy and rules to allow your intelligence agencies to physically penetrate our embassy building."

His reply, according to my notes, was: "Ya dumayu, chto eto tak" (I think that's the way it is).[8] And he added, "When you report to the president, you should also tell him about the devices we found in our embassy building in Washington"—a request Shultz omitted from his account of the meeting.

Shevardnadze also assured Shultz that he had been misinformed if he had been told that the U.S. embassy had been penetrated. The discrepancy between what was believed in Washington and what Shultz was being told in Moscow was troubling. Were the Soviet leaders continuing to purvey bald-faced lies, even face-to-face in private? Or did they have a basis for what they were saying? As American officials learned gradually over the next few months, what Shevardnadze and Gorbachev were saying had a factual basis, even if it was not the whole truth. The KGB had not physically penetrated the U.S. embassy in Moscow—at least not for several years. The KGB had started installing a sophisticated listening system in the new embassy building, but the system had not been finished.

Most officials in Washington who were told of Gorbachev's statement considered it further evidence of Soviet lying. Gorbachev would have been more convincing if he had said simply, "Yes, we tried to bug the new embassy, but you caught us before we finished the job. You tried to bug ours, but we fixed it. So what else is new, and what's the big deal?"*

So far as Gorbachev was concerned, the noise over alleged penetration of the U.S. embassy was a totally artificial issue, deliberately created by elements in the Reagan administration to impede solution of the real problems. He failed to recognize that, however distorted some U.S. allegations may have seemed, a real issue existed. The Soviet Union had bloated its diplomatic establishments with intelligence officers to an extent matched by no other country, was much more aggressive than the United States in attempts

---

lic commotion in Washington since he had been told that the Soviet Union and the United States followed essentially the same practices.

* In 1991, shortly before the Soviet Union collapsed, Vadim Bakatin, then—briefly—head of the KGB, delivered to Robert Strauss, my successor as U.S. ambassador, the Soviet plans for installing a listening system in the new U.S. embassy. These plans probably contained nothing that the United States did not already know from its meticulous examination of the structure, but Bakatin's action—which Gorbachev approved—was, nevertheless, a gesture of goodwill. Actually, so long as the Soviet Union (and, subsequently, the Russian Federation) had moles in the CIA and the FBI, they did not need listening devices in the U.S. embassy in Moscow to thwart U.S. intelligence operations. They could learn everything directly from headquarters!

to recruit spies, and did not shrink from planting evidence on innocent Americans, as the treatment of Nicholas Daniloff showed.

Fortunately, however, Shultz's meetings in Moscow in April 1987 dealt largely with the real issues and had more constructive results than the exchanges on embassy bugging. Shultz confirmed that Gorbachev had decided he could conclude an INF treaty even if there was no agreement on the other issues discussed at Reykjavík. Shultz also conducted a detailed discussion of the most important questions on all four points of the American agenda.

In addition to his meetings with Gorbachev and Shevardnadze, Shultz had a good discussion of economics with Prime Minister Nikolai Ryzhkov, whom he had met in Stockholm a year and a half earlier. (Shultz concluded perceptively that Ryzhkov knew the Soviet system needed reform, but did not grasp that the system itself rather than management of it required change.) Also, for the first time, an American secretary of state was interviewed at length on national television, giving Shultz an opportunity to explain to the Soviet public the reasons for American policy.

For both sides, the meetings Shultz had in Moscow then attenuated the rancor that had arisen following the disagreements over what was agreed at Reykjavík. Not only were arms control negotiations back on track, but the four-point U.S. agenda had become the actual framework for discussions. Shevardnadze accepted human rights as a legitimate subject for discussion. Although there was no meeting of minds on most regional conflicts, a dialogue had been established on each of them and the Americans were no longer told that discussion was pointless since these conflicts were merely an inevitable process of national liberation. Gorbachev and Shevardnadze seemed eager to widen contacts, both official and private. Jamming had ceased on broadcasts of the Voice of America and the BBC, though not yet on those of Radio Liberty.

The upshot was that Shultz came back to Washington more convinced than ever that the United States could move its agenda with the Soviet leaders and that there was a good chance of arranging the summit in Washington before the end of the year. This was important if Reagan was to visit the Soviet Union in 1988, the last year of his presidency. The disputes over spying and embassy bugging were still very much in the public eye in the United States, but gradually dissipated in the minds of senior officials as the evidence mounted that many assumptions made in early 1987 had no basis.

The meeting may have made an even deeper impression on Gorbachev. Although he debated Shultz vigorously on the points at issue, he recognized the secretary of state's commitment to finding solutions and his absolute integrity. He observed subsequently, "I realized, maybe for the first time, that I was dealing with a serious man of sound political judgement."9

Contacts Expand

I ARRIVED IN Moscow as American ambassador while Margaret Thatcher was still there, just a few days before Secretary Shultz's visit. The timing was propitious, the result of chance rather than anything I could take credit for. But, arriving when I did, I had the opportunity not only to witness the Soviet reaction to Prime Minister Thatcher's visit and to participate in Secretary of State Shultz's, but to observe the expansion of U.S. and other Western contacts with the USSR in the months following. Contacts proceeded at a speed without precedent in East-West relations.

Shultz was still in Moscow when a group of members of Congress led by Speaker James Wright showed up. They were given appointments not only with Gorbachev and Shevardnadze, but also with Yegor Ligachev, then number two in the Communist hierarchy. Speaker Wright made a television address to the Soviet people and the group held a press conference covered by Soviet journalists. Previous congressional delegations had been received by senior officials, but they had not been permitted to speak to the Soviet public on television.

In his meeting with the congressional delegation, Gorbachev accused the Reagan administration of failing to take advantage of the opportunities the Soviet Union was offering. Chances for improved relations were "better than at any time since World War II," he argued, but the U.S. administration "believes the Soviet Union is in a corner and can be squeezed."10 He resented claims that the Soviet Union had been forced back to the negotiating table by U.S. firmness. "We are not that stupid," he fumed. "If we did not feel that there is a deeper interest, we would behave as we did in the past."

Several things struck me as I listened to Gorbachev's impassioned statement. First, he *did* feel "squeezed" by U.S. policy. Second, he now realized, and was willing to admit, if only implicitly, that the previous Soviet policies were not aimed at reaching agreements. Third, he saw that it was in the Soviet interest to come to terms with the United States: this was a "deeper interest" than defending the old, rigid positions taken by Soviet negotiators.

As the spring and summer progressed, the number of American visitors to Moscow, whether officials or private citizens, increased rapidly. Charles Z. Wick, director of the United States Information Agency, came in June in an effort to expand the cultural, educational, and sports exchanges that were being revived as a result of the agreements in Geneva. He was received not only by foreign ministry and media officials, but also by Alexander Yakovlev, at that time the Politburo member responsible for ideology. The American embassy had already noted that Yakovlev seemed to be shaking up the moribund Soviet media by naming new, activist, and freethinking editors to some of the most important publications. His aim seemed to be to make the Soviet media more open to new ideas, not just to purvey turgid (and increasingly ignored) Party-line propaganda.

Yakovlev complained to Wick about some of the programming on the Voice of America, but then appealed for an end to stereotypes and an increase in contacts. Wick assured Yakovlev that he would investigate allegations of mistaken reporting by VOA and take steps to correct errors. He welcomed Yakovlev's support for increasing contacts and improving the flow of information. Subsequently, both were as good as their words. The American embassy received fewer and fewer complaints about the Voice of America, not because broadcasts had been faulty in the past but because Soviet officials were more willing to tolerate views that differed from earlier propaganda lines. Exchanges, including those of young people, expanded exponentially.

Meetings between Soviet and U.S. experts on regional problems in most parts of the world, initiated earlier, became regular occurrences. Few problems had been solved, but the assistant secretaries of state and deputy ministers of foreign affairs had gotten to know each other, discussed their respective views of the issues, and were beginning to compare notes on ways the U.S. and USSR could help solve local disputes rather than exacerbating them by military aid to competing factions. The ground was being laid for agreements that subsequently ended the fighting in Nicaragua, brought independence in Namibia, ended U.S. and Soviet indirect involvement in the Angolan civil war, brought about a departure of Vietnamese troops from Cambodia, and—in less than two years—a Soviet withdrawal from Afghanistan.

There still was no system of direct contacts between Soviet and American military officers, but Yuri Dubinin, the Soviet ambassador in Washington, and I began a series of lectures in one another's military academies. Dubinin gave his first lecture at the National War College and I spoke to the officers at the senior Soviet military academy. In that lecture I spoke of the damage hypersecrecy can do to international stability by encouraging suspicion and worst-case thinking.

The Soviet government began granting Soviet citizens many more permits to leave the Soviet Union for Israel, Germany, and the United States.

When Shultz was in Moscow in April he attended a seder Rebecca and I hosted for Jewish refuseniks. When we organized a similar seder during Passover the following year, very few of the persons who attended the one in 1987 were still in the Soviet Union. Most had been allowed to emigrate.

Congressional visitors and other prominent Americans made it a point to call on Andrei Sakharov, whom Gorbachev had allowed to return to his Moscow apartment from his exile in Gorky (Nizhny Novgorod) at the end of 1986. His release encouraged the hope that other political prisoners would soon be freed. There were no longer restrictions on Sakharov's meetings with foreigners, and he advised his visitors to support Gorbachev's efforts to bring greater freedom to Soviet society.

FROM MY FIRST days as ambassador, I was given direct access to most senior Soviet officials, even in the Central Committee apparatus that had previously been out of bounds for American diplomats. Personnel shifts in Moscow facilitated the change in policy. Now that Anatoly Dobrynin headed the Central Committee International Department, he could not be barred from contact with American officials with whom he had dealt for decades in Washington. Furthermore, Shevardnadze apparently did not feel the need to monopolize official contact the way Gromyko had.

It helped, of course, that I already knew most of the officials involved— I had dealt with some for more than twenty years. In Moscow, I always did business in Russian, which meant that I could meet privately, without interpreters. Rebecca and I established Russian as the principal language for social gatherings at Spaso House, the American ambassador's residence. It was our fourth tour in Moscow, and we had many acquaintances and some real friends among Moscow intellectuals—writers, artists, actors, film and theater directors, composers and musicians. We entertained frequently, sometimes a dozen times a week or more, and tried whenever possible to mix writers and artists with officials, to encourage all to come with their spouses, and to create a relaxing atmosphere.

In establishing rapport with Soviet officials and the Soviet public, Rebecca played a critical role. She had taken the trouble to bring her Russian to a professional level after our first tour in Moscow, and developed her own network of friends among artists, photographers, journalists, and theater people. Within a year or so she not only was Moscow's most active social hostess, but also was invited to exhibit her photographs and tapestries in cities from Grozny to Ulan Ude to Vladivostok. As Gorbachev's perestroika opened Soviet media to outside influences, our activities and interviews appeared with growing frequency in the Soviet media. Normally, the emphasis was not on political topics but on our interest in Russian and non-Russian cultures of the Soviet Union.

Suddenly, attempts to establish back channels became superfluous; the American ambassador in Moscow had as broad access to Soviet officials as the Soviet ambassador did to American officials in Washington. Informal, nonbinding discussion of the issues became the order of the day. The years I had spent on the NSC staff served me well. I knew intimately the views of the president and the secretary of state—and also some of the political minefields they had to navigate. I did not have to refer every question to Washington for guidance, though I was careful to report to the secretary of state and president every significant discussion. I sent the most sensitive reports as handwritten letters carried to Washington by couriers. Distribution of these reports was carefully controlled in Washington and we had no leaks.

The earlier attempts to establish informal channels of communication had been driven by desires in both countries for direct communication with decision makers and the need to explore possible solutions without signaling a change in negotiating positions. This required avoiding leaks, the favorite weapon of bureaucratic guerrilla fighters determined to block agreements they opposed—more often for bureaucratic than substantive reasons. The access I was granted to top Soviet officials eliminated any need for informal channels.

The staff of the American embassy in Moscow provided outstanding support to the many official visitors even though embassy officers were overworked and stressed by a winter without the services of Soviet employees. The unfounded allegations of serious breaches in embassy security weighed heavily on morale, but American diplomats in Moscow did not miss a beat in following developments in the Soviet capital. Without their analysis of Gorbachev's "new thinking," it would have been most difficult for Reagan and Shultz to grasp the opportunities that were emerging to transform East-West relations. Without their close monitoring of the treatment of dissidents and refuseniks, we would not have detected promptly the improvements in Soviet practices. Without their contacts in the Soviet media, we would not have been able to take advantage of the liberalization that gave us access, denied previously.

By summer, American replacements began to arrive in force for the Soviet employees who had been removed. They improved services at the embassy as Soviet society became more open, creating opportunities for extending embassy contacts to groups previously placed out of bounds by Soviet policy.

The American embassy was particularly fortunate that John "Mike" Joyce agreed to come to Moscow as my deputy. We had worked together during previous tours, and I knew that Mike, a first-rate manager, was a fluent Russian speaker who had published articles on Soviet political culture. He and his wife, Karen, did much to restore embassy morale and to encourage the staff to make new contacts in Soviet society, not only in Moscow but also in the provinces and the non-Russian republics. Thanks to Mike's leadership and the capable officers assigned to the embassy, the American embassy in Moscow soon became not only the best-informed embassy in the Soviet Union, but arguably the finest in the entire American Foreign Service.

Shultz and Shevardnadze Bond

DEVELOPMENTS DURING THE spring and summer set the stage for Shevardnadze's trip to the United States in September. He had meetings with Reagan and Shultz in Washington, then further meetings with Shultz when both were in New York for the United Nations General Assembly. There was no repeat of the acrimony that had marked their meeting in Vienna, just after the Reykjavík summit.

From Shevardnadze's appointment in 1985, George Shultz had been determined to build a personal relationship with the proud, sociable Georgian. During one of Shevardnadze's early visits to Washington, George and O'Bie Shultz invited Eduard and Nanuli Shevardnadze to come to their home for a private, family-style evening. There was an interpreter to facilitate conversation, but no servants, no protocol, and no arguments. George grilled the meat on their patio barbecue and O'Bie served the pie she had made herself. The Shevardnadzes were touched by the personal attention and informality, the sort of hospitality for which Georgians are famous. When the Shultzes were next in Moscow, the Shevardnadzes reciprocated with a private evening at their apartment; this time Nanuli covered the table with the spicy Georgian dishes she had helped to prepare. Both started springing small surprises on the other. Once, when Shultz came to Moscow he insisted that three of us sing a translation we had made of "Georgia on My Mind" at a formal lunch Shevardnadze hosted. The music could hardly have been worse, but Shevardnadze was delighted and moved. The gesture, he wrote later, "showed respect."

Neither was so naive as to think that difficult issues could be solved by sociability. But both understood that they were much more likely to find solutions to problems if they had confidence in each other. The personal relationship both cultivated helped them weather potential crises without losing touch with each other. Their example encouraged other officials in both countries to develop closer ties with their counterparts. Gradually, the stand-off, shout-at-the-enemy debating style that had plagued U.S.-Soviet relations since World War II was supplanted by personal networking. To be sure, most officials were initially wary and even a mite touchy lest their compatriots think they were taken in by sly adversaries. Nevertheless, the example of their superiors had its effect; by 1989, American and Soviet diplomats were working in many areas virtually as colleagues. Of course, this could never have occurred unless Gorbachev had decided to open Soviet society and to begin respecting what he called the "human factor" in political relations.

Negotiations in a number of areas began to move off dead center. Gorbachev had announced in August that he would accept a global zero for INF; the principal remaining problem was the Soviet insistence that the Pershing IA missiles owned by West Germany be removed. (The United States owned the nuclear warheads.) This was a reasonable request, but one that depended on the German rather than the American government. After a time Chancellor Helmut Kohl announced that Germany would destroy these missiles if an agreement on INF was concluded.

Shevardnadze's personal charm, the reasonable spirit he showed in negotiations, and the progress toward an unprecedented arms reduction agreement would have been enough to convince George Shultz that Shevardnadze was a valuable colleague. But the evolution in Shevardnadze's attitude toward human rights in the Soviet Union made probably the most important contribution to Shultz's feeling that the two had compatible goals. Shevardnadze had always tolerated a discussion of human rights with more courtesy than Andrei Gromyko could summon, but by 1987 he began to do more than simply arranging an exit visa once in a while. He actually began to try to change the system.

He did this by creating an office in the Soviet Ministry of Foreign Affairs to deal with human rights. Its explicit aim was to bring the Soviet Union into compliance with the obligations it had assumed when Leonid Brezhnev signed the Helsinki Final Act in 1975. It was probably the first time a Soviet minister of foreign affairs dared try to influence the behavior of the KGB and other organs of repression. With Gorbachev's support, Eduard Shevardnadze did, and to a substantial degree succeeded.

Just before Shevardnadze left Washington, he suggested that Gorbachev plan to visit Washington before the end of the year. He also invited Shultz to come to Moscow in October to put the finishing touches on an INF treaty to be signed in Washington. Reagan was delighted. He had waited years for the opportunity to show a Soviet leader the United States and had begun to wonder whether that would be possible in his remaining term of office.

Gorbachev Fumbles

WHAT LOOKED LIKE a sure bet in September became a cliff-hanger in October. When George Shultz went to Moscow to finish negotiations on the INF Treaty and set the terms of Gorbachev's visit to the United States, Gorbachev balked. The talks with Shevardnadze went smoothly and Shultz assumed, when they met, that Gorbachev would approve the treaty and set a date to come to the United States.

The meeting with Gorbachev did not go as anticipated, however. Gorbachev was in a querulous mood. He insisted on finding an acceptable formula for a START agreement, including curbs on SDI, implying that an INF treaty alone would not be sufficient to justify a summit meeting in Washington. He wasted time complaining about a booklet the State Department had issued describing Soviet disinformation efforts, conveniently ignoring that the booklet was factual and the operations it described came right out of the Central Committee Secretariat that he headed. Shultz was not aware of the booklet and was astounded that Gorbachev would divert the discussion to a matter that, compared to the other issues, was trivial. The meeting ended without a firm agreement for Gorbachev to come to Washington. As Shultz left the meeting room, Gorbachev said that he would send a letter to President Reagan explaining the situation.[11]

Shultz returned to the small, acoustically secure conference room in a wing of the unfinished new embassy to discuss his report to the president. Gorbachev's behavior that day was puzzling, and Shultz commented that Gorbachev seemed a different person from the one he had dealt with before. Previously, Gorbachev had reminded him of a boxer who had never been knocked down: cocky, self-assured. That day, however, he was like a boxer who has hit the canvas.

The Soviet delegation was also shocked. Pavel Palazchenko, Gorbachev's adviser who interpreted for him at the meeting, describes the scene after Shultz left:

> The meeting ended without harsh words, but we all knew what had happened. As the Soviet side, which included Shevardnadze, Dobrynin, Akhromeyev,

Bessmertnykh, Vorontsov, and Chernyaev, went to a waiting room nearby to sit down and have tea with Gorbachev, there was a heavy silence. No one spoke for at least a couple of minutes, and when Gorbachev finally did, it was a summary of the talk that had just ended. Again, silence followed.

It was Anatoly Chernyaev, Gorbachev's assistant, who broke the silence. "So, did we try in vain? Did we bend over backward on INF and come so close to the treaty just to see the whole thing ruined now?" he asked. . . .

Gorbachev responded, "Don't boil over, Anatoly. We'll have to think over what happened, and I said I would write the president a letter. I'll do it soon."[12]

It was a few days before the Americans, and even some of Gorbachev's own team, began to learn why Gorbachev was on edge at that meeting. Just days before, Boris Yeltsin, then the Communist Party boss in Moscow, had unexpectedly offered to resign at a meeting of the Central Committee and in doing so had leveled implicit criticism at Gorbachev himself.

Shortly after Shultz left town, the Yeltsin affair became public knowledge, not in its full detail, but word spread that there had been a major dustup at the closed Central Committee meeting. For the Moscow public, Yeltsin was almost synonymous with reform. When people learned that he was being relieved as head of the Moscow Party organization, they wondered if this meant the end of perestroika. In fact, Yeltsin's departure from the leadership turned out not to be the end of reform, but rather the start of a process that was to contribute to Gorbachev's downfall and the breakup of the Soviet Union some four years later.

Shevardnadze Recovers

AT THE TIME Shultz left Moscow, on October 23, Shevardnadze was appalled at what had happened. He normally sent a deputy to see Shultz off, but this time he went to the airport himself. Both he and Shultz avoided talking to the press as if the meeting had failed. Shevardnadze then moved quickly to retrieve the situation. Shultz's plane had barely landed at Andrews Air Force Base when I was called to the foreign ministry and told that misunderstandings had occurred and that Shevardnadze wished to travel to Washington as soon as he could be received to deliver the letter Gorbachev had promised. Obviously, he intended to put summit preparations back on track.

That is precisely what happened. Shevardnadze arrived in Washington on

October 30 with Gorbachev's letter and proposed wording for a summit announcement. He avoided any demand for an agreement regarding the ABM Treaty as a prerequisite for the meeting, saying simply that the presidents would sign the INF Treaty and discuss other issues including INF and START.

American officials assumed that this had been worked out in Moscow before Shevardnadze set off for Washington. Pavel Palazchenko, who came with the group as Shevardnadze's interpreter, tells us, however, that the foreign ministry had prepared an opening presentation that "contained, in veiled form, the same old position on ABM that caused the rupture in Moscow."[13] When Shevardnadze's aide, Sergei Tarasenko, read the proposed language on the plane to Washington, he protested that the Americans would never accept it. He drafted a replacement, Shevardnadze approved it, and this was the proposal received in Washington.

Until then, such a major change in the Soviet position could have been made only after formal approval by the Politburo. Presumably, Shevardnadze checked the language with Gorbachev by telephone, but by then both he and Gorbachev were beginning to make independent decisions. Before Shevardnadze left Washington, both countries announced that Gorbachev would come to Washington on December 7 to meet with Reagan and sign the INF Treaty.

There were still treaty details that had to be resolved, however, particularly those specifying how verification would take place. Monitoring to ensure compliance was a tricky issue despite Gorbachev's repeated assurances that it would not be a problem. One more meeting by Shultz and Shevardnadze, this time in Geneva, was required before the text was ready for the presidents to sign.

The Same Sheet of Music

EVEN BEFORE GORBACHEV arrived in Washington, American negotiators began to realize that Soviet negotiators no longer resisted dealing with the issues the United States had brought to the table. Americans no longer had to insist that human rights or actions to lift the Iron Curtain had a place on the agenda. The Soviet foreign ministry began to organize discussions in the same way the Americans did. U.S. and Soviet representatives still disagreed about how to solve the problems, but they had come to agree on what they were.

The fundamental aim of diplomacy is to convince the other fellow that what you want him to do is what he needs to do. In 1987 this happened in East-West relations. By the fall of that year, all U.S.-Soviet negotiations took place within the framework of the four-part agenda Reagan had enunciated beginning in January 1984. Most Soviet citizens were not aware that it was the U.S. agenda. The Soviet leaders had adopted, step by step, many of the goals the United States had promoted.

Reagan was careful not to trumpet claims of authorship, and in fact it would be wrong to think that he had forced his agenda on an unwilling Gorbachev. As Gorbachev wrestled with the problems the Soviet Union faced, he came to see, not all at once, but over time, that many things Reagan had proposed were not unreasonable.

Pavel Palazchenko has explained how Gorbachev and Shevardnadze were able to implement an agenda that the majority of Communist Party officials would have opposed if they had understood what he was doing. The principles Gorbachev developed by 1986 "were not inconsistent with . . . previous [Soviet] rhetoric on international affairs." For that reason, "new thinking" did not arouse opposition in the Communist Party initially. Subsequently, from 1987, as Gorbachev made practical decisions to implement the ideas he had enunciated, he was able to use the methods of the old "command system" to force changes. Party apparatchiks were conditioned to follow the general secretary without question and, furthermore, many simply did not understand the probable consequences of Gorbachev's actions.[14] By 1990 this began to change, but in 1987 and 1988, Gorbachev was able to reverse a host of Soviet policies and practices with impunity.

The important thing for the United States was that Gorbachev came to understand that the goals Reagan had set forth fitted Soviet needs. It did not matter whose ideas they were originally so long as Reagan refrained from claiming victory. The Cold War protagonists were beginning to think of solutions to problems that would benefit both and to discard the old notion that any gain by one would automatically damage the other. Thus, while few of the most important issues had been solved, negotiations moved into a less confrontational framework.

Some officials were slow to recognize this important shift in the Soviet attitude. In early November, Shultz was scandalized by CIA deputy director Robert Gates's briefing on Soviet policy. Gates argued, as he had from Gorbachev's assumption of power, that Gorbachev still had the same goals as his predecessors and was trying to reform the Soviet Union only to make it stronger. Shultz felt that Gates missed the main point: whatever Gorbachev's ultimate goals might be, he was undertaking moves that would make the Soviet Union less threatening to the United States and its allies.[15] Although official CIA assessments had pointed out changes in Soviet policies throughout 1987, Gates's personal view continued to be more skeptical than that of most CIA analysts.

Both Shultz and Gates could cite evidence in support of their respective opinions. Gorbachev was still trying to do contradictory things. He was uneasy with traditional Soviet policies and had started changing them, but he nevertheless continued many of the old policies and activities. He would lecture the Politburo occasionally on the need to get out of Afghanistan, or why it was important to admit how heavily the Soviet Union was armed. But then nothing would happen for a long time. Gorbachev was changing gradually, and at times would move backward a step or two. Gates emphasized what appeared to be continuity in Soviet policy; Shultz was alert to the unmistakable signs of change and to the potential this would have for the future.

Shultz did not conceal his anger at what he considered Bob Gates's stubborn refusal to see the changes in Soviet policy. He feared that Reagan would be swayed by the pessimistic intelligence analysis. He need not have worried. Reagan, like Shultz, would base his judgment on his interactions with Gorbachev and Shevardnadze. Gorbachev's behavior in Washington would loom larger in their minds than any number of intelligence briefings.

XIII

―――――⚬―――――

GORBACHEV IN WASHINGTON

In Washington, probably for the first time, we clearly realized how much the human factor means in international politics. . . . These people are guided by the most natural human motives and feelings.
—MIKHAIL GORBACHEV to the Politburo, 1987[1]

. . . I think the whole thing was the best summit we've ever had with the Soviet Union.
—RONALD REAGAN, 1987[2]

THE MEETING IN Reykjavík appeared a psychological turning point for Reagan and Gorbachev only in retrospect. In contrast, their meeting in Washington in December 1987 was immediately recognized by most observers as a breakthrough. The INF Treaty they signed was the most significant step the United States and Soviet Union had ever taken to reverse the direction of the arms race.

However, many Americans wondered whether President Reagan could hold his own with Gorbachev. When Reagan met television anchormen a few days before Gorbachev's arrival, one cited a poll that indicated that a plurality of those questioned (45 percent) feared Reagan would "make too many compromises to Gorbachev."[3] Reagan assured the questioner that he would sign an agreement only if it was in the U.S. interest, and then observed:

Now, I think that some of the people who are objecting the most and just refusing even to accede to the idea of ever getting an understanding, whether they realize it or not, those people, basically, down in their deepest thoughts, have accepted that war is inevitable and that there must come to be a war between the two superpowers.

Well, I think as long as you've got a chance to strive for peace you strive for peace.

A few days earlier he had taken on his critics in a speech at the conservative Heritage Foundation in Washington.4 But while defending his decision to sign the INF Treaty, he spoke repeatedly of the need to preserve SDI and of unfinished business regarding the other items on the four-part agenda. It was the sort of talk that annoyed Gorbachev, but in this instance he avoided a tit-for-tat public debate. He wrote later in his memoirs: "Both partners were becoming used to each other and stopped getting worked up at every word and snubbing every remark they disliked."5

There were disappointments on Gorbachev's part even before he arrived. He had failed, during his meeting with Shultz in October, to find a formula on ABM testing that would open the door to a START agreement during Reagan's presidency. He thus had been forced to scale down his expectations for what might be achieved in Washington in terms of agreements and to defend his trip by saying that his policy of "new thinking" had the anti-Soviet forces in the West on the run. He would take with him a group of scholars, writers, and intellectuals to convince the American public that perestroika was for real. He would make sure the book his associates had drafted for him, *Perestroika,* appeared on the newsstands in English just before he arrived. He would address a joint session of Congress in a speech to be televised to the nation. It would be something of a propaganda blitz, but it wouldn't be *Soviet* propaganda.

All of this worked out except the address to a joint session of Congress. Gorbachev had gotten the idea from the Democratic leaders in Congress, who had invited him to address a joint session. However, when word got out in Washington that this was a possibility, some Republicans objected. They saw no reason to give Gorbachev a prestigious platform to speak to the American public. They said no Communist leader had ever addressed a joint session of Congress, and they saw no reason to violate that precedent.

Secretary of State Shultz, who favored an invitation to Gorbachev in part so we could be sure that Reagan would be given the opportunity to speak to the Soviet public during his return visit, tried to work out a deal quietly. He asked Soviet ambassador Yuri Dubinin not to approach Congress on the matter, but to let Shultz see what he could do. Whether because Dubinin ignored Shultz's advice or because the White House was running scared, the invitation for Gorbachev to address Congress was withdrawn. In its place, Gorbachev was offered a private meeting with congressional leaders and the opportunity to address the American public by television.

Gorbachev was offended by what he interpreted, understandably, as a slap in the face. When Shultz and Shevardnadze met in Geneva on November 23 and 24 to finish the INF Treaty, Shevardnadze made this question the first item of business. What rankled, Shevardnadze said, was the change of signals and the controversy that had arisen in the United States. Soviet media had reported the misunderstanding, and it made it seem that the administration was insulting Gorbachev even before he arrived. Although the speech was to be to Congress, it was Republicans who objected; surely a Republican president could persuade them to relent! It would not matter very much whether Gorbachev addressed Congress or not, Shevardnadze explained, if it had never been planned. The withdrawal of an invitation was a different matter, however.

Shultz put the best face possible on the arrangements that had been made, which gave Gorbachev extensive opportunities to meet Congress and the public, but the incident continued to annoy Gorbachev, as comments in his memoirs demonstrate. He also wrote that President Reagan had forgotten about his earlier suggestion to tour the United States, but that was not the case. The White House had been informed when the date was set that Gorbachev had time only for Washington and would not be able to extend his visit to see other cities. Perhaps Gorbachev was not aware that his staff had sent such a message. We learned only gradually that he did not always review messages to us.

The Meetings

GORBACHEV AND REAGAN spent more time in public events than in closed meetings with each other, but they managed to cover the key items on the four-part agenda. Most of the real negotiation was behind the scenes, by Shultz and Shevardnadze, and by joint working groups on the various issues. This time there was no misunderstanding, as there had been at Geneva in 1985, about developing an agreed statement for the two to publish. The joint statement issued upon Gorbachev's departure was one of the longest and most detailed of any emanating from a U.S.-Soviet summit. It was able to take note of substantial progress in all of the four agenda areas.

Not all the topics had been covered before the lunch Reagan hosted for Gorbachev on his last day in Washington, so it became a working lunch. It was then that Gorbachev suddenly asked Reagan if the United States would end its support for the opposition forces in Afghanistan if the Soviet Union withdrew its troops. Reagan urged Gorbachev to leave Afghanistan but did not give a clear answer to his question.

There were, therefore, still important disagreements, but Reagan's meetings with Gorbachev in Washington were notably more harmonious than they had been in either Geneva or Reykjavík. Nevertheless, the public events were collectively the most important feature of the trip. Speeches at the large State Department lunch, the formal dinner at the White House, and the dinner and breakfast hosted by the Gorbachevs at the Soviet ambassador's residence reflected the spirit of cooperation that now permeated the dialogue. Speechwriters in both countries outdid themselves in finding encouraging historical precedents and uplifting anecdotes. There were no more fights over hostile rhetoric.

Sweet talk at social events may have seemed like fluff to cynics, but both Reagan and Gorbachev were sincere in their desire to get away from the polemics of the past. The INF Treaty that they signed on December 8, Gorbachev's second day in the United States, proved that things had changed.

The INF Treaty

BY ANY OBJECTIVE standard, the INF Treaty should have been universally applauded in both countries. The opposition that existed on the part of important groups in both the United States and Soviet Union was rooted more in the suspicions the Cold War had nurtured than in any shortcomings in the treaty. Nevertheless, both Reagan and Gorbachev had to manage the opposition in their countries in order to make the treaty a reality without political damage to themselves.

Opposition in the United States was outspoken. In the Soviet Union, it was less public, but damaging to the confidence many Soviet officials had in Gorbachev's judgment. They objected not only to the fact that the Soviet Union agreed to eliminate many more weapons than the United States did, but particularly the decision to include the SS-23 (called the "Oka" in Russian) among the missiles to be eliminated. The Soviet military claimed that this missile had a range of only 400 kilometers and therefore should not be covered in an agreement to eliminate missiles with ranges between 500 and 2,000 kilometers. However, U.S. negotiators believed that the size and configuration of the Oka indicated that its range could be at least 500 kilometers. Furthermore, the United States refused to include a new missile it was developing, the "follow-on to Lance," or Lance II, on grounds that its range was only 400 kilometers.

Gorbachev settled the issue by accepting the American position over the objection of some of his military specialists. He did so because he felt that finishing the INF agreement was of the highest priority. Also, he understood that if the United States had agreed to exempt the Oka, it would certainly deploy the Lance II, thus possibly stimulating another arms race in nuclear weapons of that range. As it was, his gamble paid off: the United States never deployed the Lance II. Nevertheless, many denizens of the Soviet military-industrial complex never forgave him for making what they considered an unwarranted concession.[6]

In the United States, opponents of the INF Treaty alleged that intermediate-range nuclear missiles were necessary in Europe to provide a "ladder of deterrence" in accord with NATO's "flexible response" doctrine. This ignored the fact that the Soviet Union was eliminating many more missiles than the United States and therefore reducing the threat to NATO disproportionately. It was a striking irony that many of the persons objecting to the INF Treaty had been original supporters of the zero option. Apparently, in their eyes, the zero option was useful only so long as the Soviet Union rejected it.

Reagan took on his critics, most from the right wing of his own party, before Gorbachev arrived to sign the treaty. The critics seemed unwilling to accept victory when it was handed to them: after all, the treaty met all the significant demands they had made as the treaty was being negotiated. Nevertheless, many persons associated with the neoconservative group, along with former secretaries of state Alexander Haig and Henry Kissinger, argued against the agreement.[7] Several senators, including Malcolm Wallop, Jesse Helms, Steve Symms, Larry Pressler, and Dan Quayle, announced, even before it was signed, that they opposed it. Senator Bob Dole, the Republican leader in the Senate, accused Reagan of forcing it on U.S. allies, and was quoted as saying, "I don't trust Gorbachev," on the day Gorbachev arrived in Washington.

Although it appeared that all INF issues had been settled by Shultz and Shevardnadze at their November meeting in Geneva, the signature was almost delayed by some last-minute antics by the Soviet military. The treaty called for an exchange of photographs of the missiles to be eliminated, but the photograph brought by the Soviet delegation to Washington was not of the missile itself but of the canister in which the missile was housed until it was launched. The explanation given was that this was the form in which the missile emerged from the factory and the form in which it would be destroyed. The United States had provided a photograph of the Pershing II and, for obvious reasons, found the Soviet photograph unacceptable. How could the president sign a treaty when the Soviet military fudged on its terms even before the treaty was signed? Shultz called an urgent meeting with Shevardnadze to explain the problem and insist on a photograph of the "naked missile" before the treaty could be signed.

The issue was substantively trivial—U.S. intelligence was fully informed about the characteristics of the SS-20—but the principle was an important one. If the Soviet military was allowed to rationalize its refusal to provide the same sort of information the United States had given it, would it not continue to try to skimp on other requirements it might consider troublesome? Shevardnadze and his arms control negotiators were embarrassed by what they considered a double-cross perpetrated by their colleagues in the military-industrial complex at home. Marshal Akhromeyev, who was with the Soviet delegation in Washington, telephoned Moscow and persuaded his colleagues to fax a picture of the missile out of its canister. Shultz agreed to accept the facsimile provided an actual photograph would be supplied as soon as feasible.[8]

Everything finally came together barely in time to permit Reagan and Gorbachev to sign the treaty as scheduled on December 8. Some argued that the INF Treaty was not of great significance because it left in place the vast majority of nuclear weapons in both countries' arsenals. Its importance, however, was not primarily in the number of weapons eliminated (though the number was substantial) but in the precedents it set. For the first time, both countries agreed to reduce the number of their nuclear weapons,* to eliminate an entire class of weapons, and to do so with thorough on-site verification. Avoiding vague language that had sometimes been used in the past to obscure differences, the treaty was a marvel of detail—almost a thousand pages. With it, Reagan and Gorbachev proved that a way could be found to put the arms race in reverse.

The treaty served the political needs of both Reagan and Gorbachev even though some people in both countries opposed it. Reagan turned the tables on skeptics who had predicted that he was risking war by challenging the Soviet Union to change its policies. Gorbachev removed what he had told the Politburo was a "pistol aimed at our head" and proved that he could do business with Ronald Reagan, despite the latter's hatred of the Soviet system.

---

* SALT I and SALT II had established ceilings for deployment, but did not require reductions.

A Tricky Formula on the ABM Treaty

SOVIET AND AMERICAN delegations worked hard to find an acceptable formula so that a treaty to reduce strategic arms (START) could be drawn up in time to be signed the following year. They finally agreed that each country would reduce its strategic nuclear arsenal to 4,900 warheads.[9] Nevertheless, SDI—or, rather, Gorbachev's misperception of SDI—was still the principal stumbling block. While Reagan was willing to commit the United States not to withdraw from the ABM Treaty for ten years, there was no agreement on what the ABM Treaty permitted. Gorbachev had dropped the demand to confine SDI research to laboratories, but still insisted on the narrow interpretation of that treaty.

Shevardnadze tried to finesse the issue by suggesting that the treaty simply state that both countries would abide by the ABM Treaty as signed, without specifying what that meant. Then, if either side thought the other was violating the ABM Treaty, it would be relieved of its obligations under the treaty. Shultz turned aside the suggestion, remarking that since the United States considered the radar station under construction near Krasnoyarsk a violation of the ABM Treaty, a START treaty with the provision Shevardnadze suggested could not even come into effect.

Inasmuch as Gorbachev had indicated that he would abandon the offending radar site if other treaty terms were met, this was probably not the main reason Shultz objected. It is most unlikely that the Senate would have ratified a treaty that contained a provision that was intentionally ambiguous, and if it did, a Senate under control of the Democratic Party (as it then was) would have insisted that SDI be kept within the limits of the narrow interpretation of the ABM Treaty. For that reason, U.S. negotiators had been instructed to obtain direct or clearly implicit Soviet acceptance of the broad interpretation, and also an acknowledged right to deploy strategic defenses after ten years.

Another important issue had emerged in the START negotiations: the Soviet Union wanted to limit nuclear-armed submarine-launched cruise missiles (SLCMs). The United States refused to agree to limits because, it claimed, the limits could not be verified. Therefore, it proposed that both sides simply declare to the other what their plans were in respect to these weapons.

On this issue, the American position was absurd. It was motivated not by U.S. national interests, but by the perceived parochial interest of a military service. The U.S. Navy did not want to accept on-site inspection of its submarines and therefore claimed that limits on nuclear-armed SLCMs could not be verified. Of course they could—with on-site inspection—and the Soviet leaders knew that. The navy's reasoning was that U.S. SLCM technology was superior to Soviet SLCM technology and that Soviet specialists should not be given a peek at it. More profoundly, it reflected a reluctance by the U.S. Navy to accept any limitations whatever on its armaments.

There was logic behind the general resistance navy brass exhibited toward arms control restrictions: The U.S. Navy had worldwide responsibilities, most not related to the Soviet Union and only partially to the Cold War. The Soviet Union was a land power with little defensive need for a "blue water" navy. Therefore any attempt to negotiate a balance, much less parity, was understandably anathema. The navy argument was valid if the question had been limits on, say, aircraft carrier task forces.

But SLCMs were different. The only likely target for American nuclear-armed SLCMs of the range the USSR wished to limit was the Soviet Union. Therefore, it could not reasonably be argued that they played no role in the strategic nuclear balance. However, the irony was that the United States had much more to fear from these weapons than the Soviet Union. How many major Soviet cities would have been vulnerable to U.S. SLCMs? Murmansk, certainly. Vladivostok, also certainly. Possibly Leningrad, if the United States were so incautious as to send submarines into the well-guarded Baltic Sea. Sevastopol and Odessa, if the United States violated treaty restrictions and sent submerged subs through the Turkish Straits.

And the United States? Look at the map! On the East Coast: Boston, New York, Philadelphia, Baltimore, Washington, Norfolk (the base of the Atlantic Fleet), Charleston (a major U.S. submarine base), Savannah, Jacksonville, Miami. On the Gulf Coast: Tampa, Pensacola, New Orleans, Houston. On the Pacific Coast: San Diego (another major submarine base), Los Angeles, San Francisco, Portland, Seattle, and Anchorage. In the Pacific: Honolulu (remember Pearl Harbor?). In citing the largest coastal cities I should not omit smaller cities such as Portland, Maine; Portsmouth, New Hampshire; New London (where U.S. submarines are built) and New Haven, Connecticut; Newark and Trenton, New Jersey; both Wilmingtons (Delaware and North Carolina), and many others.

While U.S. SLCM technology was superior to that of the Soviets, so was U.S. MIRV technology in 1972 when the air force insisted that MIRVs not be limited. By the early 1980s, when the Soviet Union showed that it could use MIRVs more effectively than the United States (with their heavier rockets, they could design ten or more warheads with deadly accuracy against U.S. missile silos), the United States decided that it was essential to curb the right to "MIRV" and tried to force the Soviet Union to single-warhead missiles).

The U.S. Navy's resistance to SLCM limits in 1987 and 1988 was even more shortsighted than the air force's 1972 infatuation with MIRVs. Given the geographical position of the two countries, the United States inherently had a greater interest in limiting nuclear-armed SLCMs than did the Soviet Union. Incredibly, each country took a position in these negotiations that was directly contrary to its own national interest—assuming that the Cold War would continue. Did I point this out to senior officials? You bet I did. Not one disagreed with me, and not one was willing to take on the navy.

Fortunately for both countries, the Cold War was soon to end. Let us hope that terrorist groups will never get hold of a nuclear device that could be brought to a U.S. port in a boat, or if so, that the U.S. Coast Guard is adequately equipped to deal with it. The U.S. Navy's attitude toward SLCMs was evidence that it saw as its primary function not the defense of the United States, but the projection of American power abroad.

If all the other questions had been solved regarding START, Gorbachev probably would not have let the SLCM issue torpedo the agreement. Just as Reagan was willing to negotiate just about everything except SDI, Gorbachev seemed willing to come to terms on other issues if he could put limitations on SDI.

Despite the remaining disagreements, the statement Reagan and Gorbachev endorsed seemed promising. They instructed their negotiators to try to complete the START treaty "at the earliest possible date, preferably in time for signature . . . during the next meeting of leaders of state in the first half of 1988." However, the statement regarding the ABM Treaty contained some artful punctuation, the implications of which were not fully appreciated by Soviet negotiators at the time. The sentence spoke of an agreement "that would commit the sides to observe the ABM Treaty, as signed in 1972, while developing their research, development, and testing as required, which are permitted by the ABM Treaty, and not to withdraw from the ABM Treaty, for a specified period of time."[10]

American negotiators subsequently argued that the phrase "which are permitted by the ABM Treaty" was set off by commas, indicating that it was in apposition to the preceding phrase, and therefore indicated that "research, development, and testing as required [by SDI]" *was* permitted by the ABM Treaty. Soviet negotiators pointed out, however, that, in Russian, all such phrases, whether restrictive or not, are set off by commas, and therefore the passage should be read to mean that *only* research, development, and testing permitted by the ABM Treaty were acceptable. Their position remained that the narrow interpretation of the ABM Treaty was the only valid one.[11]

One-upmanship with some of the more esoteric rules of English punctuation provided a dollop of amusement for American negotiators in the otherwise mind-numbing exercise they were engaged in. But it could not conceal the fact that the sides were about as far apart on this issue as they had been when Reagan and Gorbachev left Reykjavík the year before. The word "laboratories" was no longer in play, but the issue that lay behind it seemed as intractable as ever.

Gorbachev Sees America, and Vice Versa

THE FACT THAT Gorbachev was, finally, willing to destroy more weapons than the United States and to permit highly intrusive on-site inspection impressed Reagan. Reagan's willingness to enter into any substantial arms control agreement, particularly one that was arguably more in the Soviet than U.S. interest, impressed Gorbachev. But that was not all. The conclusions Gorbachev drew from his exposure to the United States were perhaps as important for the future development of U.S.-Soviet relations as was the treaty he and Reagan signed. The crowds cheering him as he drove through the streets of Washington made a profound impression. America did not fit the stereotype Communist propaganda had fabricated and spread, and Gorbachev was perceptive enough to see that.

It was more than just cheering crowds. Gorbachev's meetings with key congressional leaders, with prominent private citizens, with businessmen, journalists, and with Washington's social elite convinced him that there was a real constituency in the United States for improved relations. He was lionized everywhere; many reacted to the platitudes he uttered as if they were revelations.

The officials who came with him did their share of networking as well. Marshal Akhromeyev helped solve the problem of the SS-20 photograph. Alexander Yakovlev, who had already begun taking the ideological shackles off the Soviet mass media, assisted Gorbachev in his meetings with intellectuals. Vladimir Kryuchkov, the head of KGB external intelligence (who would soon be appointed chairman of the KGB), met CIA deputy director Robert Gates at a small dinner hosted by Colin Powell, assistant to the president for national security. It was the first meeting of high-level CIA and KGB officials. Gates subsequently described their meeting as of "two com-

mitted foes warily circling, making a jab here, a parry there. But also beginning a dialogue between the last combatants of the Cold War."[12]

Kryuchkov and Gates did not become friends and did not expect to. But
their ability to maintain a civil conversation was indicative of the rapid expansion of personal contacts by officials on both sides, some of whom
would not have dreamed of meeting a year earlier.

For Gorbachev personally, the most important member of his delegation
was his wife, Raisa. When she called on Nancy Reagan, sparks flew. Each
resented what she interpreted as efforts by the other to upstage her. Raisa
Gorbacheva was also upset with restrictions on her activities and unfairly
blamed her American hosts; actually, it was the KGB that had limited some
of her activities. Nevertheless, she too could sense the openness, friendli-
ness, and spontaneity of the many Americans she met. She must also have
noticed that Americans, unlike most Soviet citizens, considered it natural
and laudable for a first lady to play an active public role during her husband's travels.

Basically, both Gorbachevs liked America. Most Americans also liked
what they saw: a Soviet leader who smiled, who could joke, who talked of
peace and cooperation, who had an attractive, articulate wife. Some cautious
souls, fearing that Gorbachev was out to delude a gullible public, ridiculed
the effusive welcome street crowds gave him. But Gorbachev was sincere
about his desire to bring real change to the Soviet Union and to its relations
with the rest of the world.

During their final lunch in Washington, Gorbachev told Reagan he would
never view the United States again the way he had before his trip. Judging
by his subsequent actions, he meant it. The praise he received abroad bolstered his confidence that he was on the right track.

PRESIDENT REAGAN SUMMED up his view of the Washington summit in
a toast delivered at the dinner the Gorbachevs arranged at the Soviet embassy. He recalled that on VE Day, as crowds celebrated the victory on Red
Square, a Soviet army major had said to a young American diplomat, "Now
it's time to live."* Reagan expressed pride at what he and Gorbachev had ac-

* That young American was Robert C. Tucker, who headed the Joint Press Reading Service of the
American and British embassies in Moscow. He is now an emeritus professor of politics at Princeton
University and the author of a multivolume biography of Stalin. In a private communication, Profes-
sor Tucker recalls the incident as follows: "My encounter took place on May 10, 1945, a day none of

complished, but added, "I'm convinced that history will ultimately judge this summit and its participants not on missile counts but on how far we moved together for the fulfillment of that soldier's hopes."[13]

For Reagan, normal, friendly, civilized relations were more important than stocks of weapons. Now that Gorbachev had experienced cheering American crowds, he too began to understand that simple but too often disregarded fact.

When he returned to Moscow he reported to the Politburo that the people he dealt with in Washington were "guided by the most natural human motives and feelings."[14] He no longer spoke of political dinosaurs or cavemen.

---

us then serving in the U.S. embassy will ever forget. As you know, our embassy chancery at that time was on Mokhovaia Street, across from Red Square. Uniformed Americans who went out to join the celebration taking place in Red Square were carried off on the shoulders of exultant Muscovites. A civilian attaché, I walked over and joined the crowd. My most vivid memory is of a Red Army major exclaiming to no one in particular: *Teper' pora zhit'!* (Now it is time to live!) But for the autocrat in the Kremlin, as we know, it wasn't time to live in the major's sense, but to gear up for another great war whose strong possibility was lodged, as he said on February 9, 1946, in the nature of 'imperialism,' i.e., time for a cold war with the Western powers."

XIV

MR. REAGAN GOES TO MOSCOW

*But perhaps the deepest impression I had during . . . meetings with Soviet
citizens was that they were generally indistinguishable from people . . . in
America. They were simply ordinary people who longed . . . for the
same things that Americans did: peace, love, security, a better life
for themselves and their children.*
—RONALD REAGAN, 1990[1]

*For me, Ronald Reagan's acknowledgement [that perestroika had changed the
Soviet Union] was one of the genuine achievements of his Moscow visit.*
—MIKHAIL GORBACHEV, 1996[2]

THOUGH GORBACHEV WAS disappointed that he still had no agreement from Reagan regarding the ABM Treaty, he could be satisfied with
the impression he made on the American people and information media.
Time magazine, in fact, made him "Man of the Year" for 1987 and led the
issue with a laudatory biography.[3] As for Reagan—well, the article that followed the praise of Gorbachev was entitled " 'The Roughest Year': Scandal,
War, Crash, Plague . . . and Who's in Charge?" Apparently the American
president deserved no credit for achieving an agreement he had sought since
his first year in office, one that set the United States and Soviet Union on a
course that soon brought an end to the arms race and, indeed, the Cold War
itself.

Whoever was responsible for the favorable turn in U.S.-Soviet relations,
it had taken place. George Shultz, hoping to ride on the momentum established by the Washington summit, set ambitious goals for 1988: ratification
of the INF Treaty, conclusion of a strategic arms (START) agreement, a Soviet decision to withdraw from Afghanistan, and tangible improvements in

the protection of human rights in the Soviet Union.[4] Except for START, he achieved these goals—and several others not on that list—but in January 1988, none were certain.

In Washington, the first order of business was getting the INF Treaty ratified. There was little doubt that the Senate would approve it in some form. After all, virtually all Democrats were in favor, and although the Republicans were split, enough were likely to stick with a conservative Republican president to make up sixty-seven votes in favor. There was, however, a danger of crippling amendments, reservations that would require further negotiation with Gorbachev before the treaty could come into effect. Both Democrats and Republicans had favorite ideas that, in their view, would improve the treaty. However, any change in the treaty would have undermined, fatally most likely, Reagan's credibility with Gorbachev. The latter had been told repeatedly, by representatives of both American parties, that if he made a deal with Reagan it would stick; Reagan would not suffer the rebuff inflicted on Jimmy Carter when the Senate refused to ratify SALT II. How could Ronald Reagan, the scourge of the "evil empire," be outflanked from the right?

There were times in the early months of 1988, however, when it appeared that political games in the Senate could have this effect. During the spring, managing the ratification process absorbed much of the secretary of state's attention, and also that of the president's new national security assistant, Colin Powell. Ultimately, however, they succeeded, obtaining an overwhelming (93–5) vote in favor of ratification without crippling reservations. The vote to approve the treaty came just in time for Reagan to exchange the official instruments with Gorbachev in Moscow.[5]

Preparing the Moscow Summit

FOR ONCE, THERE was no verbal wrestling over whether the Moscow summit would take place. Gorbachev did not try, as he had in 1986 and 1987, to place preconditions on the meeting. He had agreed, even before he visited Washington in December 1987, to receive Reagan in Moscow in May 1988. Although both he and Reagan had hoped that they would be able to settle on the main principles of a strategic arms agreement, Gorbachev never held Reagan's trip to Moscow hostage to this or any other specific agreement.

Shultz and Shevardnadze continued to meet frequently—almost every month. Both attempted to solve the problems that blocked a START agreement, and though they failed, it was not for lack of trying. In every other area of the relationship, however, things moved. As the year went on, they picked up speed. Most important, the Soviet Union finally agreed to withdraw its military forces from Afghanistan rapidly and, in effect, without conditions.

Afghanistan

IN SEPTEMBER 1987, Shevardnadze informed Shultz privately that a firm decision had been made by the Soviet leadership to withdraw from Afghanistan. Nevertheless, Gorbachev made no public statement and Soviet negotiators stuck generally to traditional positions. Working-level discussions of Afghanistan during the Washington summit had produced little that was new.

When Gorbachev suddenly asked Reagan, during their final lunch in Washington, whether the United States would stop supplying arms to the opposition in Afghanistan if Soviet forces were withdrawn, Reagan replied with a general comment but no clear answer. When the Soviet delegation returned to Moscow from Washington, the Soviet Ministry of Foreign Affairs asked me to clarify Reagan's answer to the question. It took a few days to get an answer from Washington, suggesting to me that the question was still a subject of debate at home. Eventually I received instructions to tell the ministry that if the Soviet Union ceased supplying the Kabul regime with arms, the answer was "yes," otherwise it would be "no."

Some diplomats like to give fancy names to simple ideas. Maybe it makes them feel important, or maybe they just want to confuse people outside the loop of a particular negotiation. In this instance, wordsmiths in the State Department began to speak of "negative symmetry" (neither the Kabul regime nor the opposition would receive arms from the outside) and "positive symmetry" (both the U.S. and the USSR would have the right to supply arms to forces in Afghanistan). For the United States, only symmetry was acceptable. Gorbachev could decide whether he wanted it to be "positive" or "negative."

The U.S. attitude was driven more by politics in Washington than by the situation in Afghanistan. Both the Soviet-supported Afghan government and the Afghan opposition were well supplied with arms. If the regime in Kabul could not defeat the opposition with the help of the Soviet army, it could hardly do so whether or not it received additional military supplies from Moscow. The main issue for the Americans had always been the Soviet military occupation of Afghanistan. If that ended, there was no good reason for the United States to continue giving arms to some Afghan factions whose aims, other than expelling Soviet military forces from their country, were remote from any American interests. Furthermore, since supplies to the Afghan opposition were funneled through Pakistan, there was a danger that the Pakistani intelligence service would pass them on to fundamentalist Islamic groups hostile to the United States.

That was not the way powerful forces in Congress, led by Senator Gordon Humphrey of New Hampshire, and prominent figures such as Zbigniew Brzezinski, President Carter's national security adviser, saw it. They insisted that the United States should not stop giving arms to the opposition so long as the Soviet Union continued to supply its friends in Kabul. The question became entangled with the ratification of the INF Treaty, with some senators demanding a firm U.S. stance on "symmetry" as a price for their vote in favor of the treaty. At one point the Senate passed a resolution that urged the president to stand firm on this issue. Most senators were probably unaware that they had allowed it to pass by acclamation, but it nevertheless was a powerful weapon in the hands of zealots more interested in punishing the Soviet Union than ending the Soviet occupation of Afghanistan and cooperating to ensure a stable government in Afghanistan not dominated by anti-Western elements.

On February 8, Gorbachev finally made a public pledge to leave Afghanistan. He announced that Soviet forces would be withdrawn from Afghanistan in ten months beginning May 15, provided an agreement was reached by March 15.

From that point, negotiations that had been sputtering along for years became frenetic. Afghanistan dominated Shultz's meetings in Moscow in February. Shevardnadze complained that the United States had switched signals now that an agreement was near; Shultz explained that he had always assumed the Soviet Union would cease military supplies to Afghanistan if the United States did, and also described the political pressures in Washington.[6] Shevardnadze was not mollified—aides explained to us that he had personally persuaded President Najibullah, who had replaced Babrak Karmal as the head of the Afghan government in 1986, to agree to a withdrawal of Soviet forces on the condition that Soviet military supplies would continue. Shevardnadze was convinced that Najibullah was genuinely trying to form a coalition government that would marginalize the fundamentalist Islamic forces favored by the Pakistani intelligence service. He could not understand why the United States failed to recognize the danger to stability in the region if Islamic fundamentalists should replace the Soviet-supported regime in Kabul.

Gorbachev's indignation over the American position was all the greater when Shultz switched signals on another key issue. Whereas Pakistani president Zia ul-Haq had earlier refused to accept a Soviet proposal to help form a coalition government in Afghanistan, he now decided that this should be done, but in a way that effectively excluded most members of the Soviet-backed regime. With some reluctance, Shultz presented the idea to Gorbachev, who ridiculed it, pointing out that the United States had previously argued that outsiders could not carry a viable government to Kabul on their bayonets. He did not add that that was precisely what the Soviet Union had tried to do.

Following Gorbachev's understandable rejection, the United States lost little time abandoning Zia's idea for a coalition government arranged in advance. Shevardnadze accepted a formula for "noninterference" by outsiders in Afghanistan that implicitly allowed the U.S. to continue its arms supplies via Pakistan. Gorbachev had decided that it would be better to withdraw Soviet troops from Afghanistan in the context of an international agreement than without one.[7]

The March 15 date Gorbachev had specified as the deadline for an agreement passed, but, after much frantic diplomacy, one was ready soon thereafter. On April 14, Shultz, Shevardnadze, and the foreign ministers of Pakistan and Afghanistan went to Geneva to sign the various agreements. Diego Cordovez, the UN representative who had worked for six years to bring the parties to a settlement, observed the ceremony with gratitude that his task was finally accomplished. Nevertheless, he could not totally repress the feeling that Pakistan's evident determination to continue arming its friends in Afghanistan—and U.S. support for this decision—would eventually boomerang. Outsiders had never been able to control Afghanistan, and those who tried inevitably came a cropper.[8]

Pakistan and Afghanistan concluded three agreements, one on "principles of mutual relations" (i.e., noninterference), a second on the return of refugees to Afghanistan, and a third on "interrelationships for the settlement of the situation relating to Afghanistan." Shultz and Shevardnadze signed a separate Declaration on International Guarantees (of the first agreement) and signed the third agreement between Afghanistan and Pakistan as witnesses.[9] Unlike the INF Treaty that defines everything precisely and tries to answer just about any question that might be raised about implementation, these short agreements were full of undefined generalities and deliberate ambiguities. They did not represent a meeting of the minds of the Afghani and Pakistani governments. It was obvious to all that the civil war in Afghanistan would continue, but when Soviet troops departed, the Kabul regime would have to fight its own battles.*

---

* Contrary to the prediction of American intelligence, Najibullah was able to stay in power in Kabul for nearly three years after the Soviet withdrawal. He was captured by the U.S.-backed mujahedin in 1992 and executed by the Pakistani-backed Taliban in 1996 following their capture of Kabul.

Despite their shortcomings, the Geneva accords on Afghanistan gave Gorbachev the political cover he needed to extract his troops. The Soviet army began to leave on May 15, as Gorbachev had promised, two weeks before Reagan arrived in Moscow. The United States had insisted that the Soviet withdrawal should be "front-loaded," with larger numbers leaving early rather than later. Gorbachev also saw that this condition was met.

THERE WERE ASPECTS of the agreement on Afghanistan that the United States subsequently had reason to regret. At the time, however, the settlement solved one of the most nettlesome problems in U.S.-Soviet relations. If Gorbachev had been willing to come to terms earlier—say, in response to Reagan's appeal following the Geneva summit—he almost certainly could have secured from the United States what he sought in 1988: termination of arms supplies to the Afghan opposition.

In fact, at that time, Gorbachev would not have needed an international agreement to leave: he could have declared victory and withdrawn. In 1985 or 1986 he would have gained much credit with the United States and many other countries if he had done that. By 1988, however, it was too late for Gorbachev to salvage much from the debacle in Afghanistan. Fighting there had gone on and been intensified for three years on his watch. One of the biggest mistakes of his career was his failure to get out of Afghanistan early in his tenure rather than trying to prove that the Soviet Union could win.

Why the delay? We can only speculate.* Possibly, Gorbachev was waiting to conclude a significant arms control treaty with the United States before leaving Afghanistan: he moved quickly after signing the INF Treaty. Anatoly Chernyaev identified an additional factor when he observed that, throughout 1985, 1986, and 1987, Gorbachev was still torn between "old thinking"—loyalty to traditional Soviet objectives, particularly solidarity with "class allies"—and the "new thinking." Afghanistan is an example of the persistence of the old thinking in Gorbachev's mind. An earlier withdrawal not only would have made it easier to solve other international problems but would have enhanced the popularity of perestroika as well.

---

* I posed this question to Gorbachev after he left office, but he never gave a clear explanation. He did say in one interview that Reagan's message in his letter following their meeting in Geneva had been "most important," but did not explain why he waited more than two years after getting that letter to act on it.

Changing the Soviet System

BY 1988, DOMESTIC reform had become Gorbachev's prime concern. He had tried to get the economy out of the doldrums by going after some of the most corrupt Communist Party officials, shifting managers, trying to enforce more "labor discipline," and discouraging heavy drinking. The anti-alcohol campaign had some positive effects: public health statistics improved and male mortality rates decreased. But it was carried out in such a heavy-handed manner that it aroused strong public opposition. The other methods were not working at all. By 1987 it had become clear that Soviet economic and social problems could not be solved by tinkering with the administrative machinery. The old machinery had to be replaced, and this meant that the fundamentals of Communist Party rule had to change.

Until the spring of 1988, Gorbachev's policies enjoyed broad support among the Communist Party elite. However, when Gorbachev's colleagues began to sense that he might be thinking about changing the way the Party ruled the Soviet Union, many of them balked. Talk about reform was one thing. Almost everybody did that. But now it seemed that Gorbachev was encouraging criticism of past practices and even the system itself, and who knew where that might lead? Some of the things Gorbachev had in mind might undermine the power of the Communist Party. Such dangerous thinking had to be stopped before it got out of hand.

Opponents went public with their misgivings in March 1988 by publishing a long article in a major newspaper that attacked muckraking and defended Stalin and his practices.[10] While Gorbachev was traveling abroad, Yegor Ligachev, his number two in the Party hierarchy, encouraged Party cells to discuss the article. When Gorbachev returned, he forced through the Politburo a statement condemning it, but the damage had been done. The fact that a powerful group of Party officials opposed Gorbachev's reforms was now obvious to all who followed Soviet politics.[11]

Nevertheless, Gorbachev, supported by Shevardnadze and Alexander Yakovlev, pressed on to define a reform agenda. They had persuaded the Central Committee to authorize a Party Conference for June 1988.* It would be an opportunity to put the highest-level Communist Party endorsement on the new policies. Yakovlev led the team assigned to draft resolutions for the Party Conference to consider.

---

* Party Congresses had been held every five years since Stalin died. They were the most authoritative organ of the CPSU. Party Conferences had not been held since Stalin's death, but presumably would have the same authority as a Congress, at least until the next Congress was held.

Although Gorbachev was more than first among equals in the Politburo, he was not an absolute dictator. There was significant opposition there to the direction his domestic policy was taking, and his critics had shown their hand. If he got what he wanted, he would have to maneuver to induce the Politburo to approve his choice of recommendations for the Party Conference.

Reagan's visit, planned for late May, could make a contribution to the reform scenario. Gorbachev had argued at home that the INF Treaty was in the Soviet interest, and that his diplomacy had forced it on a wavering Ronald Reagan. He had started a process to permit an orderly withdrawal from Afghanistan; if agreements were in place and Soviet troops headed out of Afghanistan before Reagan came to Moscow, Gorbachev could claim two foreign policy victories—Pershing missiles would no longer be aimed at their head and the Americans could no longer keep them bogged down in Afghanistan. With such achievements under his belt, who in the Politburo would dare cross him when he put forward his recommendations for the Party Conference? After all, he needed to publish the Politburo's recommendations a few weeks before the Conference to give the impression that delegates had time to consider them. That meant they would appear just before Reagan arrived in Moscow. Even his critics in the Politburo would not want him to face the American president in Moscow with the Politburo divided on key issues!

If the Reagan visit went well, Gorbachev could stand on the rostrum at the Party Conference as the leader who had eased international tension and restored Soviet prestige in the world. Few, if any, would dare object to his radical proposals no matter how much they might disagree privately. Gorbachev thus laid a trap for those who derived their power from the Soviet system and had no desire to change it. He would put them in a position where they could not say no to change.

Human Rights to the Fore

ALTHOUGH REAGAN HAD always been deeply committed to defending human rights in the Soviet Union, he had kept his most vigorous efforts private to minimize Gorbachev's exposure to charges that he was bowing to American pressure if he curbed abuses. Before his visit to Moscow, however, Reagan gave human rights more emphasis in his speeches than he had before, for several reasons. During the debate over INF ratification, he wanted to make it clear that he was not forgetting the condition of human rights in the Soviet Union in order to obtain a favorable vote on the treaty. Second, Gorbachev had, as of then, moved very slowly in freeing political prisoners and allowing more emigration. What concessions he had made were individual, not the result of changes in the system or of liberalized rules. Now that there was conspicuous progress on two parts of the American agenda (the INF Treaty and Gorbachev's decision to leave Afghanistan), Reagan hoped that a strong push for human rights and democratization during his visit would stimulate similar progress on the other two agenda topics.

When George Shultz went to Moscow in February to start preparations for Reagan's visit, one of his first acts was to call on Andrei Sakharov at his modest apartment. During the wide ranging discussion, Shultz asked whether the United States should agree to participate in an international conference on human rights in Moscow as Shevardnadze had proposed. Sakharov replied that the United States should insist that the Soviet Union first withdraw from Afghanistan and release remaining political prisoners, but if it did that, the conference Shevardnadze had proposed would be most helpful to the human rights movement in the USSR. This was a useful comment since many human rights activists in the United States believed that the U.S. should refuse to participate in such a meeting unless the Soviet government became much more liberal in permitting freedom of emigration.

Sakharov's views on human rights and arms control only partially coincided with U.S. official views. Though he supported the right of persons to emigrate if they wished, Sakharov did not consider this a priority issue; he believed there would be no barrier to emigration if legislation was changed to protect the rights of individuals. He considered it more important to encourage a change of the system than to press for the emigration of individuals or groups as an exception to regular practice. He also felt that causes such as the right to emigrate would benefit from a conference in Moscow and therefore should not be delayed until Soviet performance met Western standards.

Sakharov also had a different view of some aspects of arms control. He was a strong supporter of a sharp reduction of nuclear forces, but felt that the Strategic Defense Initiative was unwise. As a physicist, he doubted that an effective homeland defense could be devised—he noted that it would always be easier and cheaper to attack weapons based in space than to put them there in the first place. This would make any space-based defense unreliable. Since he considered SDI an impractical project, he had advised Gorbachev not to make it a stumbling block to strategic arms cuts. At the same time, he saw no reason for Reagan to hold up the cuts in order to preserve SDI. He feared that plans such as those some SDI proponents described would only stimulate dangerous countermeasures on the part of the Soviet Union.[12]

Shultz went into a meeting with Shevardnadze immediately after his call on Sakharov. Shevardnadze led off with an expression of concern about infringements on rights in the United States, mentioning specifically that the U.S. "systematically denies women and blacks the opportunity to advance." Apparently the person who drew up Shevardnadze's talking points did not realize that Rozanne Ridgway, the assistant secretary of state for European affairs, and Colin Powell, the president's assistant for national security, would be sitting at the table alongside Shultz. Shultz did not protest, however, but told Shevardnadze, "We have made real progress but have lots more work to do."[13]

It was an encouraging sign that Shevardnadze took the tack he did. Though his comments exaggerated the situation, they did refer to real problems in the United States that had not been solved totally. However, the most important point was that Shevardnadze needed to demonstrate to his Politburo colleagues that discussion of human rights was a two-way street. Shultz understood this. After all, he had invited Shevardnadze at their first meeting to criticize the state of human rights in the United States if he wished. It was also worth noting that Shevardnadze had not objected to Shultz's prior call on Sakharov. His predecessor probably would have sent Sakharov back into exile rather than tolerate his meeting an American secretary of state during an official visit.

Regional Conflicts

REAGAN NOT ONLY stepped up his public comments on the human rights situation in the Soviet Union; he also drew attention to the need to settle regional conflicts where the Soviet Union was indirectly involved. These were the focus of a speech he delivered in Springfield, Massachusetts, on April 21, the day Shultz arrived in Moscow to put final touches on the plans for Reagan's Moscow visit.[14] In it, Reagan took credit for the Soviet decision to leave Afghanistan and stressed that the United States would continue to supply the opposition in Afghanistan. Of course, Gorbachev knew that this was the American position, but was doubtless annoyed to have it stressed in a speech by the president just weeks before he was to visit Moscow. Furthermore, Reagan also concentrated on the need to oppose Soviet aggression in other areas, citing, in particular, Ethiopia and Nicaragua. These were legitimate issues, but they could have been balanced with some attention to what had already been accomplished in broadening U.S.-Soviet cooperation and the steps Gorbachev was taking to open up Soviet society.

Gorbachev was given excerpts from the speech before he met with Shultz and what he read put him in a belligerent mood. He had been impressed by the increasing pattern of private consultation on regional issues, and he particularly appreciated advance notice of the plan that Shultz intended to take to the Middle East on a forthcoming trip.[15] But portions of Reagan's Springfield speech seem to violate the still fragile pattern of consultation and hark back to evil-empire baiting. Gorbachev told Shultz the speech showed that the Reagan administration was not abandoning "stereotypes" and "reliance on force" and was moving the relationship "backward." He noted that Reagan was due to arrive in just a few weeks and wondered if he could expect a "catfight."[16]

Reagan's Springfield speech had not been vetted by his senior foreign policy advisers—neither George Shultz nor Colin Powell, who was traveling with Shultz, had seen the text—so Shultz was surprised by Gorbachev's pugnacity. But after Gorbachev had railed about the speech he calmed down; he assured Shultz that they would prepare the Moscow summit so that it would be "a major political event," and that the Soviet government and people would show "respect not only to the American people, but also to the President himself."[17]

When it was his turn to talk, Shultz ignored Reagan's speech (which convinced Gorbachev that he was embarrassed by it), but instead summarized progress in each of the four parts of the formerly U.S. but now common agenda, and assured Gorbachev of the administration's commitment to "more stable and constructive relations." Following an exchange regarding future possibilities of cooperation, Gorbachev began to talk of his plans. He assured Shultz that the Soviet Union did not "pretend to have the final truth" and did not wish to "impose our way of life on other peoples." He complimented the comments Shultz had made at an earlier meeting on economic trends in the world, the thrust of which had been that both the United States and the Soviet Union risked losing the economic competition to other countries if they persisted in an arms race that drained resources from the civilian economy. He also spoke of a new generation of leaders coming forward who understood trends in the world better than their elders. Presumably in order to speed up the generational change in the Soviet Union, he confided that he would propose firm term limits at the upcoming Party Conference.

He then turned to human rights, commenting that the United States and Soviet Union had different cultures and different attitudes toward these issues. He refused to be "taught" what was right since he was no schoolboy.

He added that there was sufficient criticism within the Soviet Union that they hardly needed more from the outside. Shultz pointed out that vigorous self-criticism occurred in the United States as well, but that both countries had signed international agreements such as the Helsinki Final Act and the Declaration of Human Rights, and therefore it was not interference to point out instances when these obligations were not honored.

As it had been with Shevardnadze in February, Gorbachev seemed primarily interested in a record that showed that he had spent more time discussing the condition of human rights in the United States than he did defending his own country's practices. He avoided saying directly what must have been on his mind: "I'm moving on these issues as fast as I can. But don't push me. Particularly in public. How can I be a leader here if you make it look like I am merely following you?"[18]

Preparing the Publics

FOLLOWING GORBACHEV'S COMMENTS to Shultz in April, Reagan became more careful about his rhetoric. He continued to call attention to problems in the relationship that needed to be solved, but did so only after he had noted the progress already achieved. Whenever questioned about Gorbachev, he answered that he was a Soviet leader different from his predecessors who seemed genuinely to desire cooperation abroad and reform at home. During May he had something to say to the public about his upcoming trip almost every day. He made some major addresses, conducted interviews with American, Soviet, and European journalists, and held question-and-answer sessions with several groups.

When he was interviewed for Soviet television, he volunteered that he had read Gorbachev's book *Perestroika* and that the views expressed there made him optimistic about the future of U.S.-Soviet relations.[19] He also provided an extensive written interview to the most popular Soviet weekly magazine, *Ogonyok,* then edited by the reformist writer Vitaly Korotich.[20] In it he said that he hoped his visit would give him a better understanding of the Soviet people, just as Gorbachev's visit to Washington had helped him understand Americans.

Gorbachev, too, made several speeches and granted interviews to American publications. He took a leaf from Reagan in stressing the potential for cooperation even as he defended the Soviet point of view on the issues still in contention.

Reagan Preps in Helsinki

REAGAN WAS DUE to arrive in Moscow on May 29, but he stopped in Helsinki for three days on the way there. This gave him an opportunity not only to adapt to the time change, but also to call on Finnish officials—who had been more cooperative with the United States than some American allies had been—to deliver a major address, and to be briefed on the topics he would discuss with Gorbachev.

Helsinki was where thirty-five countries in Europe and North America signed the document in 1975 that established agreed principles of security and human rights. It was, therefore, an appropriate place for the American president to call attention to the connection between security and protection of human rights. Reagan did so in eloquent fashion to listeners in jam-packed Finlandia Hall. While he called on Gorbachev to continue the reforms he had started, he couched his appeal in a framework of optimism. His concluding words were: "I believe that in Moscow Mr. Gorbachev and I can take another step toward a brighter future and a safer world."[21] Unlike some of his advisers, he was convinced that a reformed Soviet Union would not be a threat to world peace and was willing to concede that Gorbachev seemed to be on the right track.

Reagan needed no further briefings on the negotiations he would conduct with Gorbachev. He was mainly interested in what was happening within the Soviet Union. I was asked to fill him in on the latest developments. I had gone to Helsinki from Moscow prepared to say that Gorbachev seemed serious, but had not yet made a breakthrough to fundamental reform. Opening the information media, permitting some criticism of the past, and allowing more interaction with foreigners were all encouraging developments, but the Communist Party still held the country in an unquestioned grip and the economy was showing no sign of improvement. Unless Gorbachev had something more radical in mind, the currents he had initiated could be quickly reversed if he changed his mind or was thrown out of power.

The day before I was to brief the president, Mike Joyce, my capable deputy, called me from Moscow to alert me that the Soviet news agency had issued a set of "theses" for the upcoming Party Conference. Although the embassy would be summarizing and commenting on them, he suggested that I read them in full and arranged for the Russian text to be faxed to me in Helsinki. He was right. The theses were nothing short of revolutionary in the Soviet context. They provided evidence that Gorbachev was finally prepared to cross the Rubicon and discard the Marxist ideology that had defined and justified the Communist Party dictatorship in the Soviet Union. Of course, he did not do so directly. He still had to persuade a Party Conference to adopt the principles. But the "Theses" were an indirect refutation of the basic principles of Marxism and of the most entrenched principles of the Soviet state structure.

I made the Theses the center of my presentation. "Mr. President," I reported, "if Gorbachev means what this says—and he must mean it or he wouldn't present it to a Communist Party Conference—the Soviet Union will never be the same." We finally had evidence that Gorbachev really intended, despite occasional evidence to the contrary, to press ahead with his reforms, come what may. The Theses set forth a program that Ronald Reagan, in clear conscience, could endorse.

The Reagans in Moscow

AIR FORCE ONE landed at Moscow's Vnukovo II Airport the morning of May 29, 1988. I accompanied the Soviet chief of protocol up the ramp to greet the president and his wife before they emerged from the aircraft. After I had introduced the Soviet chief of protocol, Reagan turned to me before stepping out of the plane and asked how to pronounce a Russian phrase in his arrival statement: "Rodilsya, ne toropilsya" (roughly, I was born but didn't rush it). I drilled him on the pronunciation a couple of times but was a bit uneasy. I had not heard that particular proverb before and wondered if a speechwriter had pulled a disused phrase out of some dusty dictionary. But it was too late to change the script, and it actually didn't matter whether it was a common saying. It sounded like one, and everyone would understand what it meant: we musn't rush agreements; they will come to life when they are ready. He wanted to explain at the outset why there would be no new blockbuster agreements signed while he was in Moscow.

The Reagans descended the airplane ramp and were greeted by none other than Andrei Gromyko, still the titular chief of the Soviet state, and his wife, Lidia. The president read a short statement that included the proverb, shook hands with the greeting Soviet delegation and senior officers of the American embassy, then sped off with Nancy to meet the Gorbachevs at the Kremlin. All went according to the usual protocol, which would not be remarkable except that this time it might have been different.

Up until the day before the Reagans left Helsinki to fly to Moscow, they had intended to stop by the apartment of a refusenik couple, Tatyana and Yuri Ziman, on their way to the Kremlin. The Zimans had been on the embassy's "representation list" for several years but were still being denied exit visas. Nancy Reagan heard about them from the wife of Vladimir Feltsman, a talented pianist who had been allowed to emigrate in 1987 after years of refusal, during which he was not allowed to perform in public. It occurred to Mrs. Feltsman that the Reagans could show their support for the Zimans by stopping at the Ziman apartment on their way to the Kremlin to meet the Gorbachevs. The White House did not inform the embassy in Moscow, much less ask for advice. Apparently the idea was that the Reagans would just drop by, as if spontaneously.

The president's movements are never totally spontaneous, of course, especially in foreign countries. His activities had to be coordinated with the KGB, and when Gorbachev learned that the Reagans might drop in on a refusenik couple even before they called on him and his wife, he was furious. Several days before the Reagans were due to arrive, Alexander Bessmertnykh, then Shevardnadze's deputy, asked me to come by to discuss the visit. He told me that they had been informed of the president's desire to call on the Zimans and made it clear that this could have disastrous consequences. It would embarrass Gorbachev and ensure that any other achievements the summit might make would be overshadowed by the scandal. He added that if Gorbachev was put under this sort of pressure, it would be a very long time, if ever, before the Zimans would be allowed to leave. I asked if we could be assured that the Zimans would receive exit permission promptly provided the Reagans did not call on them. Bessmertnykh answered that he had no authority to give assurances, but he doubted that the Zimans would be allowed to leave the Soviet Union if the Reagans insisted on going to their apartment.

In Helsinki, I discussed the situation with Colin Powell and Howard Baker, the chief of staff. Both said that Nancy Reagan, not the president, was insisting on the call, but both agreed that it could backfire. They undertook to try to persuade the first lady to drop the idea. The Reagans would be meeting with a group of refuseniks and dissidents during the visit, and the Zimans were invited. That would provide an appropriate opportunity for them to demonstrate their support. Furthermore, we could assume, even without formal assurance, that the Zimans would soon be granted exit permission now that the Reagans had shown their personal interest.

So, as it turned out, the Reagans went straight from the airport to call on the Gorbachevs and met the Zimans at Spaso House later. A few weeks after the Reagans left Moscow, the Zimans received permission to leave the Soviet Union. By fall they had settled in the United States. At the time, many senior officials in both countries thought that Nancy Reagan's idea was foolhardy. However, it served its purpose, for it brought home to Gorbachev that Reagan really cared about these issues—enough to threaten disruption of a summit meeting to make his point (or, perhaps, to please his wife—but if that was the case, it was something Gorbachev could understand!).

Debates Without Rancor

IN THEIR MEETINGS, Reagan and Gorbachev dutifully covered some items on all points in the agenda. On SDI and the ABM Treaty they repeated the traditional arguments. Reagan would question why Gorbachev would oppose strategic defenses if their countries had eliminated strategic offensive weapons; Gorbachev would reply that his people suspected that SDI was a program to put offensive weapons in space. Reagan would deny that this was the case and invite Gorbachev to have inspectors at U.S. tests to verify this. Gorbachev would counter that Reagan would not force the navy to allow inspections of its submarines; how could he force the research laboratories to admit Soviet inspectors?

This time, however, these exchanges were not prolonged and they were delivered without heat. The two were like actors wearily reciting a familiar script after it had been decided to postpone indefinitely the play's opening. Since they couldn't come to closure on START and the ABM Treaty, there was no reason for either to make concessions. Still, they could not meet without saying that they had discussed the question.

Generally, both avoided pointless debates. On a growing number of issues they professed the same goals; this allowed them to focus on ways to get there rather than arguing over what the outcome should be. Gorbachev came armed with some jokes and anecdotes so that he could match Reagan when the latter called up some favorite—and not always relevant—story.

Gorbachev made one proposal during their first private meeting that failed to have the result he hoped for. He gave Reagan a paragraph of general principles that he hoped the two could agree on and announce publicly. To the nonspecialist it sounded innocuous, indeed anodyne. It contained language such as a pledge to solve disputes by peaceful means, to avoid force or the threat of force, and to follow the principle of peaceful coexistence. To professional diplomats, however, it sounded like the vague language Nixon and Brezhnev had used in 1972 in their Declaration of Principles, language that, in the U.S. view, Gorbachev's predecessors had systematically violated. Furthermore, it contained the misleading term "peaceful coexistence," which had traditionally been used to justify the Brezhnev Doctrine.*

---

* "Peaceful coexistence" was supposed to apply only to "states with different social systems." This allowed "socialist states" to follow a different principle in relations with each other, such as invading a neighbor to "preserve socialism."

Reagan gave it to his staff after the meeting in an offhanded manner. He said something like "Oh, by the way, Gorbachev wonders if we could agree to something like this. See if there is anything wrong with it." Those who were negotiating the joint statement saw nothing particularly new or useful and their Soviet counterparts did not seem to be familiar with it. Therefore the question was forgotten until Reagan's final formal meeting with Gorbachev. Late in that meeting, Gorbachev asked, "What about the statement I gave you?"

Reagan did not want to admit that he had forgotten it, so he asked for a break to discuss the matter further with his delegation. We walked away from the table and huddled in a corner of the room—Secretary Shultz, Defense Secretary Frank Carlucci, Colin Powell, and Roz Ridgway, the assistant secretary of state for Europe and principal negotiator. Ridgway was most emphatic. "It's the same old general principles that got us in trouble in the past," she said. "I don't think we should go that route. We should insist on concrete agreements."[22] Shultz was also dubious. Their comments made me a bit uneasy. I, too, had been a vigorous critic of the way these principles had been misused in the 1970s. But I thought we faced a different situation in 1988; we were getting some substantial agreements on important issues. Gorbachev seemed to need Reagan's agreement to some language of this sort, probably to convince wavering Politburo members. If so, we should have been sympathetic and tried to find words that would serve his purpose so long as they did no violence to our own positions. What he gave us could probably have been fixed with small alterations, such as specifying "peaceful coexistence of all states."

There was no time, however, to debate the question, and the corner of the conference room in the Kremlin was hardly the place to conduct a frank discussion. Therefore, I said only that I thought the language might be fixed if Gorbachev insisted on a statement of this sort, but agreed that it should not be adopted as it was. Reagan was obviously disappointed with the advice he was getting—he clearly would have preferred to humor Gorbachev—but returned to the table and said that he couldn't accept the paragraph but would prefer the language in the joint statement the working group was negotiating.

Gorbachev accepted the decision, but made it clear that he considered the rejection a personal affront. He recalls this incident in his memoirs, as does Shultz, who writes that he was proud of rejecting language "that might have been drafted by Gromyko."[23] Shultz was right that much of the language was traditional Soviet rhetoric. That was the point. Gorbachev was using some old bottles for his new wine.

After the Reagans had left Moscow I asked Alexander Bessmertnykh, who had negotiated the final statement with Roz Ridgway, why Gorbachev had not handled his proposal through diplomatic channels. I told him I could imagine ways that we might have worked out something that would serve his purposes, but it could not be done the way he did it, trying in effect to take the president by surprise. Bessmertnykh said that Gorbachev's proposal took him by surprise too. He had not been informed of it in advance and had no instructions to negotiate a statement of that sort.

Years later, I asked Gorbachev why he had handled the matter as he had. He told me that he had done so on purpose, in order to challenge Reagan to make a decision on his own. He seemed oblivious to the problem the statement presented for Reagan or to the fact that, if he had explained candidly why he needed it, Reagan would have found a way to accommodate him. But the relationship had not yet developed to the point that that was possible.

Championing Freedom

IN MOSCOW, WHAT was said by Reagan and Gorbachev to each other was less important than what Reagan said to the Soviet public. Gorbachev's rant to Shultz in April over Reagan's Springfield speech had its effect. Speechwriters were instructed to be nice. And, for once, they were, but not because they glossed over real issues. White House speechwriters finally found the right balance between candor about problems and encouragement for healthy change. The speeches were upbeat and avoided crowing about American victories, even as they gave a push to causes on the American agenda. Reagan also exhibited a remarkable degree of cultural empathy. While he concentrated on important themes on the American agenda, he did so with sensitivity to the concerns of ordinary Soviet citizens and praise for the nation's cultural values. As Shevardnadze would comment, he showed respect.

His first public meeting was at Spaso House with a group of persons who had been refused permission to emigrate or had been repressed because they had criticized the Communist system. The White House persisted in labeling the guests "dissidents," but I preferred to call them "democratic activists." Now that Gorbachev was talking about democratization, why not suggest by the terminology we used that they were supporters of his reforms, I argued. (It took a while for this idea to catch on.) Reagan's message to the group included praise for their courage and perseverance, but also assurance that things were improving and that their cause was likely to prevail before long.

When he spoke to prominent writers, artists, and musicians at the Writers' Club, he praised the achievements of glasnost but pressed for publication of some still-banned works, such as Alexander Solzhenitsyn's *The Gulag Archipelago*. The applause was genuine and prolonged. Sergei Zalygin, the editor of *Novyi Mir,* the most prestigious Soviet literary journal, caught up with me as we left the hall to say, "Tell the president we agree with him." He asked me to let the president know that *The Gulag Archipelago* would soon be published in the Soviet Union.

Before his trip to Moscow, Reagan had made several statements supporting greater religious freedom in the Soviet Union and complimenting Gorbachev for the respect he had begun to demonstrate for the Russian Orthodox Church. He had hoped to arrange a meeting with the patriarch, but negotiations with the Russian Orthodox Church hierarchy turned out to be as difficult as they had been with Gorbachev's predecessors. The patriarch was willing to meet with the president, but only if the president refused to meet some priests out of favor with the church bureaucracy, such as the dedicated democrat Father Gleb Yakunin, who—unlike most of the hierarchs—had never collaborated with the KGB.

The result was that Reagan met Father Yakunin but not Patriarch Pimen. Instead of calling on the patriarch, he visited a monastery to meet with the monks and two metropolitans (whose status is similar to cardinals in the Roman Catholic Church). In his remarks to the church people assembled, Reagan praised the freedom that the Orthodox Church had recently been granted and added that he trusted that the Ukrainian Catholic (Uniate) Church would soon be allowed to function as well. Since the Russian Orthodox Church opposed the rehabilitation of the Ukrainian Church, suppressed by Stalin, the latter appeal was not welcome. It was important, however, for Reagan to put things the way he did, on the advice of historian and Librarian of Congress James Billington, who understood the ecclesiastical and political issues involved.

The fact was that the Russian Orthodox Church had indeed suffered greatly from repression, but it had never been outlawed. And now that Gorbachev was restoring some measure of religious freedom, the Russian Orthodox Church bureaucracy was arguing against granting other religious groups the same freedom it sought and was receiving. It was important for Reagan to make clear that the United States supported religious freedom, period, not the reestablishment of Russian Orthodoxy as an exclusive state religion.[24]

Each of Reagan's public appearances was before an important group, but his address to students and faculty at Moscow State University was the centerpiece of his trip. His theme was freedom, and he electrified his audience with a vision of how their futures would be brighter as the shackles of totalitarianism were dropped. His vocabulary was quite different from Gorbachev's, but in Moscow at that time his speech rang out as a paean to Gorbachev's perestroika. The prolonged standing ovation he received was probably the most enthusiastic he had witnessed since the demonstration that followed his nomination at the Republican convention.

End of the Evil Empire

IT WAS IMPLICIT in his speeches, all of which were forward-looking and optimistic. But it took a question from a reporter to make it explicit and official. As he and Gorbachev were walking in Red Square, a journalist asked the inevitable question: "Do you still consider this an evil empire?"

"No," Reagan replied. "That was another time, another era."

Reagan's onetime reference to an "evil empire" five years back had been repeated endlessly and accepted by many to represent the sum total of his policy toward the Soviet Union. And now his denial that the term fit Gorbachev's Soviet Union spread among the Soviet population with the instantaneous speed of modern communications. It made them pay more attention to other things he said, such as his admiration for Russian women, accustomed to holding a full-time job while maintaining a household in the midst of scarcity, his love for Russian literature and music, his sympathy for the terrible human losses during World War II and to Stalin's terror.

Ronald Reagan was no enemy, but a friend who understood what they had suffered and did not blame them for the oppressors who had kept them captive. If Reagan believed the country was overcoming its past, then Gorbachev had to be doing something right, most Soviet citizens reasoned. He gave them confidence that they could accomplish what most had feared even dreaming of.

To judge from comments in his memoirs, what impressed Gorbachev most was Reagan's refusal to take credit for the changes in the Soviet Union. Gorbachev recounts that at a press conference Reagan was asked, "Who deserves credit for it—you or Gorbachev?"

"Mr. Gorbachev deserves most of the credit, as the leader of this country," Reagan replied, to Gorbachev's evident delight.[25]

Reagan's comments in Moscow in 1988 probably did more than any other single event to build support in the Soviet Union for Gorbachev's reforms. By the end of 1988, Gorbachev's popularity reached its zenith. And Reagan's? By the time he left office, and even for a year or more after, his popularity was probably greater in the Soviet Union than in any other country, including the United States—except, perhaps, in some of the captive nations of Eastern Europe.

Reagan made a deep impression on the people of the Soviet Union, but they impressed him as well. He had spoken in his January 1984 speech about an American and a Soviet couple who meet and find to their surprise that they have similar interests and desires. The idea that ordinary people everywhere have much in common was one of Reagan's bedrock convictions, and what he saw of people in Moscow reinforced it.

Of course it helped that they cheered him. Reagan was as appreciative of public adulation as was Gorbachev (what politician isn't?), and the popularity each attracted in the other's country strengthened confidence that they could solve problems together.

XV

1988: July–December

THE COLD WAR ENDS–
IN PRINCIPLE

Every nation . . . must . . . refrain from the use of force. Freedom of choice is a
sine qua non. . . . We must join forces to ensure the primacy of universal
human values.
—Mikhail Gorbachev, summarizing his speech to the United Nations, 1988[1]

The meeting [on Governors Island] was a tremendous success. . . . Gorbachev
sounded as if he saw us as partners making a better world.
—Ronald Reagan, 1990[2]

GORBACHEV WENT INTO the Communist Party Conference with strong momentum a few weeks after Air Force One took the Reagans back to Washington. He had rammed through the Central Committee most of his ideas for reform, and the glow on East-West relations that followed Reagan's visit put the hardline opposition off balance. They could no longer argue plausibly that the Soviet Union faced such threats from abroad that it could not risk any changes in the political system at home. Gorbachev had successfully fused a relaxation of Cold War tensions with domestic political reform.

The Party Conference endorsed changes of such importance that, as they were implemented, they doomed the Party's control of the country. Contested elections, real power to the elected legislature, an end to Party apparatchik control of government institutions, an independent judiciary, the presumption of innocence in criminal proceedings—most of the fundamental ideas of democratic governance—were adopted in principle. All were directly contrary to Soviet practice up to then.

How could this happen? How could a group of ruling bureaucrats, imbued with the cynicism required to survive in the ideological never-never land and dog-eat-dog politics of the Communist Party, vote for principles that would ultimately separate them from the power they had begun to assume was a birthright?

Some understood the implications of Gorbachev's proposals (they had shown this earlier in the year by publishing and praising an article defending Stalinism by Nina Andreyeva, a teacher in Leningrad) but could not bring themselves to oppose the Party's general secretary. Also, they probably thought that they would manage to block implementation of the most threatening changes. For example, elections could be ostensibly free and contested, but surely a clever Party official could see to it that he always won! Principles like the supremacy of legislatures and independence of judges were already guaranteed on paper and systematically ignored. Most officials probably assumed that Gorbachev would continue the usual practices lest his own power be undermined.

Most Communist bigwigs simply failed to grasp that Gorbachev really meant to change things. Throughout their careers they had seen high-sounding "reforms" come and go without things really changing. What could be wrong with helping a general secretary pull the wool over the eyes of a credulous foreign public? If the CIA, as Robert Gates said, thought Gorbachev was interested only in increasing Soviet power, it must know something important! There was no need to worry; these foreign-sounding ideas were all just eyewash.

So Gorbachev got most of what he wanted. The Politburo and Central Committee balked only at declaring that the Soviet Union should have a pluralistic political system. They would not endorse the idea that the Communist Party could have competitors. But, of course, if the other reforms took place, the Communist Party would not be able to avoid competitors. Most found this out only when it was too late.

Even after the Party Conference, however, Yegor Ligachev and other Party "conservatives" tried to vitiate Gorbachev's program. For a brief period there was an indirect debate over a fundamental ideological principle: was Soviet foreign policy to be based on "the common interests of mankind" or on the interests of the "proletariat" in the "international class struggle"? In late July, Shevardnadze told a conference at the Soviet Ministry of Foreign . Affairs that "peaceful coexistence" was not a form of the "class struggle." Within days, Ligachev, speaking in Gorky (Nizhny Novgorod), insisted that the "class character of international relations was paramount." Then, Alexander Yakovlev took issue with Ligachev's proposition and defended mankind's common interests in a speech in Vilnius, Lithuania.³ When I asked Shevardnadze what we should make of this debate, he assured me that Gorbachev's view was the official one, and compared Ligachev's dissent to Caspar Weinberger's arguments with George Shultz.

Contacts by senior U.S. and Soviet officials expanded rapidly. Frank Carlucci, who had replaced Caspar Weinberger as secretary of defense, promptly established contact with Dmitri Yazov, the Soviet minister of defense. They met in Bern, Switzerland, and then Carlucci came to Moscow in August to initiate a series of reciprocal visits of senior military officers. John Whitehead, deputy secretary of state, came to Moscow to review the overall state of negotiations and give them a push. Michael Armacost, an under secretary of state, was designated to coordinate the consultations on regional conflicts. These talks were beginning to show progress now that Soviet troops were leaving Afghanistan and Soviet officials began a serious search for peaceful solutions to fighting elsewhere.

Shultz and Shevardnadze continued to work on the issues that still blocked an agreement to reduce strategic offensive weapons (START). Both hoped that an agreement might be completed for Reagan and Gorbachev to sign before Reagan's term ended, but they did not succeed. Gorbachev was unwilling to allow the Strategic Defense Initiative to proceed as Reagan wished, and until he did, Reagan was not willing to accept the sort of limitations on cruise missiles that Soviet negotiators demanded.

Actually, though both Shultz and Shevardnadze were acting in good faith, most Washington officials had decided that it would be a mistake to conclude an agreement on strategic arms before there was one to reduce conventional weapons in Europe to equivalent levels. After all, an original purpose of the nuclear weapons was to compensate for the Warsaw Pact superiority in conventional weaponry. Key senators advised that a START treaty would be in trouble if it was sent for ratification before the conventional imbalance had been corrected.

Although he had supported all of the arms reduction initiatives Reagan had made, Vice President Bush was not eager to have a START agreement signed the last year of the Reagan administration. He knew that he would have to indulge in some hardline rhetoric to pacify the Republican Party's right wing and it would be difficult to fight for ratification of a major arms reduction agreement at the same time. Besides, he did not want his administration to look like a mere continuation of the Reagan administration. To him, it seemed far better to delay any START agreement until he was settled in as president and had some other achievements to his credit. Therefore, he gave no active push to these negotiations in 1988.

Gorbachev at the United Nations

DESPITE THE STALLED negotiations on strategic arms, relations with the United States and Western Europe on other issues were progressing rapidly. Gorbachev decided that it was time to gain further publicity for the Soviet Union's new policies by delivering a major speech to the United Nations.

Chernyaev has described how a group of advisers worked for weeks on the speech. As was often the habit in preparing major addresses, the group convened at a villa out of town and worked late into the night for days on end, discussing and working out language for Gorbachev to use. Gorbachev would come by from time to time, read their drafts, then dictate his own.[4] The result was an address that, as Gorbachev intended, galvanized the world's attention.

The speech set forth the principles of "new thinking" in clear terms, with emphasis on the right of countries to make their own choices. In other words, he announced a formal end to the Brezhnev Doctrine that required "socialist" states to stay "socialist," as the Soviet leaders defined the term, or else risk invasion. In this instance, freedom of choice also meant that the "international class struggle" was no longer the foundation of Soviet foreign policy.

Proclaiming these principles, already mentioned in some limited contexts, was one thing. If that had been all, the speech would have attracted only modest attention. Without concrete examples of what the Soviet Union was prepared to do, they were little more than vague promises. Therefore, what struck most observers about the speech was not its ideological content, but the announcement that the Soviet Union would reduce its armed forces by at least a half million men, without requiring any concessions from its adversaries.

Finally, Gorbachev seemed to be prepared to do what he had been talking about privately for a year and a half. The applause in the hall at the United Nations was more prolonged than any the assembled delegates could remember.

Just as he had been stirred by the public acclaim he had received in Washington the year before, Gorbachev was moved by the applause at the United Nations and the enthusiastic editorial comment in key American newspapers. Chernyaev puts it this way:

> Much has been written about the impression that Gorbachev made on the world in his UN speech. But we also have to consider the impact on him of the

world's response to his speech. . . . Having received such broad recognition and support, having been "certified" a world class leader of great authority, he could be faster and surer in shaking off the fetters of the past in all aspects of foreign policy.[5]

Reagan, Gorbachev, and Bush on Governors Island

GORBACHEV MET BOTH Reagan and President-elect George Bush on Governors Island the day after his UN speech. It was to be largely a courtesy meeting and no negotiations were planned. Just before he arrived for the meeting, however, we received the news that there had been a serious earthquake in Armenia. Gorbachev had also been informed, of course, and he told the Americans when he arrived that the earthquake had done great damage, which was still being assessed.

Since none of the people present yet knew the extent of the tragedy, it did not dominate the meeting, though it was clear that Gorbachev was concerned. The conversation was amiable with pledges from Gorbachev and Bush to continue the policies Reagan and Gorbachev had initiated.

After the three parted, news from Armenia became ever more grim. Tens of thousands were missing; an entire city had been demolished, along with much of the surrounding area. Gorbachev decided to return immediately to Moscow to deal with the catastrophe, canceling his plans for several events in New York and a visit to Cuba.

President Reagan had told Gorbachev on Governors Island that the United States was prepared to help the earthquake victims in any way it could, but Gorbachev felt then that foreign assistance would not be needed. As further reports arrived, however, it was clear that Soviet resources would be strained to the utmost. Officials in the State Department called me to say that they were preparing search-and-rescue teams to leave immediately for Armenia if the Soviet government approved.

In the past, the Soviet government—at least since World War II—had always refused foreign assistance in dealing with natural disasters. Not only did Moscow reject offers of aid, Soviet officials reacted as if they considered offers to assist an insult. "We are capable of dealing with these problems ourselves," they said, and often implied that assistance offers were motivated by a desire to make them look incompetent.

This time it was different. I had been delegated to see Gorbachev off at Kennedy Airport, and I told him that we sympathized deeply with the people in Armenia and that we were prepared to rush any assistance that could be helpful. We were waiting only for his word.

He seemed grateful, thanked me for our concern, and, though he did not request U.S. aid on the spot, said that he would let us know as soon as he returned to Moscow and was briefed fully on the situation.

A few hours after his return, the Soviet government informed all the countries that had offered help that it would be appreciated. The United States had a plane in the air with rescue workers, sniffer dogs, tents, and blankets within hours after the word was given. Julia Taft, the coordinator for disaster assistance, personally accompanied the first team to Armenia. They got there in time to rescue some people still alive in the rubble.

By changing Soviet policy on an issue that involved national pride, Gorbachev showed that he meant it when he talked of common human values. He had taken down one more barrier that had prevented normal interaction with the Soviet Union.

Gorbachev Orders Full Speed Ahead

GORBACHEV HAD NOT bothered to clear his UN speech with the Politburo before it was delivered. Immediately after his return to Moscow he and most other Soviet leaders were preoccupied with the earthquake damage in Armenia. We can also infer that not all of Gorbachev's colleagues were happy with the way he had discarded traditional Communist ideology. It was not until December 27 and 28 that the Politburo met to discuss how to implement the policies Gorbachev had set forth in his UN address.

Excerpts from the minutes of that meeting available to us[6] make clear that Gorbachev was on the defensive when he commented on his address to the United Nations. Nevertheless, the minutes contain no direct criticism of the speech by other Politburo members, and Gorbachev proceeded to order concrete steps to implement the policy he had announced.

Before his December 7 UN speech, he explained, some in the West had been claiming that perestroika was only words, designed to lull the public. But his announcement of troop cuts had "pulled the rug out from under" such critics. Now, he said, conservatives in the United States and Europe feared that Soviet "new thinking" was real and therefore would impede attempts by hardliners in the West to continue the arms race. He claimed his speech had created a tidal wave of world public opinion that had put the American military-industrial complex on the defensive. This meant that the

Soviet Union had to implement the troop cuts he had announced as quickly as possible in order to force the United States to cool the arms race.

Gorbachev also discussed his impression of George H.W. Bush, who would assume the presidency of the United States in a few weeks. Gorbachev felt that Bush was more cautious than Reagan, but that he would not deliberately "exacerbate relations" with the Soviet Union. Nevertheless, he believed that people on Bush's team "were brought up in the years of the Cold War and still do not have any foreign policy alternative to the traditional postwar course of the United States." Therefore the Soviet leaders should not expect "big breakthroughs," but should adopt an active policy that would force Bush to continue Reagan's policy of improving relations.

Yegor Ligachev, still formally number two in the Communist Party, endorsed Gorbachev's recommendations, even conceding that there were "common interests of countries with different social-economic systems," one of which was the need to reduce military budgets. One would not have known from this that he had been publicly defending the international class struggle just a few months earlier.

The only debate during the meeting seems to have been over whether the Soviet people should be informed of the size of the Soviet military. Shevardnadze argued for full disclosure of current strength and of the reductions that would be implemented. Marshal Dmitri Yazov, the defense minister, assured the group that the Soviet military leaders endorsed the force reductions Gorbachev had announced and had plans in place to implement them, including withdrawals from Eastern Europe. But he objected to Shevardnadze's demand to supply the Supreme Soviet (and thus the public) with the facts about the size of Soviet military forces. "The Americans don't tell us everything," Yazov claimed, and therefore the Soviet government should also keep some things secret. Since U.S. intelligence and NATO were well informed about the size of the Soviet military establishment, what apparently worried Yazov was admitting that figures Soviet officials had supplied in negotiations had been false.

Gorbachev agreed with Yazov that some secrets would be kept for a time, but not for the reason Yazov gave. Gorbachev felt that the Soviet public would demand to know why the Soviet leadership had so overbuilt its military establishment. If the people knew the truth, they would insist on even steeper cuts than those planned, like a 75 percent reduction, Gorbachev mused. He suggested that they wait until they had reduced their defense budget to a level "somewhat closer to the American expenditures" before coming clean about the magnitude of the military burden. "If we admit now that we cannot build a long-term economic and social policy without [cuts], we will be forced to explain why," he stated. "Today we cannot tell even the Party about it; first of all we should put things in order."

Though he opposed disclosing the true size of the military burden, Gorbachev was not in doubt about what had to be done.

He called the Soviet situation "disastrous" and remarked that year after year they had been planning military expenses "twice as large as the [planned] increase in national income." Even after national income tanked, they stuck to the plan to increase military expenditures. The result was a situation "worse than that in any other country, except maybe the poorest ones."

Shevardnadze prompted, "In Angola, for instance."

Gorbachev agreed, but pointed out that "everything is different there."

He concluded the meeting by instructing a small group, including Shevardnadze and Yakovlev, to finalize instructions to carry out the promises he had made in his speech to the United Nations.

Gorbachev's argument at this meeting adopted the logic he had used earlier in regard to the INF Treaty and the withdrawal from Afghanistan. "The Americans really want those missiles in Europe, so we'll call their bluff and accept their hypocritical proposal to eliminate them." "They want to keep us bleeding in Afghanistan, so we'll show them we can leave." And now it was "They really want an arms race"—or, sometimes, "Their military-industrial complex is trying to continue the arms race."

Whether Gorbachev really believed this is not of great importance. (He must have known that his arguments were half-truths at best.) Other considerations are more significant. First, his argument was a ploy to dodge the accusation that he was knuckling under to American pressure. Second, the result Gorbachev sought *was* in the Soviet interest, even if the reasons he gave were disingenuous. Along with political reform there was nothing the Soviet Union needed so much as a reduction of military forces and of the cost of maintaining them.

More broadly and significantly, Gorbachev's arguments at this meeting show that, in practice, he had abandoned the key tenets of Soviet Cold War psychology. There is no mention whatever of an obligation to defend the "socialist commonwealth" or to fulfill an international duty to support "progressive" revolutions. There are no references to American imperialism; the threat he cites is not that of imperialist aggression but rather a trap to lure the Soviet Union into an arms race that will ruin it. More than that, he was suggesting, clearly though implicitly, that his predecessors had pounced on the cheese in the trap. If the Soviet Union had so overbuilt its military forces that its public, had it known the facts, would demand they be slashed to a quarter of their size, then the Soviet Union bore some responsibility for the fear and hostility prevalent in the West. He had said as much in Politburo meetings the year before, but now he was doing something about it.

So far as arms control was concerned, his negotiators still sought limitations on SDI before they would agree to the reduction of strategic nuclear forces. But the imbalance of conventional weapons was a greater impediment to further nuclear reductions. Until the Soviet Union agreed to balance conventional weapons in Europe, which it finally did in 1990, it would be difficult to secure U.S. Senate approval for a strategic arms reduction treaty.

The voluntary reduction of troops and conventional weapons Gorbachev offered in December 1988 was the first major step the Soviet Union took to prove that its military doctrine had indeed been revised to stress defense. It put life into the negotiations between the two military alliances to reduce conventional weapons in Europe to comparable levels.

Outsiders, of course, did not know at the time what Gorbachev said to the Politburo toward the end of 1988. Now that we can read a record of that meeting we can see that Ronald Reagan had accurately sensed Gorbachev's attitude when they met on Governors Island. Gorbachev was indeed prepared to act as a partner, not because the United States demanded it, but because he could see that the Soviet attempt to compete with the United States had led to disaster. He had no choice but to end the Cold War and find ways to cooperate.

Psychologically and ideologically, the Cold War was over before Ronald Reagan moved out of the White House.

XVI

⸻ ∼ ⸻

WHAT THEN?

I think the Cold War is not over.
—BRENT SCOWCROFT, statement on ABC television, January 22, 1989

The Cold War Is Over
—Headline on an editorial in the *New York Times,* April 2, 1989

PRESIDENT REAGAN MAY have sensed that Gorbachev was talking like a partner when they met in December 1988, but George Bush was not so confident. Although he had assured Gorbachev that he would continue the cooperation Reagan had started as soon as political considerations permitted, he and his senior advisers were skeptical. They still suspected that Gorbachev was out to improve the Soviet economy so that the Soviet Union could more successfully pursue its traditional agenda. And, in fact, many problems still existed in East-West relations. Europe was still divided, although the Iron Curtain was riddled with leaks and Gorbachev's team was busy dismantling large portions of it. Soviet troops were not all out of Afghanistan, and the Soviet Union continued to supply arms and political support to insurgencies in Africa and Latin America. Soviet officials had begun to talk about extensive democratization but had not yet done much to bring it about. Some people who wanted to emigrate were still refused exit visas, and authorities still allowed few Soviet citizens to travel abroad. Negotiations between NATO and the Warsaw Pact to reduce conventional arms had not established a nonthreatening balance, and Gorbachev still held a strategic arms reduction pact hostage to the Strategic Defense Initiative.

Those who believed the Cold War was about an imbalance of weaponry or moves on a geopolitical chessboard argued that it was far from over. Those who were convinced that a clash of ideology lay behind the arms race and the geopolitical struggle saw it differently. If Gorbachev acted in accord with his pronouncements—that Soviet foreign policy should be based on the common interests of mankind, that a nation's right to choose its system and alliances should not be limited, and that a country could not ensure its own security at the expense of others—the Cold War would be over.

The Cold War's End Confirmed

WHEN GEORGE H.W. BUSH took the oath of office, he could not be certain that Gorbachev had made or would make the hard choices that his "new thinking" required. It would have been prudent to welcome Gorbachev's statements and say that if he meant what he said and could deliver the changes he was talking about, the Cold War would be behind us. Instead, he encouraged the view that the Cold War was not over and therefore he needed a few months to review policy toward the Soviet Union. The policy review implied that President Reagan had been too accommodating toward the end of his administration, even though, as vice president, Bush had been intimately involved in the development of Reagan's policy and had supported all Reagan's moves in regard to the Soviet Union.

President Bush needed a policy review not to understand the issues or to revise policy, but to reassure the right wing of the Republican Party that he was not soft on the Soviet Union and to find a way to distinguish his policy from Reagan's. In contrast to Reagan's attempt to unify the Republican Party by making Bush his vice president and giving senior jobs to Bush's political associates, Bush excluded most "Reaganites" from his cabinet and other senior positions. Perhaps he felt that he had to put on a show of toughness to insulate himself from right-wing criticism.

To be sure, George Bush had put Gorbachev on notice that he might have to say things in his political campaign that seemed less forthcoming than his policy would be.[1] Therefore, Gorbachev was careful not to react to statements made during the presidential campaign. However, he did not expect Bush to put the relationship on hold once he was elected. When Bush's policy review extended into months, both Gorbachev and Shevardnadze began to worry that Bush was not prepared to maintain the process that had gathered momentum in 1987 and 1988, despite the fact that Bush had assured Gorbachev at Governors Island that he would focus on expanding and deepening U.S.-Soviet cooperation.

Meanwhile, throughout 1989, reform in the Soviet Union picked up speed. An elected legislature convened in March with former dissident Andrei Sakharov playing a conspicuous role. Movements seeking greater autonomy mushroomed in many of the non-Russian republics. The Soviet media showed ever greater independence and some publications stepped up efforts to expose atrocities of the past and to criticize the extravagant Soviet military spending. Soviet troops were withdrawn from Afghanistan as promised and countries in Eastern Europe began to cast out their Communist governments. This time there was no Warsaw Pact invasion to restore "socialism," but instead invitations to the new government leaders to visit Moscow. In November the Berlin Wall was breached and then dismantled by ecstatic crowds.

All this happened before President Bush met Gorbachev on Malta in early December and, finally, resumed the active policy Reagan had followed during his final years in office. Within a year, the Iron Curtain had disappeared, the countries of East and Central Europe had elected governments, Germany was united and allowed to remain in NATO, a treaty was concluded to reduce conventional weapons in Europe to equally low levels, Shevardnadze had dropped the attempt to cripple SDI as a condition for an agreement on strategic nuclear arms,* and the Soviet Union voted in the Security Council to condemn and resist Iraq's invasion of Kuwait.[2]

Throughout 1989 and 1990 it was obvious that Gorbachev was acting in accord with the principles he had proclaimed in 1988. He had removed the ideological basis for the Cold War, and his willingness to settle contentious issues on terms the West had set proved that his change of policy had been genuine.

Who Won?

GEORGE H.W. BUSH boasted during his unsuccessful bid for a second term, "We won the Cold War!" In fact, the Cold War had ended in spirit be-

---

* The START I treaty was not signed until President Bush visited Moscow in July 1991, but its key provisions had been agreed before the end of 1990.

fore he took office as president. All he had to do was set the terms of settlement, and he hesitated for ten months to do that. The tree that bore fruit on the Bush watch had been planted and nurtured by Reagan and Gorbachev. As for winners, everyone, including the Soviet Union, won.

The Soviet Union would have benefited from the end of the Cold War if it had been able to transform itself into a pluralistic, democratic state with a government of limited powers, the rule of law, and a market economy. Gorbachev cooperated to end the Cold War because he knew the Soviet Union could not be reformed if the Cold War continued.

Reagan understood this very well. He writes in his memoirs not of a victory of one country over another but of the triumph of one idea over another. "Democracy triumphed in the cold war because it was a battle of values— between one system that gave preeminence to the state and another that gave preeminence to the individual and freedom."[3]

Gorbachev made a similar point when he wrote: "Who gained by the termination of that [cold] war? Here the answer is obvious: Every country, all the peoples of the world, benefited."[4]

It was the Communist system and the ideology that inspired it that lost the competition with liberal democracy and capitalism, not the country it held in its grip for seven decades with catastrophic results.

Repercussions

THE END OF the Cold War had a bearing on two other major developments, though it did not cause them directly: the end of Communist rule in the USSR and the collapse of the Soviet Union itself. These spectacular developments occurred in such quick succession that they are often perceived as aspects of a single event. It is a mistake, however, to consider breaking the Communist monopoly of power in the country or the subsequent disintegration of the Soviet Union as ending the Cold War. They were separate events, made possible, but not inevitable, when the Cold War ended.

Theoretically, at least, the Cold War could have ended with Communist rule intact in the Soviet Union—something Gorbachev intended when he began the process of reconciliation with the West. Also, Communist rule could have ended in the Soviet Union without the destruction of the Soviet state—something Gorbachev intended when he pressed the reforms that destroyed the Communist Party's monopoly of power.

The Communist Party Loses Control

OFFICIAL SOVIET IDEOLOGY justified the Communist Party's monopoly of power by the claim that the Party was the sole legitimate representative of the "proletarian class" in its struggle with the "bourgeois class." If, however, the Soviet state based its foreign policy ultimately on "the common interests of mankind," there was no room for the "class struggle."

By the 1970s and 1980s, most people in the Soviet Union put little stock in Marxist theory if they thought about it at all. Nor did they pay attention to the debate in 1988 over the relevance of the "international class struggle" to Soviet foreign policy. Nevertheless, it was important when Gorbachev discarded the concept in his speech at the United Nations in December 1988. Though it was not Gorbachev's intention at the time to undermine Communist Party rule in the Soviet Union—he still hoped to convert the Party to one that could govern the country through democratic processes—in fact he removed the ideological cornerstone of Communist dictatorship.

Politics is not always, or even often, determined by logic, and there was no automatic connection between renunciation of the class struggle hypothesis and the dissolution of the Party dictatorship. If Stalin had decided to renounce the class struggle and substitute some other pretext for his dictatorship, that would have changed little—at least during his lifetime. But Gorbachev did more than revise ideology; he went on to attack the system that guaranteed a Communist monopoly of power. The opening of the information media to critical articles about the past and introduction of contested elections in 1989 created pressures that placed the Communist bosses on the defensive. By 1990 they had little choice but to agree to Gorbachev's proposals to create a presidency (which gave Gorbachev authority to bypass the party Politburo) and to remove the constitutional sanction of the Communist Party as the sole legal political party. None of this, however, would have happened if the general secretary of the CPSU had not insisted upon it. So thorough was the Communist Party's control of the country, and so authoritative was the general secretary's position in the Party, that no other individual or group could have peacefully liberated the Soviet Union from the Party's dictatorship.

Communist rule ended in the Soviet Union not because of Western pressure or because the Cold War was over. It ended because its leader came to understand that the system under which the Soviet Union had been ruled since the Bolshevik Revolution was a barrier to its future development. When the Party proved incapable of adapting itself to a different system of rule, to political openness and democracy, its rule had to be destroyed. Such was the logic of Gorbachev's actions in 1989, 1990, and 1991.

When, having been pushed from the center of power, many of Gorbachev's lieutenants conspired to remove him in August 1991, Communist Party control over the country had become so weakened that their attempt brought a sudden end to the Communist Party structure that had persisted for decades.

This is not to say that the steps to end the Cold War had no influence on subsequent developments. Of course they did, for it is inconceivable that political reforms could have progressed in the Soviet Union unless the Cold War was coming to an end. Reagan's policies denied Gorbachev an easy out: to limit arms and see if that would work. Once Gorbachev understood that the arms race would not be tamed nor the country's economic ills cured without opening the country to outside influence and initiating democratic reforms, the internal reform process began in earnest. Once Gorbachev started the reform process, Reagan recognized that it was in the American interest to encourage it.

In sum, Gorbachev cooperated with Reagan to end the Cold War, and Reagan cooperated with Gorbachev to legitimize the democratic process with the Soviet public. But it was Mikhail Gorbachev, not Ronald Reagan or George H.W. Bush, who ended Communist rule in the Soviet Union.

The Soviet Union Falls Apart

A MULTI-PART television "docudrama" on the Cold War produced by Sir Jeremy Isaacs and shown on CNN pictures the breakup of the Soviet Union as the event marking the end of the Cold War. When I advised the producer before the film's release that this was a misrepresentation of history, he objected, arguing that the collapse of the Soviet Union provided a more dramatic close to the series than ending at an earlier point. He was doubtless correct if his criterion was dramatic effect. But drama and history are separate genres and to distort the latter in the interest of the former is inexcusable in a production that pretends to be documentary.[5]

The fact is that the Cold War ended well before the Soviet Union collapsed. Even if one holds that it did not end until all the major problems engendered by the Cold War were solved, one can hardly argue that it continued after that.

The Soviet Union collapsed as a state *despite* the end of the Cold War, not because of it. The end of the Cold War gave its leaders an opportunity to reform its system of governance without pressures from outside. Their failure to do so can be attributed to the inherent difficulty of the task as well as opposition by much of the Communist Party and tactical mistakes by President Gorbachev.[6]

Of course, those reforms that undermined the Communist Party's control of the country created conditions that made the subsequent breakup of the Soviet Union possible. To the degree that they were stimulated by a desire to end the Cold War, there is a link going back to President Reagan's four-part agenda. But it was not the United States or the West that brought the Soviet Union down. In 1991 both American and West European leaders would have preferred to see the Soviet Union preserved as a democratic federation (minus the Baltic countries, of course) than broken up, as actually occurred. That is why President George Bush advised the non-Russian Soviet republics in August 1991 to endorse Gorbachev's union treaty.[7]

Ultimately, Mikhail Gorbachev deserves credit for the fact that the Soviet collapse was peaceful in its core areas. By relinquishing power peacefully when the leaders of most Soviet republics demanded it, Gorbachev set an important precedent for the future in both Russia and Ukraine, the two most populous Soviet republics.

Why Did the Cold War End When It Did?

THE ULTIMATE COLLAPSE of the Soviet system was probably inevitable, but it was not inevitable that the Cold War would end when it did, or that it would end peacefully. Many explanations that have been offered for the Cold War's end are not convincing. Most focus on one factor and give little attention to others that were crucial. Several things had to happen for the Cold War to end when and as it did.

The United States had to convince the Soviet leader that his country would not be allowed to win an arms race, or benefit from ending it without other changes in policy. The Soviet leader also had to understand that his country's interests required not only different policies but fundamental reform of the Soviet system. When that happened, it was important for the United States to support the reform process as best it could, avoiding any demand for "regime change." Face-to-face meetings between the Soviet and American leaders and their policy makers were essential to move the U.S.-Soviet dialogue in a constructive direction. Under these conditions, the overwhelming suspicion characteristic of the Cold War was gradually replaced by trust—not blind trust, but trust supported and reinforced by proof that promises were kept.

These developments alone, however, would not have ended the Cold War unless both American and Soviet leaders had possessed the political stature and tactical skill at home to make their agreements stick. Once Ronald Reagan and Mikhail Gorbachev occupied the highest political office in their respective countries, the process this book describes became possible. Their decisions ultimately brought the Cold War to an end.

The set of ideas, beliefs, and characteristics that Reagan brought to his office enabled him to deal effectively with Gorbachev. He understood that the Cold War was ultimately about ideology. He saw both the arms race and geopolitical competition as symptoms of an ideological struggle, not its causes. Unlike many of his advisers, he believed the Soviet system could change. Reagan welcomed and supported Gorbachev's reforms because he thought that a more open Soviet Union with an informed and empowered public would not threaten the United States or its neighbors. He believed in his ability to persuade, but he was not an arrogant know-it-all. He welcomed opportunities to learn more, not only about the issues but also, and particularly, about the nature and philosophy of the people he dealt with.

His greatest asset was his character. He dealt with others, whether friends, adversaries, or subordinates, openly and without guile. Transparency of intent is so unusual among political leaders that many observers, to this day, fail to recognize it and to appreciate the contribution it made to Reagan's effectiveness.

And Gorbachev? He, too, came to office with a combination of ideas and character traits that was unique among Soviet leaders. When experience conflicted with theory, he was willing to question the theory. He was convinced that the Soviet Union could not go on as it had and needed to change. Like Reagan, he was confident of his ability to communicate and convince. He was a master at manipulating Communist Party officials to prevent their blocking change even when his reforms undermined their power. Unlike Reagan, he was often devious about his ultimate political purpose. If he had declared his intentions openly, he would have been removed from office as soon as the Politburo learned what he really had in mind.

Gorbachev's thinking evolved under the pressure of events. "New thinking" replaced "old thinking" over a period of years, not all at once. By 1990, Gorbachev became the first Soviet leader to put the interests of the country as he understood them above those of the Communist Party. He was the only Soviet or Russian leader in history to use force last, not first, to solve serious political problems. He was the only Soviet leader to place principle above personal rule. He left office without any attempt to preserve his position by using force against his opponents.

Neither Reagan nor Gorbachev played a perfect hand. In 1987, Reagan was weakened and distracted by the Iran-Contra scandal. The personnel changes that occurred in its wake delayed decisions that could have produced treaties on strategic and conventional arms in 1988. Gorbachev could have moved faster to remove Soviet troops from Afghanistan, and could have dropped his opposition to SDI without damage to Soviet interests. Nevertheless, overall, it is difficult to see how the problems could have been solved much faster given their complexity and the entrenched special interests on both sides.

It Took More Than Two

RONALD REAGAN AND Mikhail Gorbachev made indispensable contributions to ending the Cold War, but they could not have done it alone. As we have seen, their foreign ministers, George Shultz and Eduard Shevardnadze, were far more than lieutenants carrying out their superior's orders. Without their efforts neither the American president nor the Soviet general secretary would have gotten his priorities right, and neither would have been able to implement what he wanted to do. Both Shultz and Shevardnadze took on forces in their respective governments that would have blocked agreements, pushed their superiors in the right direction, and often absorbed the heat from controversial decisions. Just as Reagan and Gorbachev brought unique combinations of assets to the task, so did Shultz and Shevardnadze. It is hard to imagine a different pair of foreign ministers who could have achieved what they did.*

Shultz and Shevardnadze also could not have fulfilled their missions without help from inside and outside the organizations they headed. Both selected professional diplomats to do most of the detailed work required in reaching sound agreements. Both also developed some support outside their departments: Shultz had the support more often than he realized of the president's assistant for national security (on Soviet matters, at least); Shevardnadze received important public support from academic think tanks and elements in the Soviet mass media that Alexander Yakovlev (as the Politburo member supervising ideology) had liberated from rigid Party control. He also usually could count on the support of Gorbachev's personal assistant, Ana-

---

* George H.W. Bush's secretary of state, James A. Baker III, also worked effectively with Shevardnadze, but that was under different circumstances. The Cold War had ended in principle, and what remained was intricate "cleanup" diplomacy.

toly Chernyaev—at least after the foreign ministry adopted Gorbachev's "new thinking." Nevertheless, outside the State Department and the Soviet Ministry of Foreign Affairs, most of the government bureaucracy in both countries was not helpful in finding ways to improve U.S.-Soviet relations. Bureaucrats and political appointees in the United States had to be pushed by Reagan; the Communist Party bureaucracy and military establishment had to be pushed by Gorbachev. In both countries, as often as not, those being pushed resisted.

George Shultz followed Alexander Haig's practice of using the American embassy in Moscow actively both to advise on policy and to help execute it. As a result, by the late 1980s, the U.S. government was better informed about developments in the Soviet Union than even Gorbachev, who was often fed false information by the KGB. The embassy was also able to mount an extensive public relations effort in the Soviet Union, using the Soviet media when Gorbachev opened them to outside influences. By the time Reagan left office, American prestige in the Soviet Union had reached a peak not seen since the height of World War II—and not matched since. This greatly facilitated Gorbachev's efforts to come to terms with the United States.

One thing is striking about the decision-making style of both Reagan and Gorbachev. Neither was skilled at managing his bureaucracy—a task left to others—but both were determined to make up their own minds regarding critical issues. Both were capable of reading position papers and then deciding it would be best to follow a different course. Both valued the counsel of a few trusted advisers more than the cautious analyses emerging from the governmental machinery. Both were willing to take political risks, and both were skilled in judging the degree of risk in their respective, very different societies. They didn't always get things right, but on the most critical issues, they finally did.

Why the Misunderstanding?

AS I NOTED at the beginning of this narrative, there are those who give all credit to ending the Cold War to Reagan. There are those who give all credit to Gorbachev. There are those who think neither was responsible; it just expired on its own, they imply, though they usually obscure the absurdity of their judgment with technical mumbo jumbo.

Why is it that, over a decade after the Cold War ended, so many divergent opinions are current regarding its end? There are probably as many reasons as there are views, and a single observer can have more than one motivation. Ignorance of some of the moves and developments I have recounted may lie at the root of many distorted impressions. Other factors are also at play: political partisanship, intellectual arrogance, and wounded *amour-propre* come immediately to mind. It is difficult for some Democrats in the United States and adherents of left-wing parties in Europe to admit that they were wrong about Reagan. Many still entertain a caricature of him as a stupid, ill-informed, reckless politician who stumbled his way through his presidency with inexplicable luck. Persons who criticized the policies that led to the end of the Cold War are often unwilling to admit that their judgment could have been flawed. Those who claimed that Reagan was risking war by confronting the Soviet leaders, or that he should not have linked arms reduction with other issues, or that a nuclear freeze was better than pressing for an actual reduction of weapons often have trouble recognizing that their policies would not have worked—given the nature of the Soviet leadership at the time—and that Reagan's policies actually did.

Persons who give all the credit to Reagan also operate out of a sense of partisanship. They make the mistake of assuming that the pressure Reagan exerted on the Soviet Union was so great that Gorbachev had no choice but to capitulate. Some attribute everything to a single factor, often exaggerated to the point of fetish: the claim that SDI brought the Cold War to an end and the Soviet Union down, as well as the judgment that the Soviet economy would have collapsed even if Gorbachev had not tried to reform it.

Within the Soviet Union, the tendency has been to associate the end of the Cold War with the collapse of the Soviet Union, and to attribute both to malign U.S. efforts. Demagogues charge that Gorbachev was taken in by Reagan and Bush, whose main aim was to destroy the Soviet Union and weaken Russia. Their successors, according to this line of reasoning, are intent on reducing Russia to a colony and to elevating the United States to the world hegemon.

While views differ regarding responsibility for ending the Cold War, it is now obvious to all but a few on the irrational fringes of politics that the Cold War is over.

EPILOGUE

*Given the current interdependence between nations, security can only be
thought of as security in common.*
—MIKHAIL GORBACHEV, 2000[1]

T HE PERSONAL CONTACTS between Mikhail Gorbachev and Ronald
Reagan continued after Reagan left office. The Reagans called on the
Gorbachevs when the latter were in San Francisco during their 1990 visit to
the United States. In September 1990 the Reagans went to Moscow a second
time, on the invitation of the Gorbachevs, but they stayed at Spaso House, as
they had in 1988. Reagan met for several hours with Gorbachev, addressed
the new Supreme Soviet (parliament), and held a seminar with Moscow
University students. Gorbachev hosted the Reagans at dinner and the Reagans invited the Gorbachevs to lunch at Spaso House.

Instead of the heated negotiations of the past, the meetings were cordial
and relaxed. The president* and former president were in general agreement
on the international questions they discussed, and both interspersed their
comments with jokes. Gorbachev had expanded the repertory of anecdotes

---

* The Soviet legislature had created the office of president earlier that year and Gorbachev held it con-
currently with that of general secretary of the Communist Party of the Soviet Union.

he had assembled for the meeting in 1988 and actually told as many jokes as Reagan. As a consequence, the meeting was frequently punctuated by hearty laughter. To those of us privileged to be present, they seemed to be acting like two old friends, now very much on the same wavelength. Gorbachev spoke at length of his attempt to move the Soviet Union to a more open political system and complained of the difficulties he faced in changing people's habits.[2]

The onset of Reagan's Alzheimer's disease soon ended the possibility of a meaningful personal relationship, but Gorbachev continued to give Reagan credit for cooperating to end the Cold War. During a dinner attended by Gorbachev in Cambridge, England, in 2001, I heard a British academic remark that he had always considered Ronald Reagan "rather an intellectual lightweight." Gorbachev demurred. "You are wrong," he countered. "President Reagan was a man of real insight, sound political judgment, and courage."

As already noted, George H.W. Bush, with Mikhail Gorbachev's cooperation, completed the process that Reagan and Gorbachev had started to end the Cold War. As a consequence, today we live in a world vastly different from the one that conditioned our perceptions in the decades following World War II. By the early 1990s, no reasonable person could doubt that the Cold War was over. Every element in Reagan's four-point agenda had been implemented: strategic nuclear weapons were being cut by 50 percent; chemical weapons were outlawed; Russia had pledged to shut down all production of biological weapons; there was no longer Soviet military intervention away from its borders; the Iron Curtain had long since disappeared; Russian citizens could travel anywhere they wished if they had the price of the ticket; the Russian press was no longer censored or controlled by the government; the rights of Russian citizens were generally protected; and elections were reasonably free.

Nevertheless, political leaders in both the United States and Russia did little to reorient their bureaucracies toward the new threat that loomed: international terrorism. Instead, most intelligence resources were still directed at the same old Cold War tasks. Both the United States and Russia continued to maintain large nuclear arsenals on alert when they no longer had a rationale. The U.S. Senate refused to ratify a ban on nuclear tests that would have deterred development of nuclear weapons by others. Such practices and decisions left both the United States and Russia ill prepared to protect their citizens from the acts of suicidal terrorists.

Even though the Cold War has been over for more than a decade, the world is not as safe as either Reagan or Gorbachev hoped it would be. Their

recent successors have failed to continue the process of rapid nuclear disarmament they started and the first President Bush supported. It is also clear
that, until September 11, 2001, they misunderstood the threats that faced the
civilized world as the twenty-first century began.

Russian mishandling of the rebellion in Chechnya has resulted in terrorist outrages that persist. The United States long ignored the dangerous implications of the Taliban victory in Afghanistan in the mid-1990s, a victory
made possible by elements in Pakistan that had been used by the United
States to deliver arms to the forces resisting the Soviet occupation. The
"positive symmetry" of 1988 had perversely led to an Afghanistan controlled by anti-Western religious fanatics who sheltered and helped train terrorists directed at both the United States and Russia.

Both Reagan and Gorbachev had hoped that by now we would have
a world largely free of nuclear weapons. Unfortunately, we do not, and
while we no longer fear a sudden nuclear attack from a rival superpower, we
are vulnerable to attacks by terrorists. The nuclear arsenals retained by the
United States, Russia, China, Great Britain, France, and Israel, and recently
acquired by India and Pakistan, cannot defend any of those countries against
terrorists. But if any of the weapons in their stockpiles, or those developed
elsewhere, reach the wrong hands, any of the current nuclear powers could
be victims of devastating attacks by terrorists.

The United States still has not found a way to fulfill Reagan's dream of
creating a defense against ballistic missiles, but since its withdrawal from
the ABM Treaty in 2002, Americans cannot blame treaty restrictions if that
goal continues to elude it. In any event, defenses against ballistic missiles
would not protect the United States from a terrorist attack. Terrorists are
much more likely to deliver nuclear and other weapons of mass destruction by low-tech methods, such as small planes, boats, or trucks, than by
missiles.

One cannot avoid the conclusion that, over the last decade, both American and Russian political leaders have failed to take full advantage of the opportunities that Reagan, Gorbachev, and the first President Bush created.
The world might be a safer place if today's leaders studied more carefully
the achievements and mistakes of their predecessors, not for partisan debate
but for insight into the ingredients of successful diplomacy.

A good place to start would be to examine the way Ronald Reagan dealt
with the potentially mortal danger the Soviet Union's weapons posed: not by
threatening military action or demanding "regime change," but by patient diplomacy backed up by economic as well as military strength. They might
also review Shevardnadze's warnings in 1988 of the danger Islamic funda-

mentalists in Afghanistan would pose if they were armed following the Soviet military departure. And as our policy makers reflect on the dangers that face us, they might also turn some attention to Gorbachev's adage (to which Reagan would have agreed heartily) that no country can ensure its own security without regarding the security of others.

If there is a lesson in the outcome of the Cold War other than the fallacy of Marxist ideology and the bankruptcy of the Communist system of rule, it is that a country cannot for long guarantee its own safety by the military domination of others. Security in today's world, as Mikhail Gorbachev came to understand, can be found only if countries cooperate to achieve it.

ACKNOWLEDGMENTS

Most of the research and much of the writing of this book was done while I was George F. Kennan Professor at the Institute for Advanced Study in Princeton, New Jersey. I am indebted to the Institute for Advanced Study for the favorable conditions it created for research and writing. I am also grateful to my colleagues on the faculty of the institute, particularly those in the School of Historical Studies and School of Social Sciences, for the support and intellectual stimulation they provided during my time with them. Several institute members—George Mirsky, Eduard Ivanyan, Jonathan Haslam, Vera Tolz, and Robert English—read portions of the manuscript and shared with me their own research that was relevant to my topic.

Throughout my thirty-five years in the American Foreign Service, George F. Kennan, whom I met only late in my career, provided both inspiration and example. It was a signal honor to occupy a chair bearing his name. Residence in Princeton also gave me the opportunity to consult with him frequently. Ambassador Kennan made the effort, in the centennial year of his life, to read an early draft of this book. His suggestions have helped me correct some errors and to improve the book in several ways. My intellectual debt to him, of course, goes well beyond his advice on this particular manuscript.

During the early part of my research (1996–98) Dr. Nina Khrushcheva, a great-granddaughter of Nikita Khrushchev who was then a graduate student at Princeton University, served as my research assistant not only for this book but also for other projects relating to contemporary Russia and its culture. My executive secretary, Terrie Bramley, kept my calendar, made appointments for interviews, arranged my frequent travel, and organized a scholarly conference with consummate efficiency and charm.

The original suggestion for a book on the evolution of U.S. and Soviet policy during the Reagan administration came from Dr. David Hamburg, then president of the Carnegie Corporation of New York. Both he and his successor, Dr. Vartan Gregorian, continued to offer encouragement during the years I worked on the manuscript. Scholars at the Carnegie Endowment for International Peace in Washington, D.C., and at the Carnegie Moscow Center were invariably helpful to me, not only with advice, but in making contacts and arranging appointments. Dr. Thomas Blanton facilitated my use of the documents available at the National Security Archive, housed in the library of George Washington University in Washington, D.C. Svetlana Savranskaya was particularly helpful in selecting and reproducing documents for me. The Ronald Reagan Presidential Library in California also cooperated by providing copies of declassified records of the Reagan-Gorbachev summit meetings.

As I noted in the Foreword, President Gorbachev and members of his institute in Moscow have given enormous help regarding the evolution of Soviet policy during the Reagan administration. President Gorbachev made himself available for a series of interviews, as did Anatoly Chernyaev, Pavel Palazchenko, Vadim Medvedev, and Georgy Shakhnazarov, before his sudden and untimely death in 2002. Eduard Shevardnadze took time from his demanding duties as president of the Republic of Georgia to answer questions regarding the development of his views. Former foreign minister Alexander Bessmertnykh was always generous with his time and advice, as was Sergei Tarasenko, formerly Shevardnadze's personal assistant. Alexander Yakovlev not only granted several interviews but also read portions of the manuscript and provided perceptive comments. Interviews in Moscow with Alexander Tsypko, Vadim Zagladin, and Tankred Golempolsky clarified for me a number of questions that had puzzled me.

Several friends and associates read all or portions of the manuscript and made helpful suggestions: Robert C. McFarlane, Ambassador Richard T. Davies, Ambassador Willard A. DePree, Professor Archie Brown of Oxford University, the Reverend Donald Schomacker, Professor Robert C. Tucker, Paul Mott, and Mary O'Brien. I also benefited from the comments of my students at Princeton University who read portions of an early draft. Jessica Jacobson, in particular, offered an insightful critique. Dr. James G. Matlock, my eldest son, provided stylistic advice and compiled an index to my first draft, which helped me find errors and repetitions. His brothers, Hugh, David, and Joseph Matlock, also read an early draft and offered helpful suggestions. Scott Moyers, my editor at Random House during the early stages of work on the book, provided important encouragement, as did my literary agent, Fifi Oscard. Robert Loomis, who kindly undertook the final editing of the book, provided just the right measure of tactful comment that helped me understand and correct some significant weaknesses.

Among the many persons who assisted me in one way or another, none was as important as my wife, Rebecca Matlock. Her support for my diplomatic and academic activities has been irreplaceable. With her help, I secured the friendship and confidence of most of the persons who figure in this book. Her contribution went even further: She cheerfully read several drafts of the book. Her sharp eye has saved me from embarrassing errors and has reduced the reader's exposure to infelicitous expressions which I seem unable, on my own, to expunge from my writing.

Needless to say, none of the people I consulted are responsible for, or necessarily share, the opinions I express.

NOTES

Foreword

1. Reagan, *An American Life* (New York: Simon & Schuster, 1990), p. 572.
2. Peter Schweizer, *Victory: The Reagan Administration's Secret Strategy That Hastened the Collapse of the Soviet Union* (New York: Atlantic Monthly Press, 1994).
3. See, for example, Beth A. Fischer, *The Reagan Reversal: Foreign Policy and the End of the Cold War* (Columbia: University of Missouri Press, 1997).

CHAPTER I
1981–82: Reagan's Challenge

1. *Weekly Compilation of Presidential Documents,* vol. 17, no. 25, p. 636.
2. Ibid., no. 53, pp. 1419–20.
3. Ibid., vol. 18, no. 19, p. 601.
4. Ibid., vol. 17, no. 5, pp. 66–67.
5. Ibid., vol. 18, no. 19, p. 639.
6. Statement to the French television network Antenne 2, Feb. 23, 1981; text in *Department of State Bulletin,* April 1981, p. 15.
7. Speech of Apr. 24, 1981, to the American Society of Newspaper Editors; text in *Department of State Bulletin,* June 1981, p. 6.
8. Speech of Apr. 27, 1982; text in *Department of State Bulletin,* June 1982, p. 43.
9. Speech at Eureka College, Eureka, Illinois, May 9, 1982; *Weekly Compilation of Presidential Documents,* vol. 18, no. 19, p. 599.
10. This and the quotations that follow are from Special National Intelligence Estimate (SNIE) 11-2-81, "Soviet Support for International Terrorism and Revolutionary Violence," issued by the Director of Central Intelligence on May 27, 1981. Most of it, including all the key judgments, has been declassified.
11. Ibid., p. 18.
12. Dmitri Volkogonov, *Autopsy for an Empire: The Seven Leaders Who Built the Soviet Regime* (New York: Free Press, 1998), p. 353.
13. See, for example, the following telegrams from the American embassy in Moscow to the Department of State (all now declassified): "Soviet Policy Toward Poland," 81 Moscow 04783 (Apr. 7, 1981); "Soviet Strategy Toward Poland," 81 Moscow 07032 (May 21, 1981); "Soviet Policy Toward Poland," 81 Moscow 08202 (June 13, 1987); "Looking Ahead on Poland: The View from Moscow," 81 Moscow 11577 (Aug. 18, 1981).
14. *Department of State Bulletin,* June 1982, p. 43.

15. Interview of Mar. 3, 1981, on CBS News; a transcript was published in *Weekly Compilation of Presidential Documents,* vol. 17, no. 10, pp. 232–33.
16. Ronald Reagan, *An American Life* (New York: Simon & Schuster, 1990), pp. 271–73; Anatoly Dobrynin, *In Confidence: Moscow's Ambassador to America's Six Cold War Presidents* (New York: Random House, 1995), pp. 492–93.
17. Dobrynin, *In Confidence,* p. 493.
18. Alexander M. Haig, Jr., *Caveat: Realism, Reagan, and Foreign Policy* (New York: Macmillan, 1984), pp. 95–96.

CHAPTER II
1981–82: Moscow's Truculence

1. Anatoly Dobrynin, *In Confidence: Moscow's Ambassador to America's Six Cold War Presidents* (New York: Random House, 1995), p. 478.
2. Ibid., p. 495.
3. *Bulletin: Cold War International History Project* 4 (Washington, D.C.: Woodrow Wilson International Center for Scholars, Fall 1994): 81.
4. Dmitri Volkogonov, *Sem' vozhdei: Galereya liderov SSSR v 2-kh knigakh* (Moscow: Novosti, 1996), 2: 65; English translation: *Autopsy for an Empire: The Seven Leaders Who Built the Soviet Regime* (New York: Free Press, 1998), p. 301.
5. The Russian text of Ustinov's speech can be found in *Pravda,* Nov. 7, 1981; comments from the U.S. embassy in Moscow are in 81 Moscow 15544, Nov. 6, 1981.
6. See, for example, the exchange reported by Jacques Attali in his *Verbatim,* vol. 1, *1981–1986* (Paris: Fayard, 1993), p. 63.
7. See, for example, the State Department record of Schmidt's meeting with Haig shortly after martial law was declared in Poland: Memorandum of Conversation: Secretary Haig's Breakfast Meeting with FRG Chancellor Schmidt, Jan. 6, 1982.
8. See, for example, the assessment in her memoirs: Margaret Thatcher, *The Downing Street Years* (New York: HarperCollins, 1993), pp. 157–58.
9. Ibid., p. 166.
10. See Paul H. Nitze's account of attitudes at the time in his *From Hiroshima to Glasnost: At the Center of Decision—A Memoir* (New York: Grove Weidenfeld, 1989), pp. 366–69.
11. Aleksandr G. Savel'yev and Nikolai N. Detinov, *The Big Five: Arms Control Decision Making in the Soviet Union* (Westport, Conn.: Praeger, 1995), pp. 55–59.
12. Ibid., pp. 55–56.
13. Both Nitze and Kvitsinsky have described this effort and the reaction of their respective governments. See Nitze, *From Hiroshima to Glasnost,* and Julij A. Kwizinskij, *Vor dem Sturm: Erinnerungen eines Diplomaten* (Berlin: Siedler Verlag, 1993). Although the two accounts disagree on several secondary points, such as who said precisely what at what time and who was responsible for leaks to the press, they are in agreement regarding the substance of the proposals and the reactions of their governments.
14. Nitze, *From Hiroshima to Glasnost,* p. 380.
15. Kwizinskij, *Vor dem Sturm,* p. 305 ff.
16. Nitze, *From Hiroshima to Glasnost,* pp. 388–89.
17. Volkogonov, *Autopsy for an Empire,* p. 299.
18. Ibid., pp. 299–300.

19. John Drexel, ed., *The Facts on File Encyclopedia of the 20th Century* (New York: Facts on File, 1991), p. 12.
20. Dobrynin, *In Confidence,* p. 527.
21. "Andropov . . . was one of those who were unable to break through the barrier of old ideas and values." (Mikhail Gorbachev, *Memoirs* [New York: Doubleday, 1996], p. 153.)

CHAPTER III
1983: Summit Hopes Dashed

1. Statement broadcast on Soviet radio and television, published in *Pravda,* Sept. 29, 1983.
2. NSDD-75 has been declassified in full and a facsimile of the original document was published as an appendix in Robert C. McFarlane, *Special Trust* (New York: Cadell & Davies, 1994), pp. 372–80.
3. George P. Shultz, *Turmoil and Triumph: My Years as Secretary of State* (New York: Scribner, 1993), pp. 166–67.
4. See Ibid., pp. 164–65; Anatoly Dobrynin, *In Confidence: Moscow's Ambassador to America's Six Cold War Presidents* (New York: Random House, 1995), pp. 517–21.
5. John Pollock describes the two families, the reasons for their desire to emigrate, and their previous experiences in his *The Siberian Seven* (Waco, Tex.: Word Books, 1980).
6. Shultz, *Turmoil and Triumph,* p. 165.
7. See *New York Times,* Jan. 4, 1963, Sec. 1, p. 8.
8. Max M. Kampelman, *Entering New Worlds: The Memoirs of a Private Man in Public Life* (New York: HarperCollins, 1991), pp. 270–71.
9. The text of the speech is in *Weekly Compilation of Presidential Documents,* vol. 19, no. 12, pp. 442–48.
10. See Frances FitzGerald, *Way Out There in the Blue: Reagan, Star Wars and the End of the Cold War* (New York: Simon & Schuster, 2000), p. 20.
11. *Weekly Compilation of Presidential Documents,* vol. 19, no. 12, p. 448.
12. Reagan states in his memoirs that he never believed in the possibility of an "impenetrable shield." (*An American Life* [New York: Simon & Schuster, 1990], p. 608.)
13. Shultz, *Turmoil and Triumph,* pp. 261–64, 266–67.
14. *Department of State Bulletin,* July 1983, p. 69.
15. See, for example, Shultz, *Turmoil and Triumph,* p. 274.
16. See Paul Henze, *The Plot to Kill the Pope* (New York: Scribner, 1985).
17. Andrei Gromyko, *Memoirs* (New York: Doubleday, 1989), pp. 298–301.
18. Murray Sayle has given the most accurate review of what actually happened and the Soviet disinformation in his "Closing the File on Flight 007," *The New Yorker,* Dec. 13, 1993, pp. 90–101. At the time, however, some Western observers accepted the Soviet falsehoods without question. In his *Shootdown: Flight 007 and the American Connection* (New York: Viking, 1986), R. W. Johnson, identified as a "Fellow in Politics" at Oxford University, not only accepts all the Soviet calumnies but invents some of his own. It is all the more remarkable that a respected American publisher published this farrago of blatant lies.
19. Statement published in *Pravda* and *Izvestiya,* Sept. 29, 1983. English translation in the *Current Digest of the Soviet Press,* vol. 35, no. 39, Oct. 26, 1983.

20. The message was delivered informally by Sergei Vishnevsky, a *Pravda* correspondent with direct ties to the Central Committee. I describe it in detail in Jack F. Matlock, Jr., *Autopsy on an Empire: The American Ambassador's Account of the Collapse of the Soviet Union* (New York: Random House, 1995), p. 83.
21. Clark told friends at the time that Michael Deaver, deputy chief of staff in the White House, had convinced Nancy Reagan that Clark was not up to the job. See McFarlane, *Special Trust*, pp. 254–56; also FitzGerald, *Way Out There in the Blue*, pp. 230–35.
22. Shultz, *Turmoil and Triumph*, p. 320.

CHAPTER IV
1984: Reagan Prepares; Moscow Dawdles

1. Address from East Room of the White House, text in *Weekly Compilation of Presidential Documents*, vol. 20, no. 3, pp. 40–45.
2. Statement by Oleg Grinevsky at a conference on understanding the end of the Cold War at Brown University, May 7–10, 1998.
3. "Vystuplenie R. Reigana," *Izvestiya*, Jan. 17, 1984.
4. Statement at a conference on understanding the end of the Cold War at Brown University, May 7–10, 1998.
5. Reagan quotes extensively from these exchanges, as well as earlier ones with Brezhnev and Andropov, in his memoirs, *An American Life* (New York: Simon & Schuster, 1990).
6. Christopher Andrew and Oleg Gordievsky, *Comrade Kryuchkov's Instructions: Top Secret Files on KGB Foreign Operations, 1975–1985* (Stanford, Calif.: Stanford University Press, 1993), p. 97.
7. Extensive excerpts from the letter, along with the entire handwritten postscript, are included in Reagan, *An American Life*, pp. 595–98.
8. "The Pentagon's Shultz-Bashing," *Washington Post*, Mar. 21, 1984.
9. *Newsweek*, Apr. 23, 1984, p. 21.
10. *Weekly Compilation of Presidential Documents*, vol. 20, no. 23, p. 832.
11. Ibid., no. 26, p. 945.
12. Lou Cannon, "Reagan Uses Speech to Castigate Soviets, Propose Non-Arms Pacts," *Washington Post*, June 28, 1984, pp. A17, A27.
13. In addition to extensive excerpts from the speech, the *New York Times* of June 28, 1984, carried a lengthy report by Steven R. Weisman and a separate analysis by Bernard Gwertzman.
14. See, for example, *New York Times*, June 30, 1984, p. 4.
15. A White House press release on July 27, 1984, explained that TASS had misrepresented the U.S. position, which was that "we have accepted the Soviet proposal for discussions in Vienna in September without preconditions." On August 1, McFarlane announced again that the United States was prepared to accept the Soviet proposal and had so informed the Soviet government in diplomatic channels. (*Department of State Bulletin*, September 1984, p. 25.)
16. Reagan, *An American Life*, p. 605.
17. Victor Israelyan, *On the Battlefields of the Cold War: A Soviet Ambassador's Confession* (University Park: Pennsylvania State University Press, 2003), pp. 348–52.
18. Gorbachev told me of this in a conversation in March 2000 when I asked if he had been aware of our efforts to contact him in 1984. Dobrynin informed Gorbachev after he be-

came general secretary that Gromyko had pocketed the messages and later complained to Dobrynin that they had been sent.

19. Reagan, *An American Life,* p. 606.

20. Mikhail Gorbachev, *On My Country and the World* (New York: Columbia University Press, 2000), p. 172.

CHAPTER V
1985: Gorbachev in Power

1. From Gorbachev's address to Soviet citizens upon leaving office; text from Mikhail Gorbachev, *Memoirs* (New York: Doubleday, 1996), p. xxvii.

2. Ronald Reagan, *An American Life* (New York: Simon & Schuster, 1990), p. 614.

3. See Gorbachev, *Memoirs,* pp. 164–66.

4. At the time, some observers, claiming to have inside information, reported that Gorbachev had won his office by a 5–4 vote, and would have lost if all members of the Politburo had been present. (Vladimir Shcherbitsky and Dinmukhamed Kunayev, the Party leaders of Ukraine and Kazakhstan, respectively, who were not sympathetic to Gorbachev, were absent.) Robert D. English summarizes the various reports of this process in his *Russia and the Idea of the West: Gorbachev, Intellectuals and the End of the Cold War* (New York: Columbia University Press, 2000), pp. 195–98.

5. Alexander Yakovlev, *Omut pamyati* (Moscow: Vagrius, 2000), p. 443.

6. Dmitri Volkogonov, *Autopsy for an Empire: The Seven Leaders Who Built the Soviet Regime* (New York: Free Press, 1998), p. 448.

7. Reagan, *An American Life,* p. 615. The meeting, which I attended, took place in the Oval Office on April 19, 1985.

8. Interview with Sergei Tarasenko, Jan. 19, 2001.

9. See, for example, Reagan's account: *An American Life,* p. 615.

10. For other instances of Weinberger's refusal to implement an order from the president, see Robert C. McFarlane, *Special Trust* (New York: Cadell & Davies, 1994), pp. 270–71.

11. Caspar Weinberger, *Fighting for Peace: Seven Critical Years in the Pentagon* (New York: Warner, 1990), p. 331.

12. The full text of this speech is in *Pravda* and *Izvestiya* of May 9, 1985.

13. *Weekly Compilation of Presidential Documents,* vol. 21, no. 19, p. 602 ff.

14. Edmund Morris gives a vivid description of the controversy surrounding Reagan's visit to Bitburg in his *Dutch: A Memoir of Ronald Reagan* (New York: Random House, 1999). See especially pp. 522–31.

15. *Weekly Compilation of Presidential Documents,* vol. 21, no. 24, pp. 771–74.

16. I describe this meeting in my *Autopsy on an Empire: The American Ambassador's Account of the Collapse of the Soviet Union* (New York: Random House, 1995), pp. 51–52.

17. See also George P. Shultz, *Turmoil and Triumph: My Years as Secretary of State* (New York: Scribner, 1993), pp. 563–64.

18. Ibid., p. 574.

19. Eduard Shevardnadze, *Moi vybor: V zashchitu demokratii i svobody* (Moscow: Novosti, 1991), pp. 79–80. English translation: *The Future Belongs to Freedom* (New York: Free Press, 1991), pp. 38–39.

20. Anatoly Gromyko describes in detail his father's distress in his *Andrei Gromyko: v labirintakh Kremlya: vospominaniia i razmyshleniia syna* (Moscow: Avtor, 1997).
21. Interview with Alexander Bessmertnykh, Jan. 19, 2001.

CHAPTER VI
1985: Enter Shevardnadze

1. George P. Shultz, *Turmoil and Triumph: My Years as Secretary of State* (New York: Scribner, 1993), p. 702.
2. Eduard Shevardnadze, *The Future Belongs to Freedom* (New York: Free Press, 1991), p. 49.
3. Robert M. Gates, *From the Shadows: The Ultimate Insider's Story of Five Presidents and How They Won the Cold War* (New York: Simon & Schuster, 1996), p. 341.
4. Robert D. English describes their views in detail in Chapter 6 of his *Russia and the Idea of the West: Gorbachev, Intellectuals and the End of the Cold War* (New York: Columbia University Press, 2000).
5. Mikhail Gorbachev and Zdeněk Mlynář, *Conversations with Gorbachev* (New York: Columbia University Press, 2002), pp. 49–50.
6. Aleksandr G. Savel'yev and Nikolai N. Detinov describe the operations of the group in their book *The Big Five: Arms Control Decision Making in the Soviet Union* (Westport, Conn.: Praeger, 1995).
7. For the view of Soviet experts, see ibid., p. 91.
8. Shultz, *Turmoil and Triumph,* pp. 589–94.

CHAPTER VII
1985: Geneva: The First Skirmish

1. Mikhail Gorbachev, *Memoirs* (New York: Doubleday, 1996), p. 403.
2. Comment regarding his objectives at the Geneva summit meeting: Ronald Reagan, *An American Life* (New York: Simon & Schuster, 1990), p. 12.
3. The results of an NBC/*Wall Street Journal* poll were: Eighty-three percent thought the Geneva summit a "good idea" versus 10 percent who disapproved. Nineteen percent thought the meeting would "produce an agreement that will slow down the military build-up," while 69 percent thought it would not. (Quoted in an unclassified Information Memorandum from Assistant Secretary Bernard Kalb to Secretary of State Shultz, Oct. 31, 1985.)
4. The Office of Research in the U.S. Information Agency summarized these views in a report of Nov. 13, 1985, entitled "Major West European Press on U.S.-Soviet Relations."
5. Mikhail Gorbachev, *On My Country and the World* (New York: Columbia University Press, 2000), pp. 177–79.
6. Gorbachev, *Memoirs,* p. 407.
7. Ibid., p. 406.
8. Reagan, *An American Life,* p. 644.
9. Robert C. McFarlane, *Special Trust* (New York: Cadell & Davies, 1994), pp. 329–33.
10. Reagan, *An American Life,* pp. 646–48.

11. Gorbachev, *On My Country and the World,* p. 179.

12. Ibid., pp. 184–85.

CHAPTER VIII

1986: Geneva Recedes; Complications Mount

1. Mikhail Gorbachev, *Memoirs* (New York: Doubleday, 1996), p. 412.

2. Ronald Reagan, *An American Life* (New York: Simon & Schuster, 1990), p. 651.

3. Joseph G. Whelan describes these negotiations in a report he authored for the Committee on Foreign Affairs of the U.S. House of Representatives: *Soviet Diplomacy and Negotiating Behavior—1979–88: New Tests for U.S. Diplomacy* (Washington, D.C.: U.S. Government Printing Office, 1988), 2: 492–98.

4. Tarasenko recounted the background of Gorbachev's January 1986 proposal to a conference at Brown University, May 7–10, 1998.

5. See, for example, Chernyaev's comment: "I can pinpoint the exact time when Gorbachev placed his stake on a direct dialogue with the American leadership. It was at the very beginning of 1986. Hence the famous declaration about a nuclear-free world by the year 2000." (Anatoly S. Chernyaev, *Shest' let s Gorbachevym* [Moscow: Izdatel'skaya gruppa "Progress" "Kul'tura," 1993], p. 78; English translation: *My Six Years with Gorbachev* [University Park: Pennsylvania State University Press, 2000], p. 59.)

6. Anatoly S. Chernyaev, *Moya zhizn' i moyo vremya* (Moscow: Mezhdunarodnye otnosheniya, 1995), p. 443.

7. Chernyaev, *Shest' let,* p. 65; *My Six Years,* p. 49.

8. Chernyaev, *Shest' let,* pp. 67–68; *My Six Years,* p. 51.

9. Reagan, *An American Life,* p. 655.

10. *Soviet Noncompliance,* ACDA Publication 120, March 1986.

11. Ibid., p. ii.

12. Chernyaev, *Shest' let,* p. 79; *My Six Years,* p. 60.

13. George P. Shultz, *Turmoil and Triumph: My Six Years as Secretary of State* (New York: Scribner, 1993), pp. 578–82.

14. See Mikhail Gorbachev, *Memoirs* (New York: Doubleday, 1996), pp. 189–93; Alexander Yakovlev, *Omut pamyati* (Moscow: Vagrius, 2000), pp. 253–55; Chernyaev, *Shest' let,* pp. 86–88; *My Six Years,* pp. 65–67.

15. Television address of May 14, 1986; text in *Pravda,* May 15, 1986.

16. Chernyaev, *Shest' let,* pp. 78–80; *My Six Years,* pp. 59–61.

17. Eduard Shevardnadze, *Moi vybor: V zashchitu demokratii i svobody* (Moscow: Novosti, 1991), pp. 103–106; English translation: *The Future Belongs to Freedom* (New York: Free Press, 1991), pp. 54–56.

18. The quotation is translated from the summary text of the conversation in Jacques Attali, *Verbatim,* vol. 2, *1986–1988* (Paris: Fayard, 1995), p. 112. Though not identical in wording, it tracks with the Russian summary cited by Chernyaev, *Shest' let,* p. 102; *My Six Years,* p. 76.

19. Gorbachev, *Memoirs,* pp. 429–30.

20. Chernyaev, *Shest' let,* p. 102; *My Six Years,* p. 76.

21. Chernyaev, *Shest' let,* p. 104; *My Six Years,* p. 77.

CHAPTER IX
1986: A Crisis and a New Proposal

1. Diary entry quoted in Ronald Reagan, *An American Life* (New York: Simon & Schuster, 1990), p. 667.
2. Anatoly S. Chernyaev, *Shest' let s Gorbachevym* (Moscow: Izdatel'skaya gruppa "Progress" "Kul'tura," 1993), p. 109; English translation: *My Six Years with Gorbachev* (University Park: Pennsylvania State University Press, 2000), p. 81.
3. Reagan, *An American Life,* pp. 666–69, 672–74.
4. Conversations on this subject have been reconstructed from notes I made at the time.
5. Robert M. Gates, *From the Shadows: The Ultimate Insider's Story of Five Presidents and How They Won the Cold War* (New York: Simon & Schuster, 1996), p. 366.
6. This and subsequent conversations have been reconstructed from notes and a vivid memory. Though paraphrased, they retain both the substance and mood.
7. I describe the Chautauqua meeting in more detail in my *Autopsy on an Empire: The American Ambassador's Account of the Collapse of the Soviet Union* (New York: Random House, 1995), pp. 102–104. An English translation of my speech was published by the Department of State: Jack F. Matlock, Jr., "U.S.-Soviet Relations: Background and Prospects," Current Policy No. 870. Washington, D.C.: Department of State, 1986.
8. Daniloff's moving description of his ordeal and of his family background can be found in his book *Two Lives, One Russia* (Boston: Houghton Mifflin, 1988).
9. Chernyaev, *Shest' let,* p. 105; *My Six Years,* p. 78.
10. A detailed description of these negotiations can be found in John Borawski, *From the Atlantic to the Urals: Negotiating Arms Control at the Stockholm Conference* (Washington, D.C.: Pergamon-Brassey, 1988).
11. George P. Shultz, *Turmoil and Triumph: My Six Years as Secretary of State* (New York: Scribner, 1993), p. 739.
12. Ibid., pp. 733–50.
13. Chernyaev, *Shest' let,* pp. 107–108; *My Six Years,* p. 80.
14. Chernyaev, *Shest' let,* p. 109; *My Six Years,* p. 81.
15. Chernyaev, *Shest' let,* pp. 110–11; *My Six Years,* pp. 81–83.
16. Chernyaev, *Shest' let,* pp. 112–13; *My Six Years,* pp. 83–84.

CHAPTER X
1986: Reykjavík: Wrestlers in the Ring

1. Ronald Reagan, *An American Life* (New York: Simon & Schuster, 1990), p. 675.
2. Mikhail Gorbachev, *Memoirs* (New York: Doubleday, 1996), pp. 415–16.
3. The official U.S. record of the meeting has been declassified and is available from the Ronald Reagan Presidential Library. The Soviet notes have been published in the journal *Mirovaya ekonomika i mezhdunarodnye otnosheniya (MEMO),* nos. 4, 5, 7, and 8, 1993. Direct quotations from Reagan are generally based on the American notes, which are usually more detailed than the Soviet notes, but in a few instances the Soviet notes recorded a phrase or sentence missing from the U.S. record, in which case it was used. Quotations from Gorbachev are based on the Soviet notes unless they omit a comment recorded in the U.S. notes.
4. Quoted from the Soviet notes, which track with the somewhat more detailed American record.

CHAPTER XI
1986: Reykjavík: Recriminations

1. Ronald Reagan, *An American Life* (New York: Simon & Schuster, 1990), p. 679.
2. Politburo document of that date, quoted in Dmitri Volkogonov, *Sem' vozhdei: Galereya liderov SSSR v 2-kh knigakh* (Moscow: Novosti, 1996), 2; 307; English translation: *Autopsy for an Empire* (New York: Free Press, 1998), pp. 494–95.
3. This is a paraphrase from a vivid memory and brief notes I made at the time.
4. He made this statement several times in personal interviews.
5. Don Oberdorfer, *From the Cold War to a New Era: The United States and the Soviet Union, 1983–1991* (Baltimore: Johns Hopkins University Press, 1999), pp. 209–10.
6. Hendrik Hertzberg discusses this possibility in his "Star Wars, or The Sting," *The New Yorker,* May 15, 2000, pp. 92–96.
7. Moscow TASS in English, Nov. 10, 1986, as reported by the Foreign Broadcast Information Service.
8. Private communication from Roald Sagdeyev.
9. Eduard Shevardnadze, *Moi vybor: V zashchitu demokratii i svobody* (Moscow: Novosti, 1991), p. 158; English translation: *The Future Belongs to Freedom* (New York: Free Press, 1991), p. 89.
10. Mikhail Gorbachev, *On My Country and the World* (New York: Columbia University Press, 2000), p. 195.
11. Reagan, *An American Life,* p. 683.

CHAPTER XII
1987: A Common Agenda

1. Notes of Politburo sessions on Feb. 23 and 26, 1987, Archive of the Gorbachev Foundation.
2. Statement at a conference on understanding the end of the Cold War, Brown University, May 7–10, 1998.
3. Margaret Thatcher, *The Downing Street Years* (New York: HarperCollins, 1993), p. 481.
4. Mikhail Gorbachev, *Memoirs* (New York: Doubleday, 1996), p. 434.
5. Anatoly Chernyaev's notes from the Politburo session of May 8, 1987, National Security Archive, George Washington University.
6. *Weekly Compilation of Presidential Documents,* vol. 23, no. 14, p. 361 ff.
7. My quotations from this meeting, unless noted otherwise, are from notes I took at the time. Shultz describes the meeting in some detail in his *Turmoil and Triumph: My Years as Secretary of State* (New York: Scribner, 1993), pp. 889–95. Gorbachev offers a shorter account in his *Memoirs* (New York: Doubleday, 1996), pp. 439–42.
8. Gorbachev's interpreter made the reply, which Shultz recorded as "Yes, this is precisely so," more categorical. (Shultz, *Turmoil and Triumph,* p. 890.)
9. Gorbachev, *Memoirs,* p. 440.
10. These and other quotations are based on my notes of the meeting.
11. The Soviet minutes of the meeting were published in *Mirovaya ekonomika i mezhdunarodnaya otnosheniya (MEMO),* nos. 10–11, 1993. Shultz describes it in his *Turmoil and Triumph,* pp. 995–1001.
12. Pavel Palazchenko, *My Years with Gorbachev and Shevardnadze: The Memoir of*

a Soviet Interpreter (University Park: Pennsylvania State University Press, 1997), p. 73.

13. Ibid., p. 74.

14. Ibid., pp. 81–82.

15. Shultz, *Turmoil and Triumph,* pp. 1002–1004. Robert Gates defends the CIA's assessments in his memoirs, *From the Shadows: The Ultimate Insider's Story of Five Presidents and How They Won the Cold War* (New York: Simon & Schuster, 1996), p. 422.

CHAPTER XIII

1987: Gorbachev in Washington

1. Anatoly S. Chernyaev, *Shest' let s Gorbachevym* (Moscow: Izdatel'skaya gruppa "Progress" "Kul'tura," 1993), pp. 188–89; English translation: *My Six Years with Gorbachev* (University Park: Pennsylvania State University Press, 2000), p. 142.

2. Ronald Reagan, *An American Life* (New York: Simon & Schuster, 1990), p. 701.

3. *Weekly Compilation of Presidential Documents,* vol. 23, no. 48, p. 1425.

4. Ibid., pp. 1391–99.

5. Mikhail Gorbachev, *Memoirs* (New York: Doubleday, 1996), p. 447.

6. Georgy Korniyenko, Gromyko's first deputy, was one of Gorbachev's most ardent critics, as he shows in his memoirs, *Kholodnaya voina* (Moscow: Mezhdunarodnaya otnosheniya, 1995) and in the book he co-authored with Marshal Akhromeyev, *Glazami marshala i diplomata* (Moscow: Mezhdunarodnaya otnosheniya, 1994). On the other hand, General Nikolai Detinov, a member of the senior Soviet advisory group during the negotiations, believes that Gorbachev's decision was absolutely correct and fully in accord with Soviet interests. See Aleksander G. Savel'yev and Nikolai N. Detinov, *The Big Five: Arms Control Decision Making in the Soviet Union* (Westport, Conn.: Praeger, 1995), pp. 127–28.

7. See, for example, the scathing comments by Kenneth L. Adelman, Reagan's director of the Arms Control and Disarmament Agency (Adelman, *The Great Universal Embrace: Arms Summitry—A Skeptic's Account* [New York: Simon & Schuster, 1989], pp. 242–43). He points out the irony in Kissinger's critique since Kissinger had said in 1979, "It is also necessary that either the Soviet nuclear threat in theater nuclear forces against Europe be eliminated [which I do not see possible] or that an immediate effort be made to build up our theater nuclear forces." These words clearly implied that U.S. "theater nuclear forces" would not be necessary if the Soviet Union eliminated its forces of that type directed against Europe. Eventually, Dr. Kissinger gave some qualified support to ratification.

8. In fact, it took officials in the Soviet foreign ministry nearly a month to extract the photograph from the defense ministry. See also Pavel Palazchenko, *My Years with Gorbachev and Shevardnadze: The Memoir of a Soviet Interpreter* (University Park: Pennsylvania State University Press, 1997), pp. 76–77.

9. George P. Shultz, *Turmoil and Triumph: My Years as Secretary of State* (New York: Scribner, 1993), p. 1014.

10. *Weekly Compilation of Presidential Documents,* vol. 23, no. 49, p. 1495.

11. For a more detailed description of differences in the Russian and English versions, see Savel'yev and Detinov, *The Big Five,* pp. 179–80.

12. Robert M. Gates, *From the Shadows: The Ultimate Insider's Story of Five Presidents and How They Won the Cold War* (New York: Simon & Schuster, 1996), p. 426.
13. *Weekly Compilation of Presidential Documents,* vol. 23, no. 49, p. 1492.
14. Chernyaev, *Shest' let,* pp. 188–89; *My Six Years,* p. 142.

CHAPTER XIV
1988: Mr. Reagan Goes to Moscow

1. Ronald Reagan, *An American Life* (New York: Simon & Schuster, 1990), p. 709.
2. Mikhail Gorbachev, *Memoirs* (New York: Doubleday, 1996), p. 457.
3. *Time,* Jan. 4, 1988.
4. George P. Shultz, *Turmoil and Triumph: My Years as Secretary of State* (New York: Scribner, 1993), p. 1080.
5. Ibid., pp. 1080–1086. George Shultz describes the process in detail.
6. Ibid., pp. 1086–1090.
7. Diego Cordovez and Selig S. Harrison provide the most detailed and reliable account of these negotiations in *Out of Afghanistan: The Inside Story of the Soviet Withdrawal* (New York: Oxford University Press, 1995).
8. See ibid., p. 387.
9. See ibid., appendix, for texts of these agreements.
10. *Sovetskaya Rossiya,* Mar. 13, 1988, p. 3
11. See Jack F. Matlock, Jr., *Autopsy on an Empire: The American Ambassador's Account of the Collapse of the Soviet Union* (New York: Random House, 1995), pp. 119–21.
12. I acted as interpreter for Shultz and Sakharov at this meeting and have summarized Sakharov's views from my notes. Shultz reports on major portions of Sakharov's comments in *Turmoil and Triumph,* p. 1095. However, he omits any mention of Sakharov's views on SDI and on the best strategy for dealing with the emigration issue.
13. Ibid., p. 1096.
14. The text is in *Weekly Compilation of Presidential Documents,* vol. 24, no. 16, pp. 503–11.
15. See Gorbachev, *Memoirs,* p. 451.
16. Shultz, *Turmoil and Triumph,* p. 1097. Also see Gorbachev, *Memoirs,* pp. 452–53.
17. Shultz, *Turmoil and Triumph,* p. 1097.
18. Shultz reports this conversation in considerable detail in his memoirs. Ibid., pp. 1097–1100.
19. See "Interview with Soviet Television Journalists Valentin Zorin and Boris Kalyagin, May 20, 1988," *Weekly Compilation of Presidential Documents,* vol. 24, no. 22, pp. 686–92.
20. A Ukrainian poet and magazine editor, Korotich had been recruited by Alexander Yakovlev in 1986 to take over *Ogonyok.* Korotich quickly made it one of the most aggressive reformist publications.
21. *Weekly Compilation of Presidential Documents,* vol. 24, no. 22, pp. 677–82.
22. A paraphrase from memory.
23. Gorbachev, *Memoirs,* p. 458; Shultz, *Turmoil and Triumph,* p. 1105.
24. Edmund Morris, Reagan's biographer who was present at Danilov Monastery, charac-

terizes his reference to the Ukrainian Catholics as a gaffe (*Dutch: A Memoir of Ronald Reagan* [New York: Random House, 1999], p. 634). It was nothing of the kind. Reagan understood very well what he was saying and why.
25. Gorbachev, *Memoirs,* p. 457.

CHAPTER XV
1988: The Cold War Ends—in Principle

1. Mikhail Gorbachev, *Memoirs* (New York: Doubleday, 1996), p. 460.
2. Ronald Reagan, *An American Life* (New York: Simon & Schuster, 1990), p. 720.
3. For details, see Jack F. Matlock, Jr., *Autopsy of an Empire: The American Ambassador's Account of the Collapse of the Soviet Union* (New York: Random House, 1995), pp. 142–48.
4. Anatoly Chernyaev, *My Six Years with Gorbachev* (University Park: Pennsylvania State University Press, 2000), p. 200.
5. Ibid., p. 202.
6. Woodrow Wilson International Center for Scholars, *Bulletin: International Cold War History Project,* 12–13 (Fall/Winter 2001), pp. 24–29.

CHAPTER XVI
What Then?

1. When riding to the airport with Gorbachev at the end of Gorbachev's visit to Washington in December 1987, Bush told him that some of the things said during the upcoming political campaign should be disregarded. In other words, he would need to indulge in a certain amount of anti-Soviet rhetoric. See Pavel Palazchenko, *My Years with Gorbachev and Shevardnadze: The Memoir of a Soviet Interpreter* (University Park: Pennsylvania State University Press, 1997), pp. 79–80.
2. The end-game diplomacy of Bush and Gorbachev is described well in Don Oberdorfer, *From the Cold War to a New Era: The United States and the Soviet Union, 1983–1991* (Baltimore: Johns Hopkins University Press, 1998), and by Robert L. Hutchings, *American Diplomacy and the End of the Cold War: An Insider's Account of U.S. Policy in Europe, 1989–1992* (Washington, D.C.: Woodrow Wilson Center Press, 1997).
3. Ronald Reagan, *An American Life* (New York: Simon & Schuster, 1990), p. 715.
4. Mikhail Gorbachev, *On My Country and the World* (New York: Columbia University Press, 2000), p. 53.
5. A critique and defense of the film can be found in Arnold Beichman, ed., *CNN's Cold War Documentary: Issues and Controversy* (Stanford, Calif.: Hoover Institute Press, 2000).
6. I describe this process at length in Jack F. Matlock, Jr., *Autopsy of an Empire: The American Ambassador's Account of the Collapse of the Soviet Union* (New York: Random House, 1995).
7. Speech in Kiev, Aug. 1, 1991.

Epilogue

1. Mikhail Gorbachev, *My Country and the World* (New York: Columbia University Press, 2000), p. 251.

2. Igor Korchilov interpreted for the Reagans during their Moscow visit in 1990. He described Reagan's speeches and meetings in detail in his *Translating History: Thirty Years on the Front Lines of Diplomacy with a Top Russian Interpreter* (New York: Scribner, 1997), pp. 333–77.

BIBLIOGRAPHY

A. Documents

(1) Official American documents and the text of speeches were obtained from:

Ronald Reagan Presidential Library: Memoranda of Conversation recording the summit meetings in Geneva, Reykjavík, Washington, and Moscow.

Department of State, Freedom of Information Act Electronic Reading Room (www.foia. state.gov) for declassified State Department documents.

For statements by the president and White House announcements: *Weekly Compilation of Presidential Documents.*

Department of State Bulletin, for speeches by secretary of state and other senior American officials.

Declassified American intelligence reports are available from the National Security Archive, George Washington University, and on the Internet at www.cia.gov/csi. Among the reports published in hard copy are those in the following volumes:

Fischer, Benjamin B., ed. *At Cold War's End: U.S. Intelligence on the Soviet Union and Eastern Europe, 1989–1991.* Washington, D.C.: Center for the Study of Intelligence, Central Intelligence Agency, 1991.

Haines, Gerald K., and Robert E. Leggett, eds. *CIA's Analysis of the Soviet Union, 1947–1991.* Washington, D.C.: Center for the Study of Intelligence, Central Intelligence Agency, 2001.

The text of much of the correspondence between Reagan and the Soviet leaders can be found in Reagan's autobiography, *An American Life,* listed below with other memoirs.

(2) Official Soviet documents and the text of speeches were obtained from:

Translations of Politburo minutes and other relevant documents have been published by the Cold War International History Project, Woodrow Wilson International Center for Scholars in its *Bulletin*. Russian originals are available in the National Security Archive at George Washington University, Washington, D.C., and at the Gorbachev Institute in Moscow.

Reykjavík Summit:
Mirovaya ekonomika i mezhdunarodnye otnosheniya (*MEMO*), nos. 4, 5, 7, and 8, 1993.

Shultz Meeting with Gorbachev, April 1987:
Mirovaya ekonomika i mezhdunarodnye otnosheniya (*MEMO*), nos. 10–11, 1993.

The Soviet notes on several of Gorbachev's meetings with Western leaders, and also on his meeting in the Soviet foreign ministry in May 1986, and other private communications have been published in German translation in Michail S. Gorbatschow, *Gipfelgespräche: Geheime Protokolle aus meiner Amtszeit*. Berlin: Rowohlt, 1993.

The Russian text of Gorbachev's speeches and articles can be found in M. S. Gorbachev, *Izbrannye rechi i stat'i*, 7 vols. Moscow: Izdatelstvo politicheskoi literatury, 1987–1990. They also were reported, usually the day after they were delivered, in *Pravda* and *Izvestiya*. English translations were often published in the *Current Digest of the Soviet Press*.

Soviet intelligence reports:

Andrew, Christopher, and Oleg Gordievsky. *Comrade Kryuchkov's Instructions: Top Secret Files on KGB Foreign Operations, 1975–1985*. Stanford, Calif.: Stanford University Press, 1993. Numerous other reports are quoted or summarized in the volumes listed below by Dmitri Volkogonov and those co-authored by Christopher Andrew.

B. Memoirs and Studies by Persons Involved in Diplomacy, Policy Making, or Espionage:

Adelman, Kenneth L. *The Great Universal Embrace: Arms Summitry—A Skeptic's Account*. New York: Simon & Schuster, 1989.

Akhromeyev, Sergei F., and Georgy M. Korniyenko. *Glazami marshala i diplomata: Kriticheskii vzglyad na vneshniuiu politiku SSSR do i posle 1985 goda*. Moscow: Mezhdunarodnaye otnosheniya, 1992.

Alexandrov-Agentov, A. M. *Ot Kollontay do Gorbacheva: Vospominanie diplomata, sovetnika A. A. Gromyko, pomoshchnika L. I. Brezhneva, Yu. V. Andropova, K. U. Chernenko i M. S. Gorbacheva*. Moscow: Mezhdunarodnye otnosheniya, 1994.

Andrew, Christopher, and Oleg Gordievsky. *KGB: The Inside Story of Its Foreign Operations from Lenin to Gorbachev*. London: Hodder & Stoughton, 1990.

Andrew, Christopher, and Vasili Mitrokhin. *The Sword and the Shield: The Mitrokhin Archive and the Secret History of the KGB*. New York: Basic Books, 1999.

Arbatov, Georgi. *The System: An Insider's Life in Soviet Politics*. New York: Times Books, 1992.

Attali, Jacques. *Verbatim*, vol. 1, *1981–1986;* vol. 2, *1986–1988*. Paris: Fayard, 1993–95.

Chernyaev, Anatoly S. *Moya zhizn' i moyo vremya*. Moscow: Mezhdunarodnye otnosheniya, 1995.

———. *Shest' let s Gorbachevym: Po dnevnikovym zapisam*. Moscow: Izdatel'skaya gruppa "Progress" "Kul'tura," 1993. English translation: *My Six Years with Gorbachev*. University Park: Pennsylvania State University Press, 2000.

Cordovez, Diego, and Selig S. Harrison. *Out of Afghanistan: The Inside Story of the Soviet Withdrawal*. New York: Oxford University Press, 1995.

Deaver, Michael K. *A Different Drummer: My Thirty Years with Ronald Reagan*. New York: HarperCollins, 2001.

Dobrynin, Anatoly. *In Confidence: Moscow's Ambassador to America's Six Cold War Presidents*. New York: Random House, 1995.

Gates, Robert M. *From the Shadows: The Ultimate Insider's Story of Five Presidents and How They Won the Cold War*. New York: Simon & Schuster, 1996.

Gorbachev, Mikhail. *On My Country and the World*. New York: Columbia University Press, 2000.

————. *Memoirs.* New York: Doubleday, 1996.

————. *Perestroika: New Thinking for Our Country and the World.* New York: Harper & Row, 1987.

————. *Zhizn' i reformy,* 2 vols. Moscow: Novosti, 1995. Translated in full in German: Michail Gorbatschow, *Erinnerungen.* Berlin: Siedler Verlag, 1995. The abridged English translation (*Memoirs*) contains those sections of greatest interest to the American reader:

————, and Zdeněk Mlynář. *Conversations with Gorbachev: On Perestroika, the Prague Spring, and the Crossroads of Socialism.* New York: Columbia University Press, 2002.

Gorbacheva, Raisa. *I Hope: Reminiscences and Reflections.* New York: HarperCollins, 1991.

Gromyko, Anatoly. *Andrei Gromyko v labirintakh Kremlya: vospominaniia i razmyshleniia syna.* Moscow: Avtor, 1997.

Gromyko, Andrei. *Pamyatnoye,* 2 vols. Moscow: Izdatel'stvo politicheskoi literatury, 1988. Abridged English translation: *Memoirs.* New York: Doubleday, 1989.

Haig, Alexander M., Jr. *Caveat: Realism, Reagan, and Foreign Policy.* New York: Macmillan, 1984.

Hyland, William G. *Mortal Rivals: Superpower Relations from Nixon to Reagan.* New York: Random House, 1987.

Israelyan, Victor. *On the Battlefields of the Cold War: A Soviet Ambassador's Confession* University Park: Pennsylvania State University Press, 2003.

Kalugin, Oleg, with Fen Montaigne. *The First Directorate: My 32 Years in Intelligence and Espionage Against the West.* New York: St. Martin's, 1994.

Kampelman, Max M. *Entering New Worlds: The Memoirs of a Private Man in Public Life.* New York: HarperCollins, 1991.

Korchilov, Igor. *Translating History: Thirty Years on the Front Lines of Diplomacy with a Top Russian Interpreter.* New York: Scribner, 1997.

Korniyenko, G. M. *Kholodnaya voina: Svidetel'stvo ee uchastnika.* Moscow: Mezhdunarodnye otnosheniya, 1995.

Kvitsinsky, Yuli. *Vremya i sluchai: Zametki professionala.* Moscow: Olma, 1999, which was published earlier in a German translation: Kwizinskij, Julij A. *Vor dem Sturm: Erinnerungen eines Diplomaten.* Berlin: Siedler Verlag, 1993.

Ligachev, Yegor. *Inside Gorbachev's Kremlin.* New York: Pantheon, 1993.

McFarlane, Robert C. *Special Trust.* New York: Cadell & Davies, 1994.

Medvedev, Vadim. *V Komande Gorbacheva: Vzglyad iznutri.* Moscow: Bylina, 1994.

Meese, Edwin, III. *With Reagan: The Inside Story.* Washington, D.C.: Regnery Gateway, 1992.

Nitze, Paul H., with Ann M. Smith and Steven L. Rearden. *From Hiroshima to Glasnost: At the Center of Decision—A Memoir.* New York: Grove Weidenfeld, 1989.

Palazchenko, Pavel. *My Years with Gorbachev and Shevardnadze: The Memoir of a Soviet Interpreter.* University Park: Pennsylvania State University Press, 1997.

Powell, Colin, with Joseph E. Persico. *My American Journey.* New York: Random House, 1995.

Reagan, Nancy, with William Novak. *My Turn: The Memoirs of Nancy Reagan.* New York: Random House, 1989.

Reagan, Ronald. *An American Life: The Autobiography.* New York: Simon & Schuster, 1990.

Regan, Donald T. *For the Record: From Wall Street to Washington.* New York: Harcourt Brace Jovanovich, 1988.

Rodman, Peter W. *More Precious Than Peace: The Cold War and the Struggle for the Third World.* New York: Scribners, 1984.

Sagdeyev, Roald Z. *The Making of a Soviet Scientist: My Adventures in Nuclear Fusion and Space from Stalin to Star Wars.* New York: Wiley, 1994.

Sakharov, Andrei. *Vospominaniya.* New York: Chekhov, 1990. English translation: *Memoirs.* New York: Knopf, 1990.

Savel'yev, Aleksandr G., and Nikolai N. Detinov. *The Big Five: Arms Control Decision Making in the Soviet Union.* Westport, Conn.: Praeger, 1995.

Shakhnazarov, Georgy. *S Vozhdyami i bez nikh.* Moscow: Vagrius, 2001.

———. *Tsena svobody: Reformatsiya Gorbacheva glazami ego pomoshchnika.* Moscow: Zevs, 1993.

Shevardnadze, Eduard. *Moi vybor: V zashchitu demokratii i svobody.* Moscow: Novosti, 1991. English translation: *The Future Belongs to Freedom.* New York: Free Press, 1991.

Shultz, George P. *Turmoil and Triumph: My Years as Secretary of State.* New York: Scribner, 1993.

Simons, Thomas W., Jr. *The End of the Cold War?* New York: St. Martin's, 1990.

Strober, Deborah Hart, and Gerald S. Strober. *Reagan: The Man and His Presidency.* Boston: Houghton Mifflin, 1998. (Comments by persons who worked with Reagan.)

Sukhodrev, V. M. *Yazyk moi—drug moi: Ot Khrushcheva do Gorbacheva.* Moscow: Olimp, 1999.

Tannenwald, Nina, ed. *Understanding the End of the Cold War, 1980–87: An Oral History Conference.* Providence, R.I.: Watson Institute for International Studies, Brown University, 1998. The conference was held May 7–10, 1998.

Thatcher, Margaret. *The Downing Street Years.* New York: HarperCollins, 1993.

Weinberger, Caspar. *Fighting for Peace: Seven Critical Years in the Pentagon.* New York: Warner, 1990.

Wohlforth, William C., ed. *Cold War Endgame: Oral History, Analysis, Debates.* University Park: Pennsylvania State University Press, 2003.

———. *Witnesses to the End of the Cold War.* Baltimore: Johns Hopkins University Press, 1996.

Yakovlev, Alexander. *Gor'kaya chasha.* Yaroslavl: Verkhne-Volzhskoye knizhnoye izdatel'stvo, 1994.

———. *Muki prochteniya bytiya: Perestroika, nadezhdy, i realnosti.* Moscow: Novosti, 1991.

———. *Omut pamyati.* Moscow: Vagrius, 2000.

———. *Predislovie, Obval, Posleslovie.* Moscow: Novosti, 1992. English translation: *The Fate of Marxism in Russia.* New Haven: Yale University Press, 1993.

C. Books and Articles by Journalists and Scholars

Barrett, Laurence I. *Gambling with History: Ronald Reagan in the White House.* Garden City, N.Y.: Doubleday, 1983.

Beichman, Arnold, ed. *CNN's Cold War Documentary: Issues and Controversy.* Stanford, Calif.: Hoover Institution Press, 2000.

Borawski, John. *From the Atlantic to the Urals: Negotiating Arms Control at the Stockholm Conference.* Washington, D.C.: Pergamon-Brassey, 1988.

Breslauer, George W. *Gorbachev and Yeltsin as Leaders*. New York: Cambridge University Press, 2002.

Brown, Archie. *The Gorbachev Factor*. New York: Oxford University Press, 1996.

Brzezinski, Zbigniew, ed. *Promise or Peril: The Strategic Defense Initiative*. Washington, D.C.: Ethics and Public Policy Center, 1986.

Burlatsky, Fedor. *Russkie gosudari epokha reformatsii: Nikita Smely, Mikhail Blazhenny, Boris Krutoi*. Moscow: Shark, 1996.

Cannon, Lou. *President Reagan: The Role of a Lifetime*. New York: PublicAffairs, 2000.

Cronin, James E. *The World the Cold War Made: Order, Chaos, and the Return of History*. New York: Routledge, 1996.

Dallek, Robert. *Ronald Reagan: The Politics of Symbolism. With a New Preface*. Cambridge, Mass.: Harvard University Press, 1999.

Dallin, Alexander. *Black Box: KAL 007 and the Superpowers*. Berkeley: University of California Press, 1985.

Daniloff, Nicholas. *Two Lives, One Russia*. Boston: Houghton Mifflin, 1988.

Doder, Dusko, and Louise Branson. *Gorbachev: Heretic in the Kremlin*. New York: Viking, 1990.

Drexel, John, ed. *The Facts on File Encyclopedia of the 20th Century*. New York: Facts on File, 1991.

D'Souza, Dinesh. *Ronald Reagan: How an Ordinary Man Became an Extraordinary Leader*. New York: Free Press, 1997.

Ekedahl, Carolyn McGiffert, and Melvin A. Goodman. *The Wars of Eduard Shevardnadze*. University Park: Pennsylvania State University Press, 1997.

English, Robert D. *Russia and the Idea of the West: Gorbachev, Intellectuals and the End of the Cold War*. New York: Columbia University Press, 2000.

Evangelista, Matthew. *Unarmed Forces: The Trans-National Movement to End the Cold War*. Ithaca, N.Y.: Cornell University Press, 1999.

Fischer, Beth A. *The Reagan Reversal: Foreign Policy and the End of the Cold War*. Columbia: University of Missouri Press, 1997.

FitzGerald, Frances. *Way Out There in the Blue: Reagan, Star Wars and the End of the Cold War*. New York: Simon & Schuster, 2000.

Forsberg, Tuomas. "Power, Interests, and Trust: Explaining Gorbachev's Choices at the End of the Cold War." *Review of International Studies* 25, no. 4 (1999): 603–22.

Gaddis, John Lewis. *The United States and the End of the Cold War: Implications, Reconsiderations, Provocations*. New York: Oxford University Press, 1992.

———. *We Now Know: Rethinking Cold War History*. New York: Oxford University Press, 1997.

Garthoff, Raymond L. *Détente and Confrontation: American-Soviet Relations from Nixon to Reagan*. Washington, D.C.: Brookings Institution Press, 1985.

———. *The Great Transition: American-Soviet Relations and the End of the Cold War*. Washington, D.C.: Brookings Institution Press, 1994.

———. *A Journey Through the Cold War: A Memoir of Containment and Coexistence*. Washington, D.C.: Brookings Institution Press, 2001.

Grachev, Andrei. *Gorbachev*. Moscow: Vagrius, 2001.

Halliday, Fred. "Soviet Foreign Policymaking and the Afghanistan War: From 'Second Mongolia' to 'Bleeding Wound.' " *Review of International Studies* 25, no. 4 (1999): 675–92.

Hazan, Baruch A. *Gorbachev and His Enemies: The Struggle for Perestroika*. Boulder, Colo.: Westview, 1990.

Henze, Paul. *The Plot to Kill the Pope*. New York: Scribner, 1985.

Herf, Jeffrey. *War by Other Means: Soviet Power, West German Resistance, and the Battle of the Euromissiles*. New York: Free Press, 1991.

Hersh, Seymour M. *"The Target Is Destroyed": What Really Happened to Flight 007 and What America Knew About It*. New York: Random House, 1986.

Hogan, Michael J., ed. *The End of the Cold War: Its Meaning and Implications*. New York: Cambridge University Press, 1992.

Hough, Jerry. *Russia and the West: Gorbachev and the Politics of Reform*. New York: Simon & Schuster, 1988.

Hunter, Robert W. *Spy Hunter: Inside the FBI Investigation of the Walker Espionage Case*. Annapolis, Md.: Naval Institute Press, 1999.

Hutchings, Robert L. *American Diplomacy and the End of the Cold War: An Insider's Account of U.S. Policy in Europe, 1989–1992*. Washington, D.C.: Woodrow Wilson Center Press, 1997.

Johnson, R. W. *Shootdown: Flight 007 and the American Connection*. New York: Viking, 1986.

Kaiser, Robert G. *Why Gorbachev Happened: His Triumphs and His Failure*. New York: Simon & Schuster, 1991.

Kokoshin, Andrei A. *Soviet Strategic Thought, 1917–91*. Cambridge, Mass.: MIT Press, 1998.

Kramer, Mark. "Ideology and the Cold War." *Review of International Studies* 25, no. 4, (1999): 539–76.

Lewin, Moshe. *The Gorbachev Phenomenon: A Historical Interpretation*. Berkeley: University of California Press, 1988.

Mandelbaum, Michael, and Strobe Talbott. *Reagan and Gorbachev*. New York: Vintage, 1987. A Council on Foreign Relations book.

Matlock, Jack F., Jr. *Autopsy on an Empire: The American Ambassador's Account of the Collapse of the Soviet Union*. New York: Random House, 1995.

Medvedev, Zhores A. *Gorbachev*. New York: Norton, 1986.

Mendelson, Sarah E. *Changing Course: Ideas, Politics, and the Soviet Withdrawal from Afghanistan*. Princeton: Princeton University Press, 1998.

Morris, Edmund. *Dutch: A Memoir of Ronald Reagan*. New York: Random House, 1999.

Oberdorfer, Don. *From the Cold War to a New Era: The United States and the Soviet Union, 1983–1991*. Baltimore: Johns Hopkins University Press, 1998.

Odom, William E. *The Collapse of the Soviet Military*. New Haven: Yale University Press, 1998.

Paterson, Thomas G. *On Every Front: The Making and Unmaking of the Cold War*, rev. ed. New York: Norton, 1992.

Patman, Robert G. "Reagan, Gorbachev, and the Emergence of 'New Political Thinking.' " *Review of International Studies* 25, no. 4 (1999): 577–602.

Pemberton, William E. *Exit with Honor: The Life and Presidency of Ronald Reagan*. Armonk, N.Y.: Sharpe, 1998.

Pipes, Richard. *Survival Is Not Enough: Soviet Realities and America's Future*. New York: Simon & Schuster, 1984.

Pollock, John. *The Siberian Seven*. Waco, Tex.: Word Books, 1980.

Powers, Thomas. *Intelligence Wars: American Secret History from Hitler to al-Qaeda.* New York: New York Review Books, 2002.

Richmond, Yale. *Cultural Exchange and the Cold War: Raising the Iron Curtain.* University Park: Pennsylvania State University Press, 2003.

Ruge, Gerd. *Michail Gorbatschow: Biographie.* Frankfurt-am-Main: S. Fischer, 1990.

Sayle, Murray. "Closing the File on Flight 007." *The New Yorker,* Dec. 13, 1993, pp. 90–101.

Schöllgen, Gregor. *Geschichte der Weltpolitik von Hitler bis Gorbatschow, 1941–1991.* Munich: C. H. Beck, 1996.

Schweizer, Peter. *Victory: The Reagan Administration's Secret Strategy That Hastened the Collapse of the Soviet Union.* New York: Atlantic Monthly Press, 1994.

Sheehy, Gail. *The Man Who Changed the World: The Lives of Mikhail S. Gorbachev.* New York: HarperCollins, 1990.

Sprinkle, Robert Hunt. "Two Cold Wars and Why They Ended Differently." *Review of International Studies* 25, no. 4 (1999): 623–40.

Suri, Jeremi. "Explaining the End of the Cold War: A New Historical Consensus?" *Journal of Cold War Studies* 4, no. 4 (Fall 2002): 60–92.

Talbott, Strobe. *The Master of the Game: Paul Nitze and the Nuclear Peace.* New York: Knopf, 1988.

———. *The Russians and Reagan.* New York: Vintage, 1984. A Council on Foreign Relations book.

Tatu, Michel. *Gorbatchev: L'U.R.S.S. va-t-elle changer?* Paris: Le Centurion, 1987.

Volkogonov, Dmitri. *Sem' vozhdei. Galereya liderov SSSR v 2-kh knigakh.* Moscow: Novosti, 1996. English translation: *Autopsy for an Empire: The Seven Leaders Who Built the Soviet Regime.* New York: Free Press, 1998.

Whelan, Joseph G. *Soviet Diplomacy and Negotiating Behavior—1979–88: New Tests for U.S. Diplomacy.* Published for the Committee on Foreign Affairs of the U.S. House of Representatives. Washington, D.C.: U.S. Government Printing Office, 1988.

———. *Soviet Diplomacy and Negotiating Behavior—1988–90: Gorbachev-Reagan-Bush Meetings at the Summit.* Published for the Committee on Foreign Affairs of the U.S. House of Representatives. Washington, D.C.: U.S. Government Printing Office, 1991.

White, Stephen. *Gorbachev in Power.* New York: Cambridge University Press, 1990.

Wise, David. *Spy: The Inside Story of How the FBI's Robert Hanssen Betrayed America.* New York: Random House, 2002.

Zubok, Vladislav M. "Gorbachev and the End of the Cold War: Perspectives on History and Personality." *Cold War History* 2, no. 2 (2002): 61–100.

INDEX

Page numbers beginning with 329 refer to endnotes.

ABOUT THE AUTHOR

First posted to Moscow in 1961, career diplomat JACK F. MATLOCK, JR., was American's man on the scene for most of the Cold War. A scholar of Russian history and culture, Matlock was President Reagan's choice for the crucial post of ambassador to the Soviet Union. He is the author of *Autopsy on an Empire: The American Ambassador's Account of the Collapse of the Soviet Union.* Matlock now divides his time between Princeton, New Jersey, and his wife's farm in Booneville, Tennessee.

ABOUT THE TYPE

This book was set in Times Roman, designed by Stanley Morison specifically for *The Times* of London. The typeface was introduced in the newspaper in 1932. Times Roman has had its greatest success in the United States as a book and commercial typeface, rather than one used in newspapers.